CROSSED™

VOLUME 9

parts 1-6: GRAVE NEW WORLD
DANIEL WAY story EMILIANO URDINOLA art

part 7: THE WIZARD OF AUS
SIMON SPURRIER story GABRIEL ANDRADE art

FERNANDO HEINZ softcover art
GABRIEL ANDRADE hardcover art
DIGIKORE STUDIOS colors
JAYMES REED letters

chapter breaks
JACEN BURROWS, FERNANDO HEINZ,
MIGUEL A. RUIZ, CHRISTIAN ZANIER, MATT MARTIN,
GABRIEL ANDRADE, EMILIANO URDINOLA

COLLECTING CROSSED: BADLANDS #44-49, 2013 Special

WILLIAM CHRISTENSEN editor-in-chief
MARK SEIFERT creative director
JIM KUHORIC managing editor
DAVID MARKS director of events
ARIANA OSBORNE production assistant

CROSSED CREATED BY GARTH ENNIS

AVATAR™

www.crossedcomic.com www.avatarpress.com www.twitter.com/avatarpress

CROSSED Volume 9. May 2014. Published by Avatar Press, Inc., 515 N. Century Blvd. Rantoul, IL 61866.

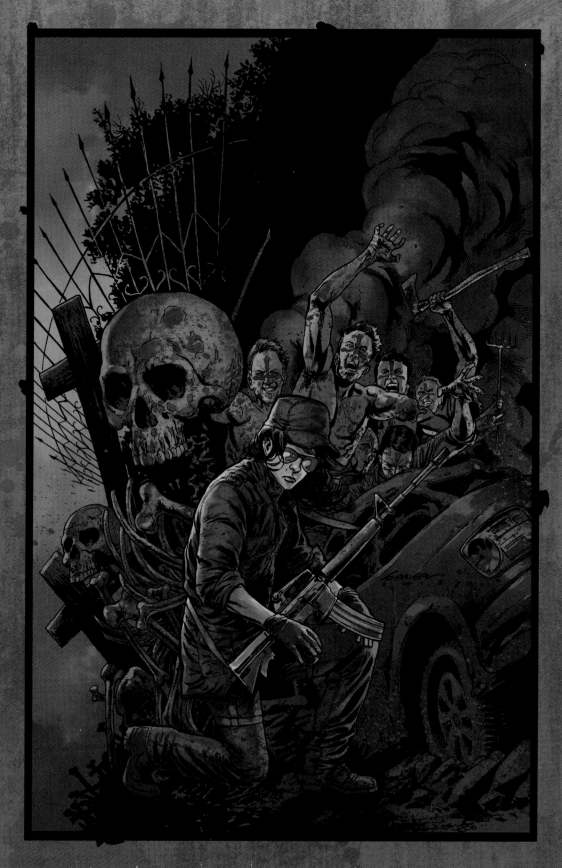

GRAVE NEW WORLD

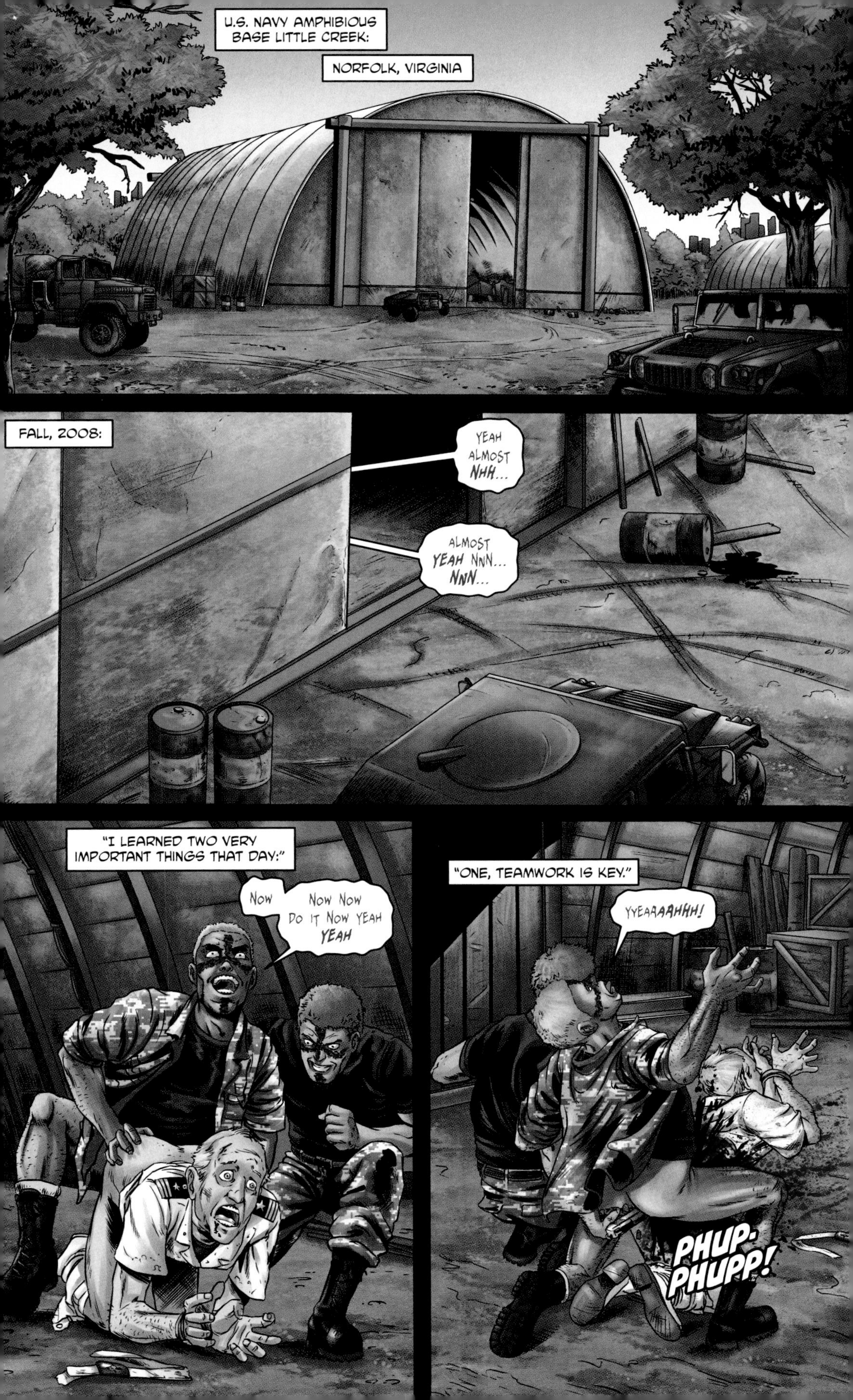
U.S. NAVY AMPHIBIOUS BASE LITTLE CREEK:
NORFOLK, VIRGINIA
FALL, 2008:
YEAH ALMOST NHH...
ALMOST YEAH NNN... NNN...
"I LEARNED TWO VERY IMPORTANT THINGS THAT DAY:"
Now
Now Now Do it Now YEAH YEAH
"ONE, TEAMWORK IS KEY."
YYEAAAAHHH!
PHUP-PHUPP!

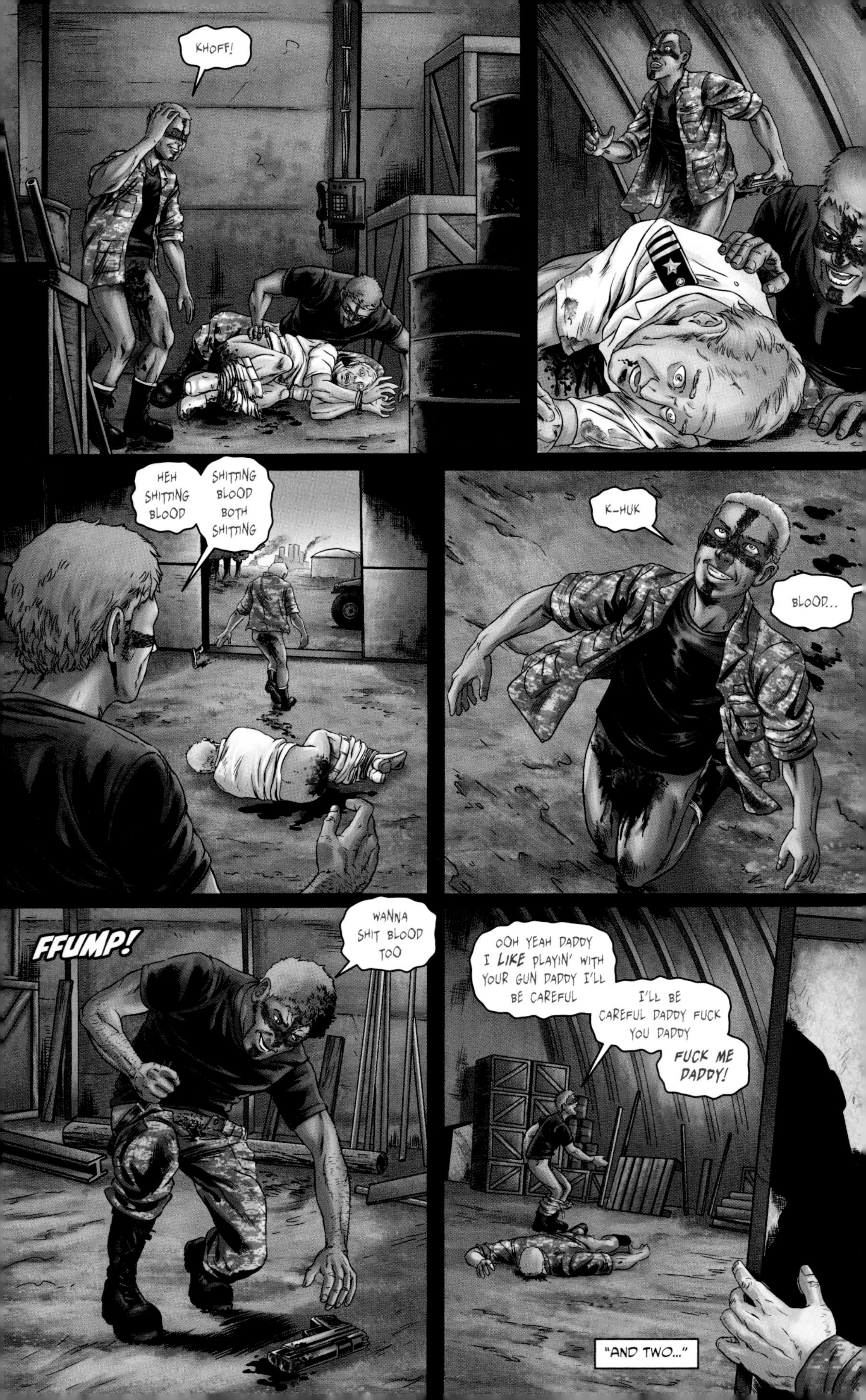
KHOFF!
HEH SHITTING BLOOD
SHITTING BLOOD BOTH SHITTING
K-HUK
BLOOD...
FFUMP!
WANNA SHIT BLOOD TOO
OOH YEAH DADDY I LIKE PLAYIN' WITH YOUR GUN DADDY I'LL BE CAREFUL
I'LL BE CAREFUL DADDY FUCK YOU DADDY
FUCK ME DADDY!
"AND TWO..."

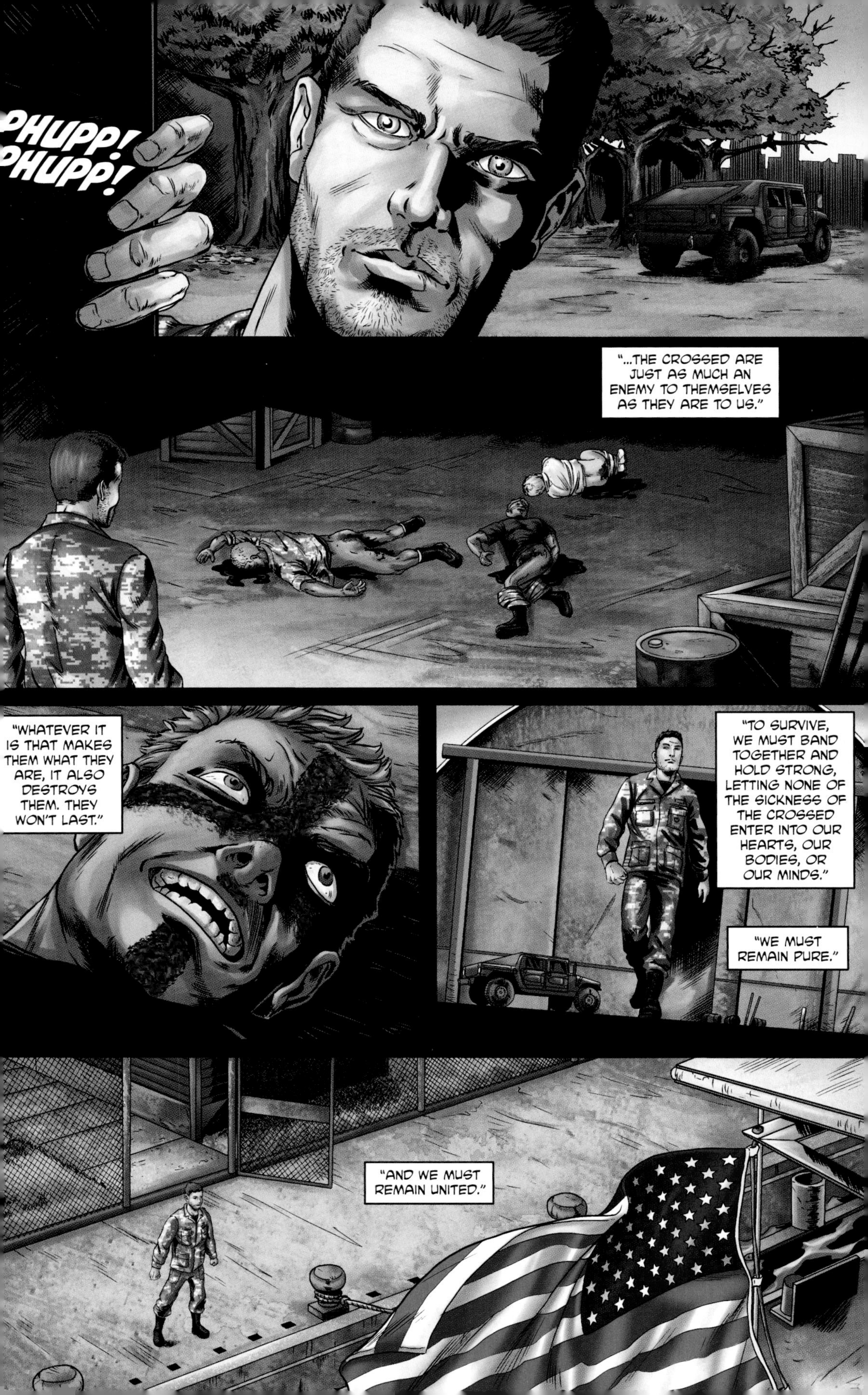
PHUPP! PHUPP!
"...THE CROSSED ARE JUST AS MUCH AN ENEMY TO THEMSELVES AS THEY ARE TO US."
"WHATEVER IT IS THAT MAKES THEM WHAT THEY ARE, IT ALSO DESTROYS THEM. THEY WON'T LAST."
"TO SURVIVE, WE MUST BAND TOGETHER AND HOLD STRONG, LETTING NONE OF THE SICKNESS OF THE CROSSED ENTER INTO OUR HEARTS, OUR BODIES, OR OUR MINDS."
"WE MUST REMAIN PURE."
"AND WE MUST REMAIN UNITED."

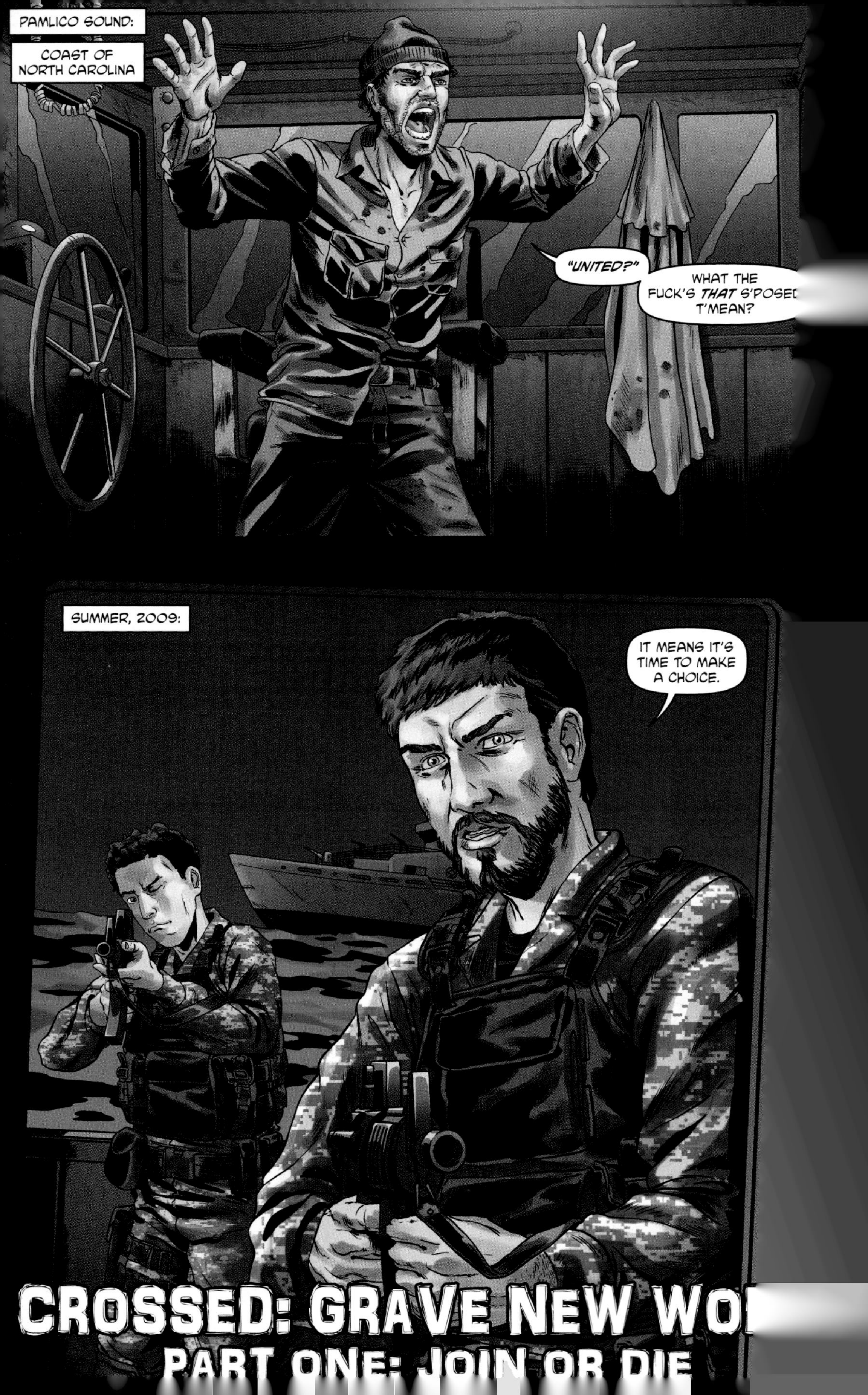
PAMLICO SOUND:
COAST OF NORTH CAROLINA
"UNITED?"
WHAT THE FUCK'S *THAT* S'POSED T'MEAN?
SUMMER, 2009:
IT MEANS IT'S TIME TO MAKE A CHOICE.
CROSSED: GRAVE NEW WO
PART ONE: JOIN OR DIE

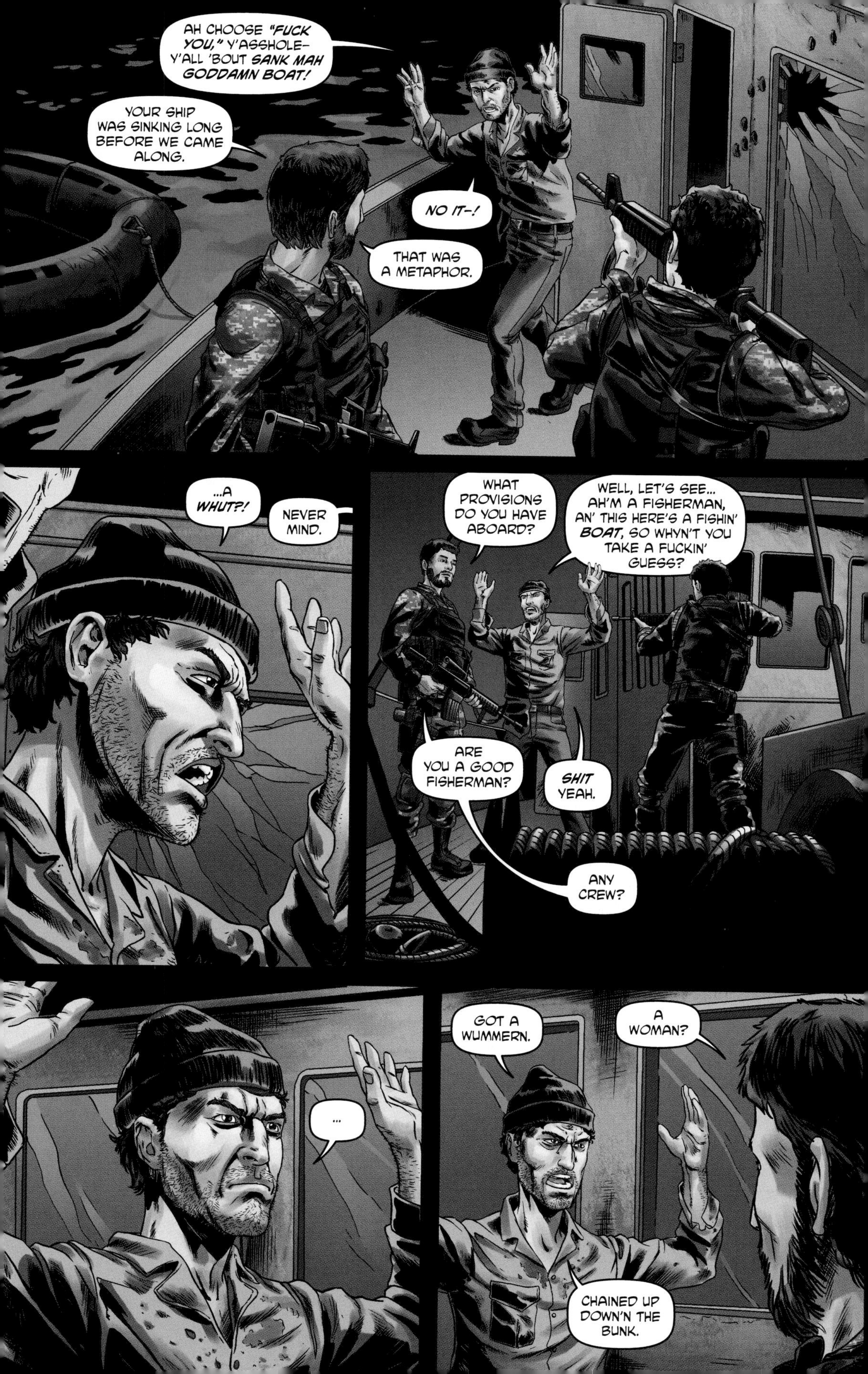
AH CHOOSE "FUCK YOU," Y'ASSHOLE– Y'ALL 'BOUT SANK MAH GODDAMN BOAT!
YOUR SHIP WAS SINKING LONG BEFORE WE CAME ALONG.
NO IT–!
THAT WAS A METAPHOR.
...A WHUT?!
NEVER MIND.
WHAT PROVISIONS DO YOU HAVE ABOARD?
WELL, LET'S SEE... AH'M A FISHERMAN, AN' THIS HERE'S A FISHIN' BOAT, SO WHYN'T YOU TAKE A FUCKIN' GUESS?
ARE YOU A GOOD FISHERMAN?
SHIT YEAH.
ANY CREW?
...
GOT A WUMMERN.
A WOMAN?
CHAINED UP DOWN'N THE BUNK.

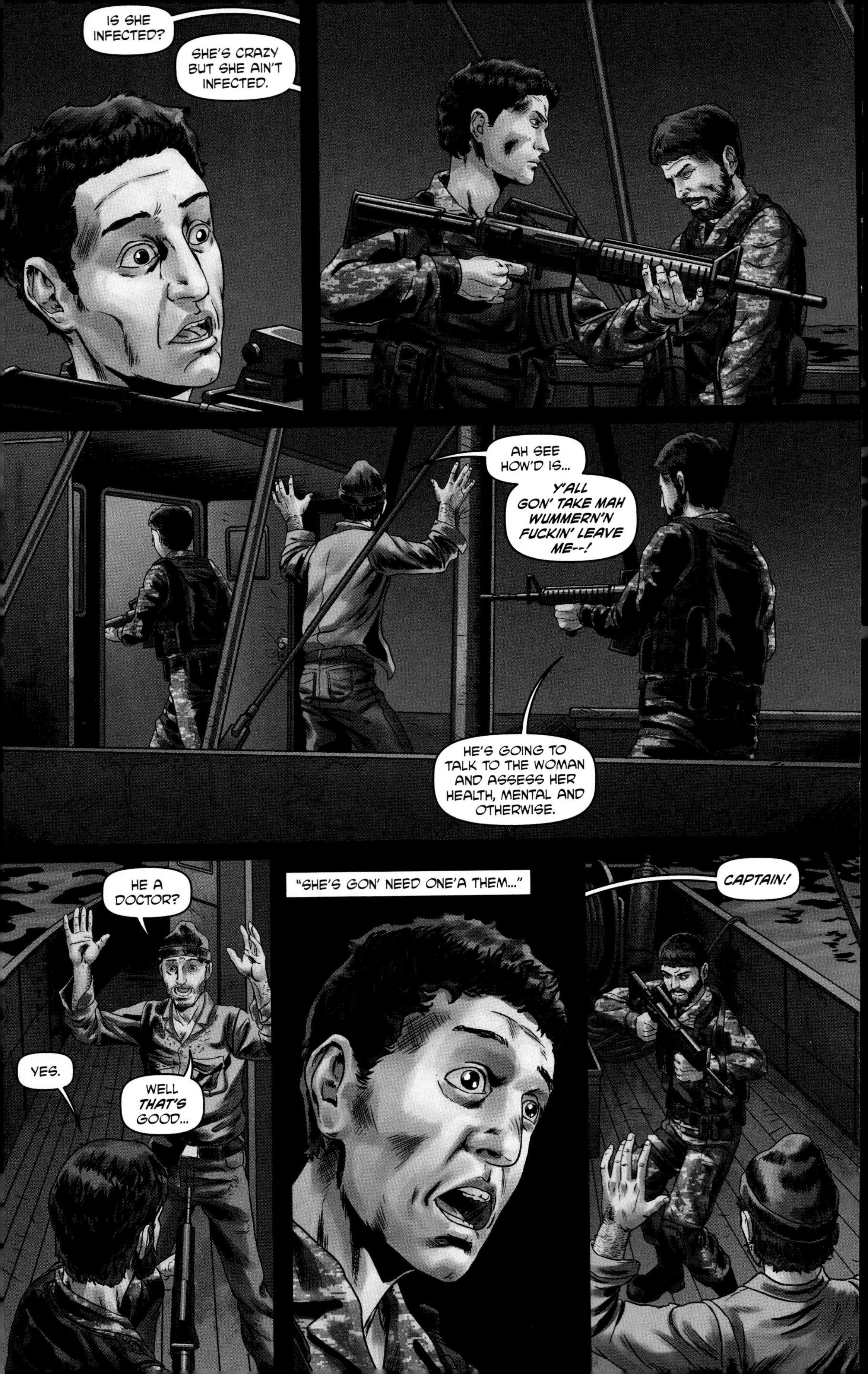

IS SHE INFECTED?
SHE'S CRAZY BUT SHE AIN'T INFECTED.
AH SEE HOW'D IS...
Y'ALL GON' TAKE MAH WUMMERN'N FUCKIN' LEAVE ME--!
HE'S GOING TO TALK TO THE WOMAN AND ASSESS HER HEALTH, MENTAL AND OTHERWISE.
HE A DOCTOR?
YES.
WELL *THAT'S* GOOD...
"SHE'S GON' NEED ONE'A THEM..."
CAPTAIN!

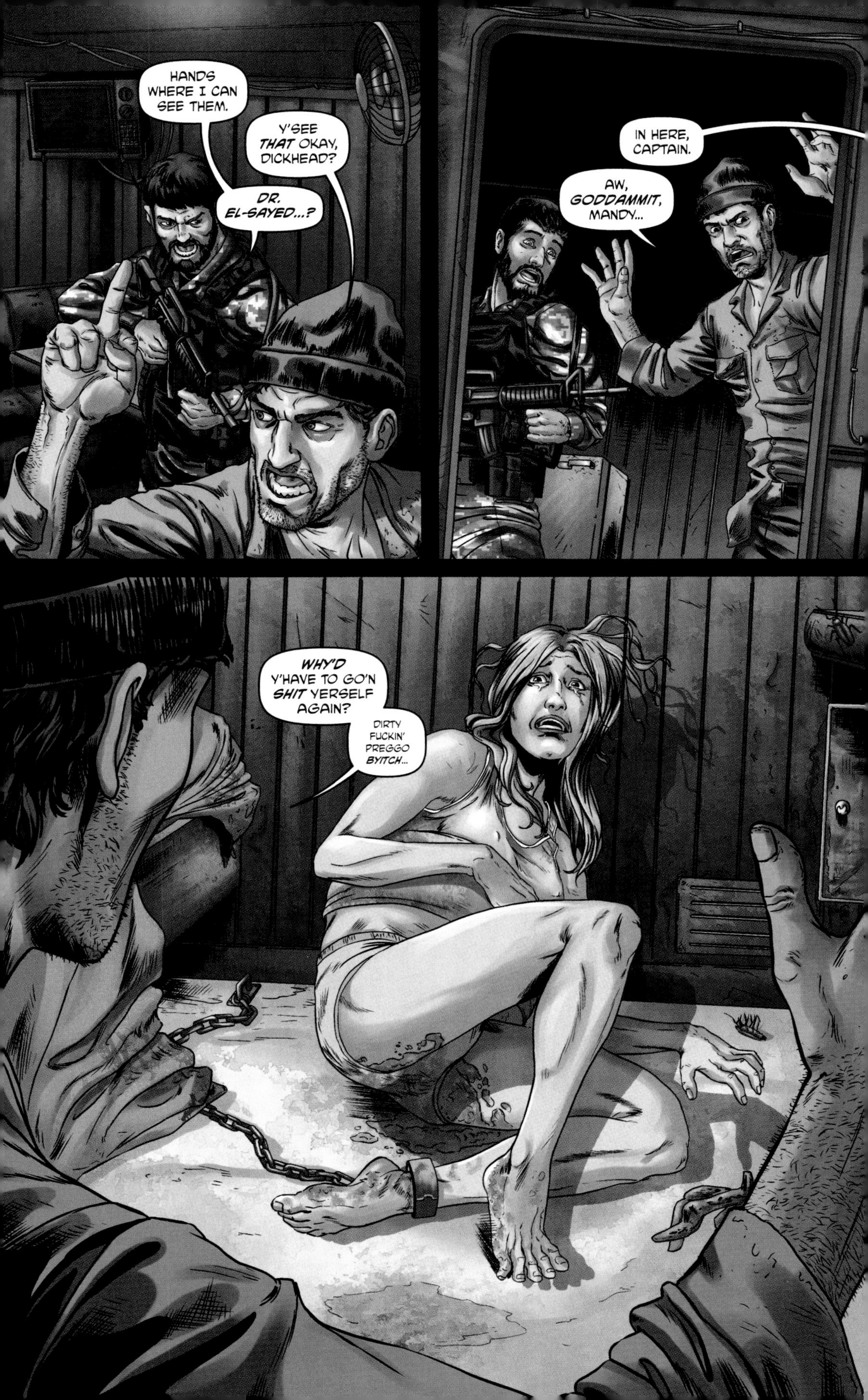
HANDS WHERE I CAN SEE THEM.
Y'SEE THAT OKAY, DICKHEAD?
DR. EL-SAYED...?
IN HERE, CAPTAIN.
AW, GODDAMMIT, MANDY...
WHY'D Y'HAVE TO GO'N SHIT YERSELF AGAIN?
DIRTY FUCKIN' PREGGO BYITCH...

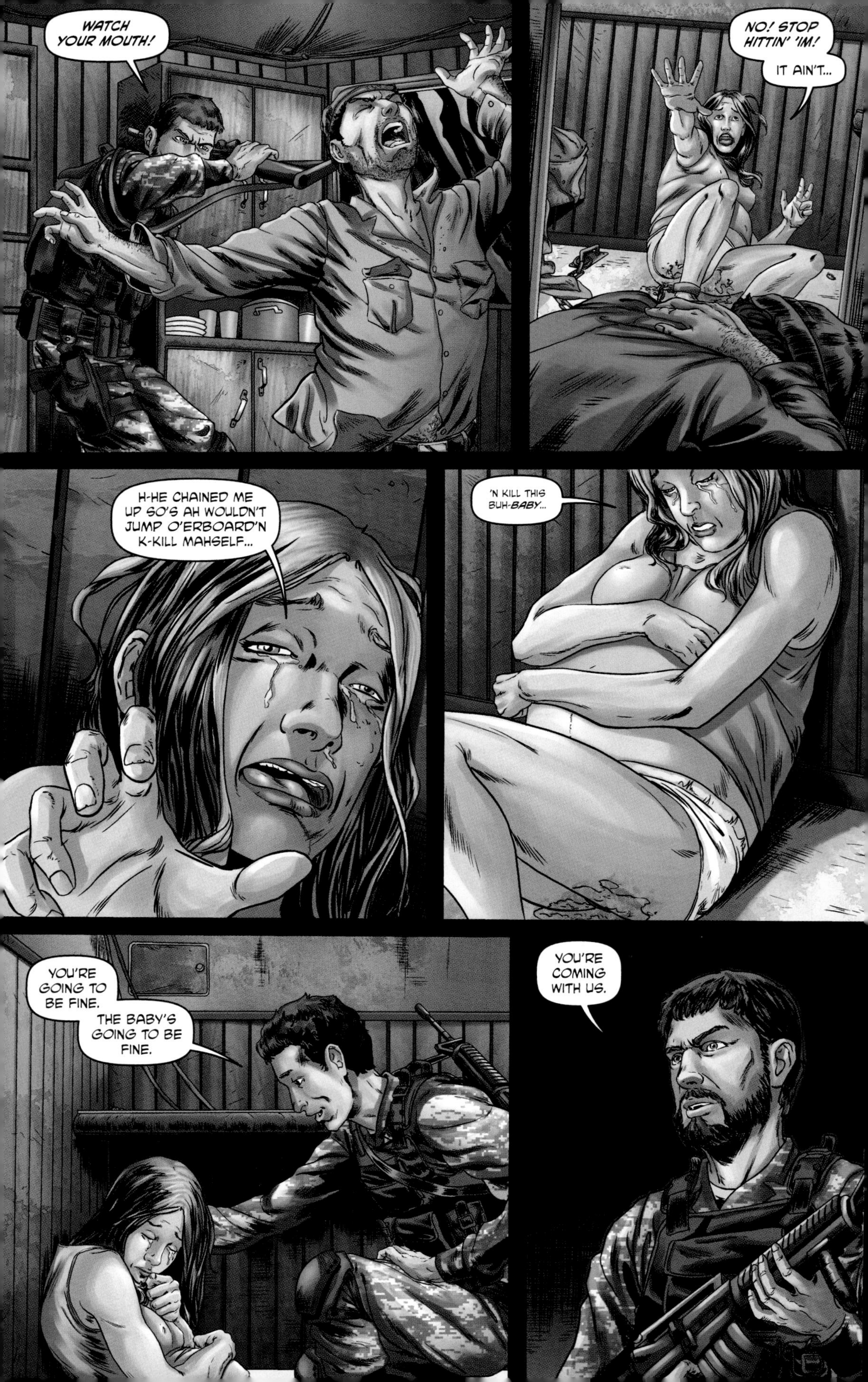
WATCH YOUR MOUTH!
NO! STOP HITTIN' 'IM!
IT AIN'T...
H-HE CHAINED ME UP SO'S AH WOULDN'T JUMP O'ERBOARD'N K-KILL MAHSELF...
'N KILL THIS BUH-BABY...
YOU'RE GOING TO BE FINE.
THE BABY'S GOING TO BE FINE.
YOU'RE COMING WITH US.

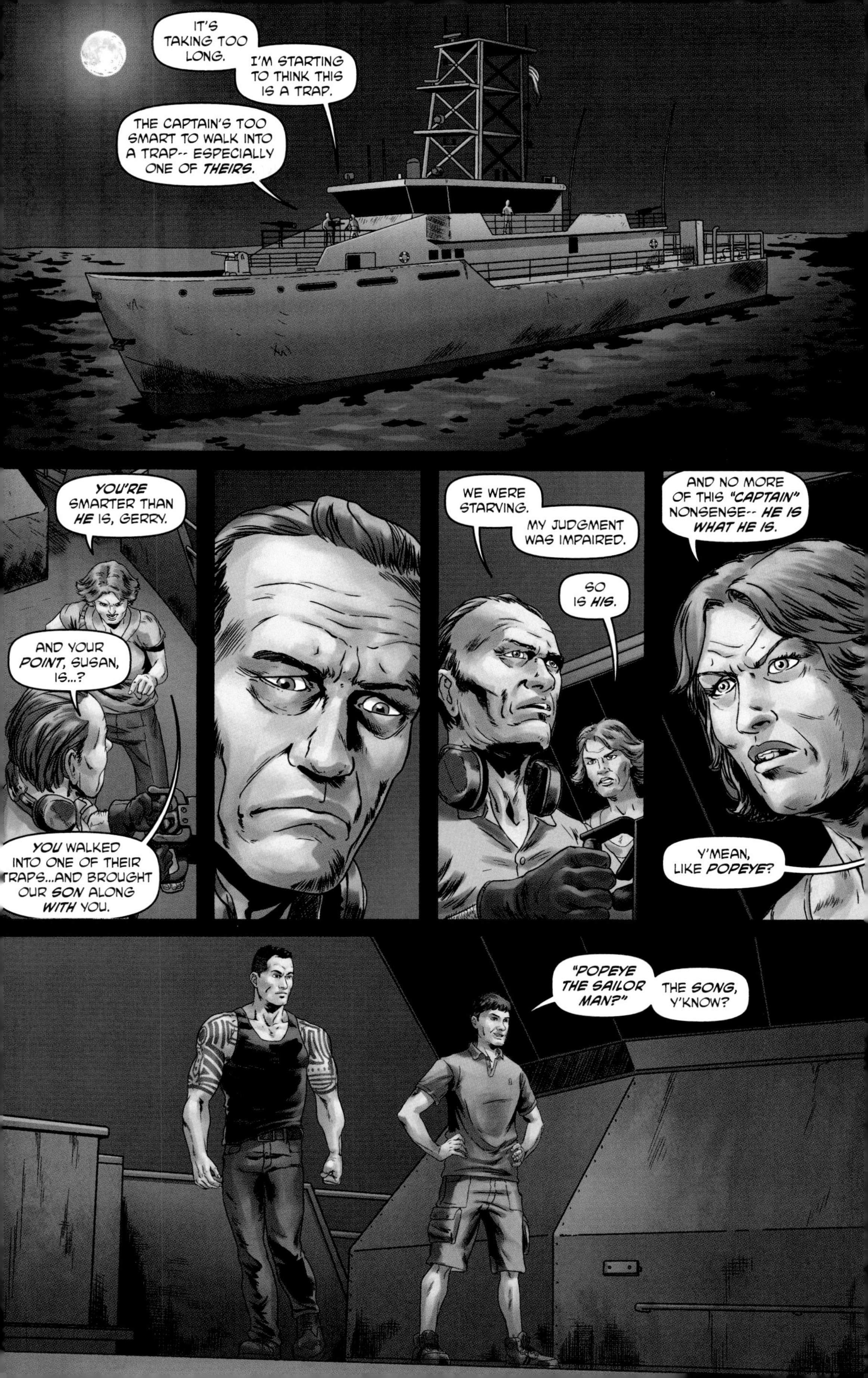

IT'S TAKING TOO LONG.
I'M STARTING TO THINK THIS IS A TRAP.
THE CAPTAIN'S TOO SMART TO WALK INTO A TRAP-- ESPECIALLY ONE OF *THEIRS*.
YOU'RE SMARTER THAN *HE* IS, GERRY.
AND YOUR *POINT*, SUSAN, IS...?
YOU WALKED INTO ONE OF THEIR TRAPS...AND BROUGHT OUR *SON* ALONG *WITH* YOU.
WE WERE STARVING.
MY JUDGMENT WAS IMPAIRED.
SO IS *HIS*.
AND NO MORE OF THIS *"CAPTAIN"* NONSENSE-- *HE IS WHAT HE IS*.
Y'MEAN, LIKE *POPEYE*?
"POPEYE THE SAILOR MAN?"
THE *SONG*, Y'KNOW?

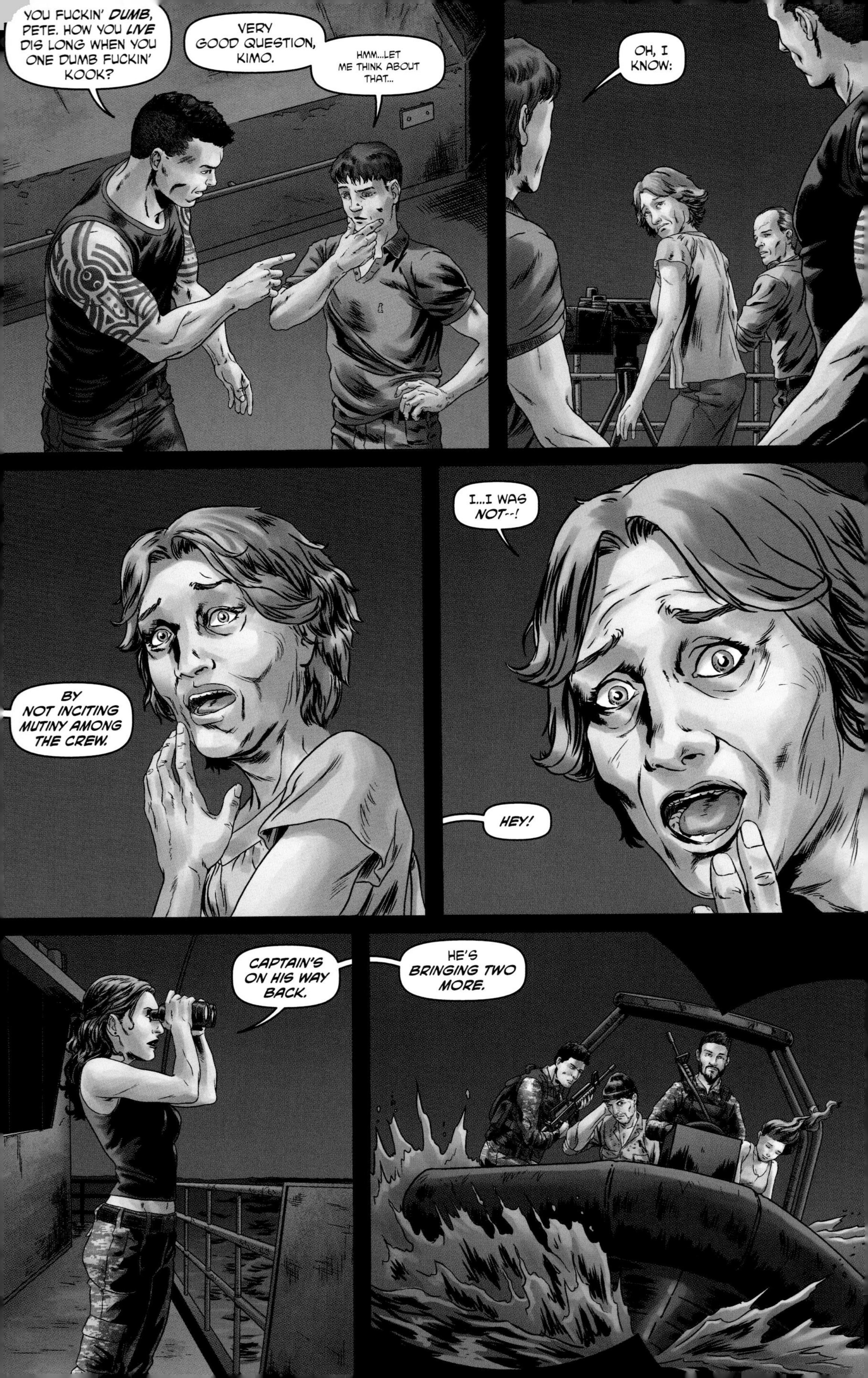
YOU FUCKIN' DUMB, PETE. HOW YOU LIVE DIS LONG WHEN YOU ONE DUMB FUCKIN' KOOK?
VERY GOOD QUESTION, KIMO.
HMM...LET ME THINK ABOUT THAT...
OH, I KNOW:
BY NOT INCITING MUTINY AMONG THE CREW.
I...I WAS NOT--!
HEY!
CAPTAIN'S ON HIS WAY BACK.
HE'S BRINGING TWO MORE.

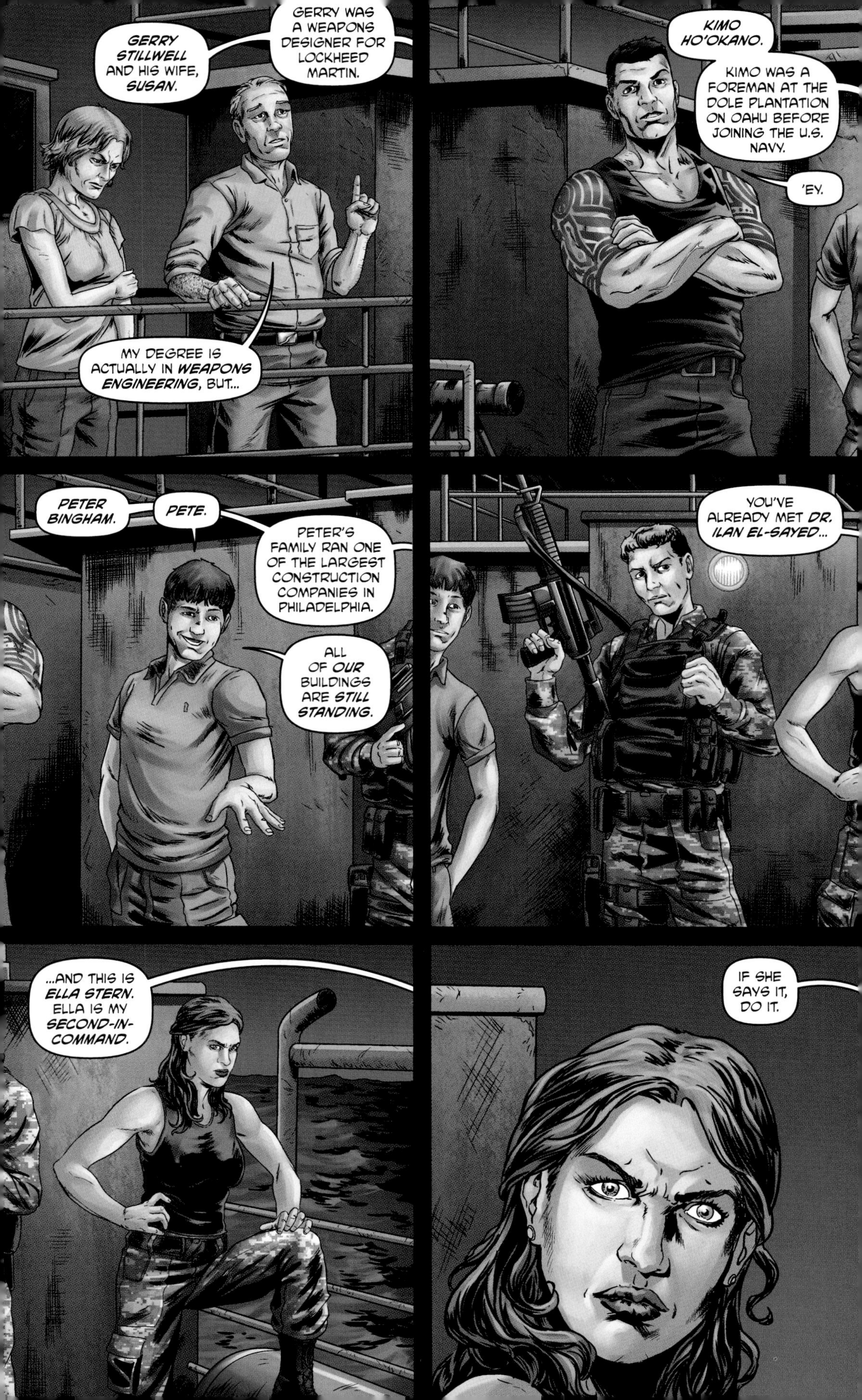
GERRY STILLWELL AND HIS WIFE, SUSAN.
GERRY WAS A WEAPONS DESIGNER FOR LOCKHEED MARTIN.
MY DEGREE IS ACTUALLY IN WEAPONS ENGINEERING, BUT...
KIMO HO'OKANO.
KIMO WAS A FOREMAN AT THE DOLE PLANTATION ON OAHU BEFORE JOINING THE U.S. NAVY.
'EY.
PETER BINGHAM.
PETE.
PETER'S FAMILY RAN ONE OF THE LARGEST CONSTRUCTION COMPANIES IN PHILADELPHIA.
ALL OF OUR BUILDINGS ARE STILL STANDING.
YOU'VE ALREADY MET DR. ILAN EL-SAYED...
...AND THIS IS ELLA STERN. ELLA IS MY SECOND-IN-COMMAND.
IF SHE SAYS IT, DO IT.

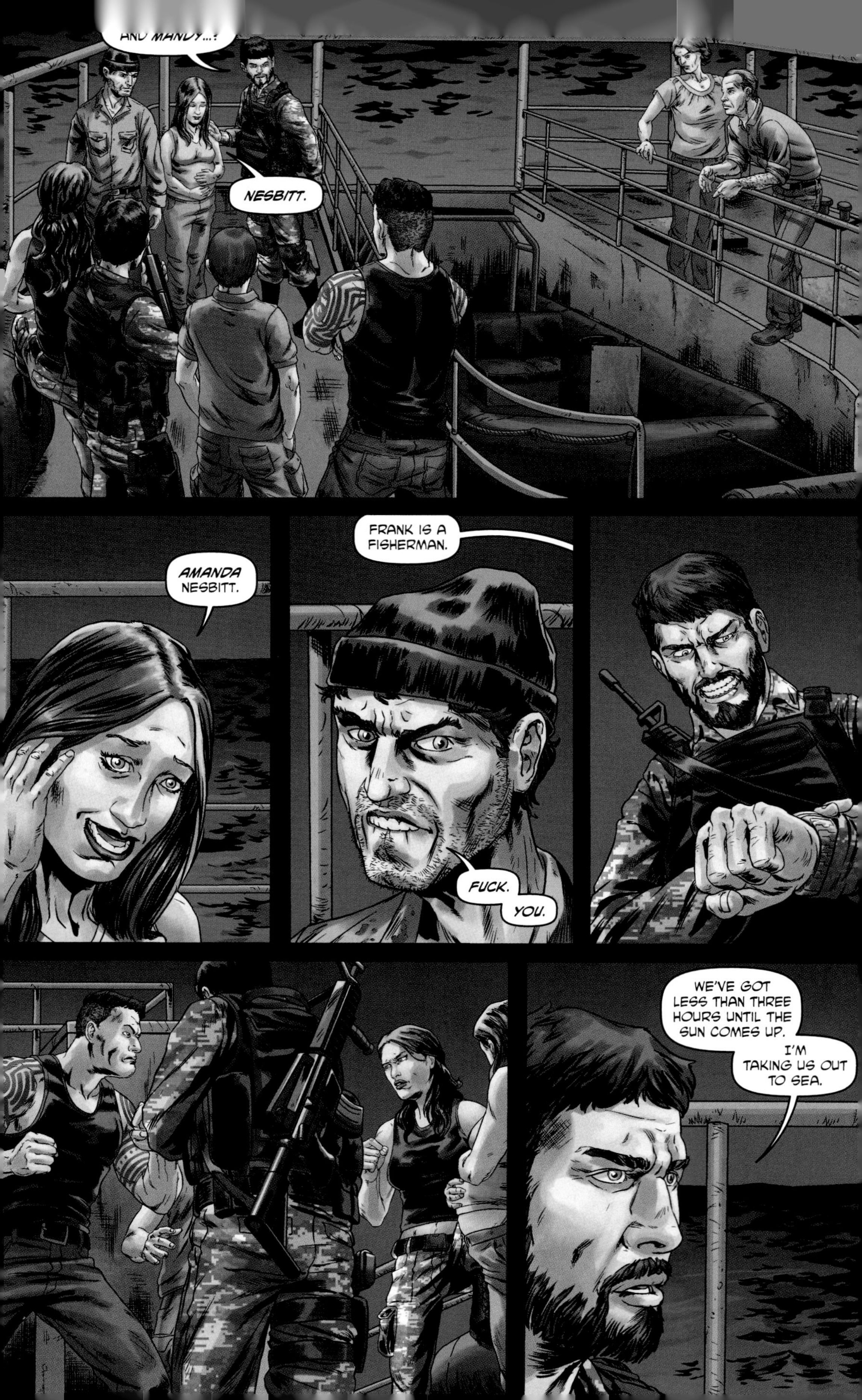
AND MANDY...?
NESBITT.
AMANDA NESBITT.
FRANK IS A FISHERMAN.
FUCK.
YOU.
WE'VE GOT LESS THAN THREE HOURS UNTIL THE SUN COMES UP.
I'M TAKING US OUT TO SEA.

FRANK, GO WITH KIMO-- HE'LL GET YOU SQUARED AWAY.

AMANDA, YOU GO WITH DR. EL-SAYED.

NAW, FUCK THAT SHIT--!

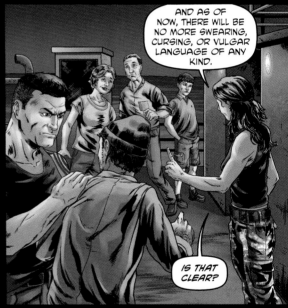

AND AS OF NOW, THERE WILL BE NO MORE SWEARING, CURSING, OR VULGAR LANGUAGE OF ANY KIND.

IS THAT CLEAR?

AYE-AYE.

WHAT KINDA SHIT...?

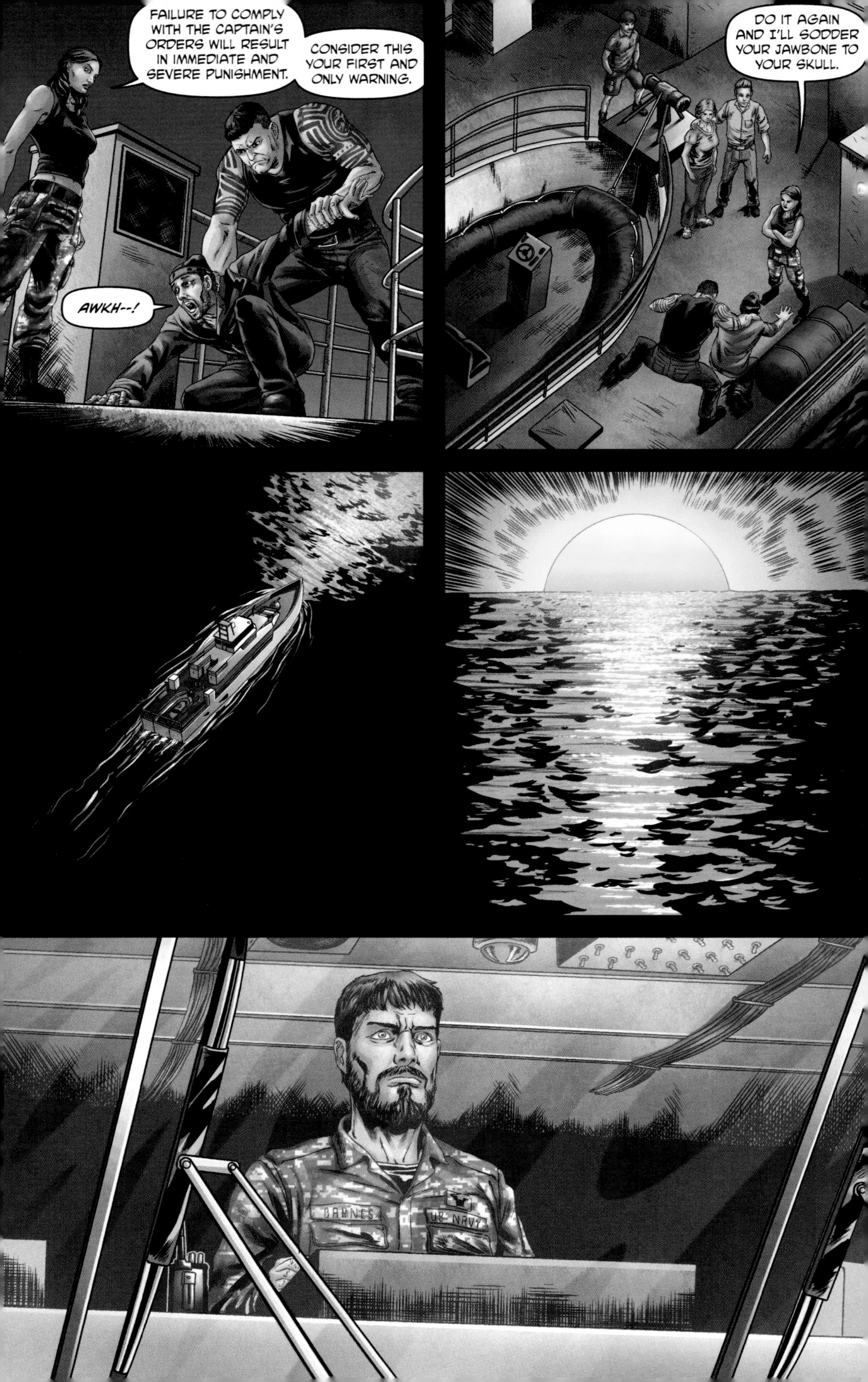
FAILURE TO COMPLY WITH THE CAPTAIN'S ORDERS WILL RESULT IN IMMEDIATE AND SEVERE PUNISHMENT.
CONSIDER THIS YOUR FIRST AND ONLY WARNING.
AWKH--!
DO IT AGAIN AND I'LL SODDER YOUR JAWBONE TO YOUR SKULL.
BARNES
US NAVY

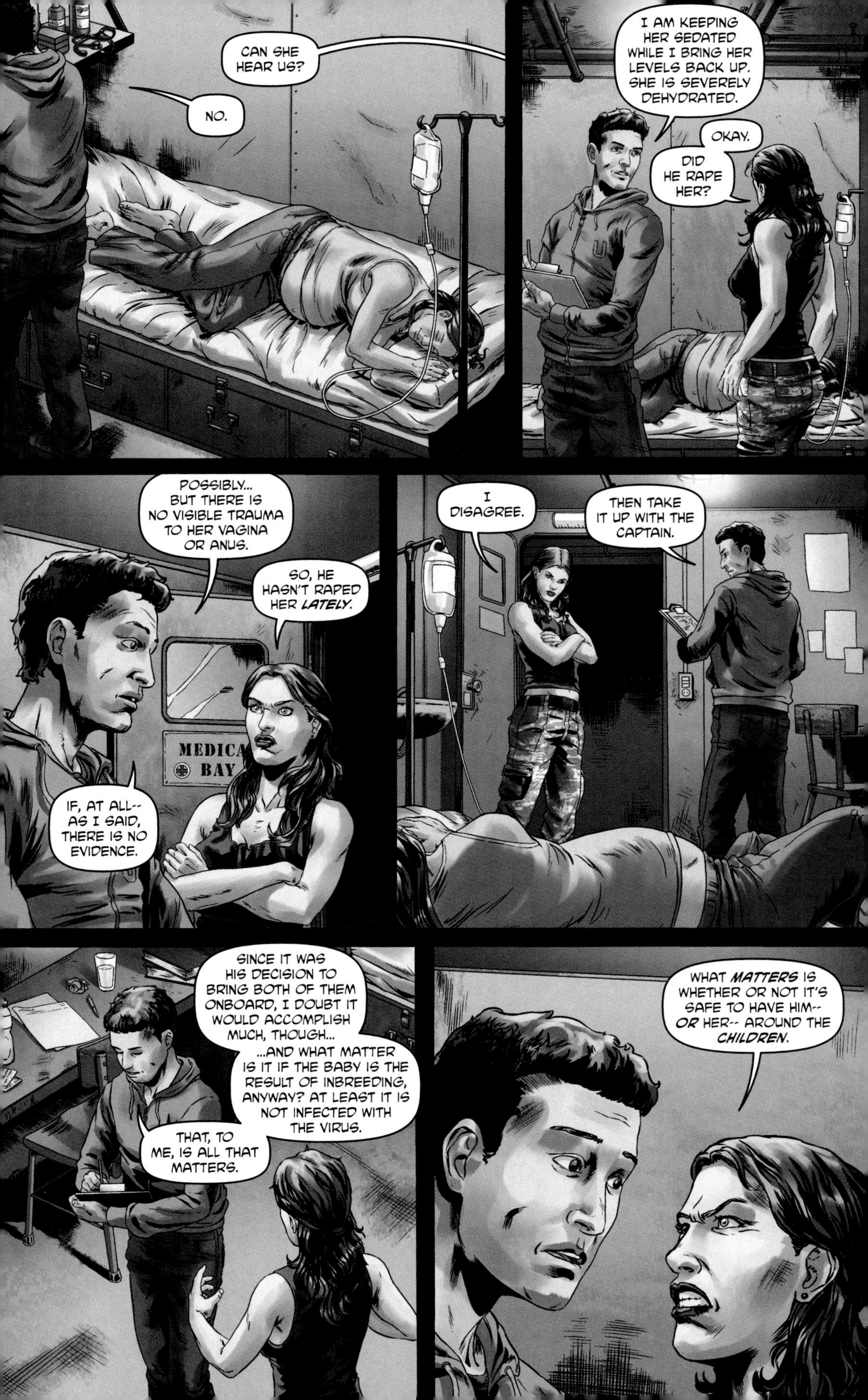
CAN SHE HEAR US?
NO.
I AM KEEPING HER SEDATED WHILE I BRING HER LEVELS BACK UP. SHE IS SEVERELY DEHYDRATED.
OKAY.
DID HE RAPE HER?
POSSIBLY... BUT THERE IS NO VISIBLE TRAUMA TO HER VAGINA OR ANUS.
SO, HE HASN'T RAPED HER *LATELY*.
MEDICAL BAY
IF, AT ALL-- AS I SAID, THERE IS NO EVIDENCE.
I DISAGREE.
THEN TAKE IT UP WITH THE CAPTAIN.
SINCE IT WAS HIS DECISION TO BRING BOTH OF THEM ONBOARD, I DOUBT IT WOULD ACCOMPLISH MUCH, THOUGH...
...AND WHAT MATTER IS IT IF THE BABY IS THE RESULT OF INBREEDING, ANYWAY? AT LEAST IT IS NOT INFECTED WITH THE VIRUS.
THAT, TO ME, IS ALL THAT MATTERS.
WHAT *MATTERS* IS WHETHER OR NOT IT'S SAFE TO HAVE HIM-- *OR* HER-- AROUND THE *CHILDREN*.

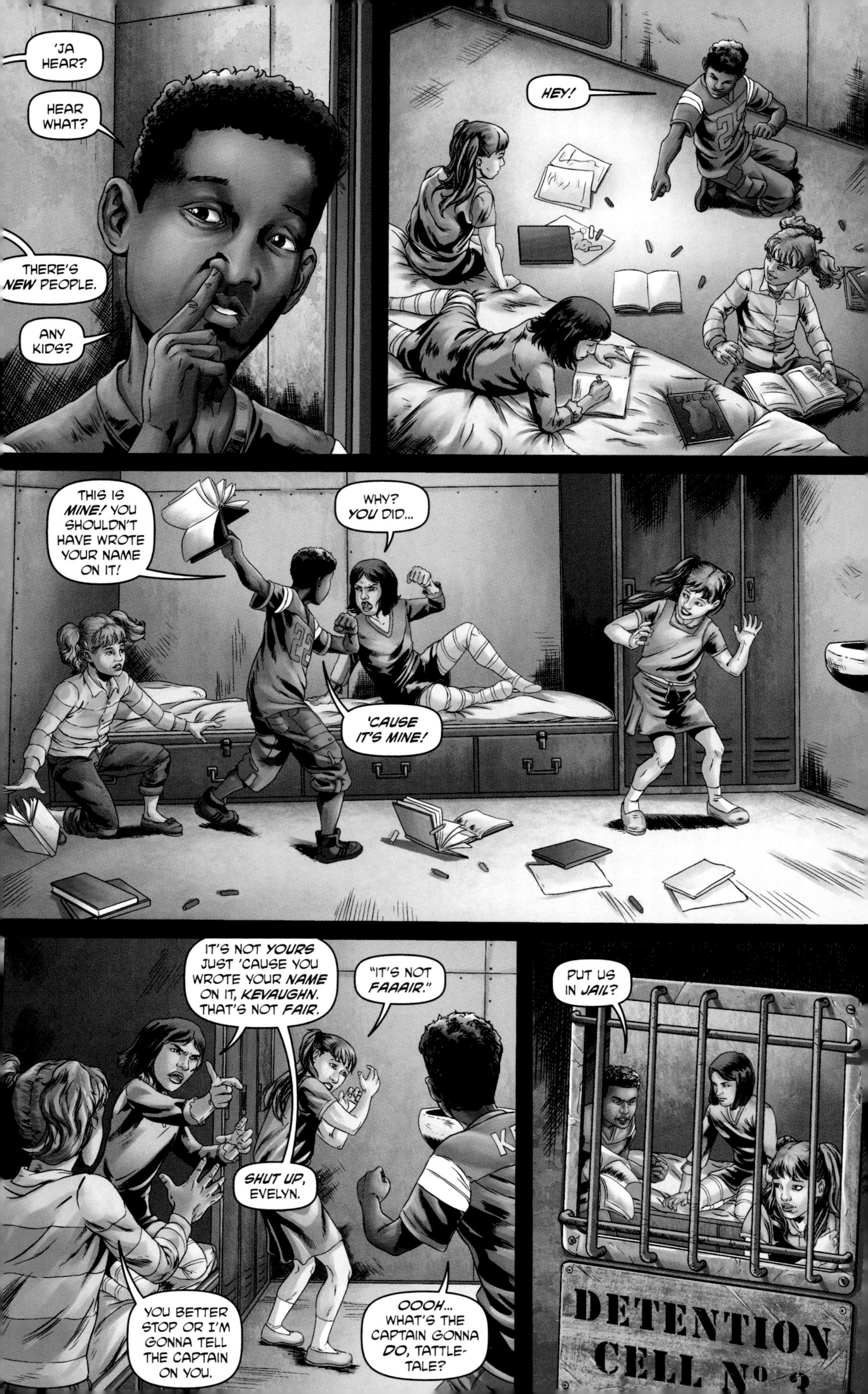

'JA HEAR?
HEAR WHAT?
THERE'S *NEW* PEOPLE.
ANY KIDS?
HEY!
THIS IS *MINE!* YOU SHOULDN'T HAVE WROTE YOUR NAME ON IT!
WHY? *YOU* DID...
'CAUSE IT'S MINE!
IT'S NOT *YOURS* JUST 'CAUSE YOU WROTE YOUR *NAME* ON IT, *KEVAUGHN*. THAT'S NOT *FAIR*.
"IT'S NOT *FAAAIR*."
SHUT UP, EVELYN.
YOU BETTER STOP OR I'M GONNA TELL THE CAPTAIN ON YOU.
OOOH... WHAT'S THE CAPTAIN GONNA *DO*, TATTLE-TALE?
PUT US IN *JAIL*?
DETENTION CELL No 3

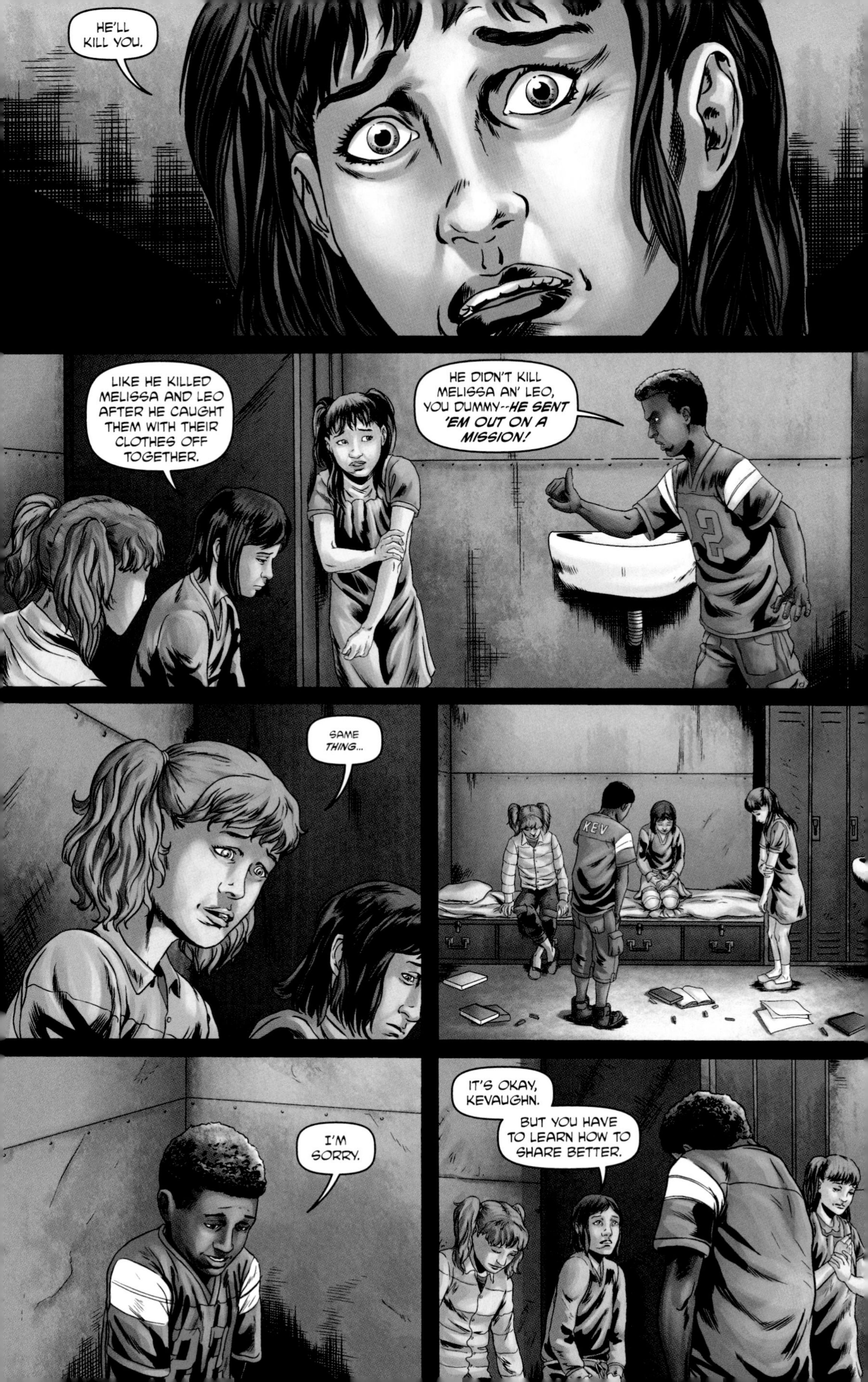
HE'LL KILL YOU.
LIKE HE KILLED MELISSA AND LEO AFTER HE CAUGHT THEM WITH THEIR CLOTHES OFF TOGETHER.
HE DIDN'T KILL MELISSA AN' LEO, YOU DUMMY--*HE SENT 'EM OUT ON A MISSION!*
SAME *THING*...
KEV
I'M SORRY.
IT'S OKAY, KEVAUGHN.
BUT YOU HAVE TO LEARN HOW TO SHARE BETTER.

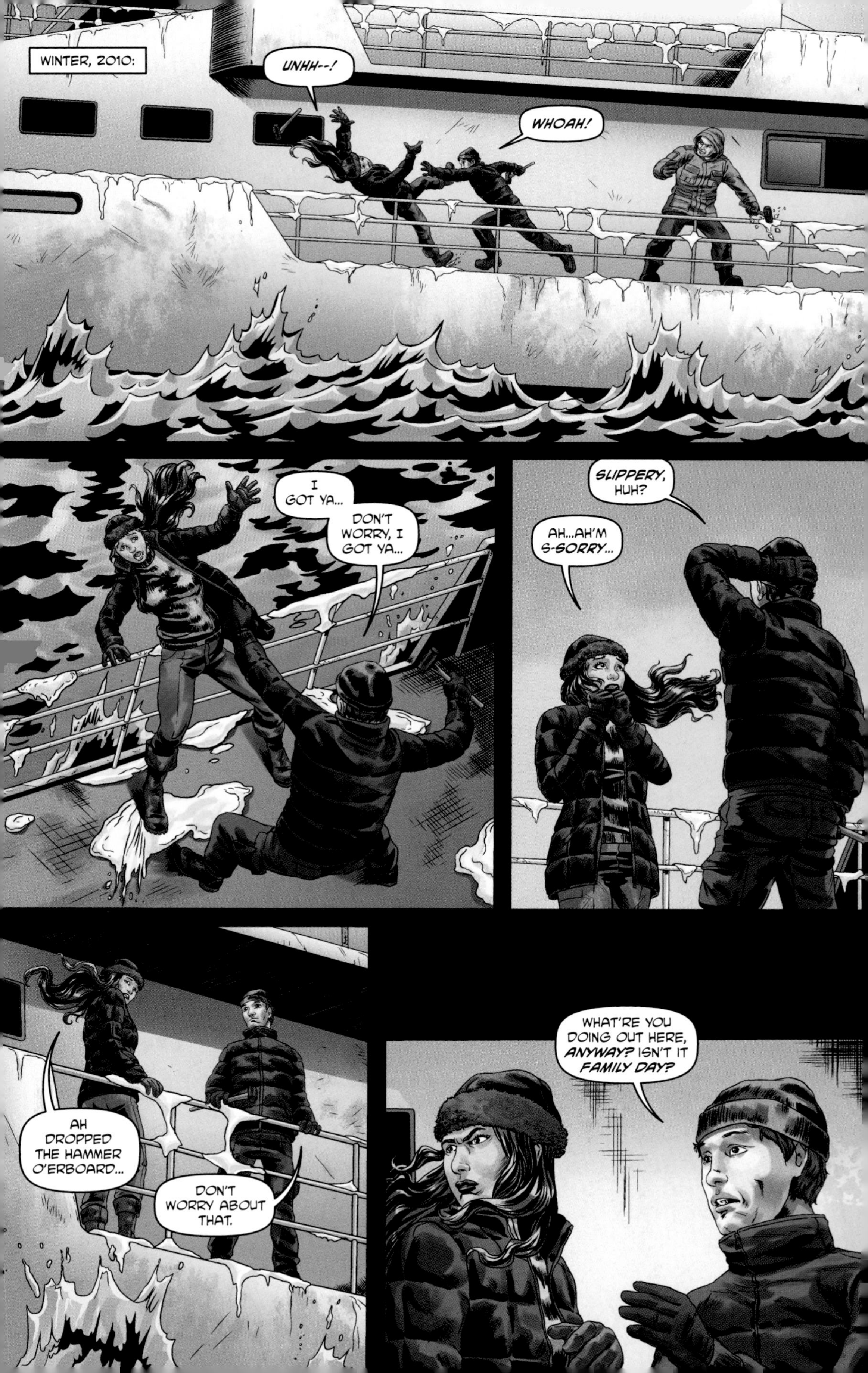
WINTER, 2010:
UNHH--!
WHOAH!
I GOT YA...
DON'T WORRY, I GOT YA...
SLIPPERY, HUH?
AH...AH'M S-SORRY...
AH DROPPED THE HAMMER O'ERBOARD...
DON'T WORRY ABOUT THAT.
WHAT'RE YOU DOING OUT HERE, ANYWAY? ISN'T IT FAMILY DAY?

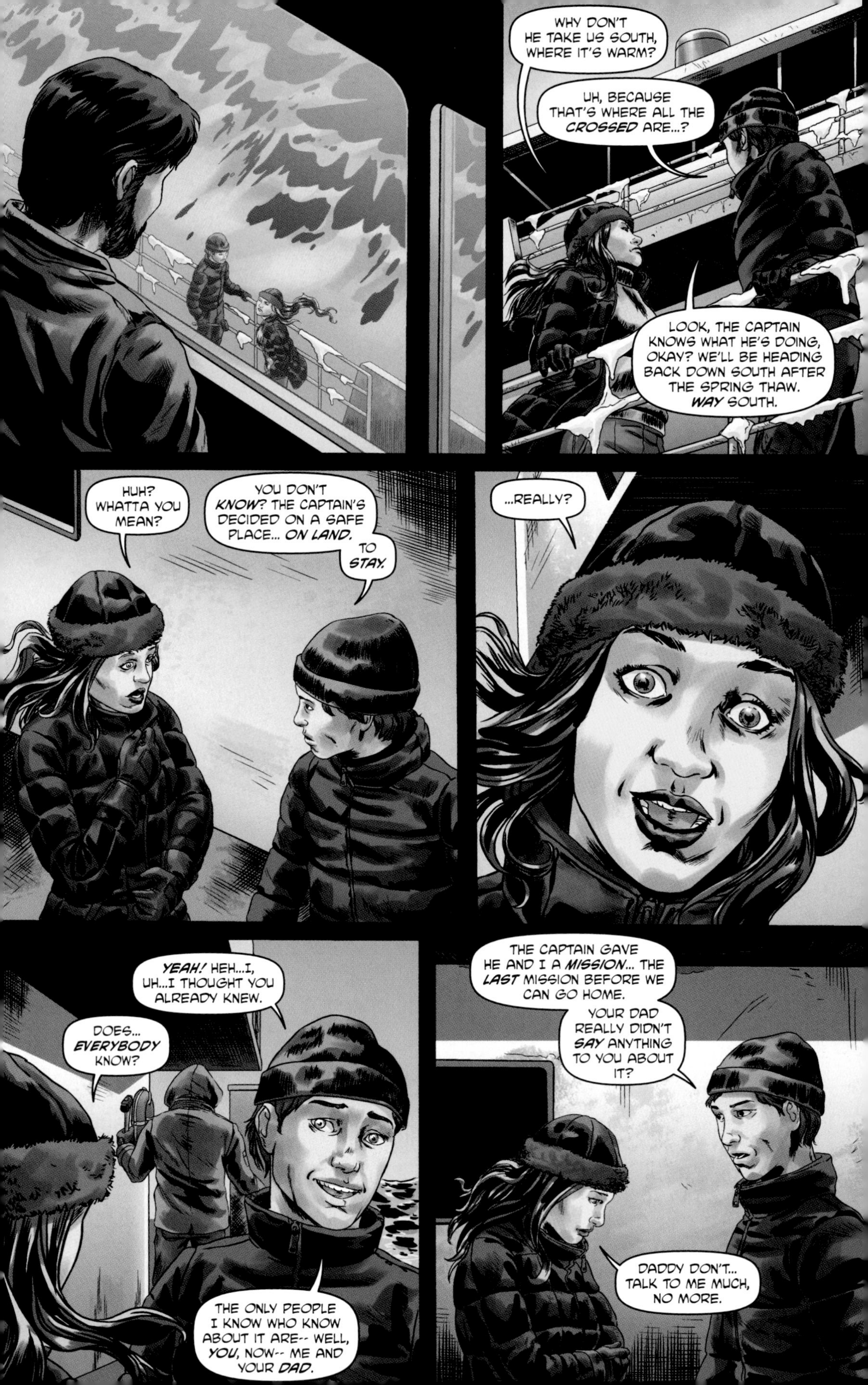

WHY DON'T HE TAKE US SOUTH, WHERE IT'S WARM?
UH, BECAUSE THAT'S WHERE ALL THE *CROSSED* ARE...?
LOOK, THE CAPTAIN KNOWS WHAT HE'S DOING, OKAY? WE'LL BE HEADING BACK DOWN SOUTH AFTER THE SPRING THAW. ***WAY*** SOUTH.
HUH? WHATTA YOU MEAN?
YOU DON'T ***KNOW***? THE CAPTAIN'S DECIDED ON A SAFE PLACE... ***ON LAND.***
TO ***STAY.***
...REALLY?
YEAH! HEH...I, UH...I THOUGHT YOU ALREADY KNEW.
DOES... ***EVERYBODY*** KNOW?
THE ONLY PEOPLE I KNOW WHO KNOW ABOUT IT ARE-- WELL, ***YOU***, NOW-- ME AND YOUR ***DAD***.
THE CAPTAIN GAVE HE AND I A ***MISSION***... THE ***LAST*** MISSION BEFORE WE CAN GO HOME.
YOUR DAD REALLY DIDN'T ***SAY*** ANYTHING TO YOU ABOUT IT?
DADDY DON'T... TALK TO ME MUCH, NO MORE.

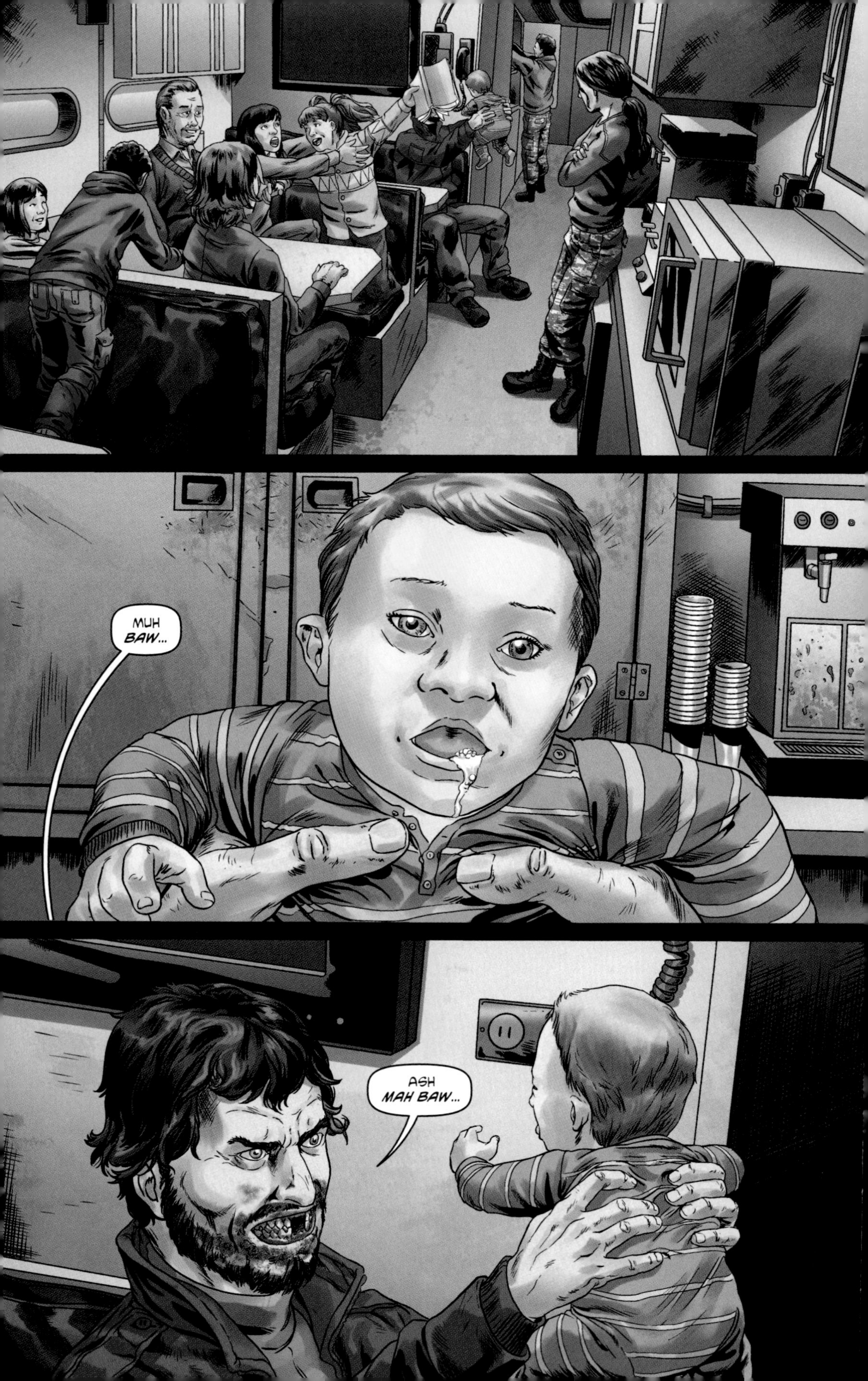
MUH BAW...
ASH MAH BAW...

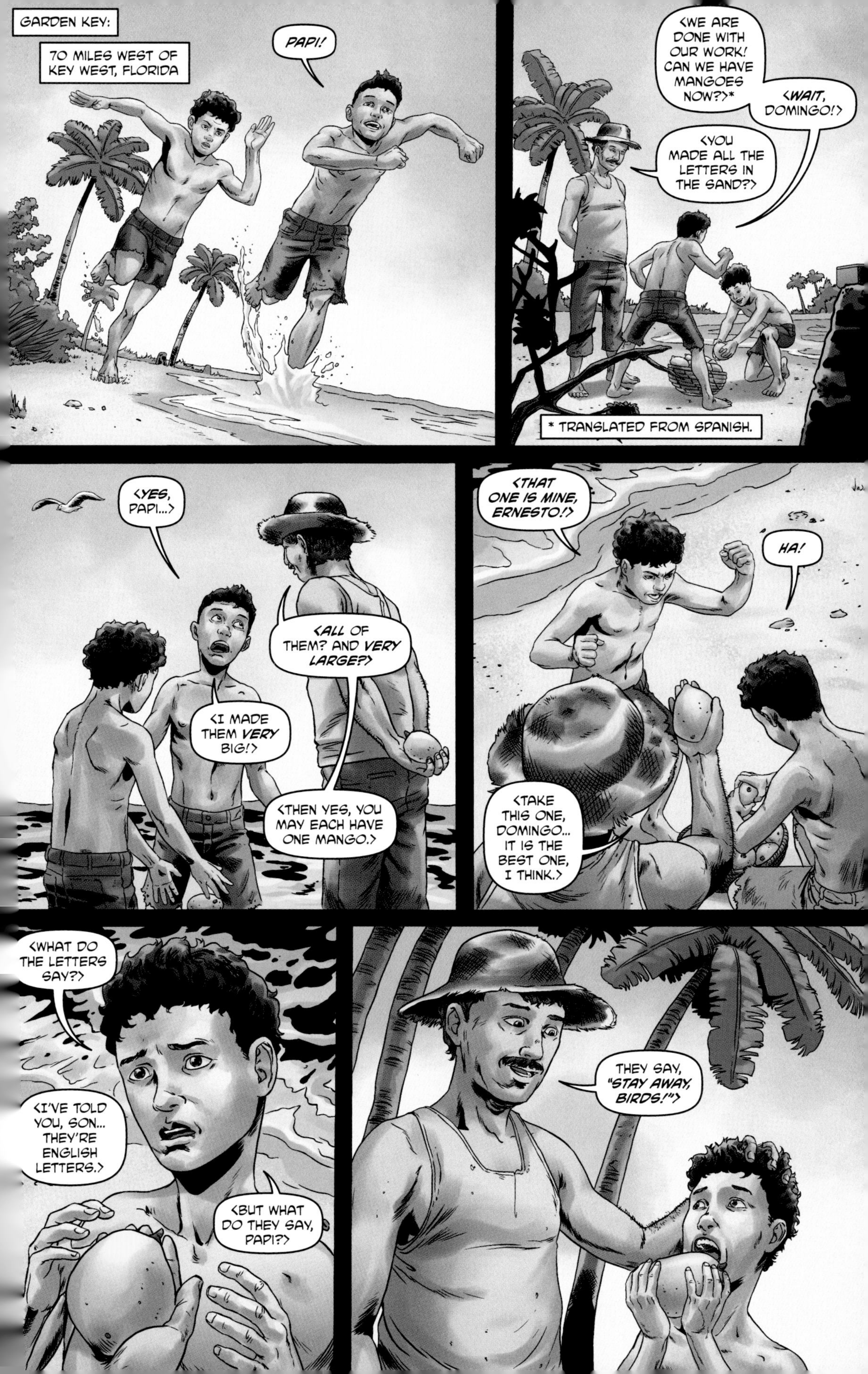
GARDEN KEY:
70 MILES WEST OF KEY WEST, FLORIDA
PAPI!
<WE ARE DONE WITH OUR WORK! CAN WE HAVE MANGOES NOW?>*
<WAIT, DOMINGO!>
<YOU MADE ALL THE LETTERS IN THE SAND?>
* TRANSLATED FROM SPANISH.
<YES, PAPI...>
<ALL OF THEM? AND VERY LARGE?>
<I MADE THEM VERY BIG!>
<THEN YES, YOU MAY EACH HAVE ONE MANGO.>
<THAT ONE IS MINE, ERNESTO!>
HA!
<TAKE THIS ONE, DOMINGO... IT IS THE BEST ONE, I THINK.>
<WHAT DO THE LETTERS SAY?>
<I'VE TOLD YOU, SON... THEY'RE ENGLISH LETTERS.>
<BUT WHAT DO THEY SAY, PAPI?>
THEY SAY, "STAY AWAY, BIRDS!">

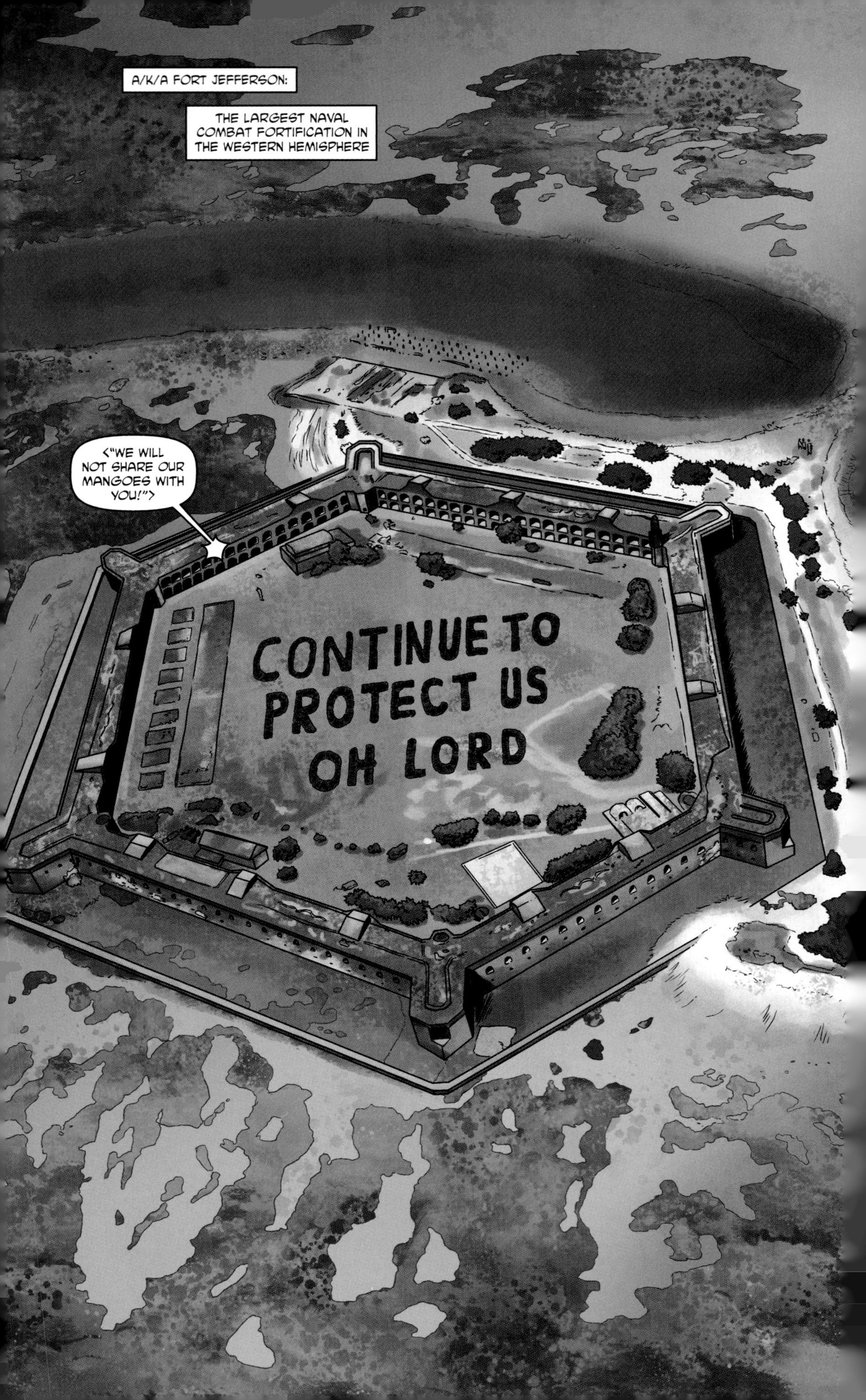
A/K/A FORT JEFFERSON:
THE LARGEST NAVAL COMBAT FORTIFICATION IN THE WESTERN HEMISPHERE
<"WE WILL NOT SHARE OUR MANGOES WITH YOU!">
CONTINUE TO PROTECT US OH LORD

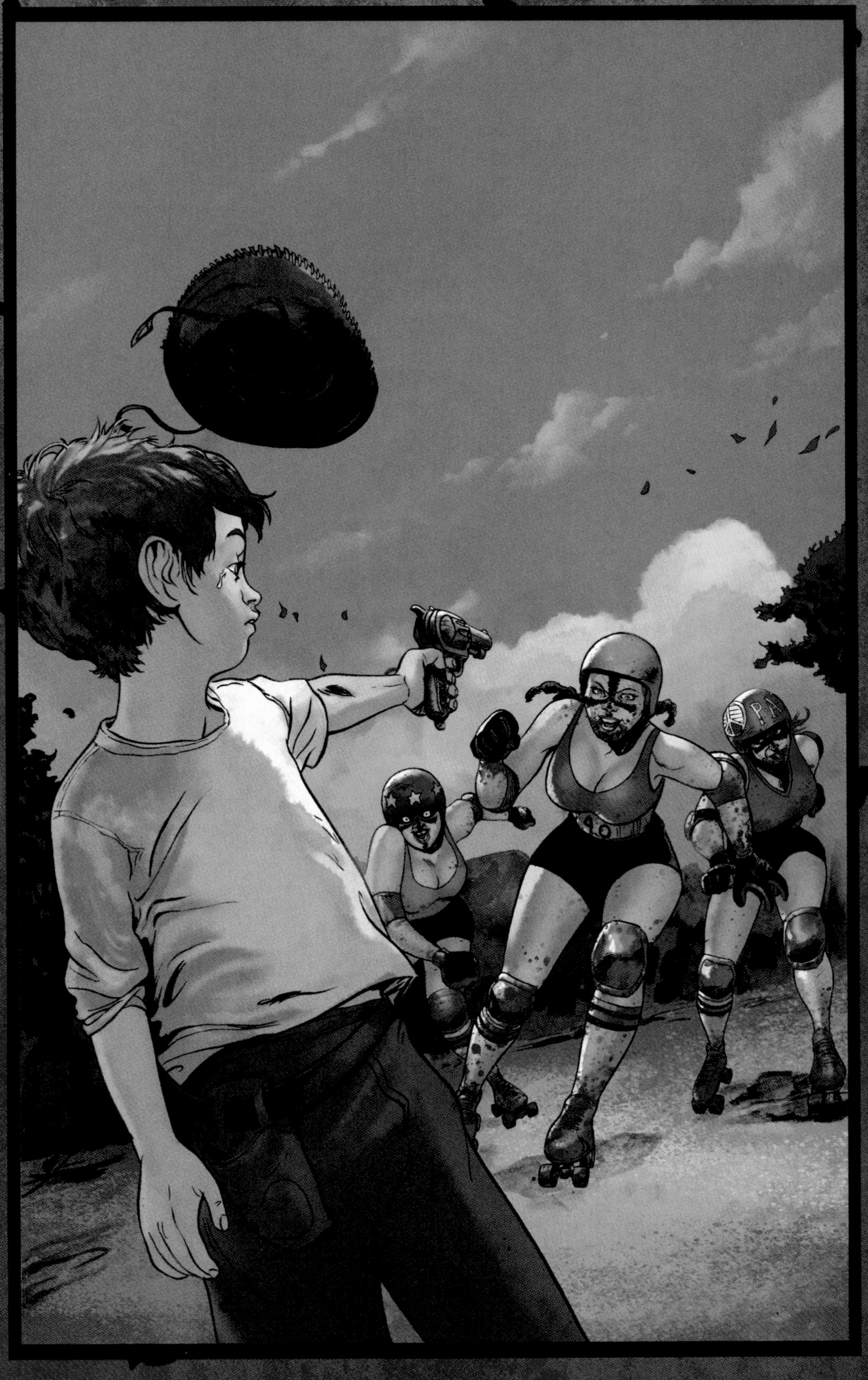

PART 2

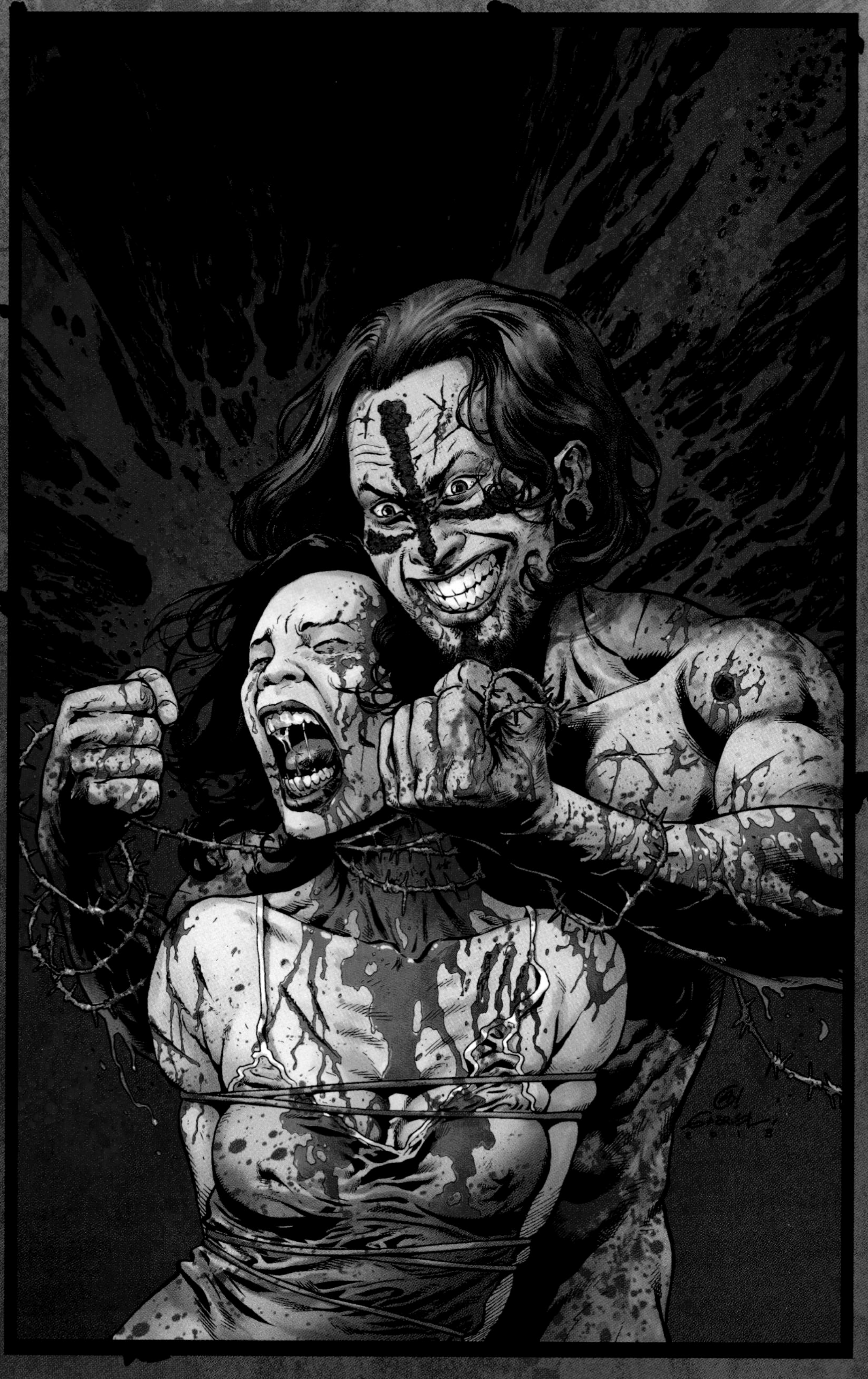

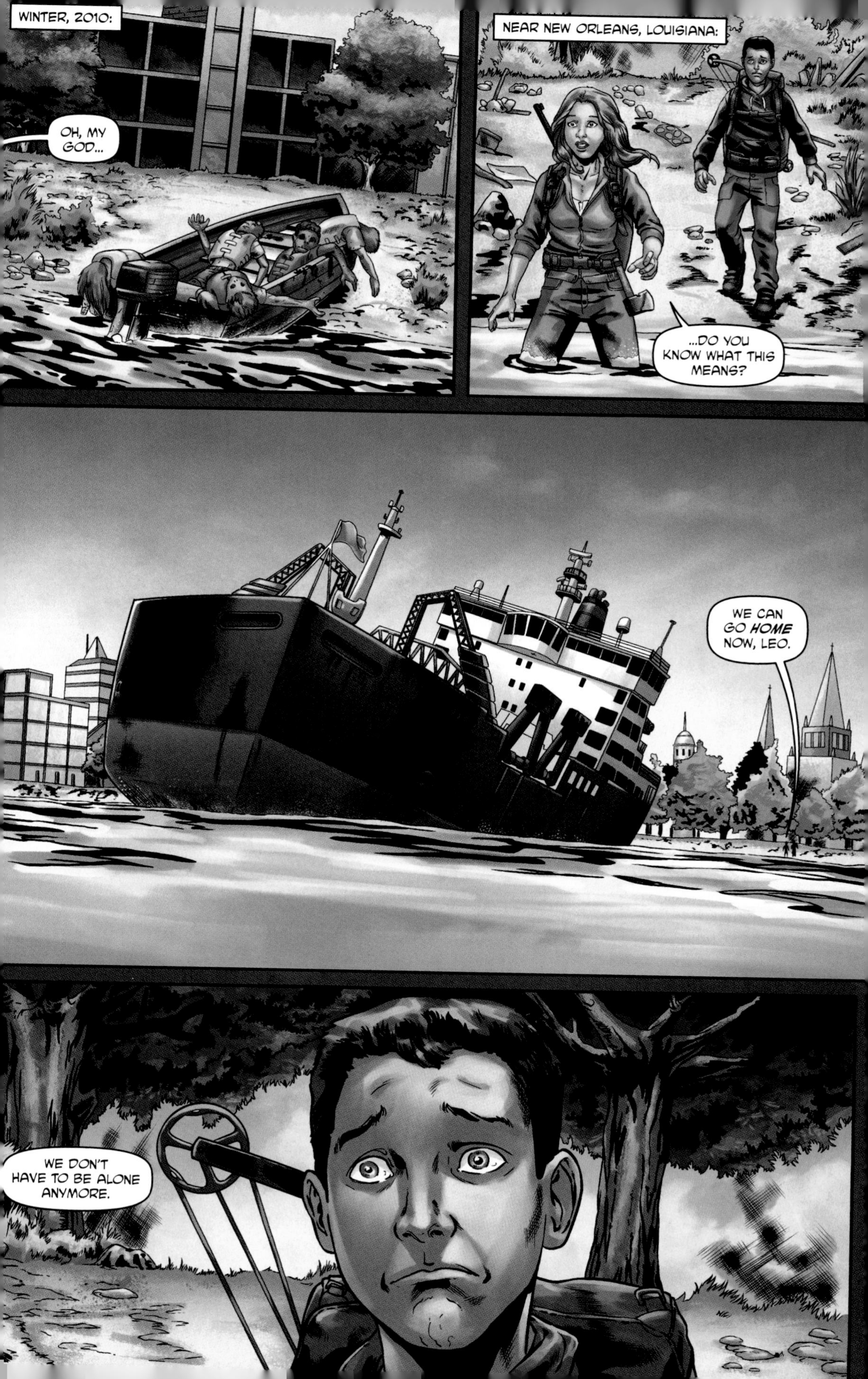
WINTER, 2010:
OH, MY GOD...
NEAR NEW ORLEANS, LOUISIANA:
...DO YOU KNOW WHAT THIS MEANS?
WE CAN GO **HOME** NOW, LEO.
WE DON'T HAVE TO BE ALONE ANYMORE.

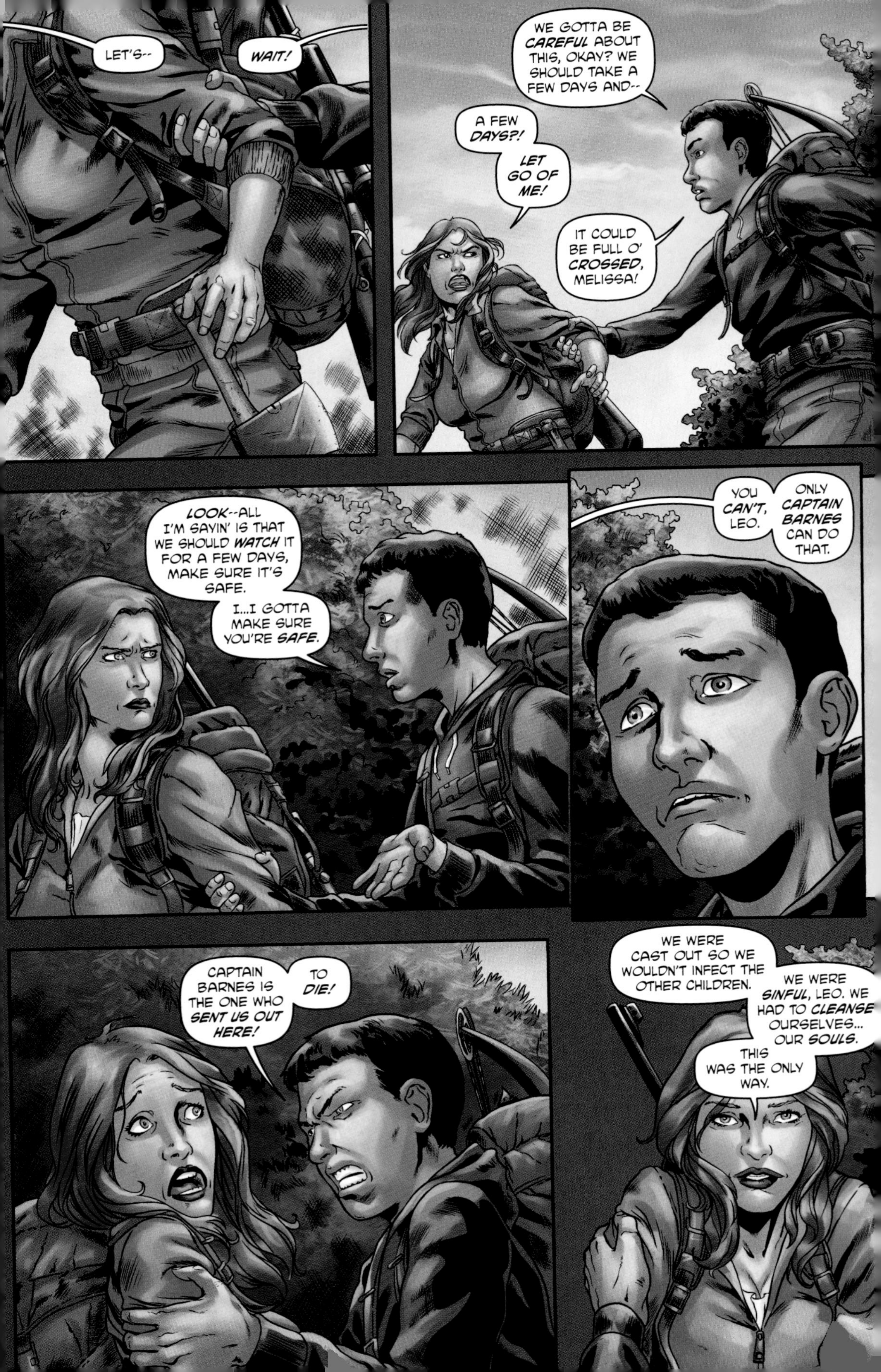

LET'S--
WAIT!
WE GOTTA BE CAREFUL ABOUT THIS, OKAY? WE SHOULD TAKE A FEW DAYS AND--
A FEW DAYS?!
LET GO OF ME!
IT COULD BE FULL O' CROSSED, MELISSA!
LOOK--ALL I'M SAYIN' IS THAT WE SHOULD WATCH IT FOR A FEW DAYS, MAKE SURE IT'S SAFE.
I...I GOTTA MAKE SURE YOU'RE SAFE.
YOU CAN'T, LEO.
ONLY CAPTAIN BARNES CAN DO THAT.
CAPTAIN BARNES IS THE ONE WHO SENT US OUT HERE!
TO DIE!
WE WERE CAST OUT SO WE WOULDN'T INFECT THE OTHER CHILDREN.
WE WERE SINFUL, LEO. WE HAD TO CLEANSE OURSELVES... OUR SOULS.
THIS WAS THE ONLY WAY.

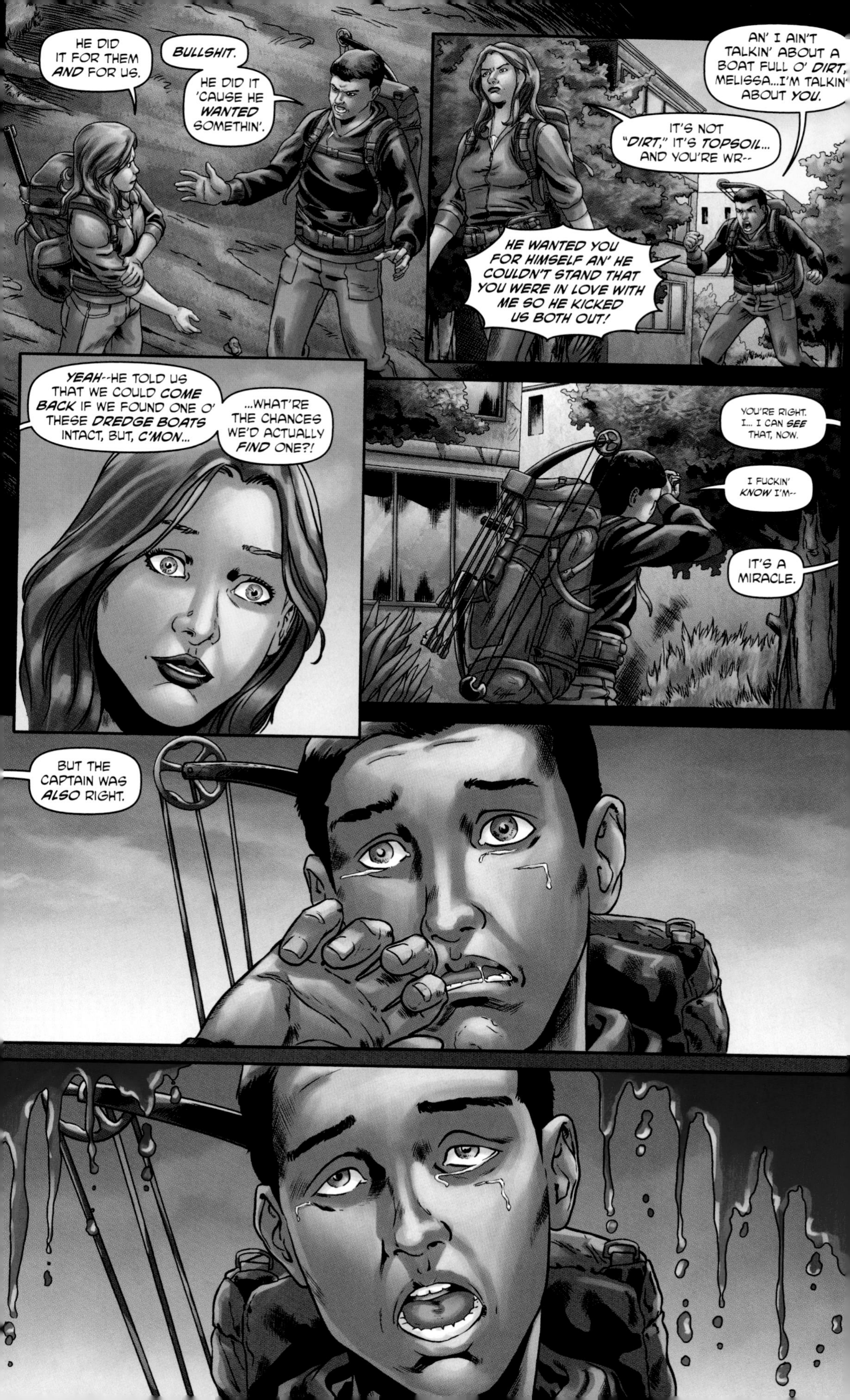
HE DID IT FOR THEM AND FOR US.
BULLSHIT.
HE DID IT 'CAUSE HE WANTED SOMETHIN'.
AN' I AIN'T TALKIN' ABOUT A BOAT FULL O' DIRT, MELISSA...I'M TALKIN' ABOUT YOU.
IT'S NOT "DIRT," IT'S TOPSOIL... AND YOU'RE WR--
HE WANTED YOU FOR HIMSELF AN' HE COULDN'T STAND THAT YOU WERE IN LOVE WITH ME SO HE KICKED US BOTH OUT!
YEAH--HE TOLD US THAT WE COULD COME BACK IF WE FOUND ONE O' THESE DREDGE BOATS INTACT, BUT, C'MON...
...WHAT'RE THE CHANCES WE'D ACTUALLY FIND ONE?!
YOU'RE RIGHT. I... I CAN SEE THAT, NOW.
I FUCKIN' KNOW I'M--
IT'S A MIRACLE.
BUT THE CAPTAIN WAS ALSO RIGHT.

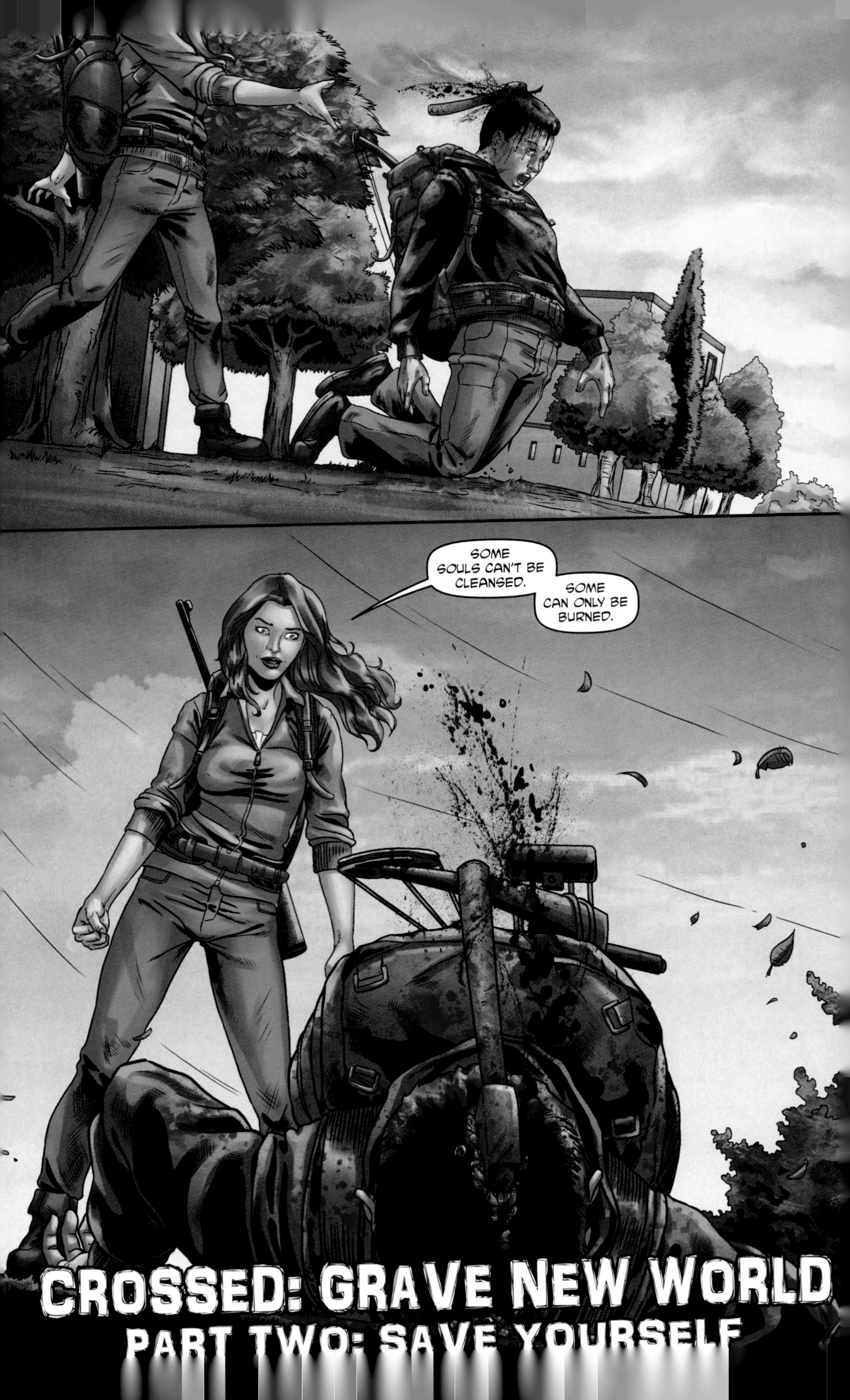
SOME SOULS CAN'T BE CLEANSED.
SOME CAN ONLY BE BURNED.
CROSSED: GRAVE NEW WORLD
PART TWO: SAVE YOURSELF

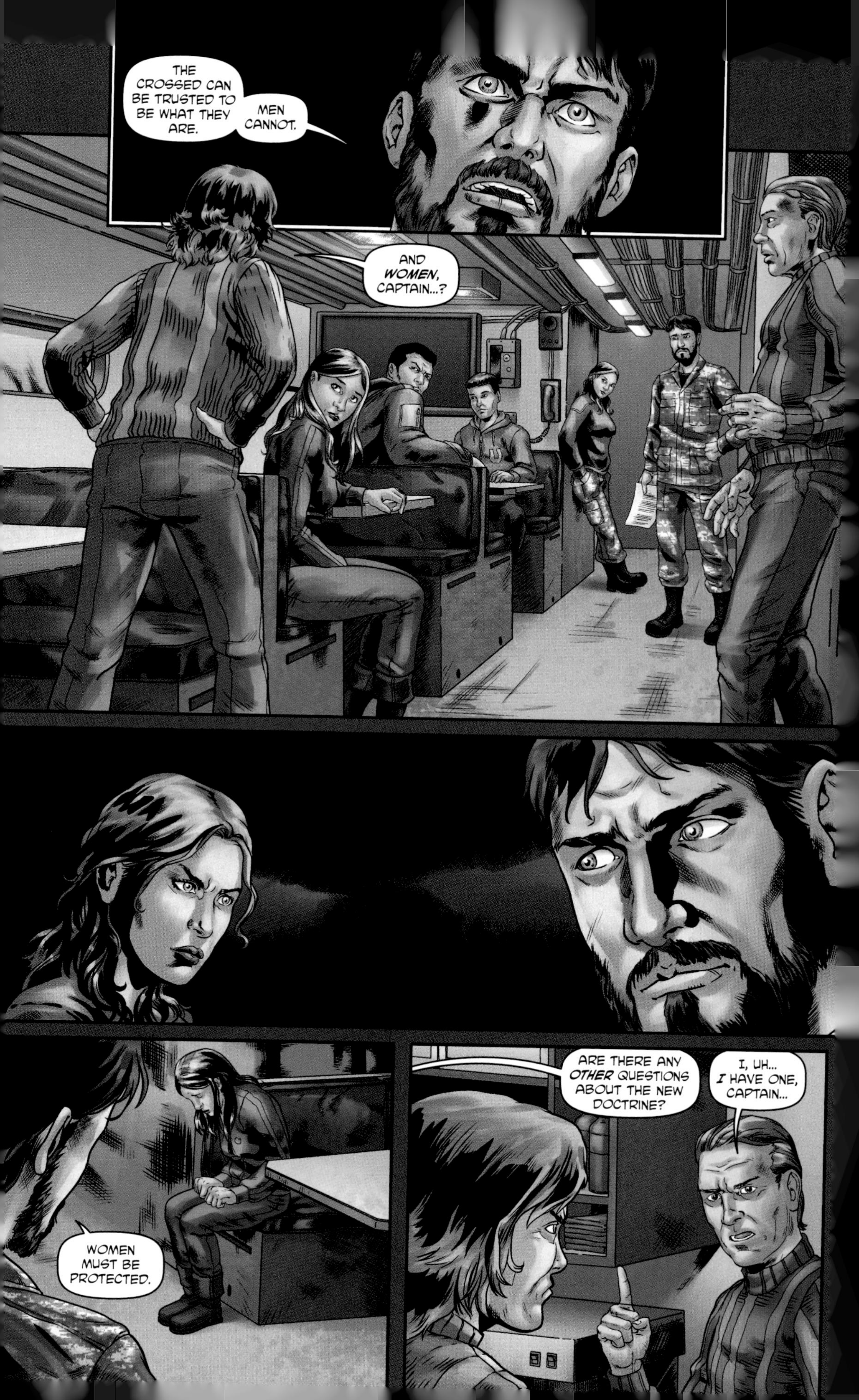
THE CROSSED CAN BE TRUSTED TO BE WHAT THEY ARE.
MEN CANNOT.
AND *WOMEN*, CAPTAIN...?
WOMEN MUST BE PROTECTED.
ARE THERE ANY *OTHER* QUESTIONS ABOUT THE NEW DOCTRINE?
I, UH... *I* HAVE ONE, CAPTAIN...

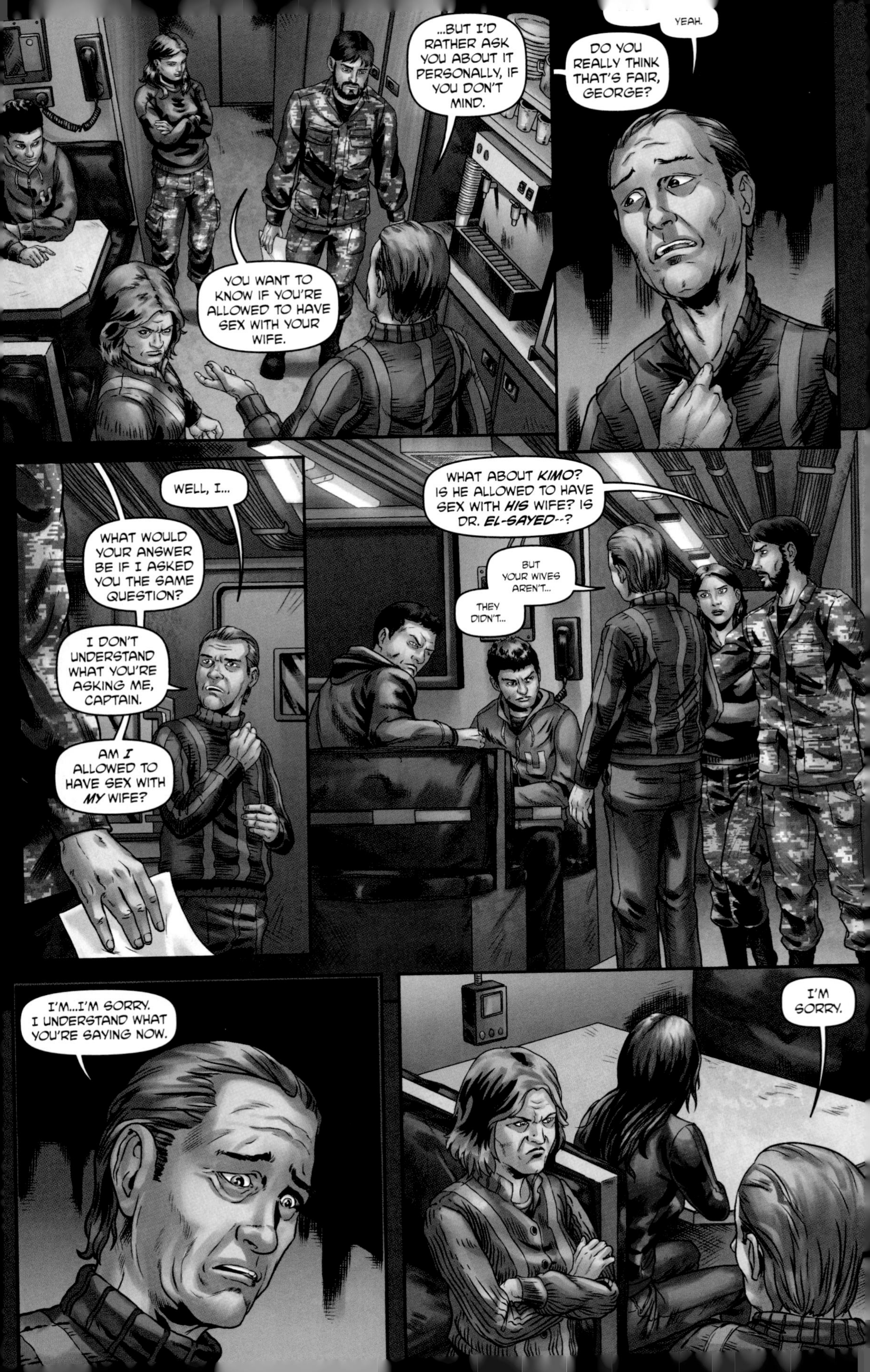
...BUT I'D RATHER ASK YOU ABOUT IT PERSONALLY, IF YOU DON'T MIND.
YOU WANT TO KNOW IF YOU'RE ALLOWED TO HAVE SEX WITH YOUR WIFE.
YEAH.
DO YOU REALLY THINK THAT'S FAIR, GEORGE?
WELL, I...
WHAT WOULD YOUR ANSWER BE IF I ASKED YOU THE SAME QUESTION?
I DON'T UNDERSTAND WHAT YOU'RE ASKING ME, CAPTAIN.
AM *I* ALLOWED TO HAVE SEX WITH *MY* WIFE?
WHAT ABOUT *KIMO*? IS HE ALLOWED TO HAVE SEX WITH *HIS* WIFE? IS DR. *EL-SAYED*--?
BUT YOUR WIVES AREN'T...
THEY DIDN'T...
I'M...I'M SORRY. I UNDERSTAND WHAT YOU'RE SAYING NOW.
I'M SORRY.

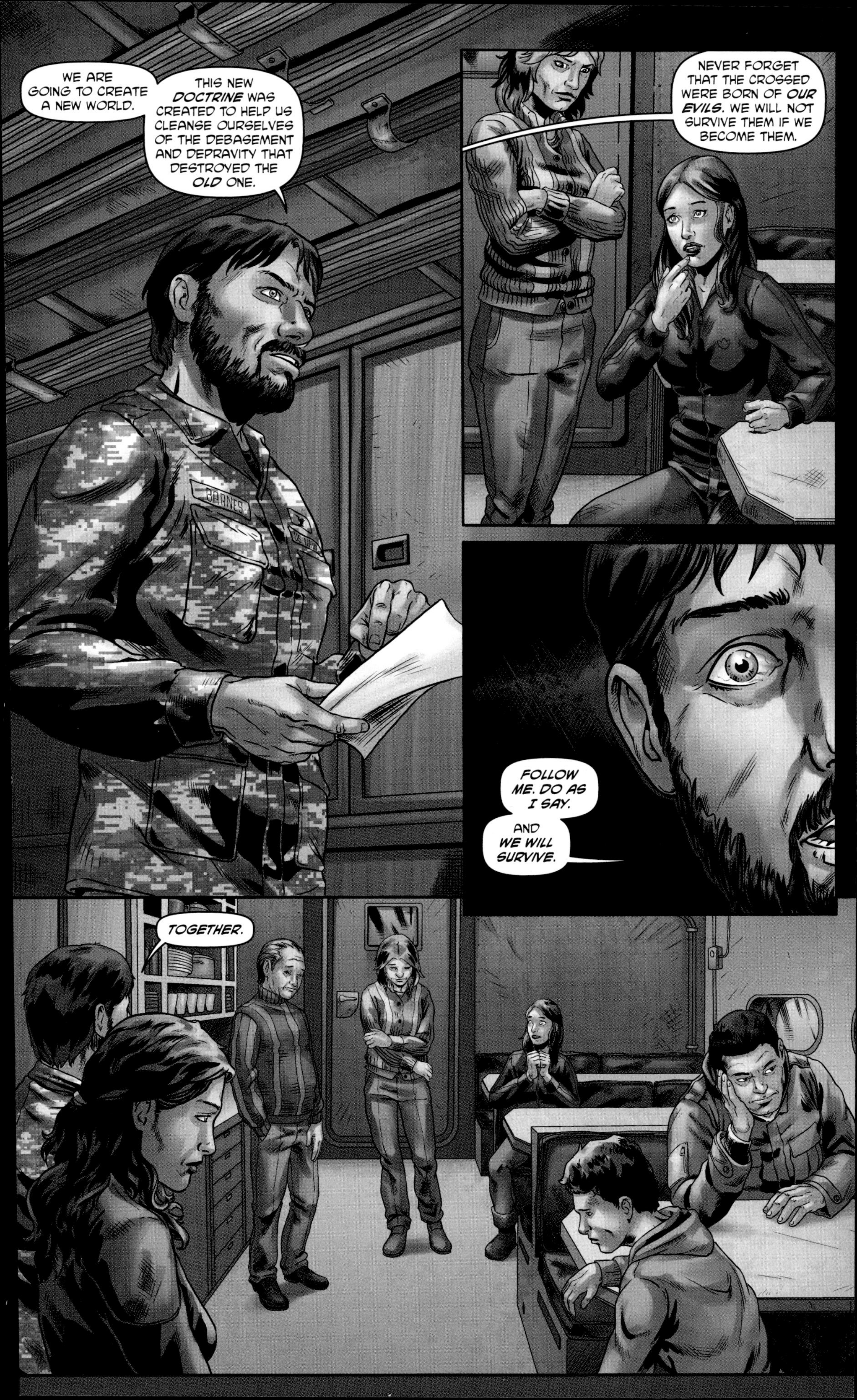

WE ARE GOING TO CREATE A NEW WORLD.
THIS NEW DOCTRINE WAS CREATED TO HELP US CLEANSE OURSELVES OF THE DEBASEMENT AND DEPRAVITY THAT DESTROYED THE OLD ONE.
NEVER FORGET THAT THE CROSSED WERE BORN OF OUR EVILS. WE WILL NOT SURVIVE THEM IF WE BECOME THEM.
FOLLOW ME. DO AS I SAY.
AND WE WILL SURVIVE.
TOGETHER.

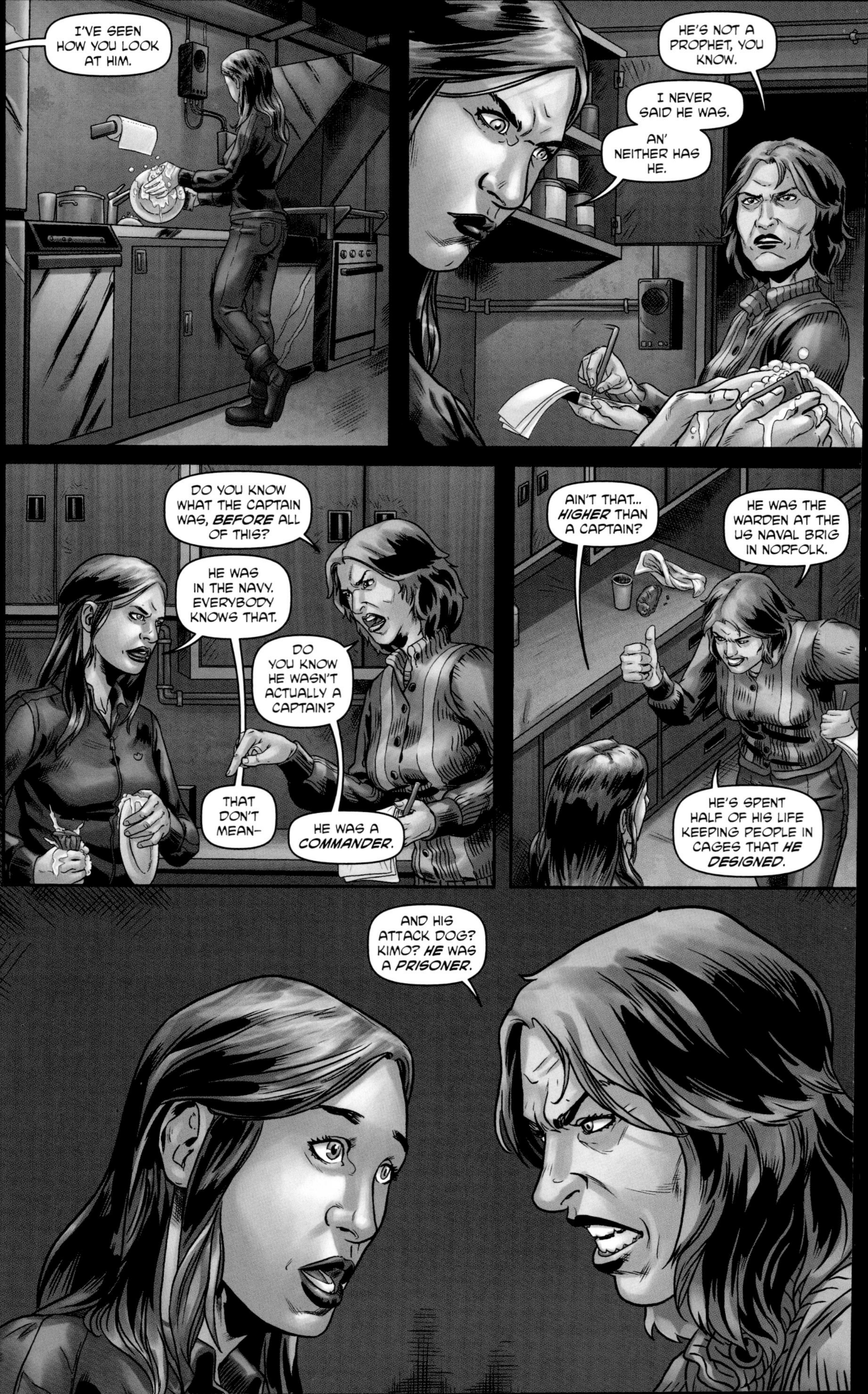

I'VE SEEN HOW YOU LOOK AT HIM.
HE'S NOT A PROPHET, YOU KNOW.
I NEVER SAID HE WAS.
AN' NEITHER HAS HE.
DO YOU KNOW WHAT THE CAPTAIN WAS, *BEFORE* ALL OF THIS?
HE WAS IN THE NAVY. EVERYBODY KNOWS THAT.
DO YOU KNOW HE WASN'T ACTUALLY A CAPTAIN?
THAT DON'T MEAN–
HE WAS A *COMMANDER*.
AIN'T THAT... *HIGHER* THAN A CAPTAIN?
HE WAS THE WARDEN AT THE US NAVAL BRIG IN NORFOLK.
HE'S SPENT HALF OF HIS LIFE KEEPING PEOPLE IN CAGES THAT *HE DESIGNED*.
AND HIS ATTACK DOG? KIMO? *HE* WAS A *PRISONER*.

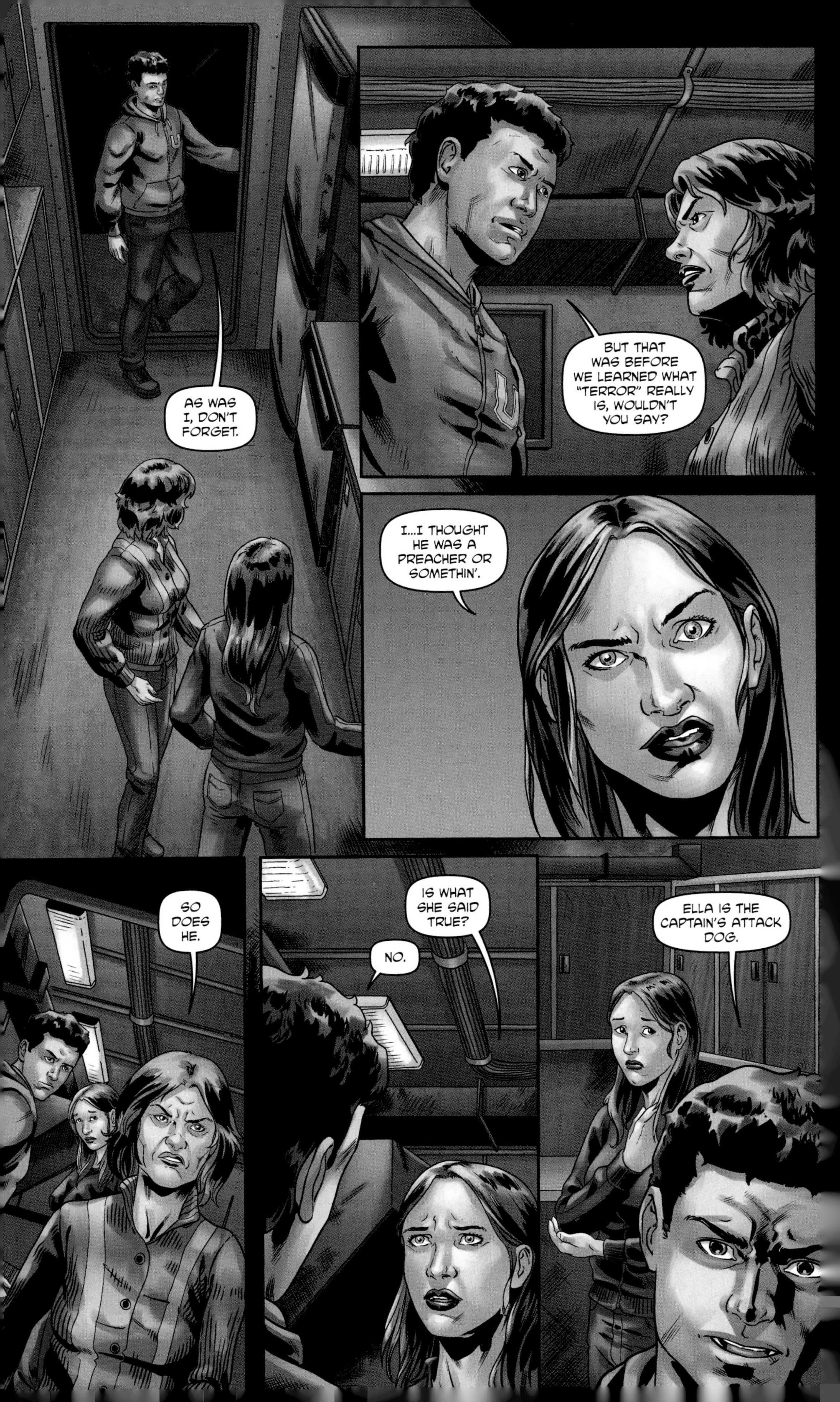
AS WAS I, DON'T FORGET.
BUT THAT WAS BEFORE WE LEARNED WHAT "TERROR" REALLY IS, WOULDN'T YOU SAY?
I...I THOUGHT HE WAS A PREACHER OR SOMETHIN'.
SO DOES HE.
IS WHAT SHE SAID TRUE?
NO.
ELLA IS THE CAPTAIN'S ATTACK DOG.

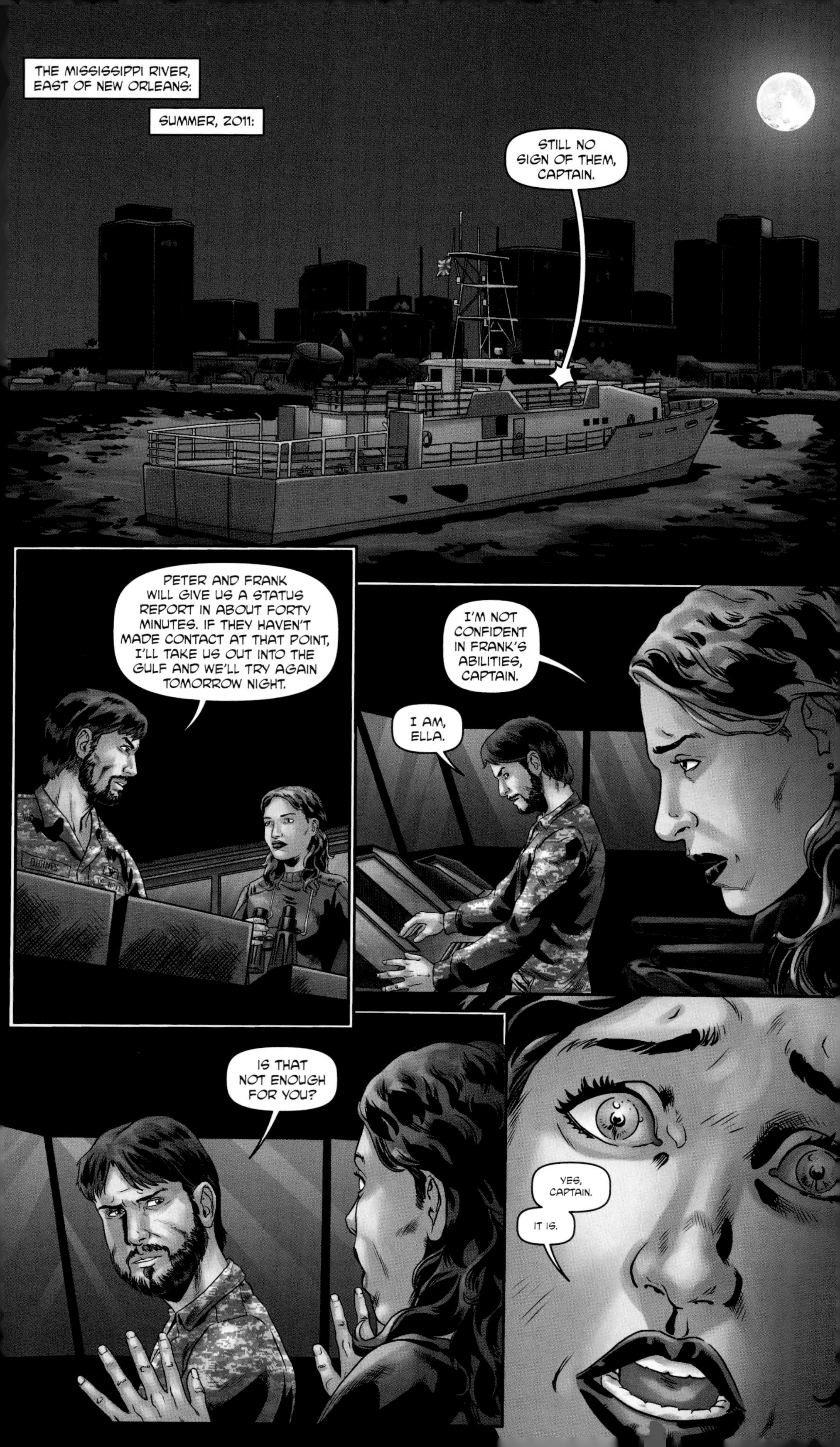
THE MISSISSIPPI RIVER, EAST OF NEW ORLEANS:
SUMMER, 2011:
STILL NO SIGN OF THEM, CAPTAIN.
PETER AND FRANK WILL GIVE US A STATUS REPORT IN ABOUT FORTY MINUTES. IF THEY HAVEN'T MADE CONTACT AT THAT POINT, I'LL TAKE US OUT INTO THE GULF AND WE'LL TRY AGAIN TOMORROW NIGHT.
I'M NOT CONFIDENT IN FRANK'S ABILITIES, CAPTAIN.
I AM, ELLA.
IS THAT NOT ENOUGH FOR YOU?
YES, CAPTAIN.
IT IS.

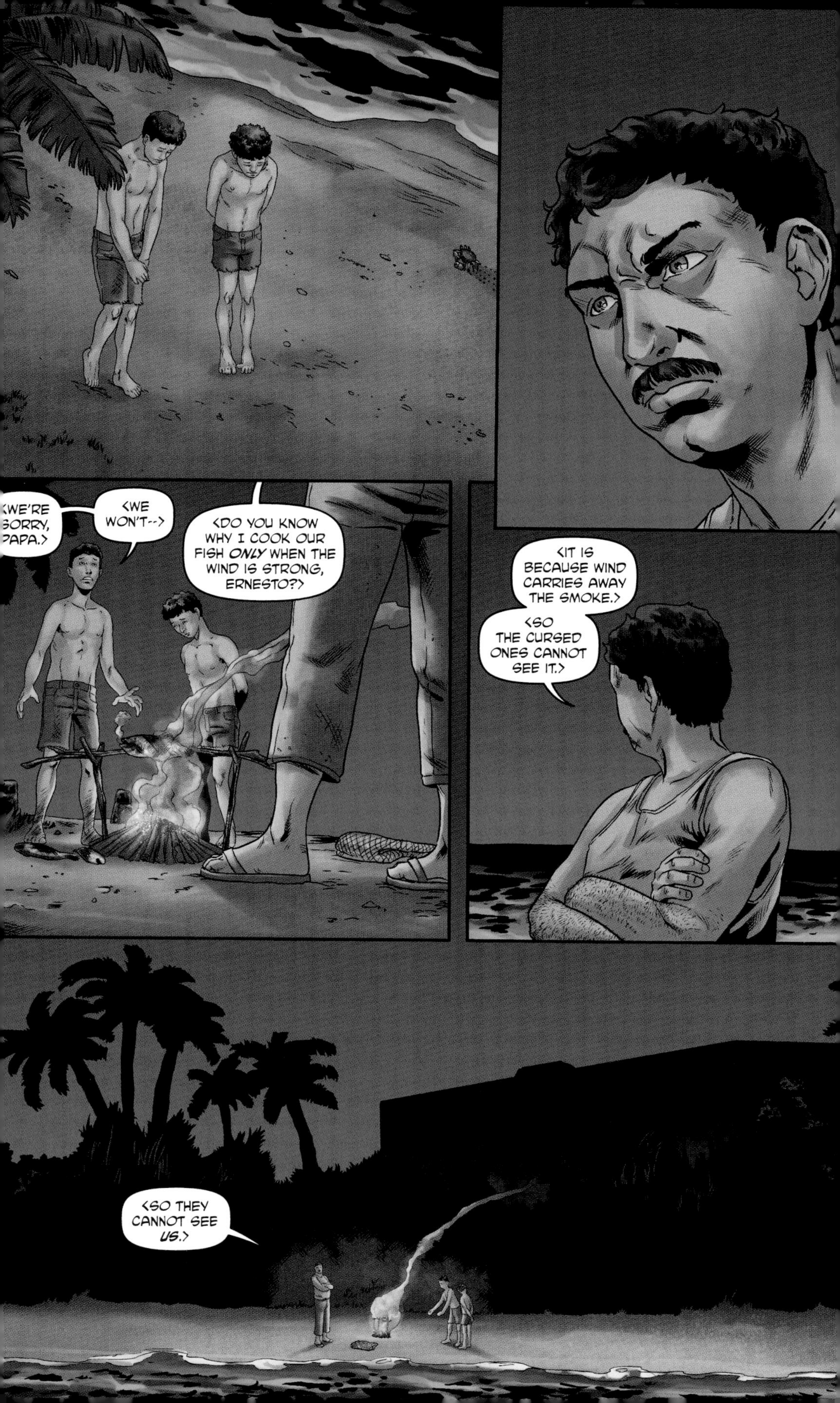

<WE'RE SORRY, PAPA.>
<WE WON'T-->
<DO YOU KNOW WHY I COOK OUR FISH ONLY WHEN THE WIND IS STRONG, ERNESTO?>
<IT IS BECAUSE WIND CARRIES AWAY THE SMOKE.>
<SO THE CURSED ONES CANNOT SEE IT.>
<SO THEY CANNOT SEE US.>

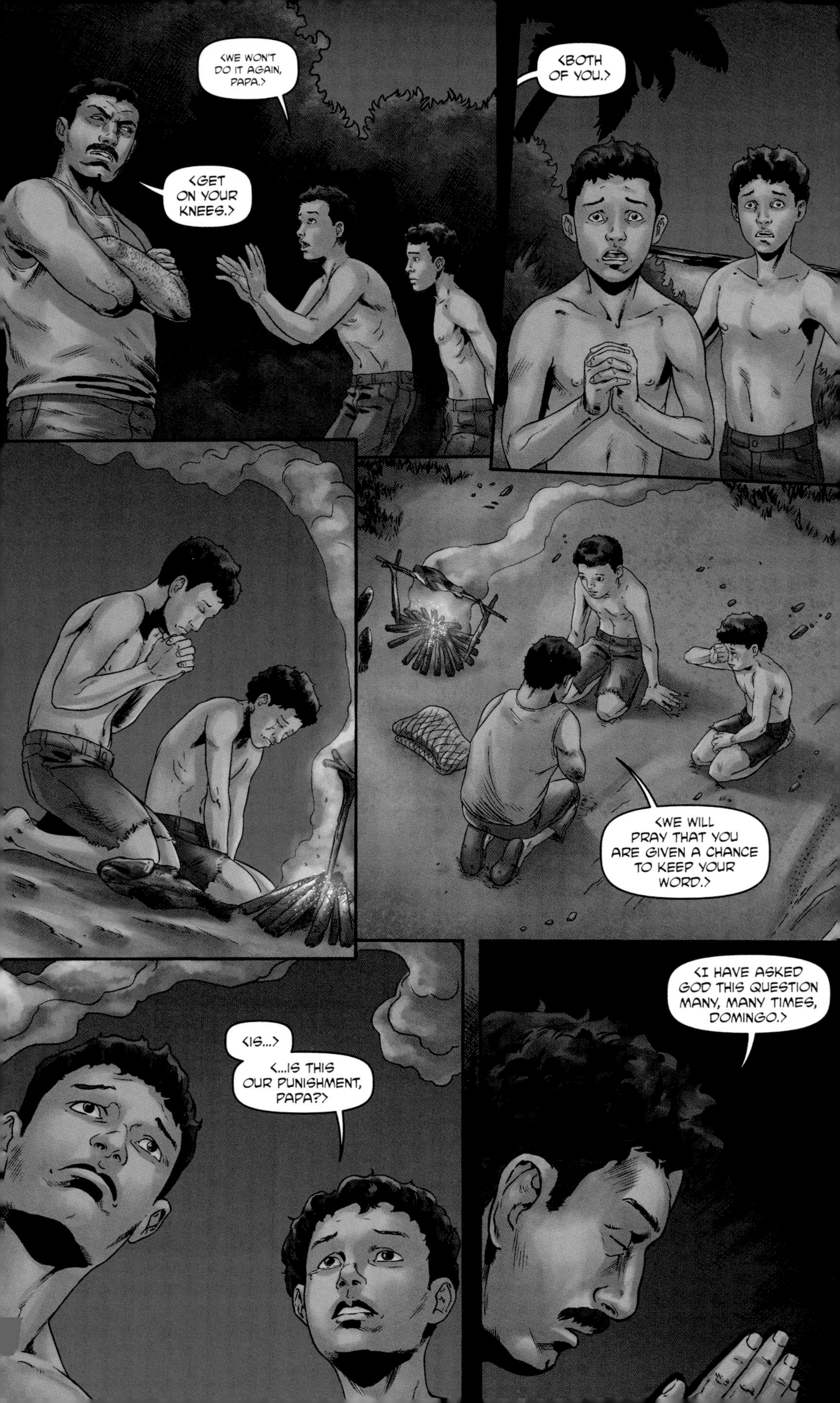

<WE WON'T DO IT AGAIN, PAPA.>
<GET ON YOUR KNEES.>
<BOTH OF YOU.>
<WE WILL PRAY THAT YOU ARE GIVEN A CHANCE TO KEEP YOUR WORD.>
<IS...>
<...IS THIS OUR PUNISHMENT, PAPA?>
<I HAVE ASKED GOD THIS QUESTION MANY, MANY TIMES, DOMINGO.>

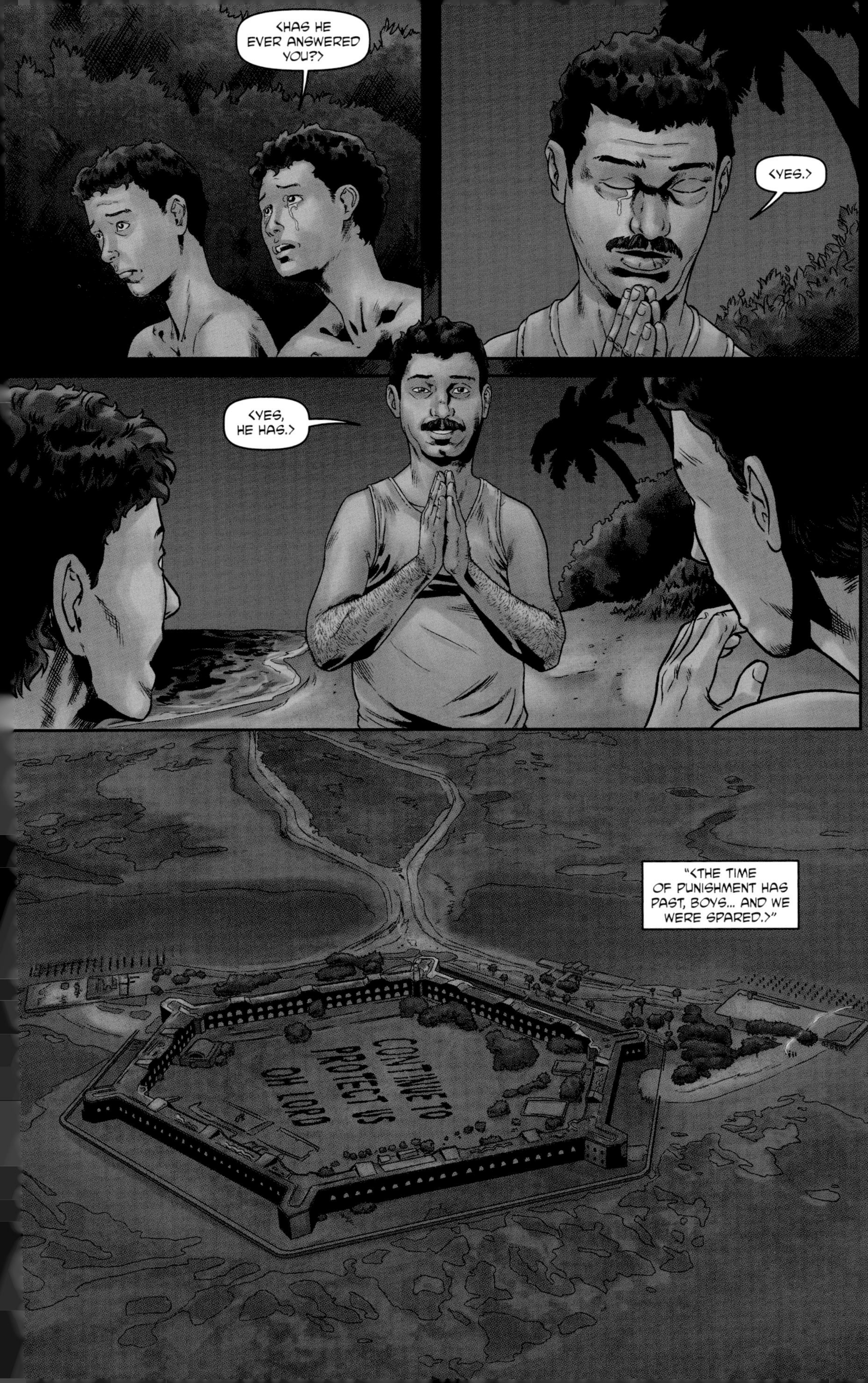
<HAS HE EVER ANSWERED YOU?>
<YES.>
<YES, HE HAS.>
"<THE TIME OF PUNISHMENT HAS PAST, BOYS... AND WE WERE SPARED.>"
CONTINUE TO PROTECT US OH LORD

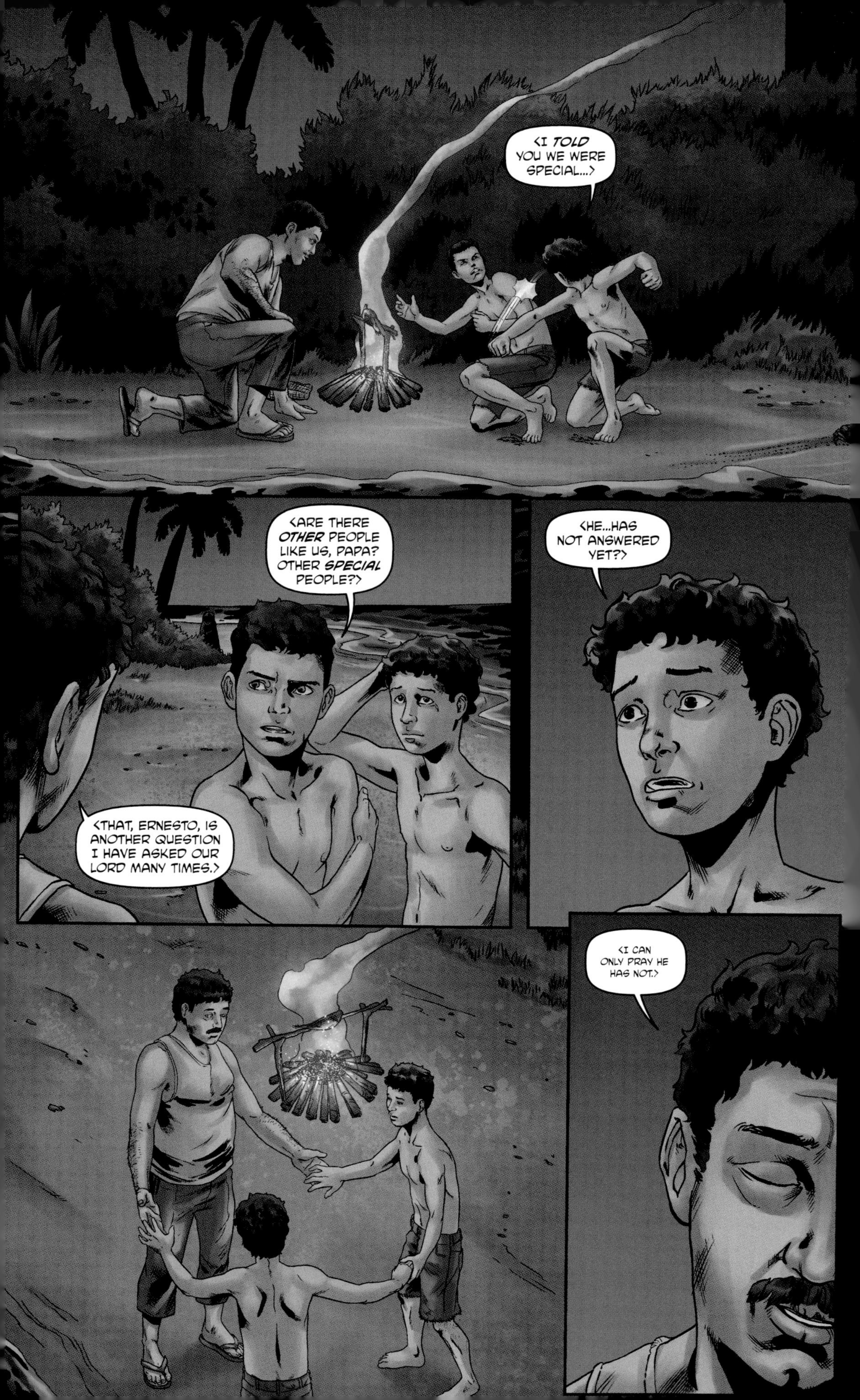

<I TOLD YOU WE WERE SPECIAL...>
<ARE THERE OTHER PEOPLE LIKE US, PAPA? OTHER SPECIAL PEOPLE?>
<THAT, ERNESTO, IS ANOTHER QUESTION I HAVE ASKED OUR LORD MANY TIMES.>
<HE...HAS NOT ANSWERED YET?>
<I CAN ONLY PRAY HE HAS NOT.>

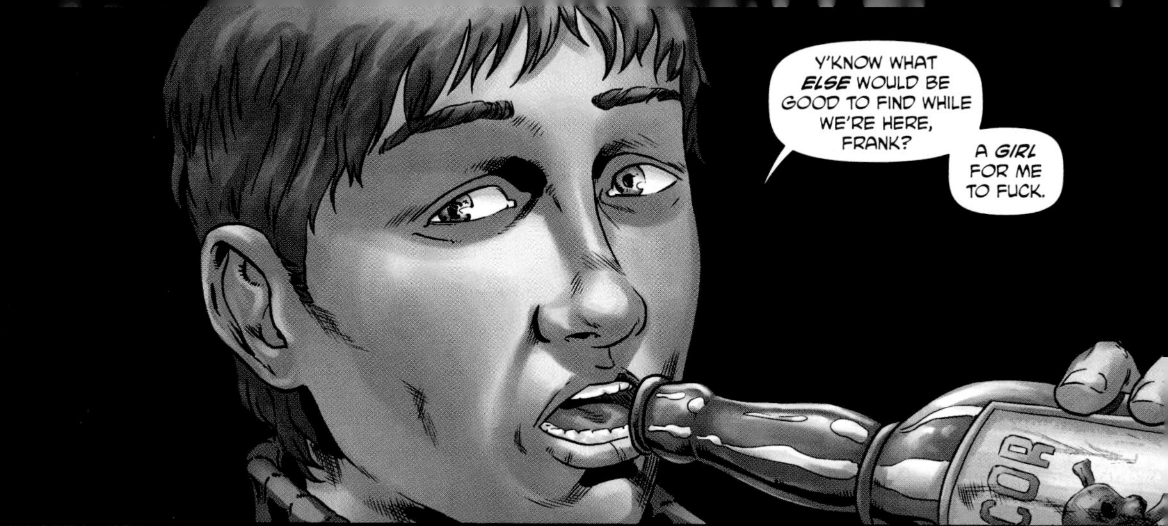
Y'KNOW WHAT ELSE WOULD BE GOOD TO FIND WHILE WE'RE HERE, FRANK?
A GIRL FOR ME TO FUCK.

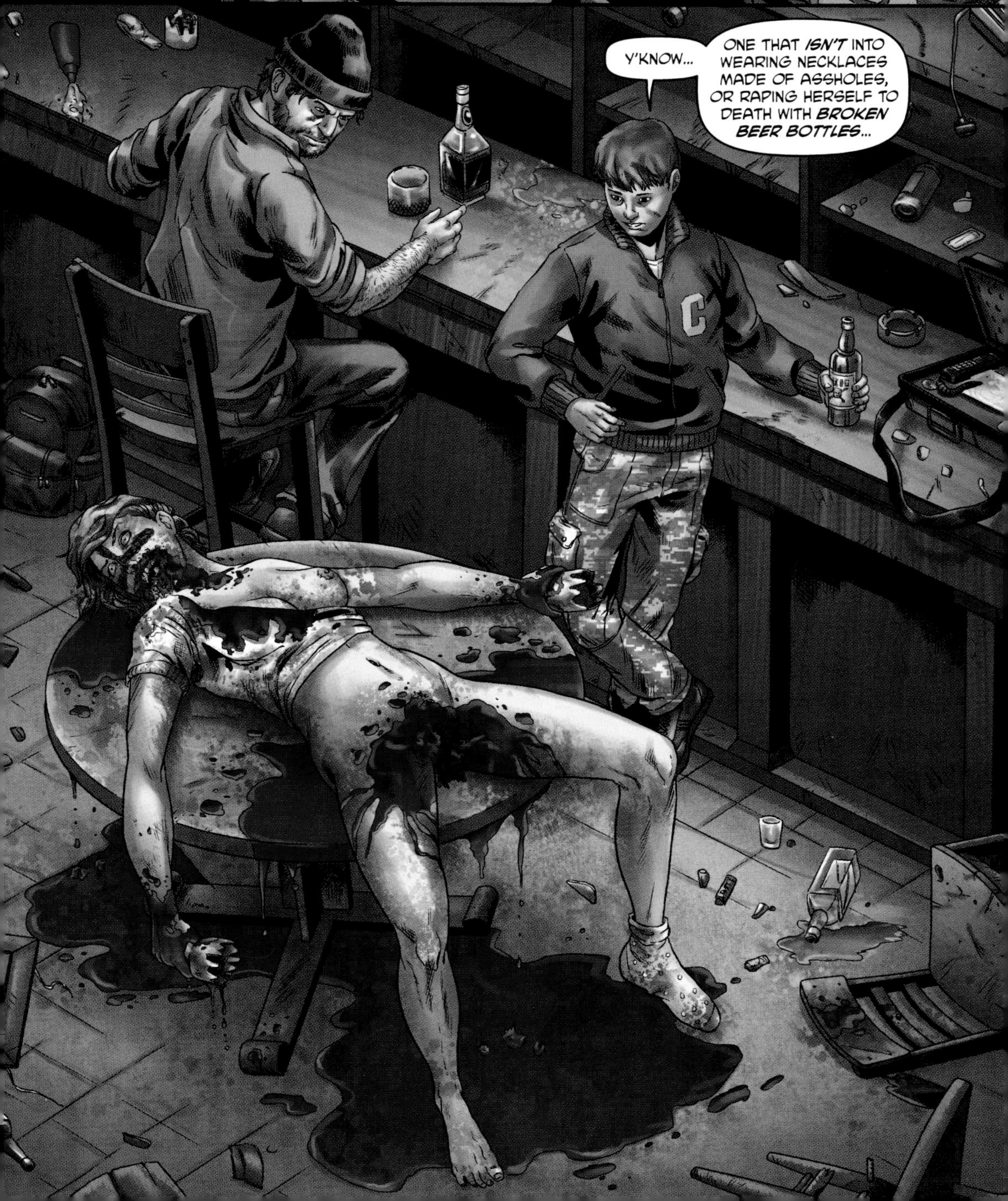
Y'KNOW...
ONE THAT ISN'T INTO WEARING NECKLACES MADE OF ASSHOLES, OR RAPING HERSELF TO DEATH WITH BROKEN BEER BOTTLES...

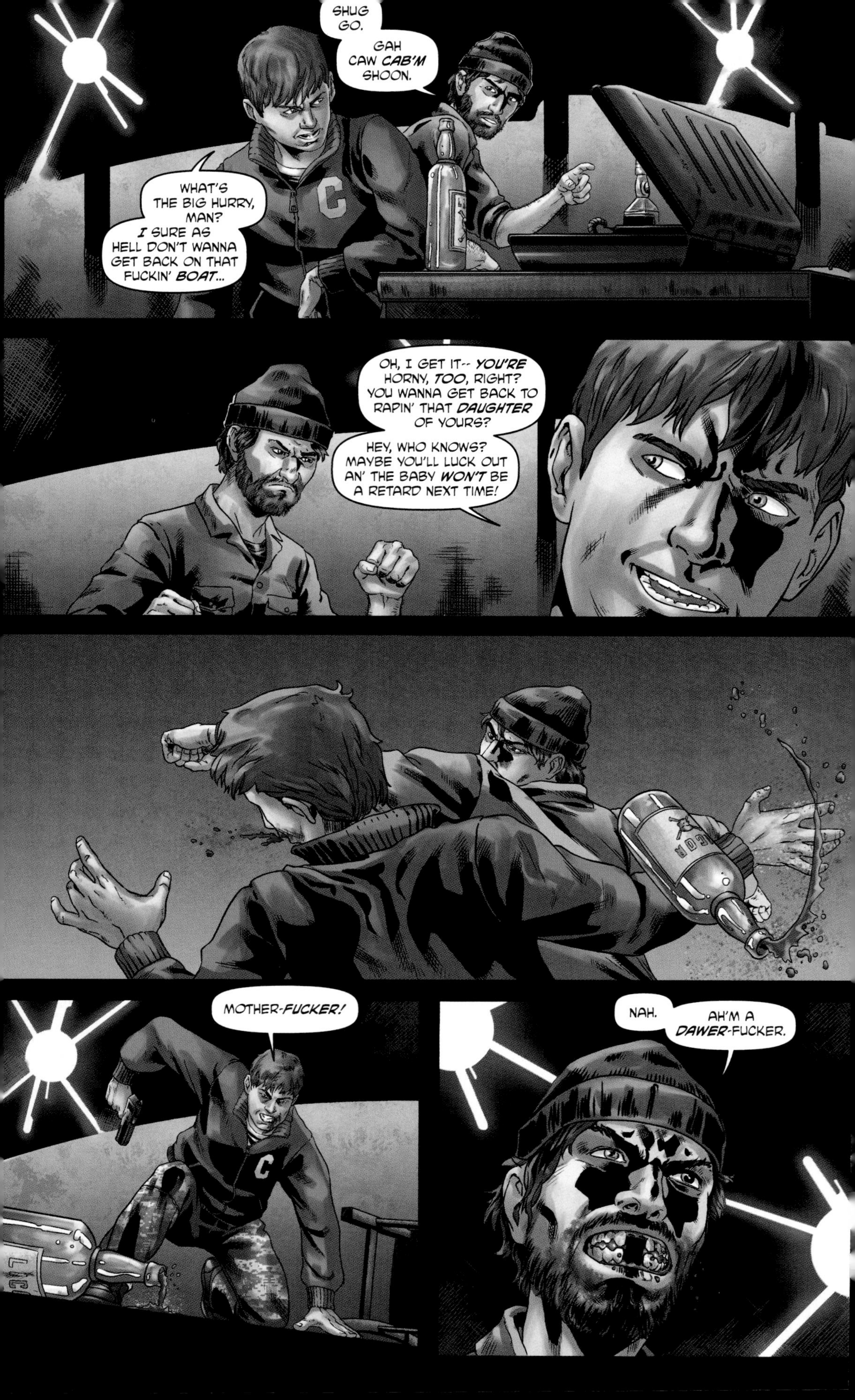

SHUG GO.
GAH CAW CAB'M SHOON.
WHAT'S THE BIG HURRY, MAN? I SURE AS HELL DON'T WANNA GET BACK ON THAT FUCKIN' BOAT...
OH, I GET IT-- YOU'RE HORNY, TOO, RIGHT? YOU WANNA GET BACK TO RAPIN' THAT DAUGHTER OF YOURS?
HEY, WHO KNOWS? MAYBE YOU'LL LUCK OUT AN' THE BABY WON'T BE A RETARD NEXT TIME!
MOTHER-FUCKER!
NAH.
AH'M A DAWER-FUCKER.

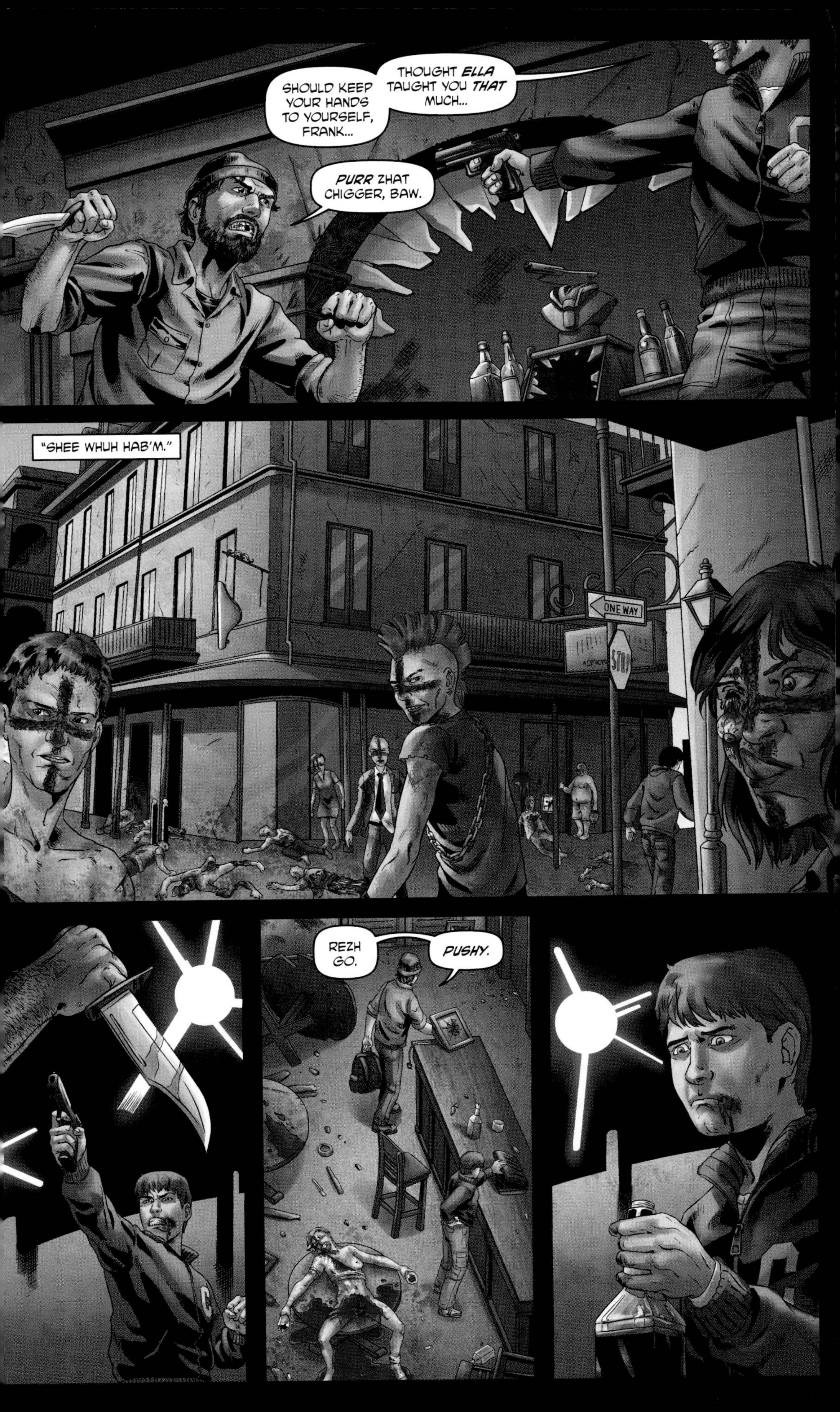
SHOULD KEEP YOUR HANDS TO YOURSELF, FRANK...
THOUGHT ELLA TAUGHT YOU THAT MUCH...
PURR ZHAT CHIGGER, BAW.
"SHEE WHUH HAB'M."
ONE WAY
REZH GO.
PUSHY.

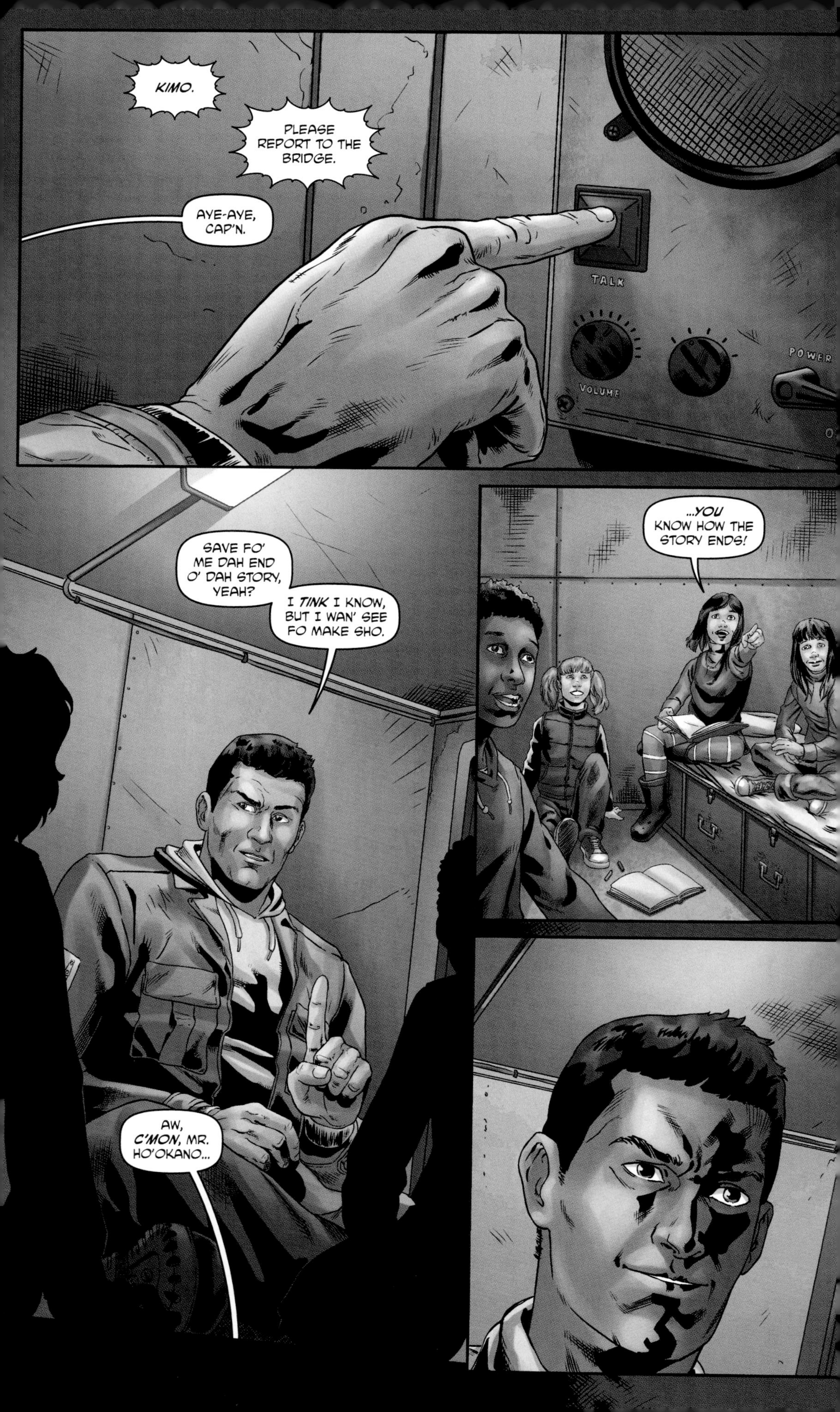
KIMO.
PLEASE REPORT TO THE BRIDGE.
AYE-AYE, CAP'N.
TALK
VOLUME
POWER
SAVE FO' ME DAH END O' DAH STORY, YEAH?
I TINK I KNOW, BUT I WAN' SEE FO MAKE SHO.
...YOU KNOW HOW THE STORY ENDS!
AW, C'MON, MR. HO'OKANO...

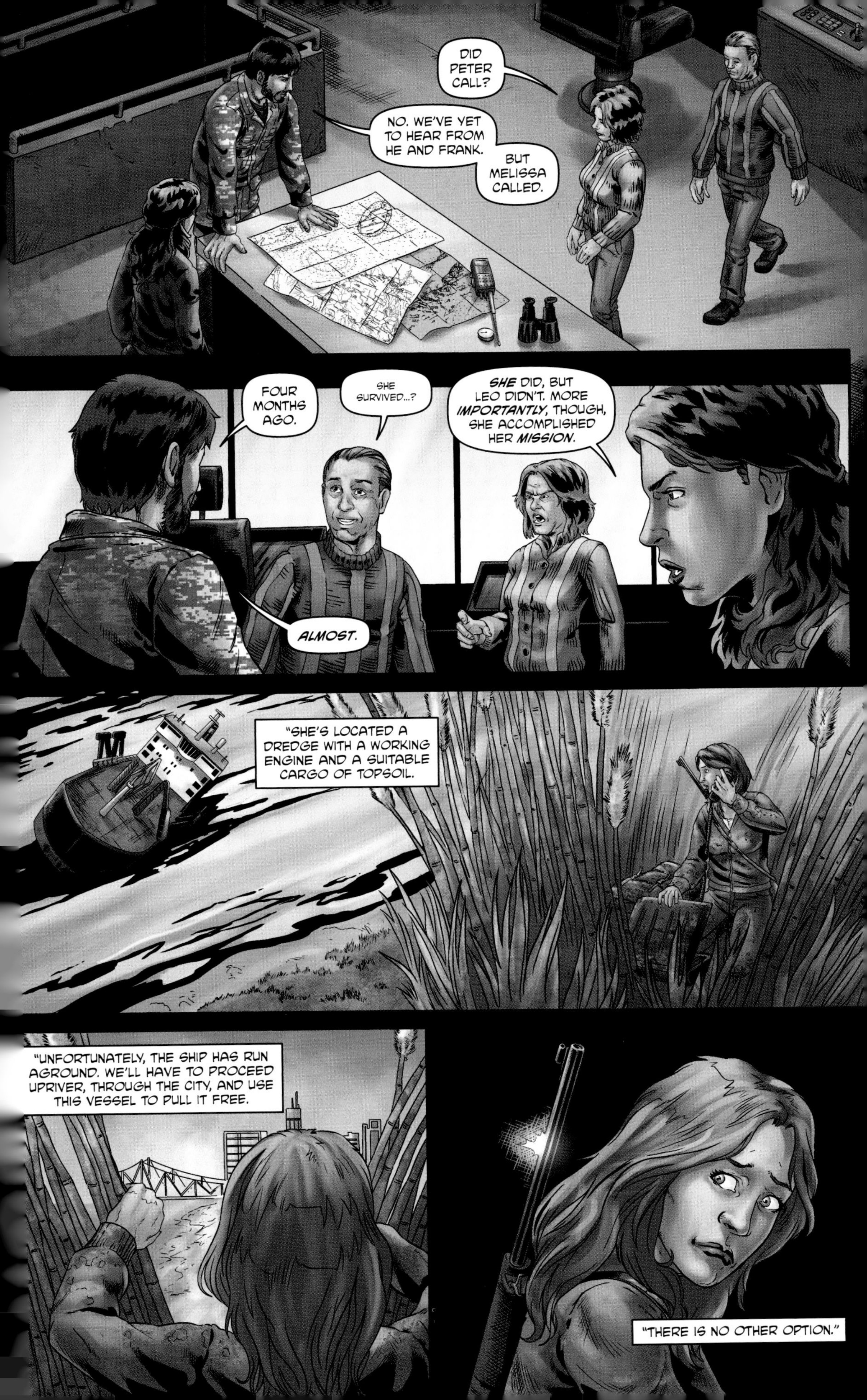
DID PETER CALL?
NO. WE'VE YET TO HEAR FROM HE AND FRANK.
BUT MELISSA CALLED.
FOUR MONTHS AGO.
SHE SURVIVED...?
SHE DID, BUT LEO DIDN'T. MORE IMPORTANTLY, THOUGH, SHE ACCOMPLISHED HER MISSION.
ALMOST.
"SHE'S LOCATED A DREDGE WITH A WORKING ENGINE AND A SUITABLE CARGO OF TOPSOIL.
"UNFORTUNATELY, THE SHIP HAS RUN AGROUND. WE'LL HAVE TO PROCEED UPRIVER, THROUGH THE CITY, AND USE THIS VESSEL TO PULL IT FREE.
"THERE IS NO OTHER OPTION."

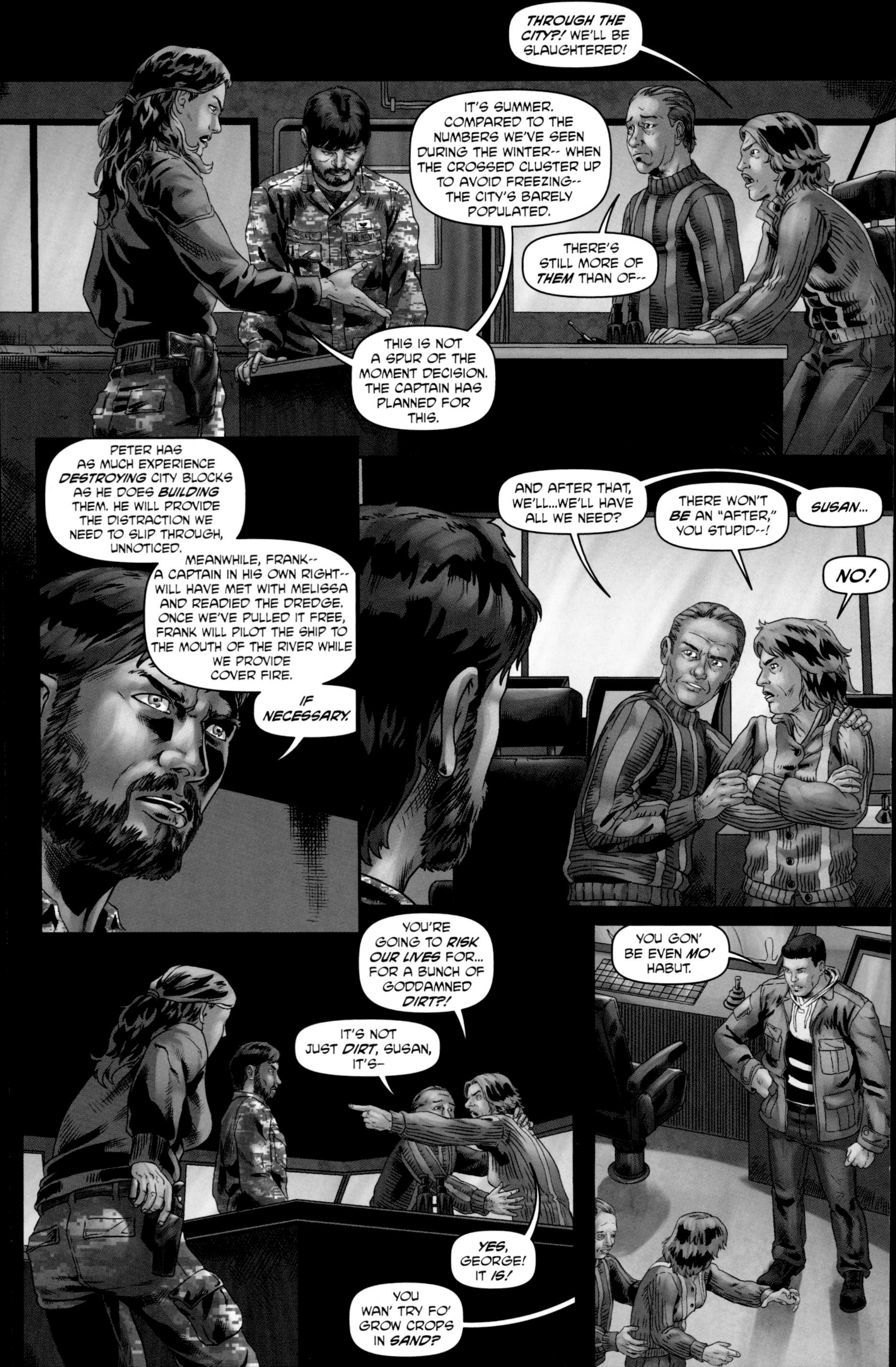

THROUGH THE CITY?! WE'LL BE SLAUGHTERED!
IT'S SUMMER. COMPARED TO THE NUMBERS WE'VE SEEN DURING THE WINTER-- WHEN THE CROSSED CLUSTER UP TO AVOID FREEZING-- THE CITY'S BARELY POPULATED.
THERE'S STILL MORE OF THEM THAN OF--
THIS IS NOT A SPUR OF THE MOMENT DECISION. THE CAPTAIN HAS PLANNED FOR THIS.
PETER HAS AS MUCH EXPERIENCE DESTROYING CITY BLOCKS AS HE DOES BUILDING THEM. HE WILL PROVIDE THE DISTRACTION WE NEED TO SLIP THROUGH, UNNOTICED.
MEANWHILE, FRANK-- A CAPTAIN IN HIS OWN RIGHT-- WILL HAVE MET WITH MELISSA AND READIED THE DREDGE. ONCE WE'VE PULLED IT FREE, FRANK WILL PILOT THE SHIP TO THE MOUTH OF THE RIVER WHILE WE PROVIDE COVER FIRE.
IF NECESSARY.
AND AFTER THAT, WE'LL...WE'LL HAVE ALL WE NEED?
THERE WON'T BE AN "AFTER," YOU STUPID--!
SUSAN...
NO!
YOU'RE GOING TO RISK OUR LIVES FOR... FOR A BUNCH OF GODDAMNED DIRT?!
IT'S NOT JUST DIRT, SUSAN, IT'S-
YES, GEORGE! IT IS!
YOU WAN' TRY FO' GROW CROPS IN SAND?
YOU GON' BE EVEN MO' HABUT.

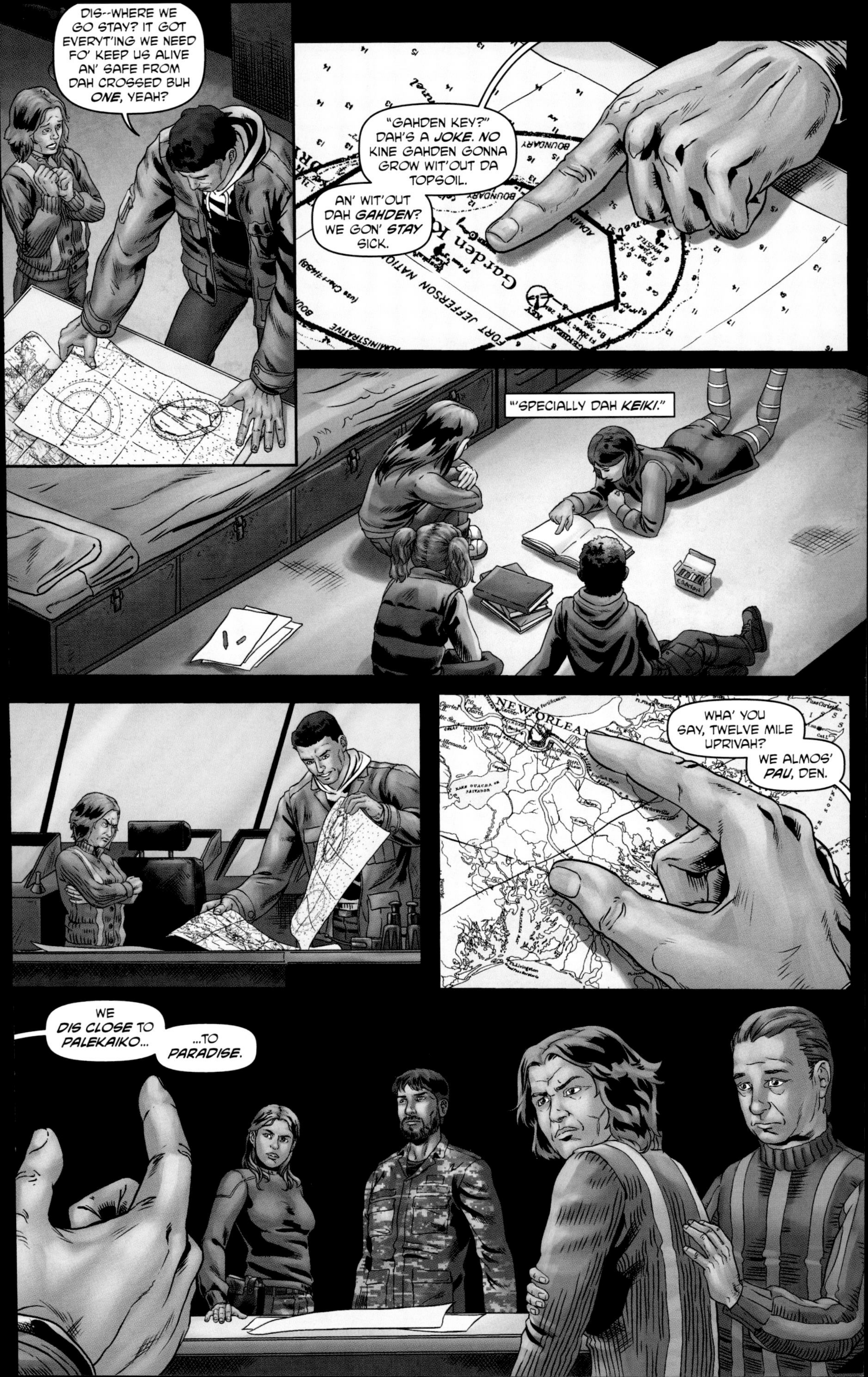
DIS--WHERE WE GO STAY? IT GOT EVERYT'ING WE NEED FO' KEEP US ALIVE AN' SAFE FROM DAH CROSSED BUH ONE, YEAH?
"GAHDEN KEY?" DAH'S A JOKE. NO KINE GAHDEN GONNA GROW WIT'OUT DA TOPSOIL.
AN' WIT'OUT DAH GAHDEN? WE GON' STAY SICK.
"'SPECIALLY DAH KEIKI."
WHA' YOU SAY, TWELVE MILE UPRIVAH?
WE ALMOS' PAU, DEN.
WE DIS CLOSE TO PALEKAIKO...
...TO PARADISE.

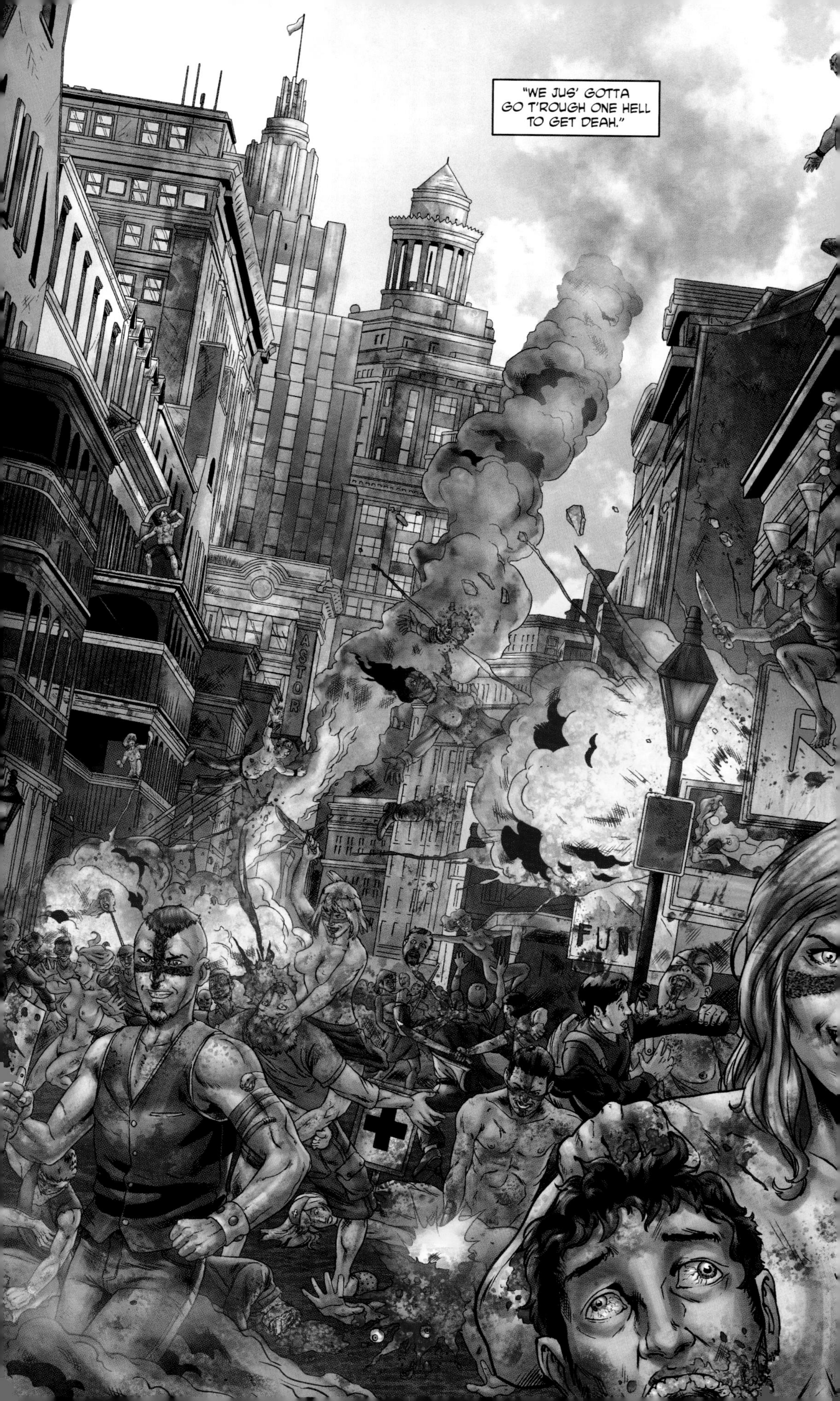
"WE JUS' GOTTA GO T'ROUGH ONE HELL TO GET DEAH."
ASTOR
FUN

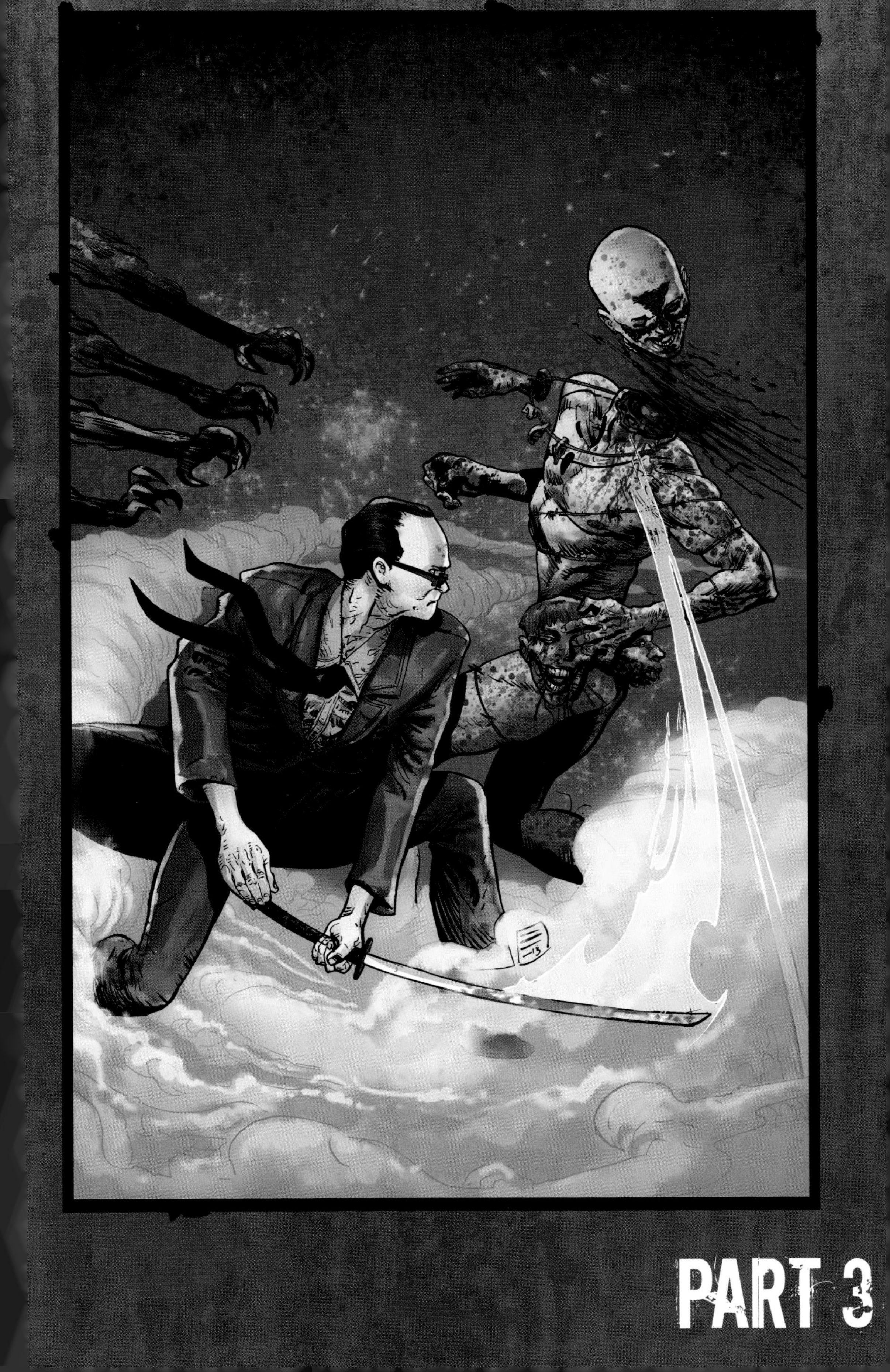

PART 3

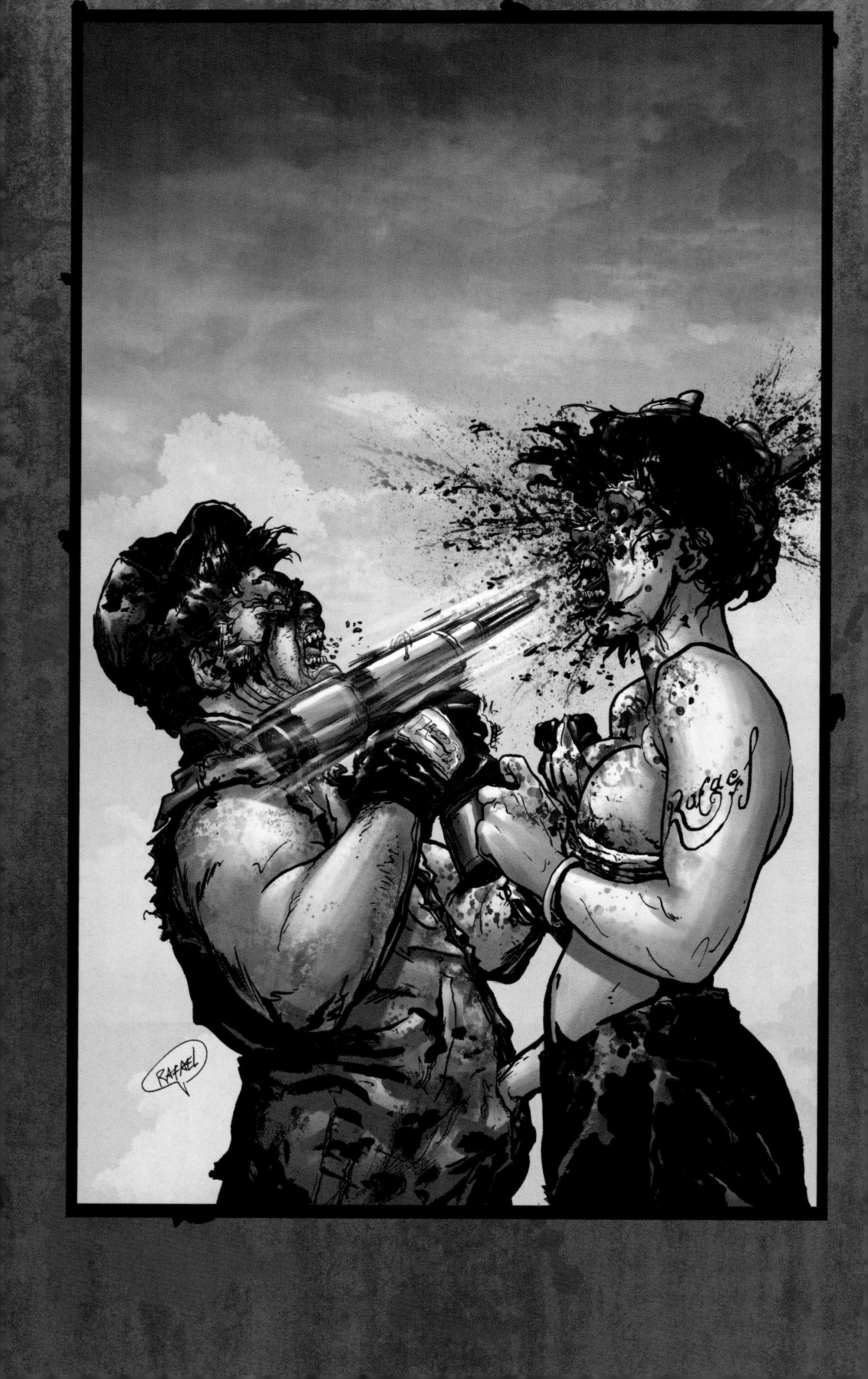
RAFAEL

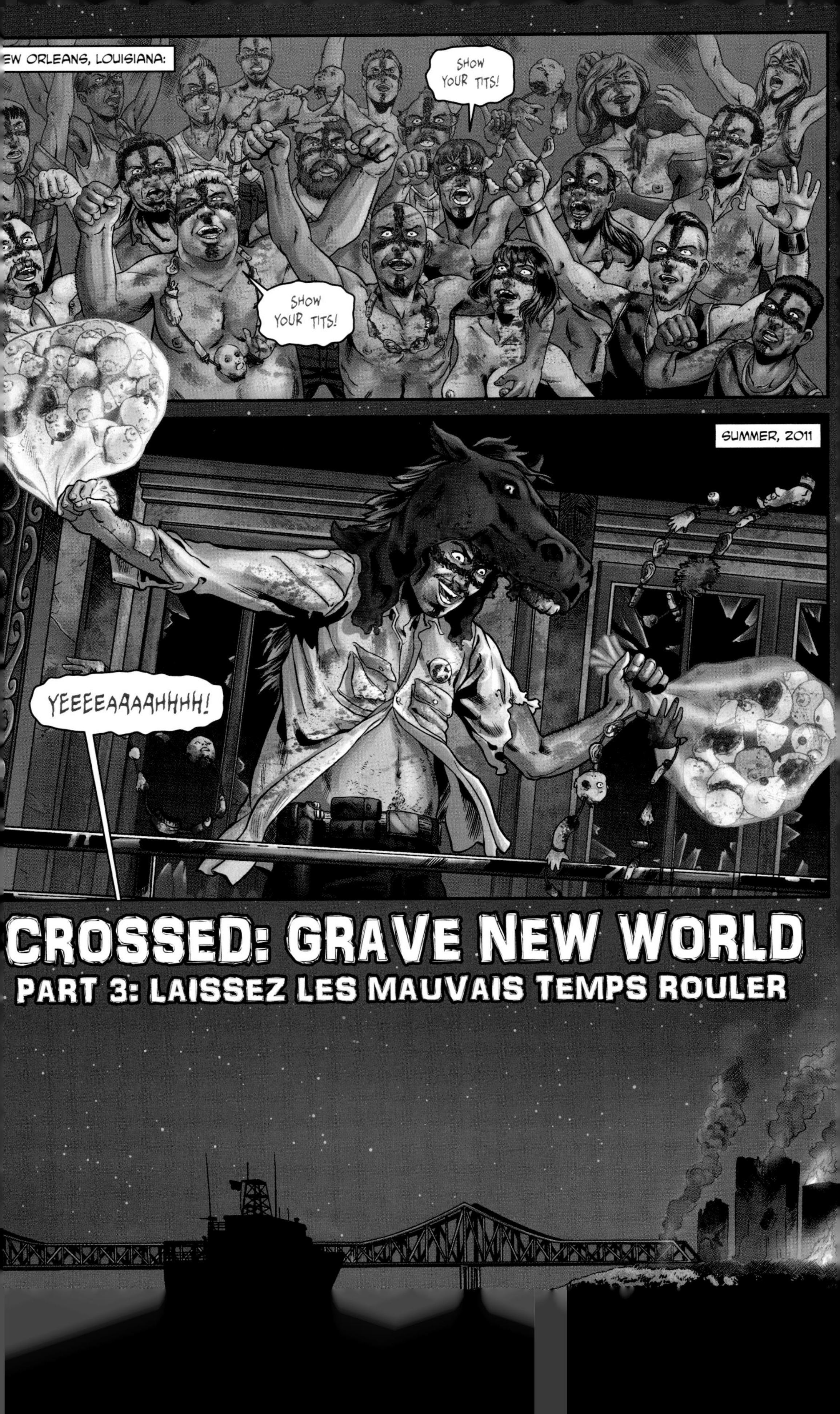
EW ORLEANS, LOUISIANA:
SHOW YOUR TITS!
SHOW YOUR TITS!
SUMMER, 2011
YEEEEAAAAHHHH!
CROSSED: GRAVE NEW WORLD
PART 3: LAISSEZ LES MAUVAIS TEMPS ROULER

"ON MY SIGNAL, PETER WILL DETONATE A SERIES OF CHARGES..."

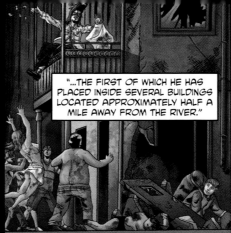

"...THE FIRST OF WHICH HE HAS PLACED INSIDE SEVERAL BUILDINGS LOCATED APPROXIMATELY HALF A MILE AWAY FROM THE RIVER."

NOW.

"THE CROSSED WILL SWARM TO THOSE LOCATIONS, ATTRACTED BY THE NOISE AND THE PROMISE OF DESTRUCTION."

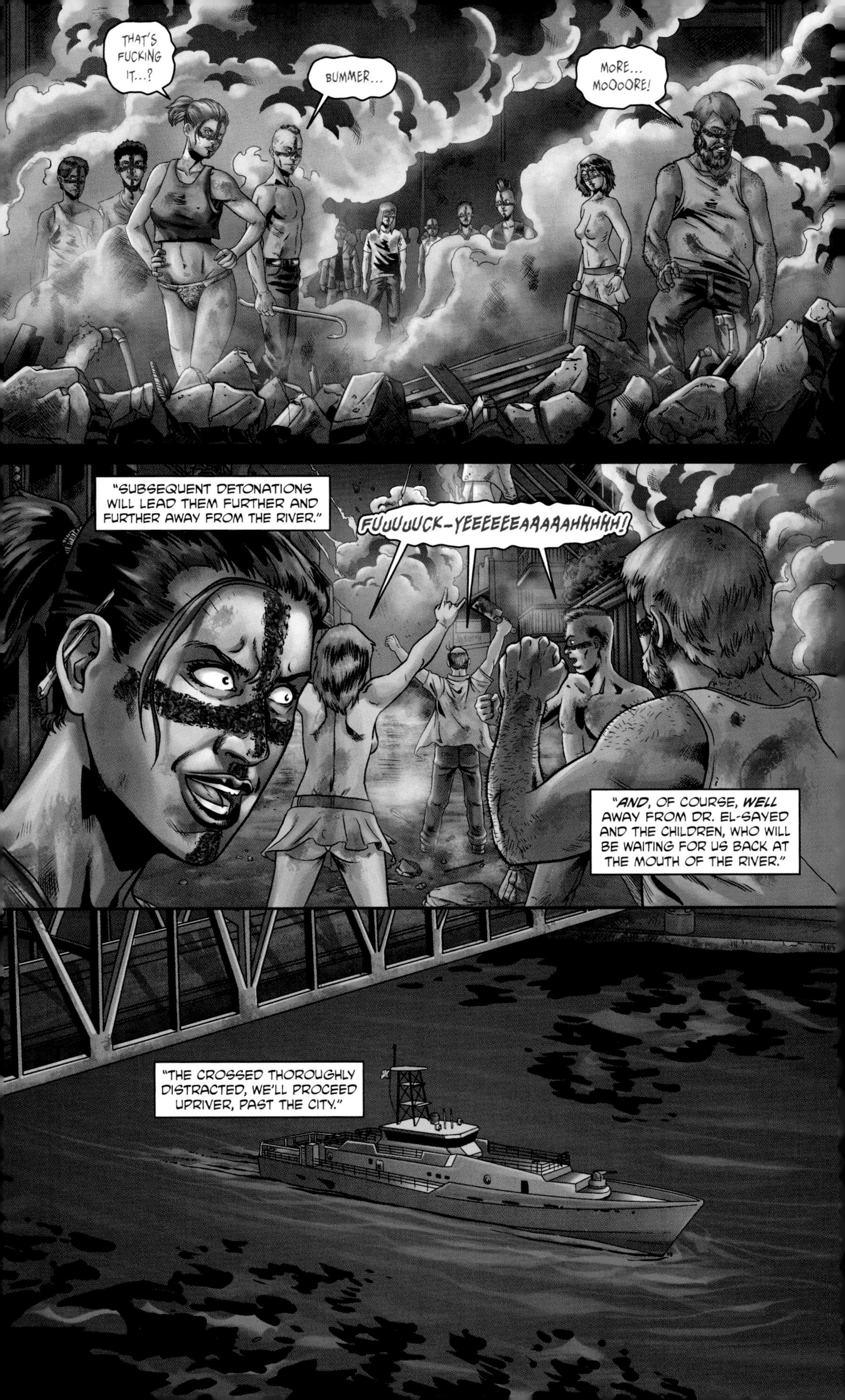
THAT'S FUCKING IT...?
BUMMER...
MORE... MOOoORE!
"SUBSEQUENT DETONATIONS WILL LEAD THEM FURTHER AND FURTHER AWAY FROM THE RIVER."
FUUUUUCK-YEEEEEEAAAAAHHHHH!
"AND, OF COURSE, WELL AWAY FROM DR. EL-SAYED AND THE CHILDREN, WHO WILL BE WAITING FOR US BACK AT THE MOUTH OF THE RIVER."
"THE CROSSED THOROUGHLY DISTRACTED, WE'LL PROCEED UPRIVER, PAST THE CITY."

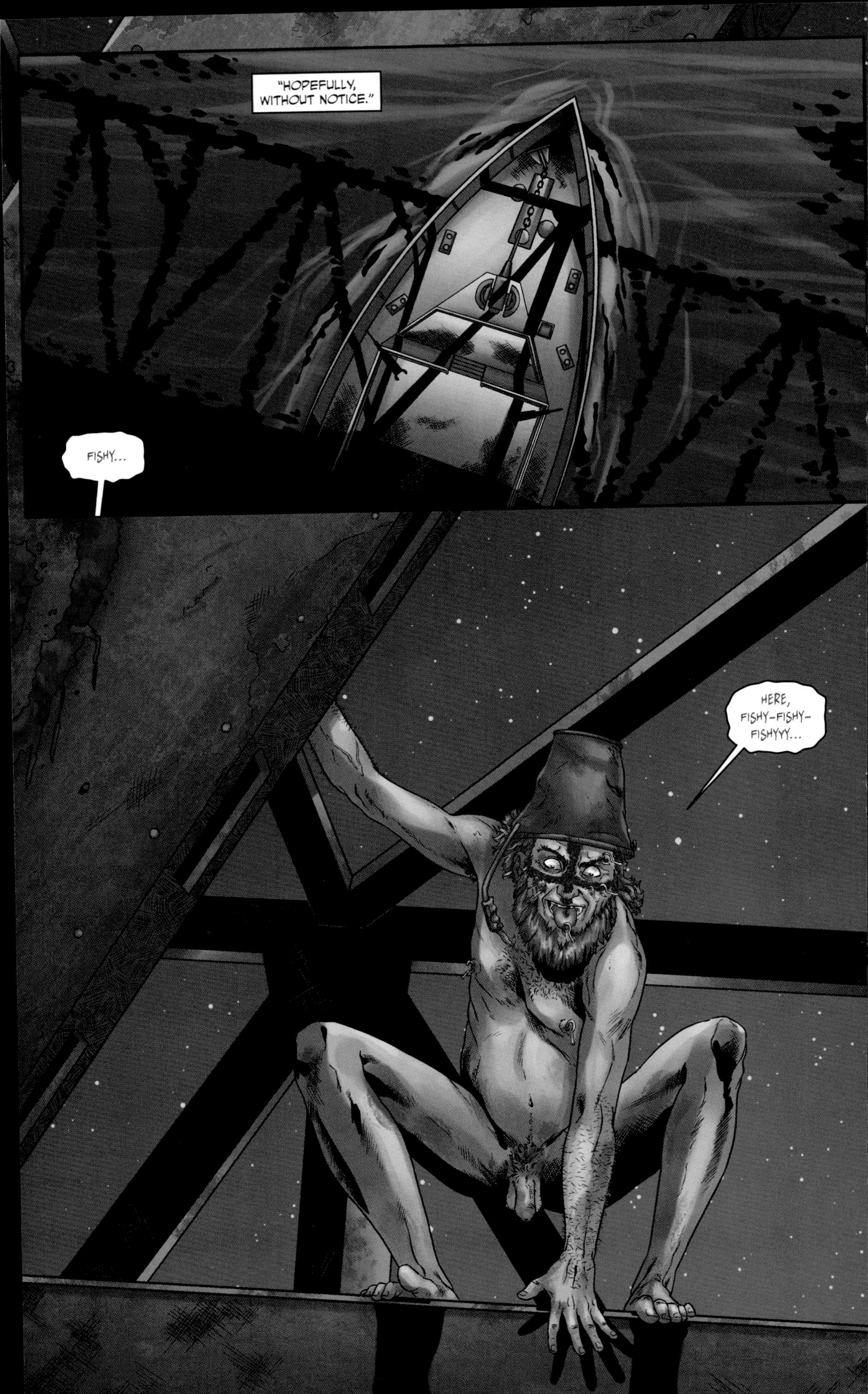
"HOPEFULLY, WITHOUT NOTICE."
FISHY...
HERE, FISHY-FISHY-FISHYYY...

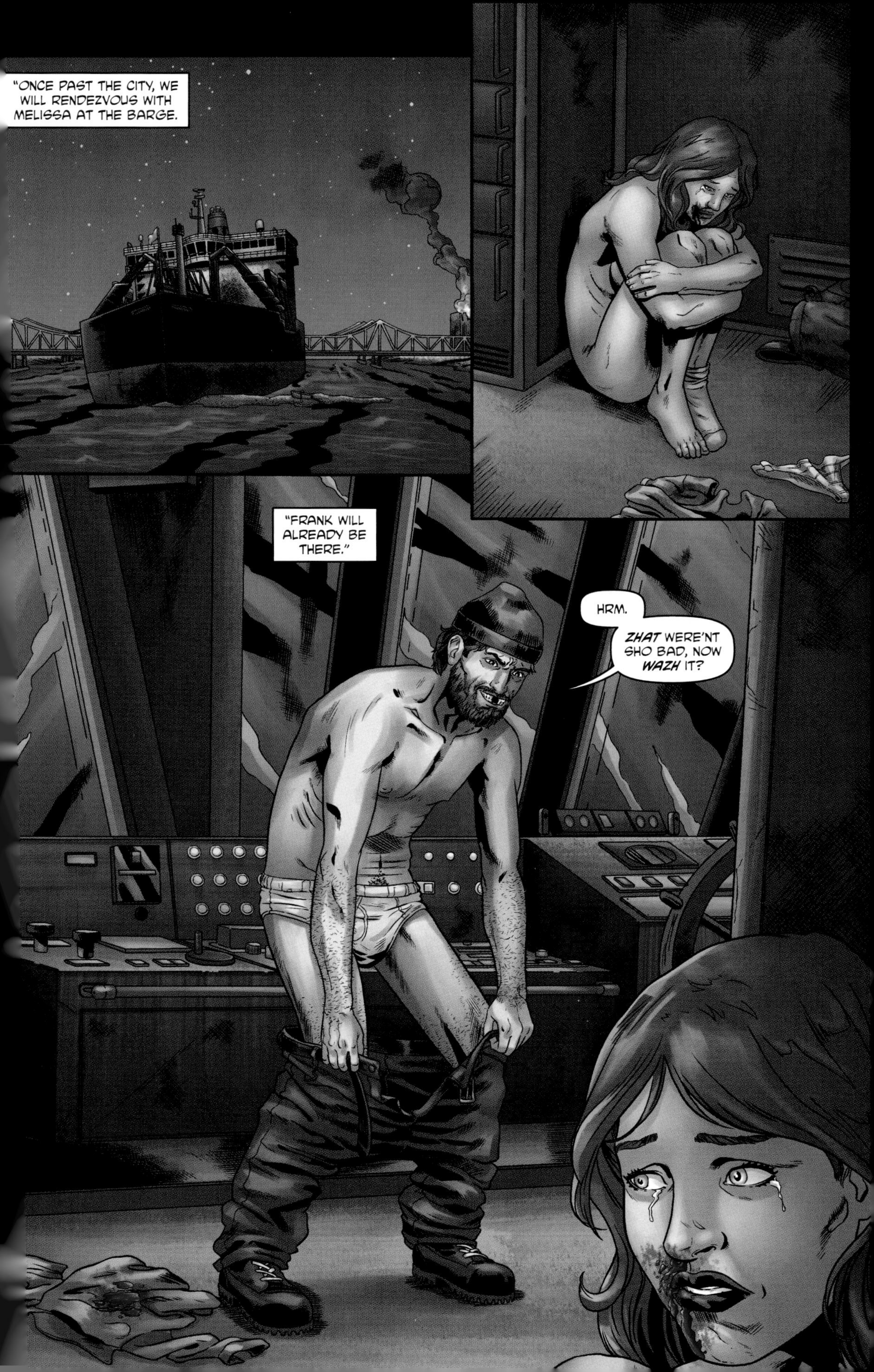
"ONCE PAST THE CITY, WE WILL RENDEZVOUS WITH MELISSA AT THE BARGE.
"FRANK WILL ALREADY BE THERE."
HRM.
ZHAT WERE'NT SHO BAD, NOW WAZH IT?

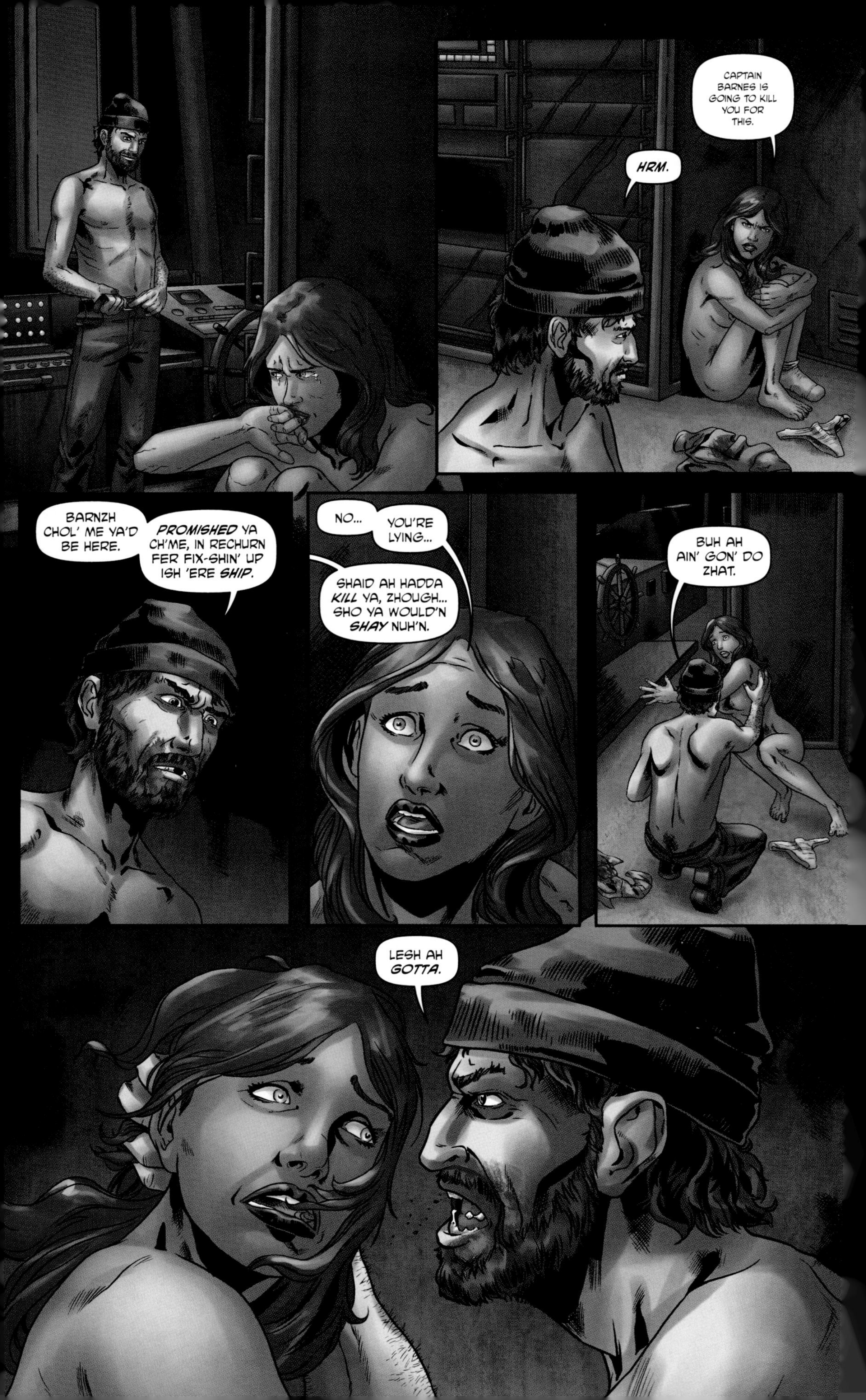
HRM.
CAPTAIN BARNES IS GOING TO KILL YOU FOR THIS.
BARNZH CHOL' ME YA'D BE HERE.
PROMISHED YA CH'ME, IN RECHURN FER FIX-SHIN' UP ISH 'ERE SHIP.
NO...
YOU'RE LYING...
SHAID AH HADDA KILL YA, ZHOUGH... SHO YA WOULD'N SHAY NUH'N.
BUH AH AIN' GON' DO ZHAT.
LESH AH GOTTA.

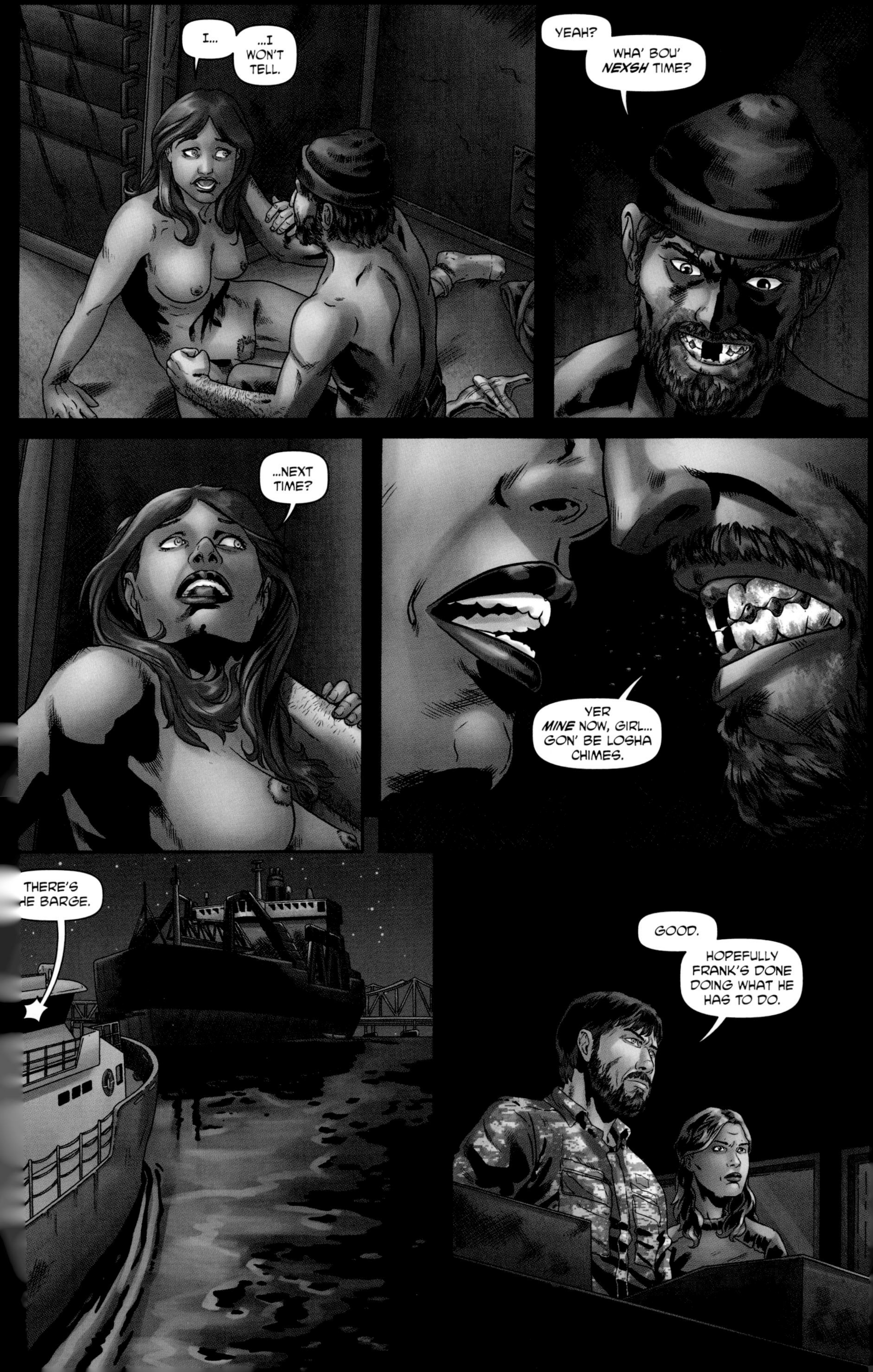
I...
...I WON'T TELL.
YEAH?
WHA' BOU' NEXSH TIME?
...NEXT TIME?
YER MINE NOW, GIRL... GON' BE LOSHA CHIMES.
THERE'S
HE BARGE.
GOOD.
HOPEFULLY FRANK'S DONE DOING WHAT HE HAS TO DO.

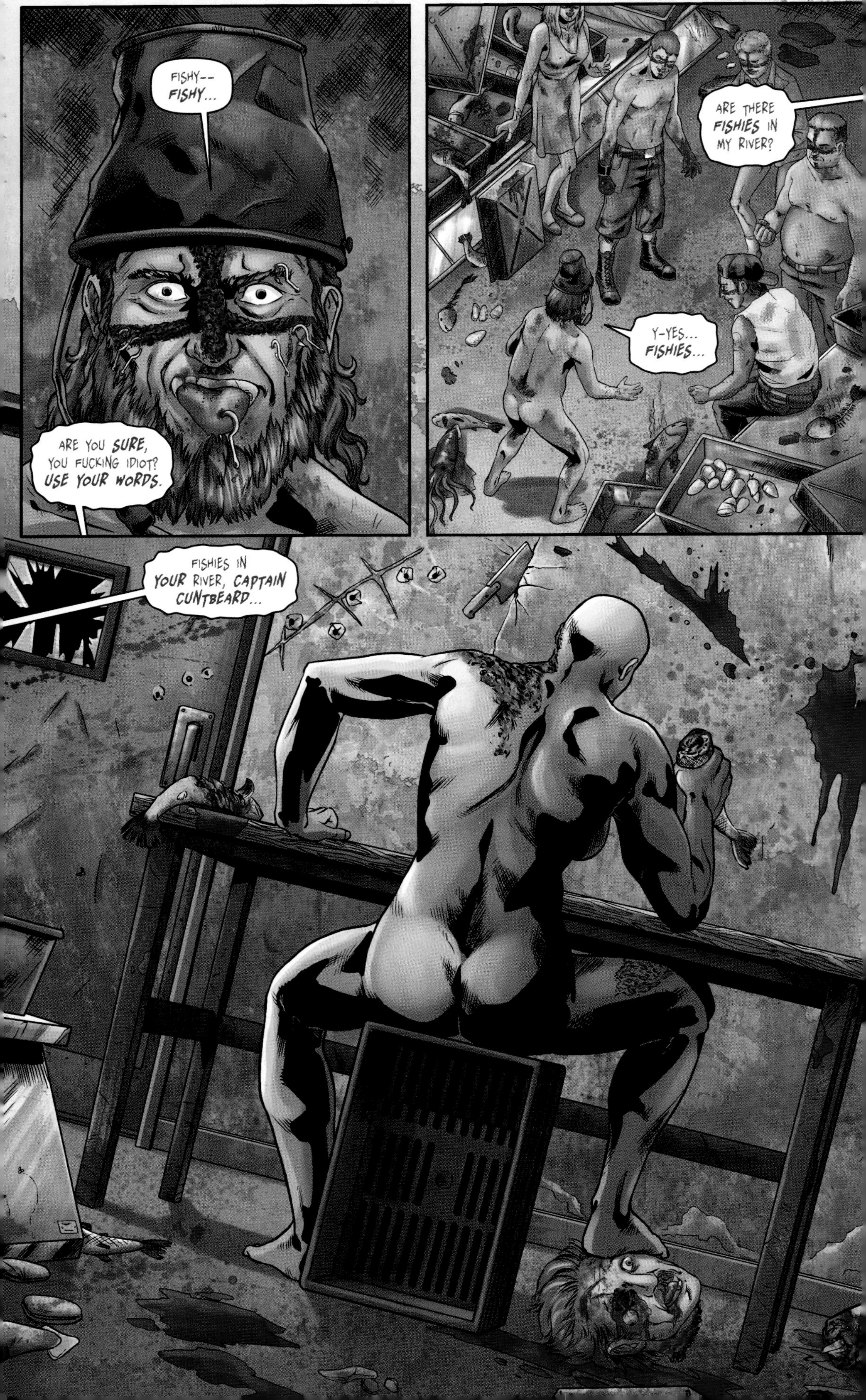
FISHY-- FISHY...
ARE YOU SURE, YOU FUCKING IDIOT? USE YOUR WORDS.
ARE THERE FISHIES IN MY RIVER?
Y-YES... FISHIES...
FISHIES IN YOUR RIVER, CAPTAIN CUNTBEARD...

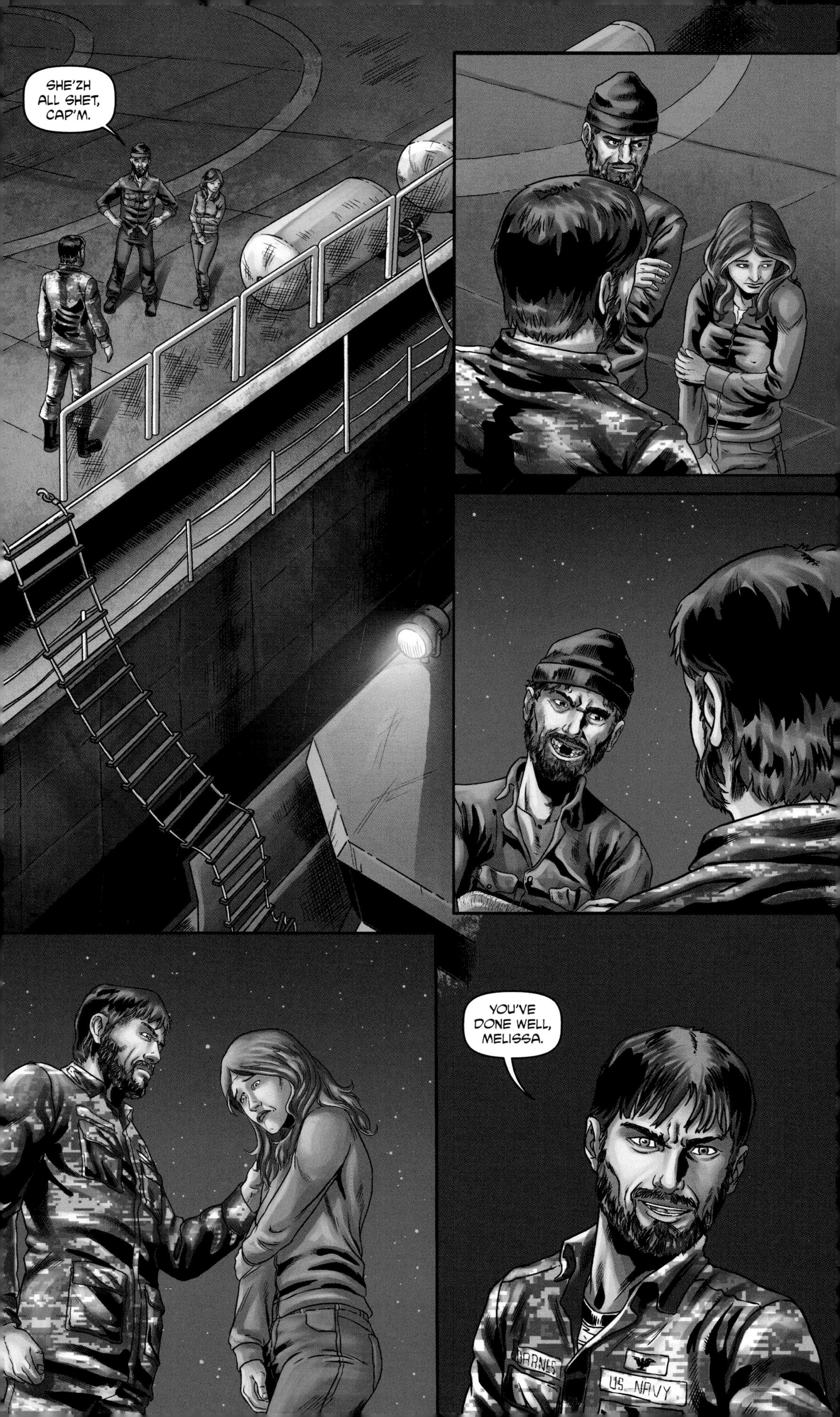
SHE'ZH ALL SHET, CAP'M.
YOU'VE DONE WELL, MELISSA.
US NAVY

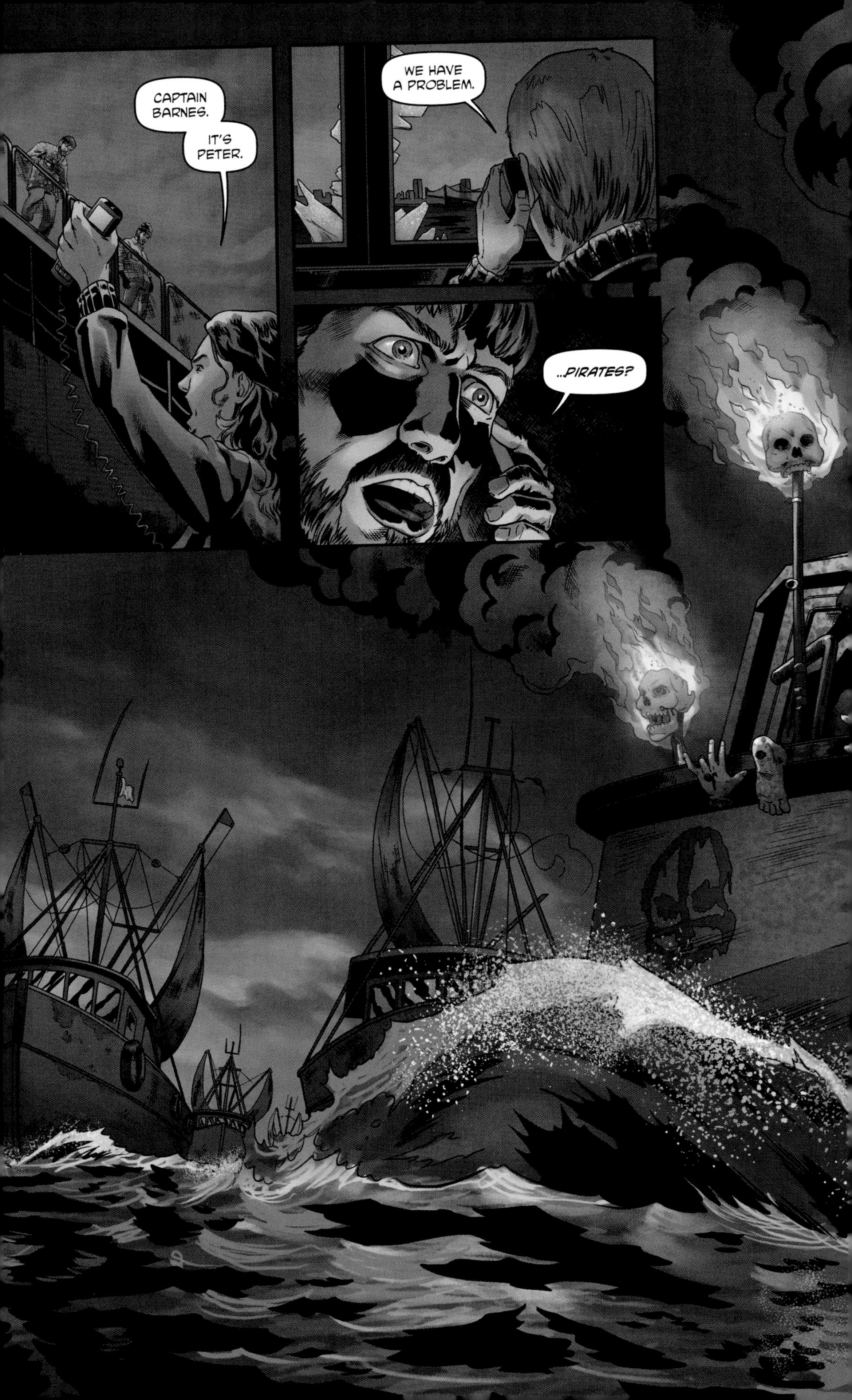
CAPTAIN BARNES.
IT'S PETER.
WE HAVE A PROBLEM.
...PIRATES?

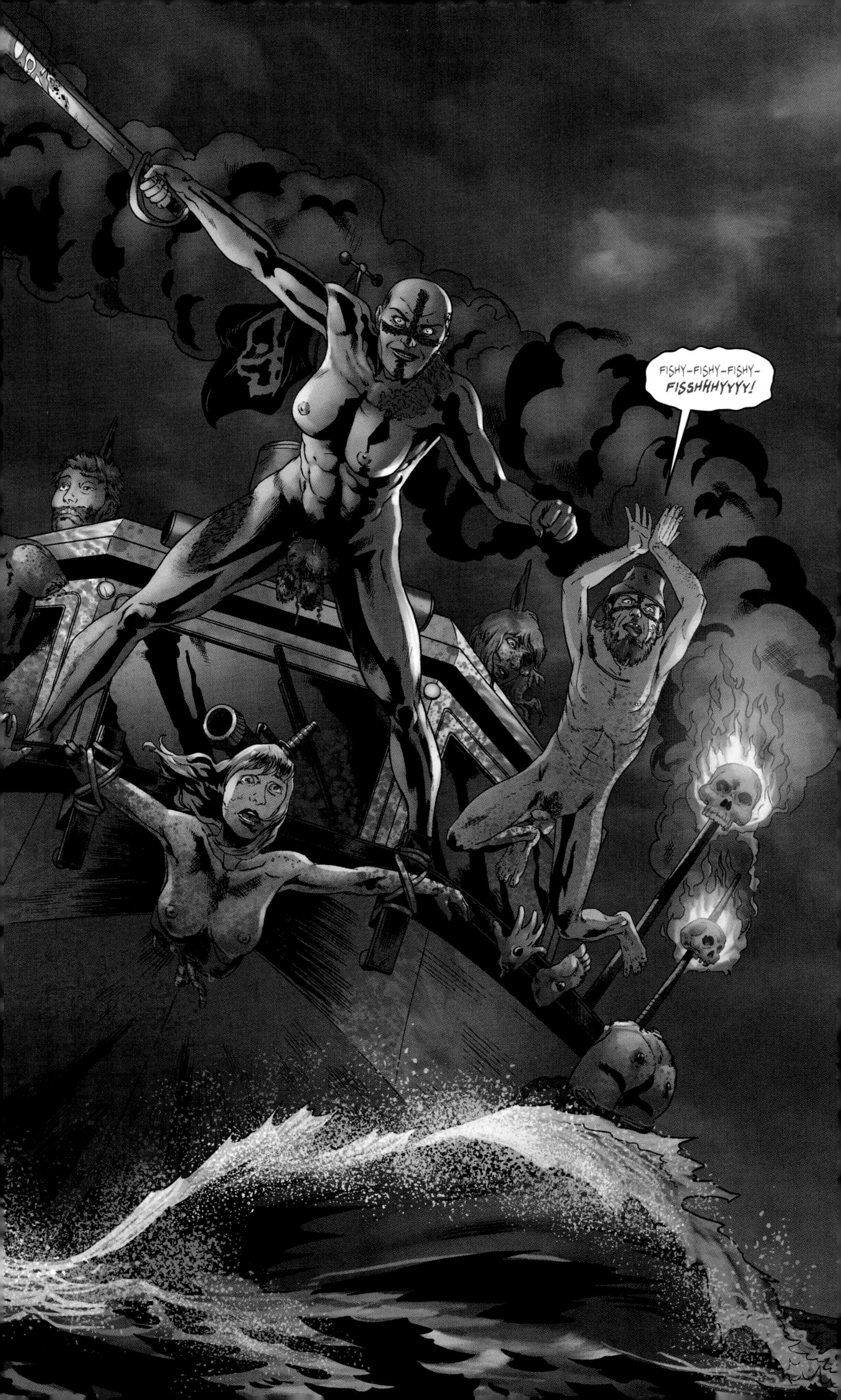
FISHY-FISHY-FISHY-
FISSHHHYYYY!

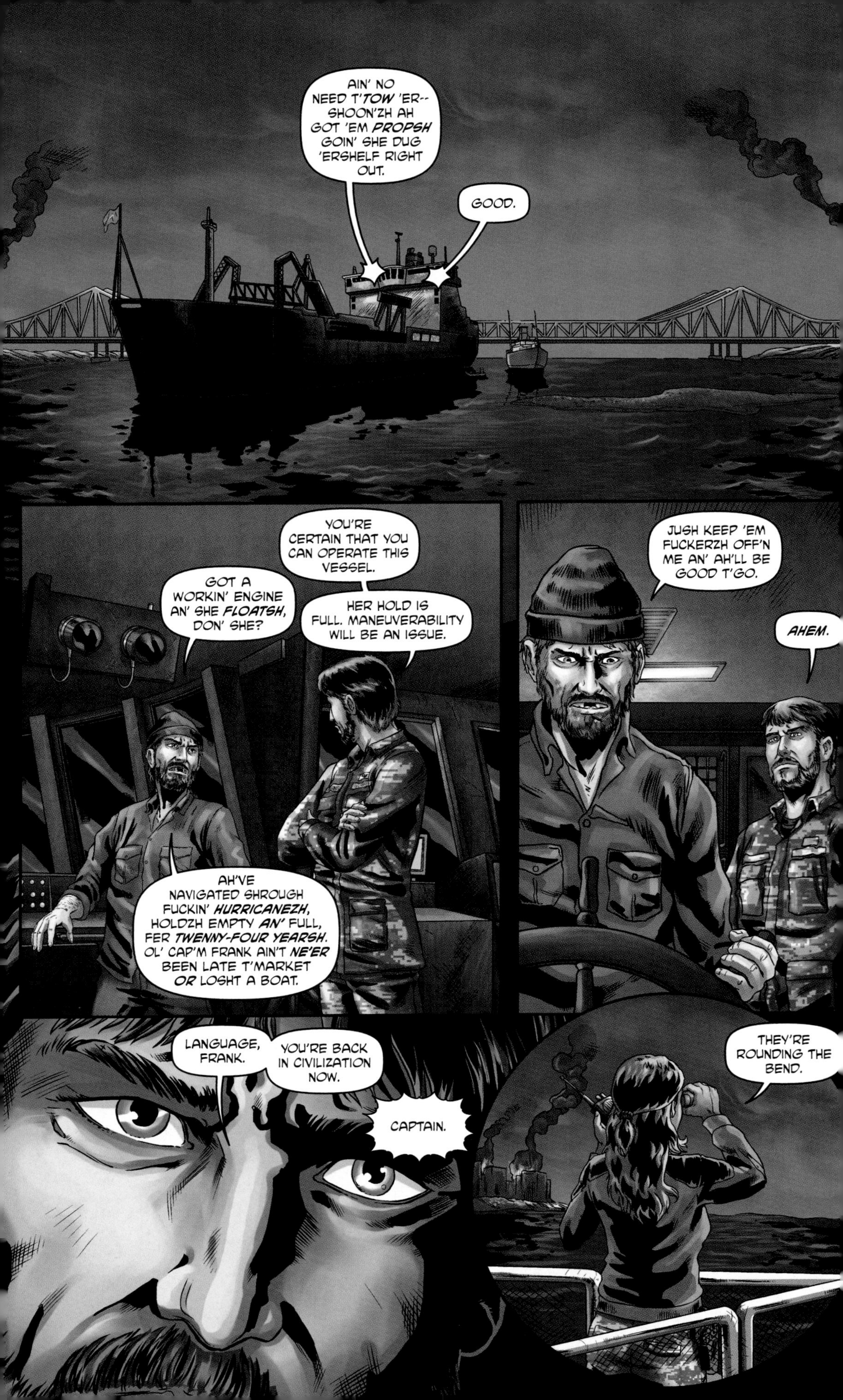
AIN' NO NEED T'TOW 'ER-- SHOON'ZH AH GOT 'EM PROPSH GOIN' SHE DUG 'ERSHELF RIGHT OUT.
GOOD.
YOU'RE CERTAIN THAT YOU CAN OPERATE THIS VESSEL.
GOT A WORKIN' ENGINE AN' SHE FLOATSH, DON' SHE?
HER HOLD IS FULL. MANEUVERABILITY WILL BE AN ISSUE.
AH'VE NAVIGATED SHROUGH FUCKIN' HURRICANEZH, HOLDZH EMPTY AN' FULL, FER TWENNY-FOUR YEARSH. OL' CAP'M FRANK AIN'T NE'ER BEEN LATE T'MARKET OR LOSHT A BOAT.
JUSH KEEP 'EM FUCKERZH OFF'N ME AN' AH'LL BE GOOD T'GO.
AHEM.
LANGUAGE, FRANK.
YOU'RE BACK IN CIVILIZATION NOW.
CAPTAIN.
THEY'RE ROUNDING THE BEND.

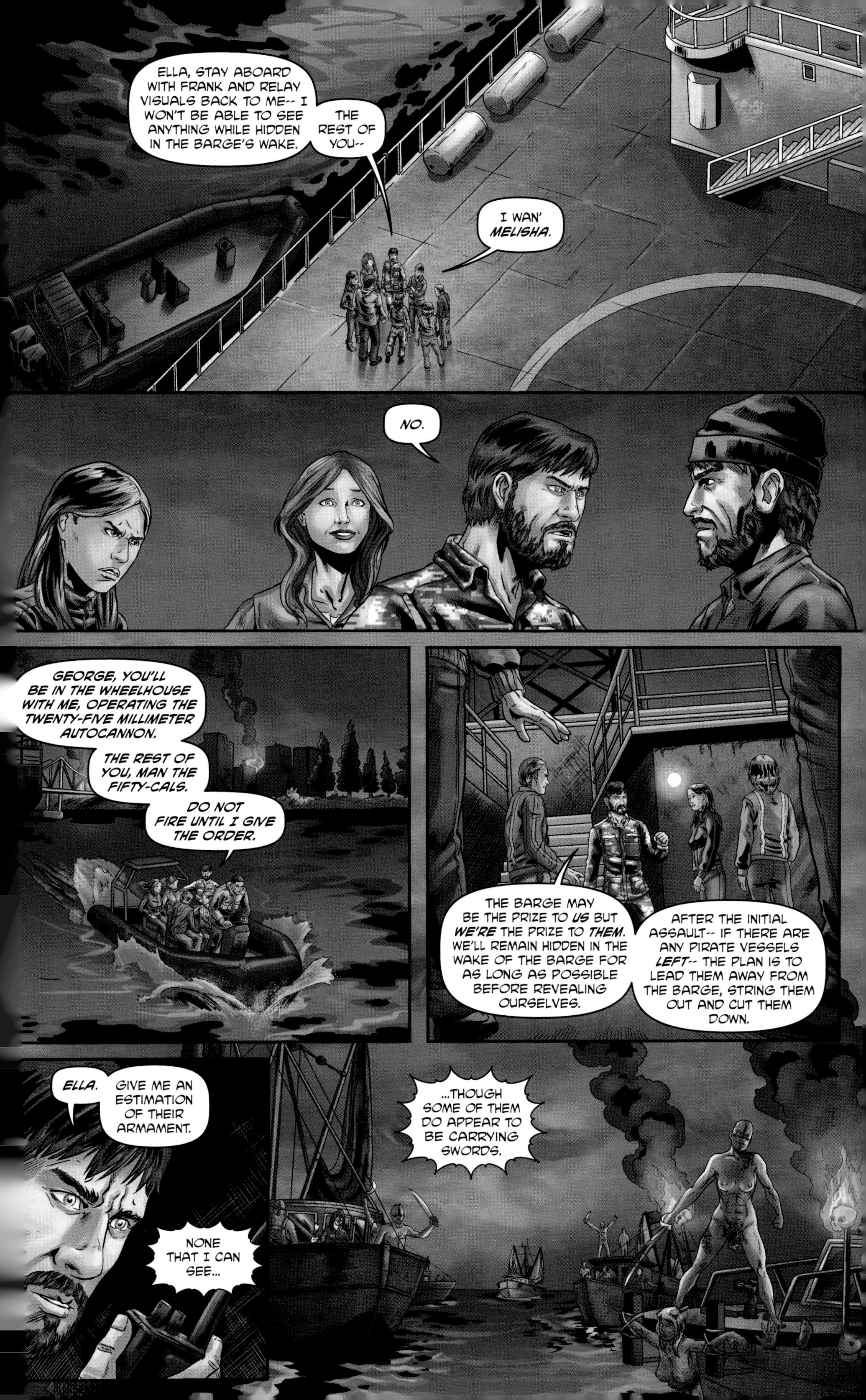
ELLA, STAY ABOARD WITH FRANK AND RELAY VISUALS BACK TO ME-- I WON'T BE ABLE TO SEE ANYTHING WHILE HIDDEN IN THE BARGE'S WAKE.
THE REST OF YOU--
I WAN' *MELISHA*.
NO.
GEORGE, YOU'LL BE IN THE WHEELHOUSE WITH ME, OPERATING THE TWENTY-FIVE MILLIMETER AUTOCANNON.
THE REST OF YOU, MAN THE FIFTY-CALS.
DO NOT FIRE UNTIL I GIVE THE ORDER.
THE BARGE MAY BE THE PRIZE TO *US* BUT *WE'RE* THE PRIZE TO *THEM*. WE'LL REMAIN HIDDEN IN THE WAKE OF THE BARGE FOR AS LONG AS POSSIBLE BEFORE REVEALING OURSELVES.
AFTER THE INITIAL ASSAULT-- IF THERE ARE ANY PIRATE VESSELS *LEFT*-- THE PLAN IS TO LEAD THEM AWAY FROM THE BARGE, STRING THEM OUT AND CUT THEM DOWN.
ELLA.
GIVE ME AN ESTIMATION OF THEIR ARMAMENT.
NONE THAT I CAN SEE...
...THOUGH SOME OF THEM DO APPEAR TO BE CARRYING SWORDS.

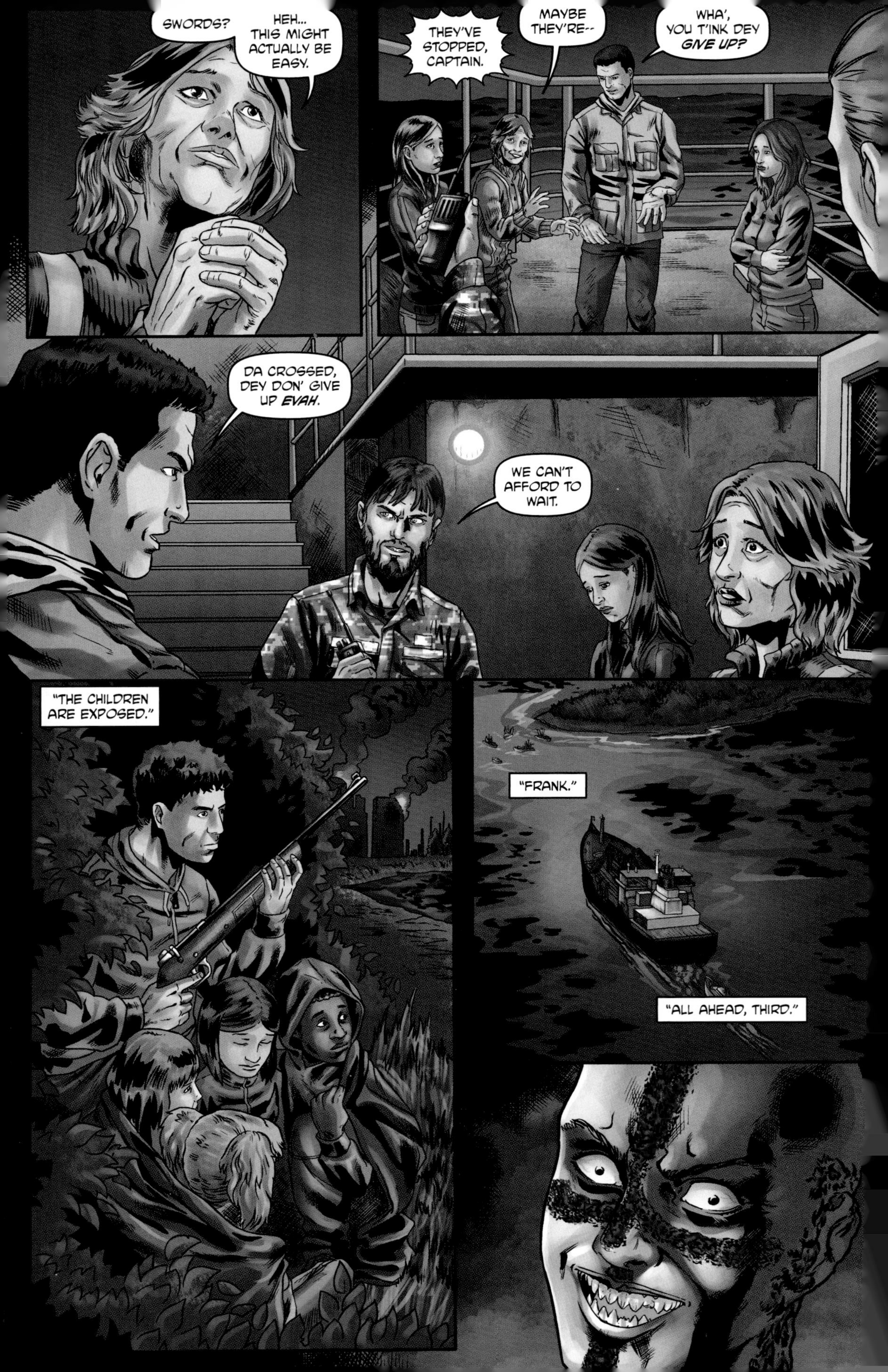
SWORDS?
HEH... THIS MIGHT ACTUALLY BE EASY.
THEY'VE STOPPED, CAPTAIN.
MAYBE THEY'RE--
WHA', YOU T'INK DEY GIVE UP?
DA CROSSED, DEY DON' GIVE UP EVAH.
WE CAN'T AFFORD TO WAIT.
"THE CHILDREN ARE EXPOSED."
"FRANK."
"ALL AHEAD, THIRD."

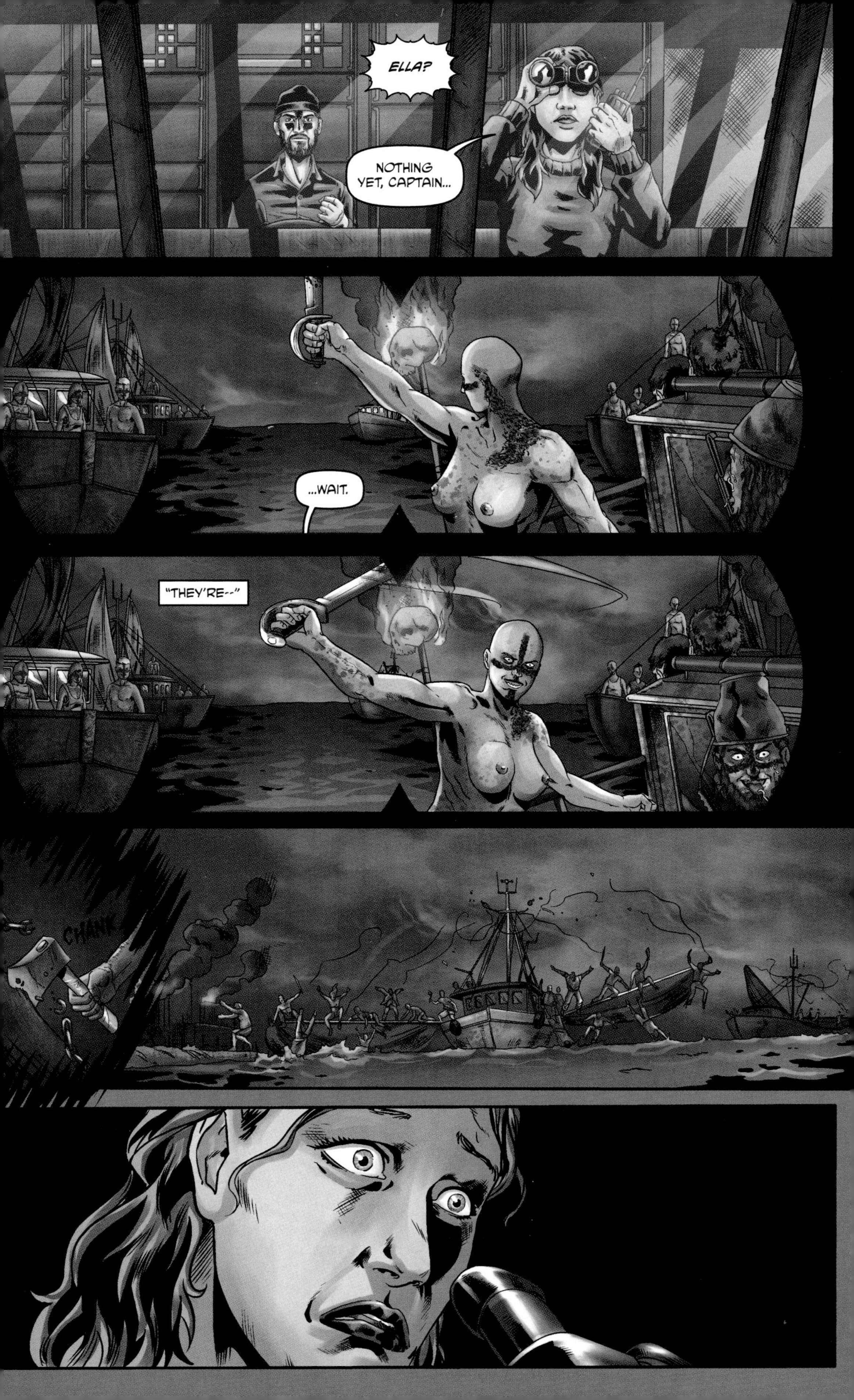
ELLA?
NOTHING YET, CAPTAIN...
...WAIT.
"THEY'RE--"
CHANK

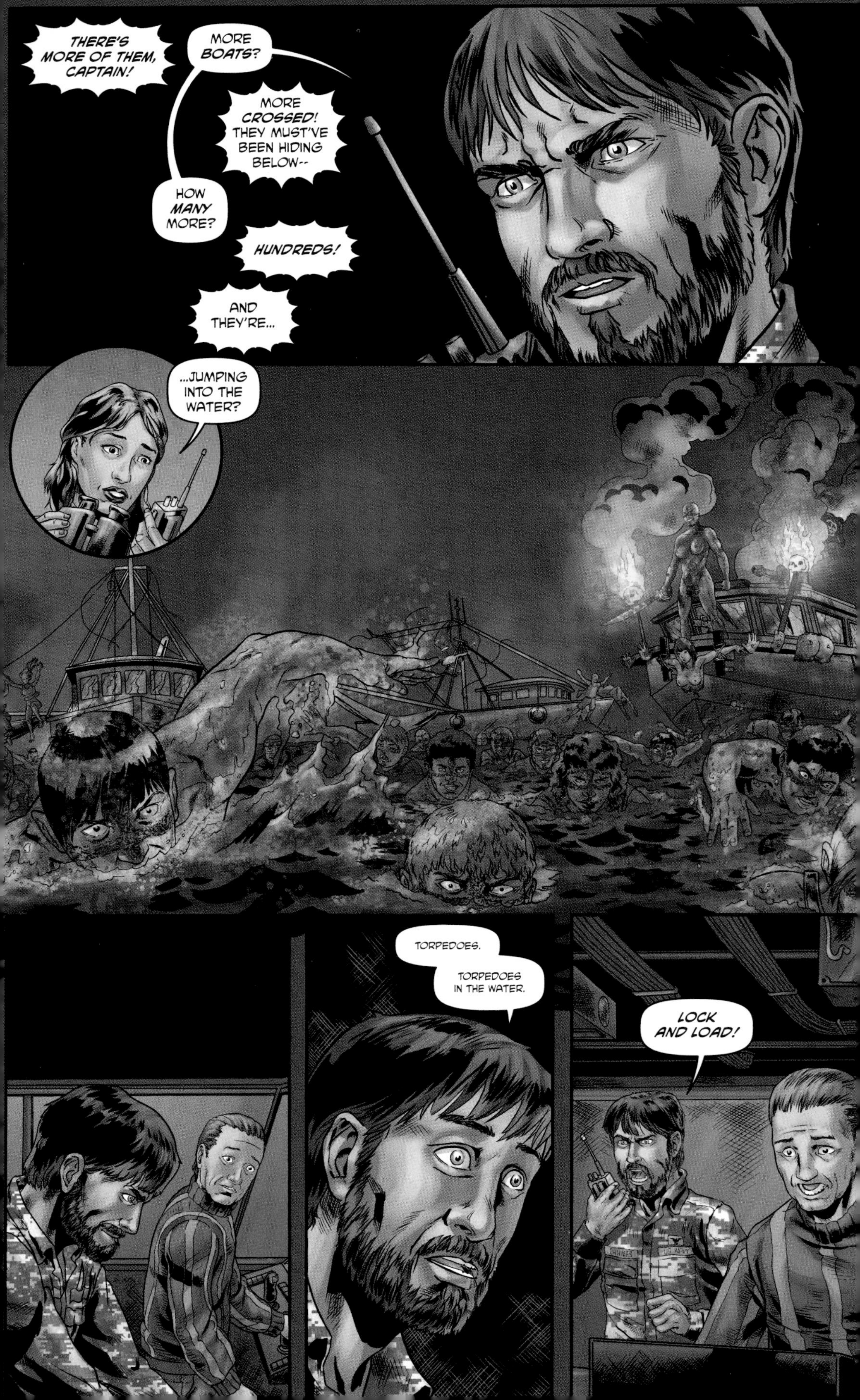
THERE'S MORE OF THEM, CAPTAIN!
MORE BOATS?
MORE CROSSED! THEY MUST'VE BEEN HIDING BELOW--
HOW MANY MORE?
HUNDREDS!
AND THEY'RE...
...JUMPING INTO THE WATER?
TORPEDOES.
TORPEDOES IN THE WATER.
LOCK AND LOAD!

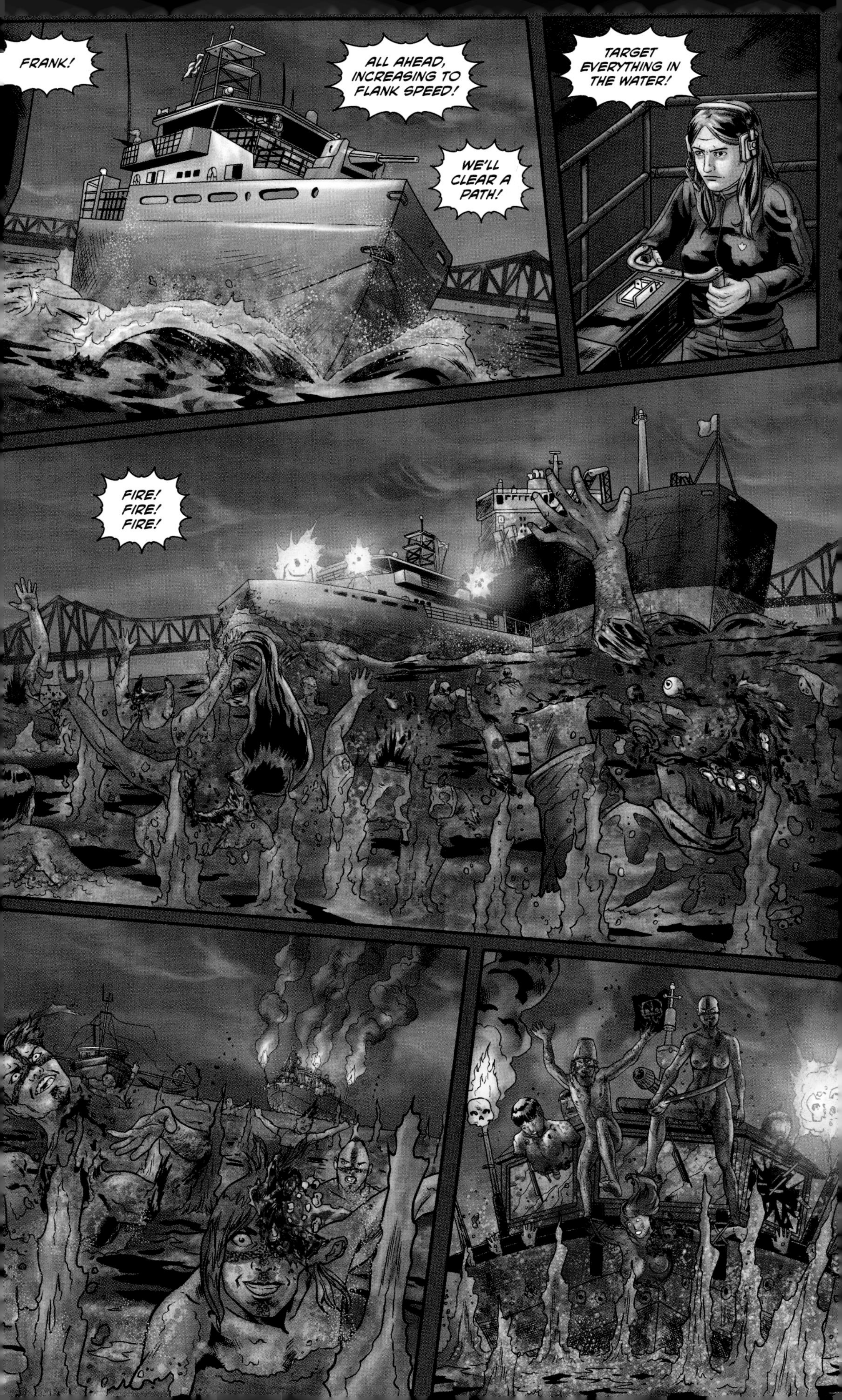
FRANK!
ALL AHEAD, INCREASING TO FLANK SPEED!
WE'LL CLEAR A PATH!
TARGET EVERYTHING IN THE WATER!
FIRE! FIRE! FIRE!

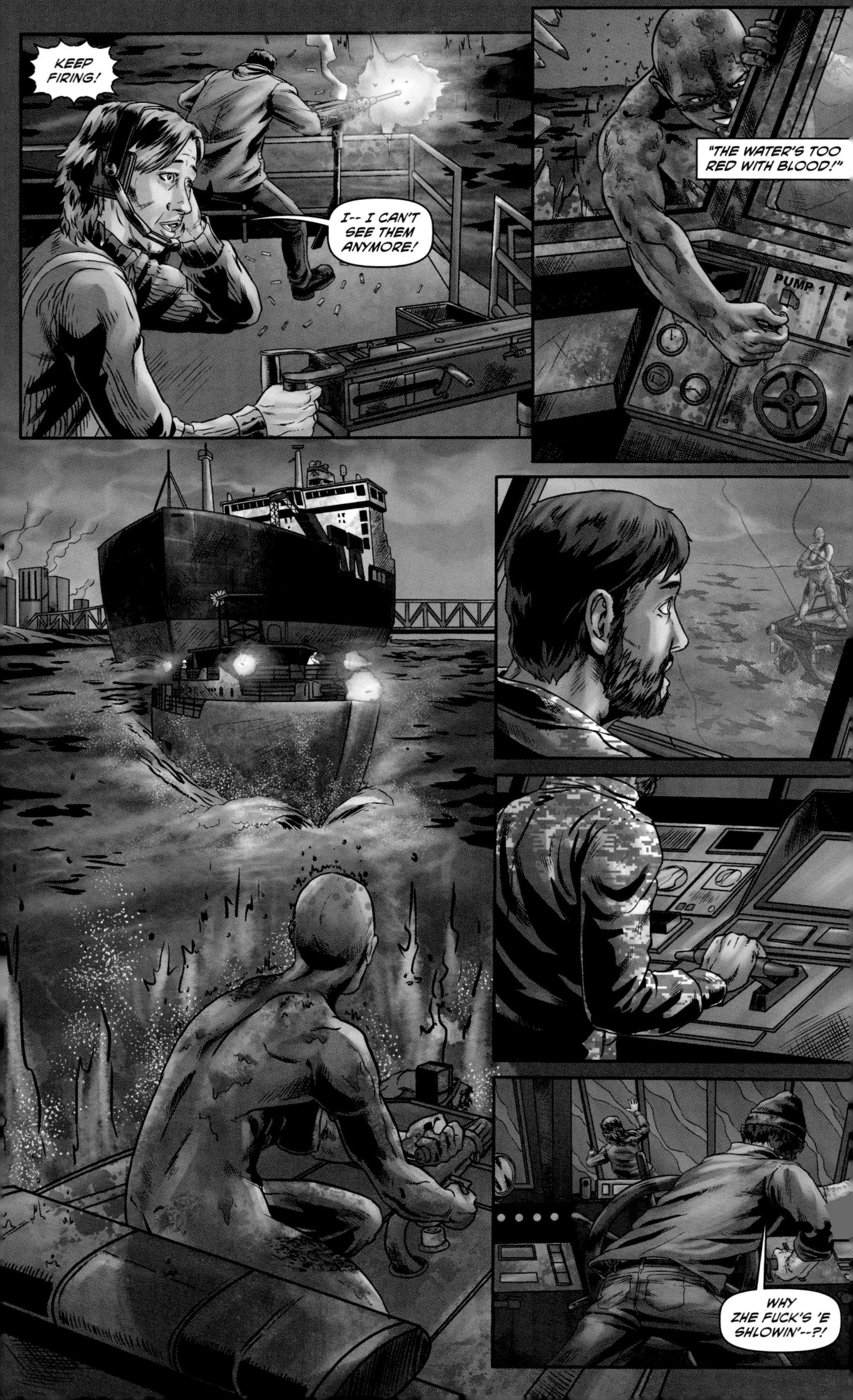
KEEP FIRING!
I-- I CAN'T SEE THEM ANYMORE!
"THE WATER'S TOO RED WITH BLOOD!"
PUMP 1
WHY ZHE FUCK'S 'E SHLOWIN'--?!

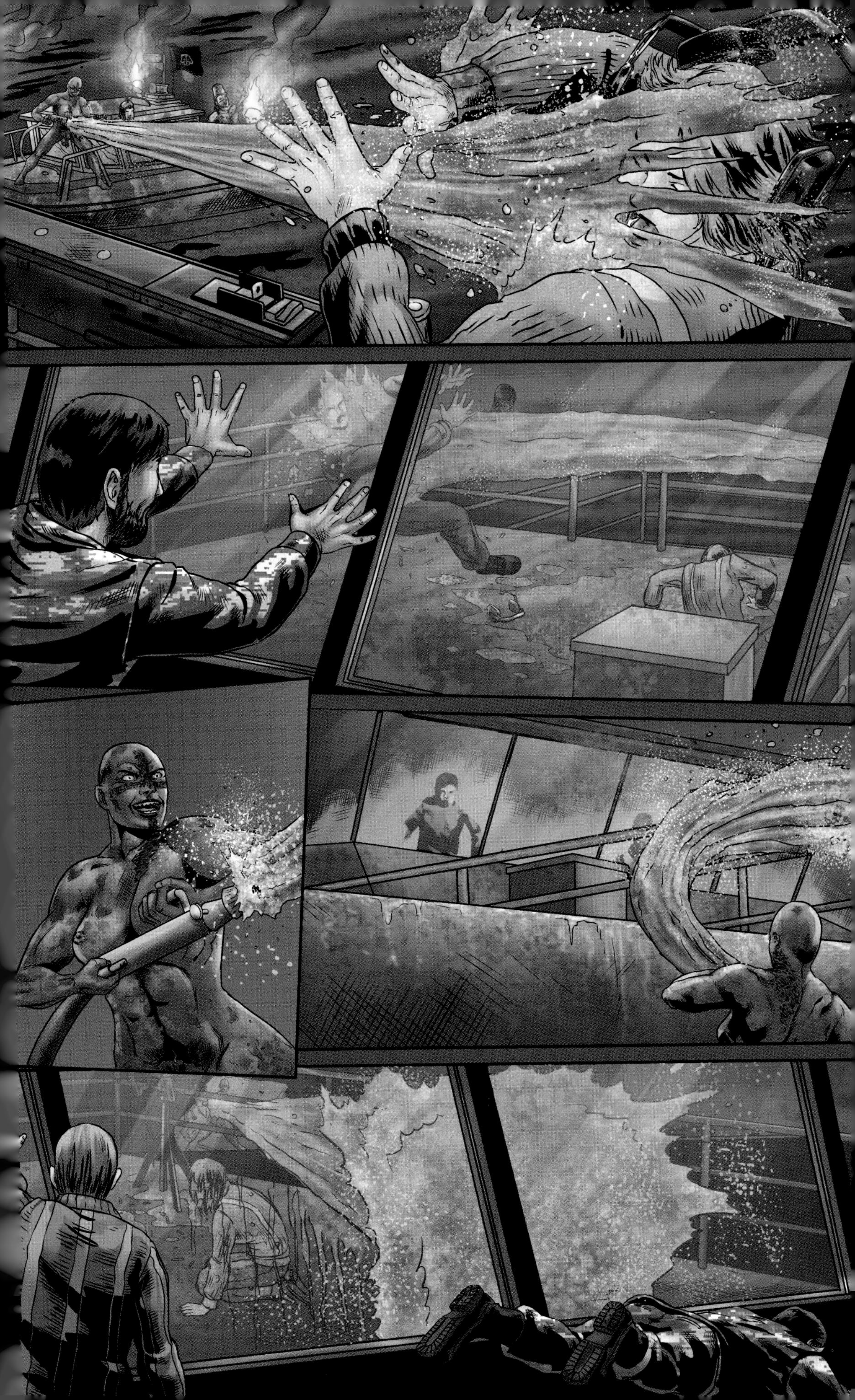

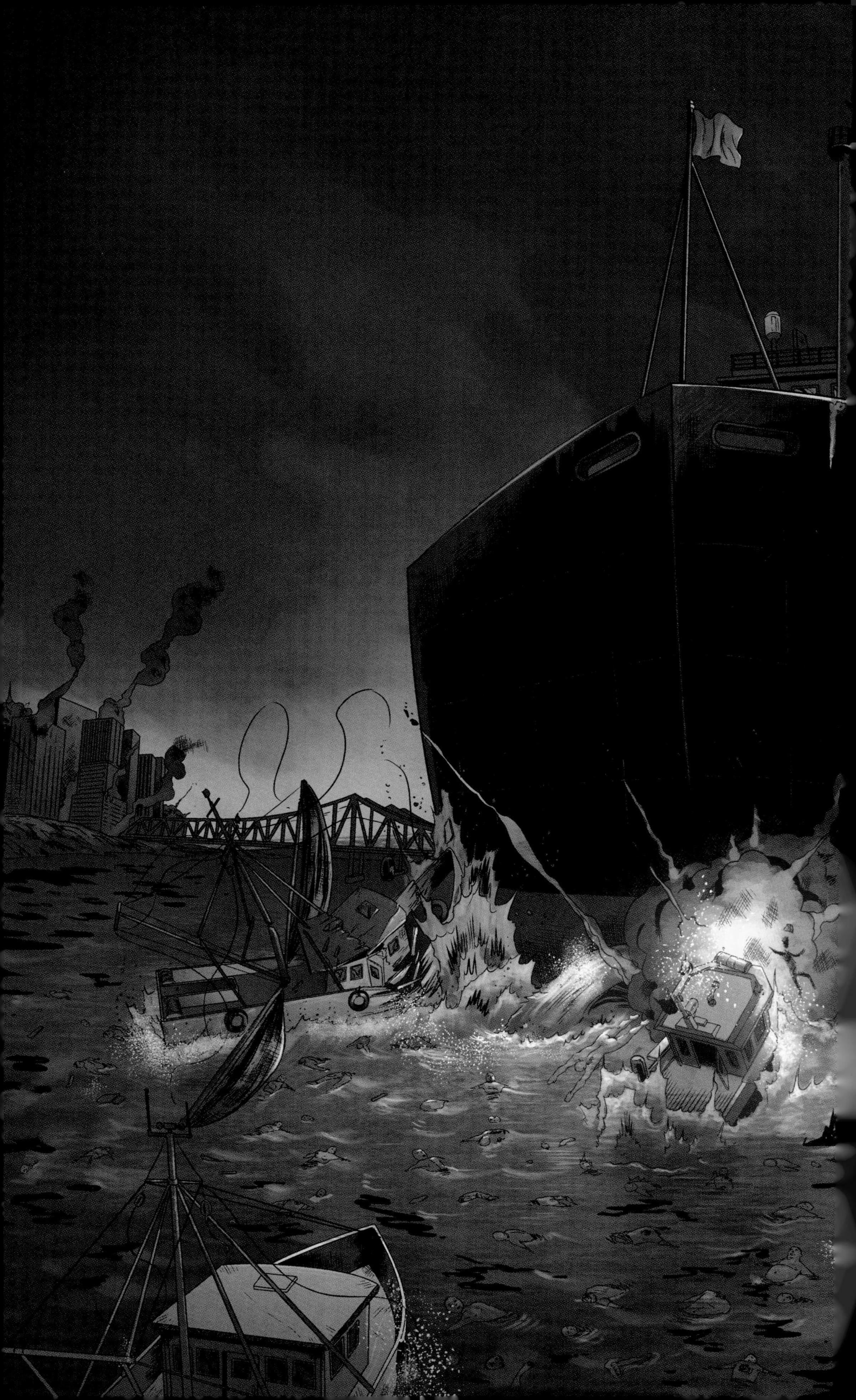

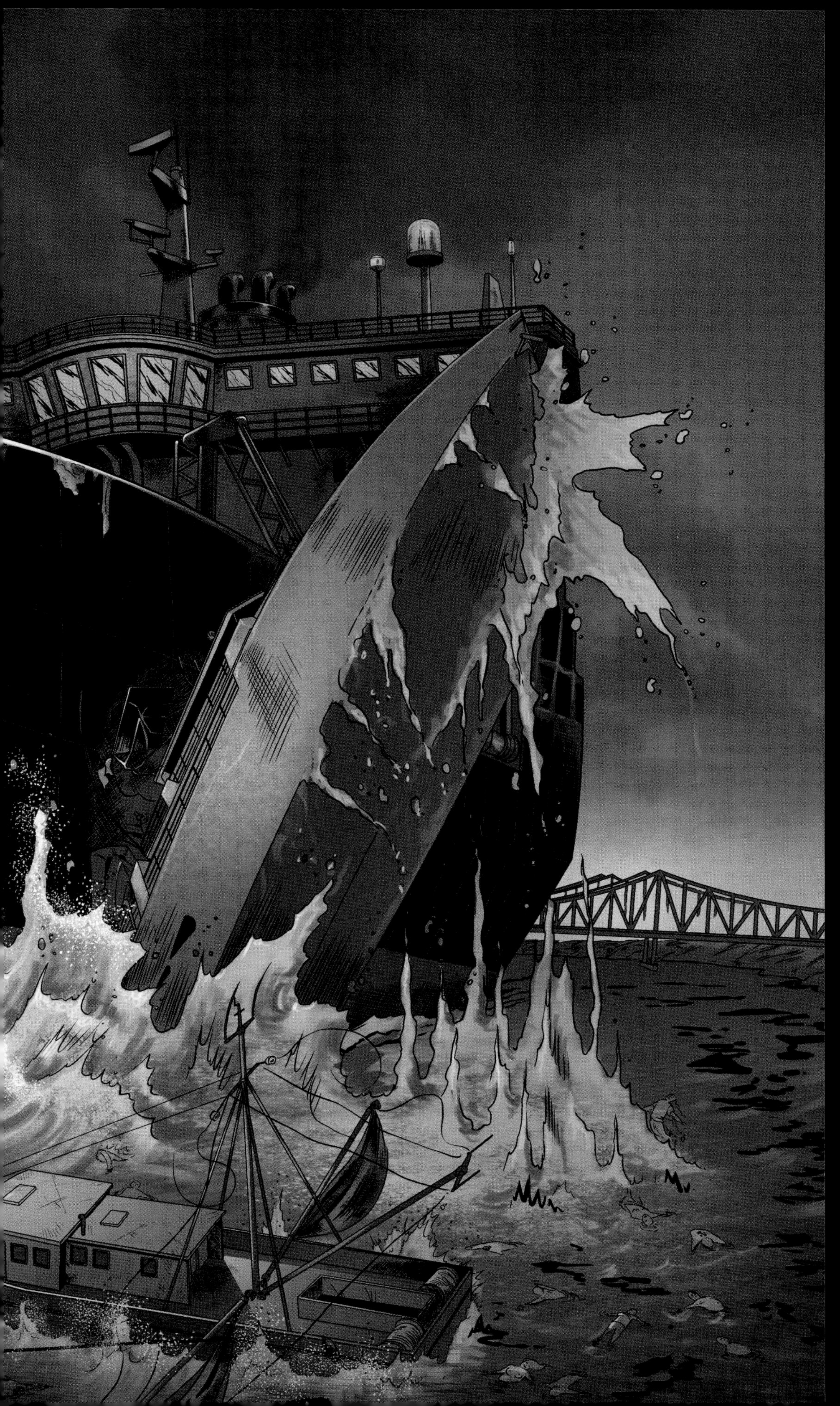

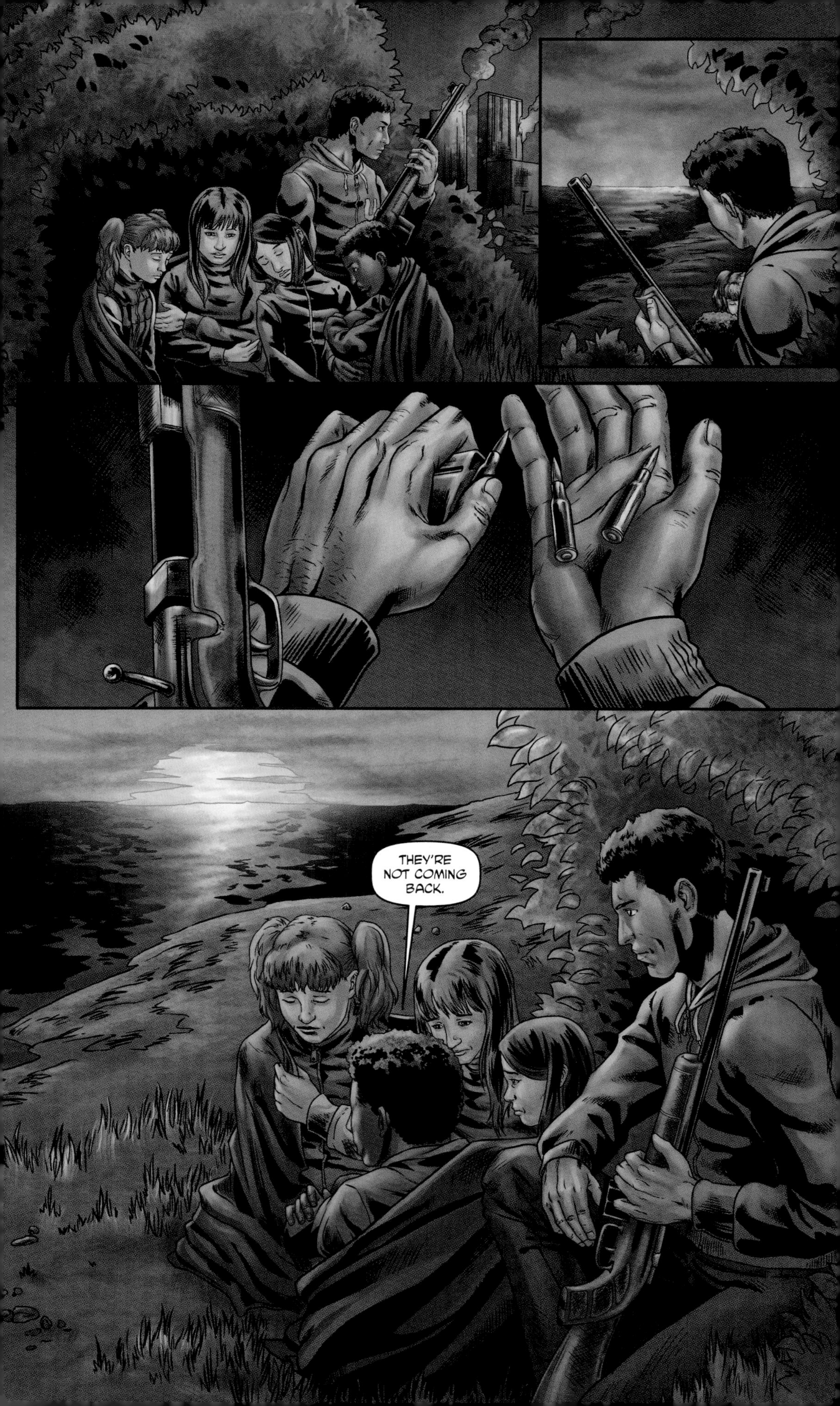
THEY'RE NOT COMING BACK.

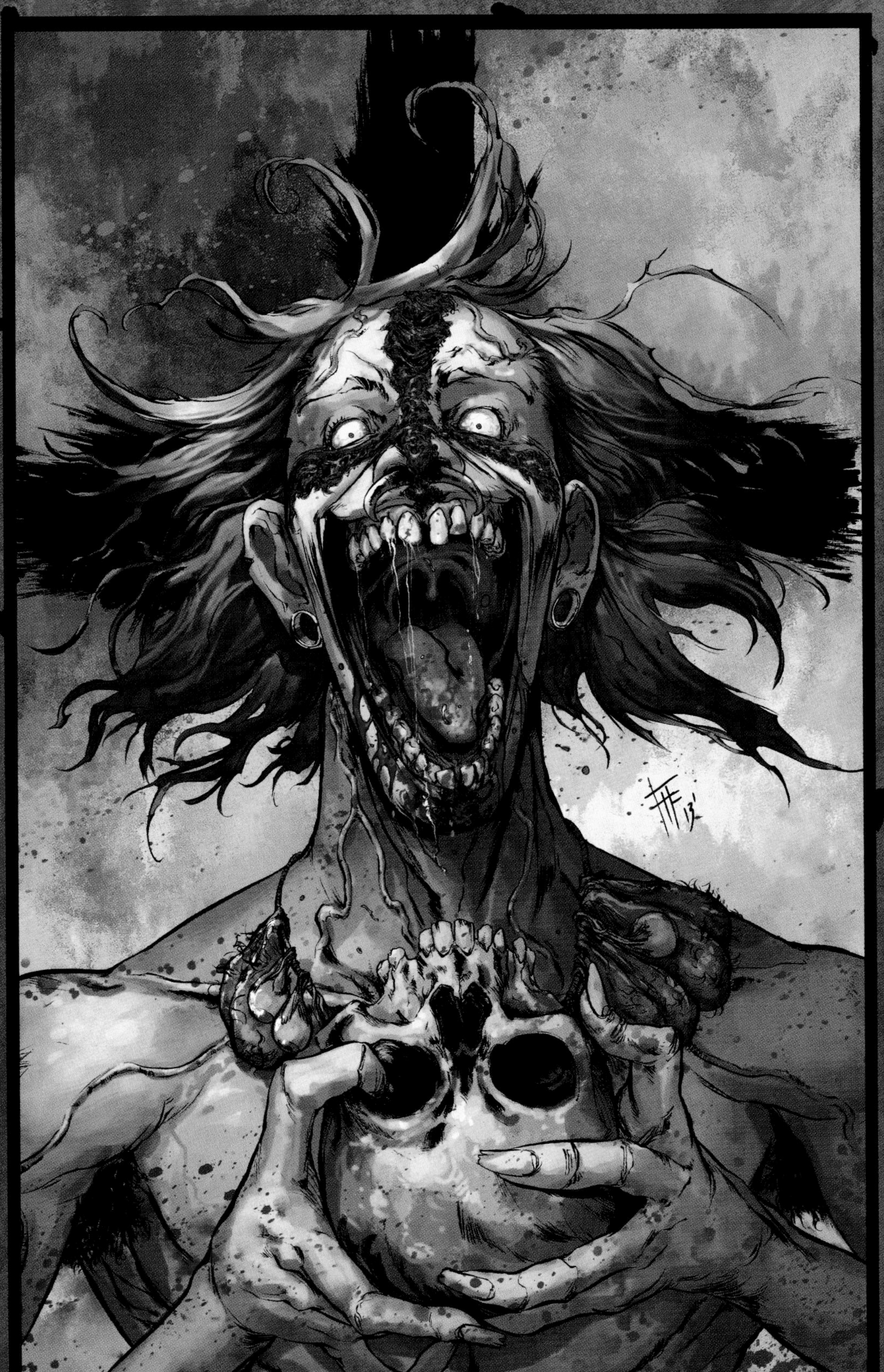

PART 4

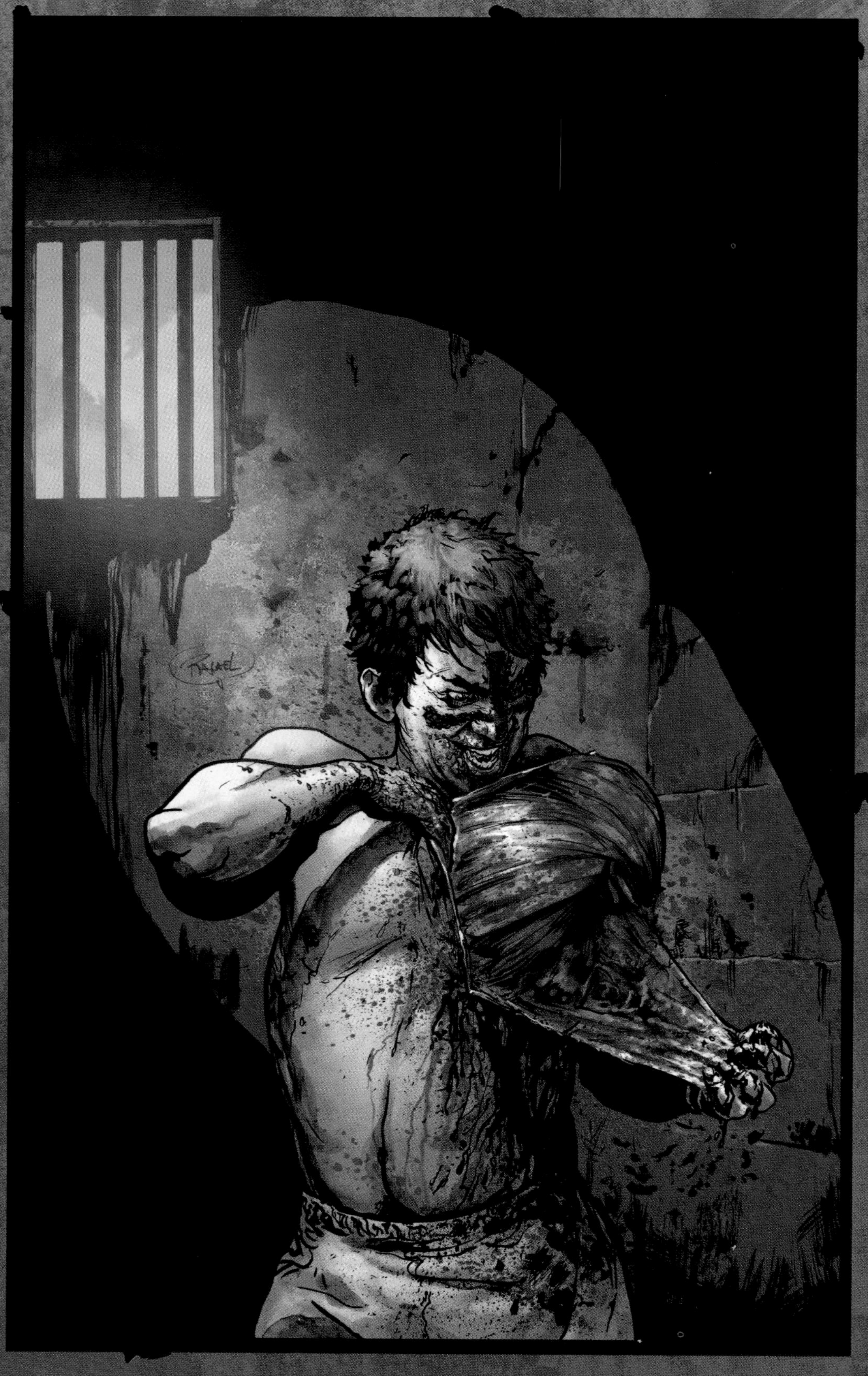

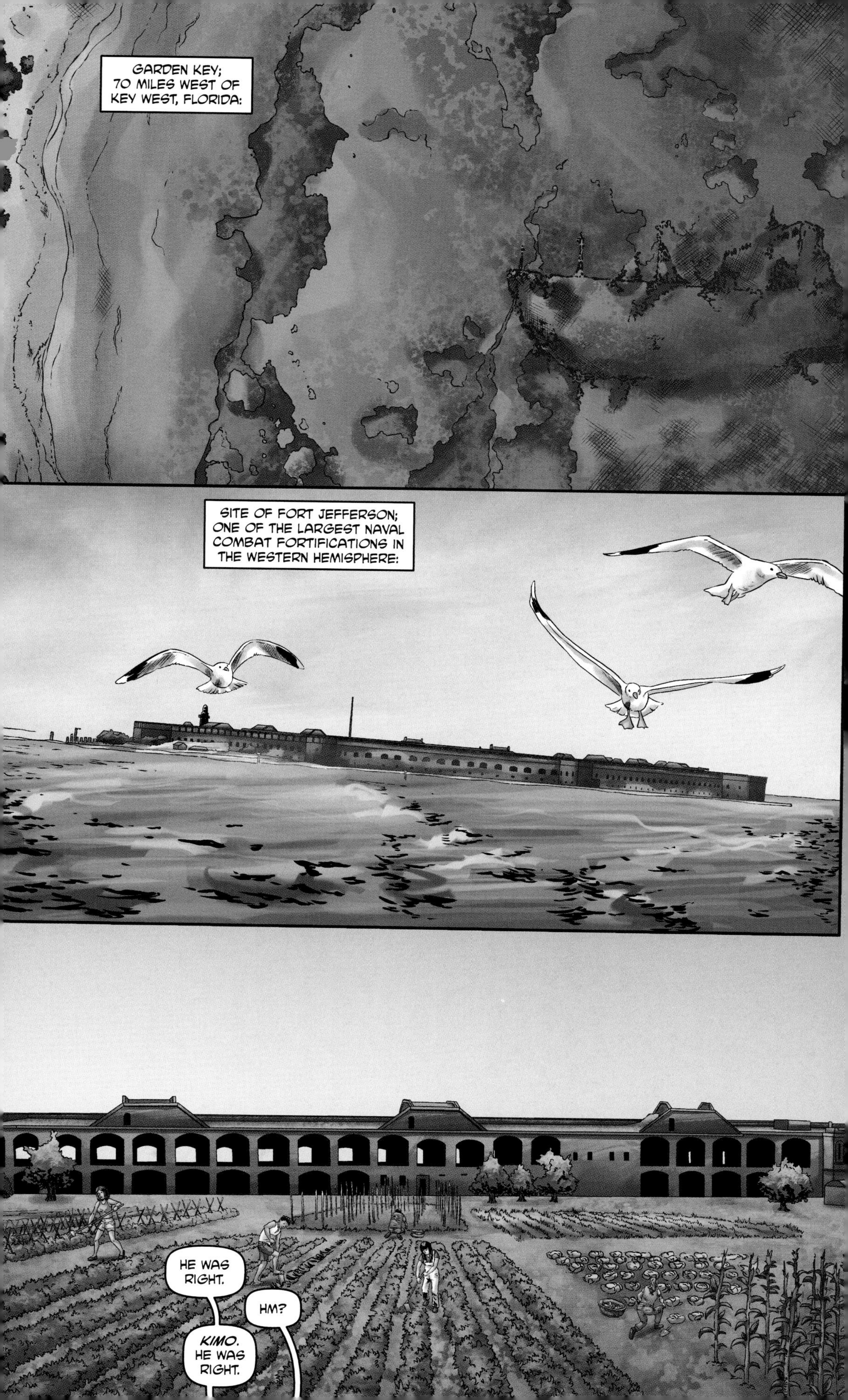
GARDEN KEY; 70 MILES WEST OF KEY WEST, FLORIDA:
SITE OF FORT JEFFERSON; ONE OF THE LARGEST NAVAL COMBAT FORTIFICATIONS IN THE WESTERN HEMISPHERE:
HE WAS RIGHT.
HM?
KIMO. HE WAS RIGHT.

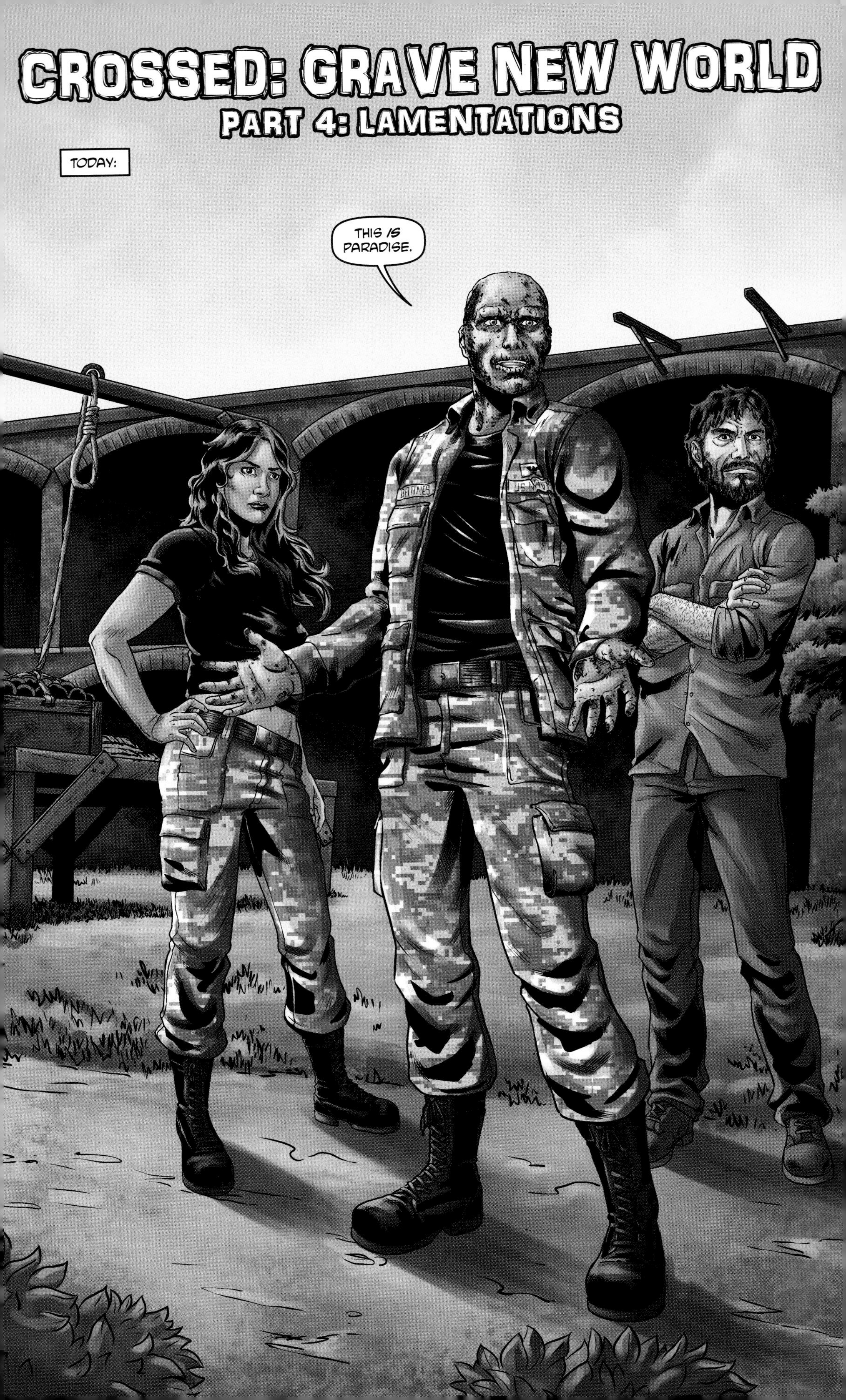
CROSSED: GRAVE NEW WORLD
PART 4: LAMENTATIONS
TODAY:
THIS IS PARADISE.

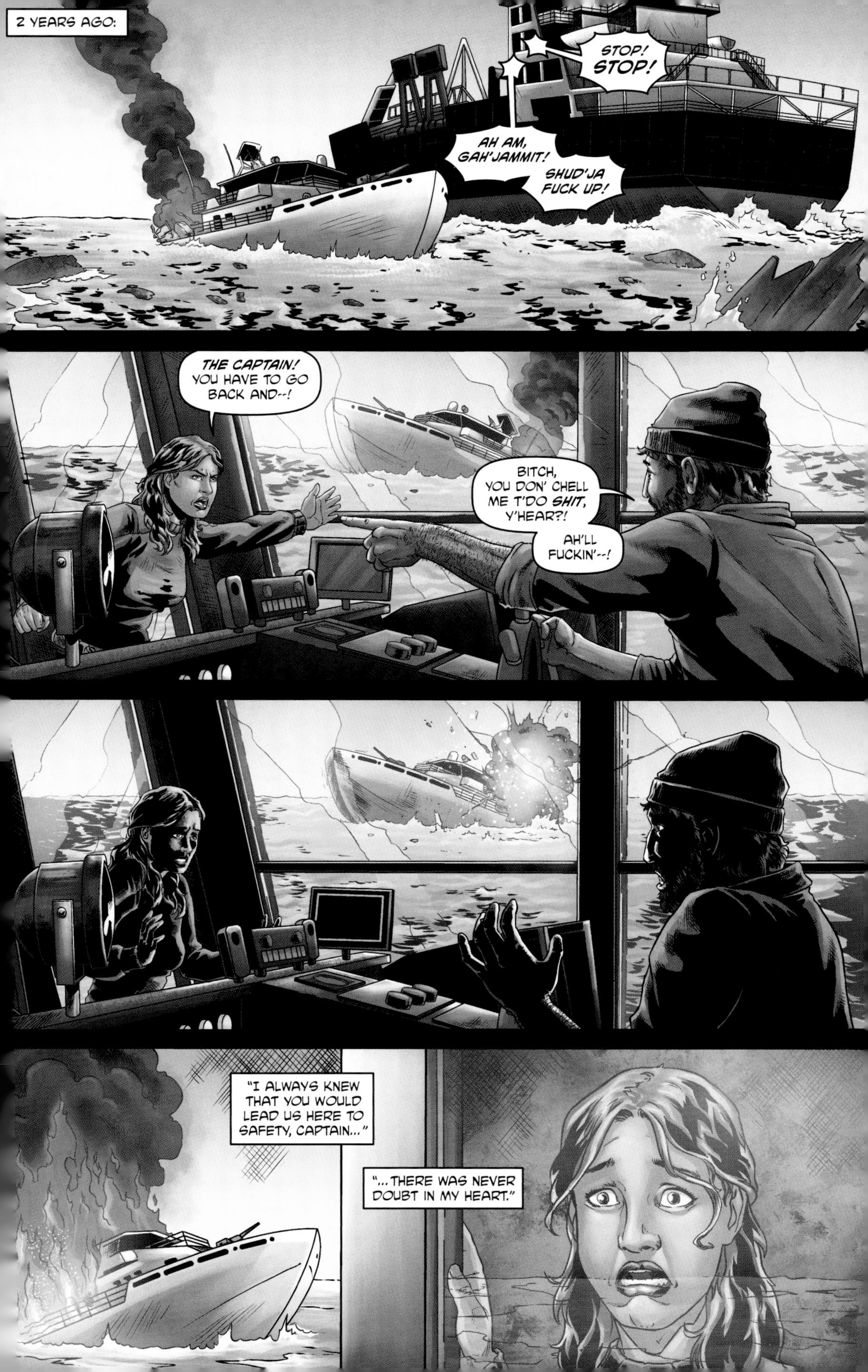
2 YEARS AGO:
STOP! STOP!
AH AM, GAH'JAMMIT!
SHUD'JA FUCK UP!
THE CAPTAIN! YOU HAVE TO GO BACK AND--!
BITCH, YOU DON' CHELL ME T'DO SHIT, Y'HEAR?!
AH'LL FUCKIN'--!
"I ALWAYS KNEW THAT YOU WOULD LEAD US HERE TO SAFETY, CAPTAIN..."
"...THERE WAS NEVER DOUBT IN MY HEART."

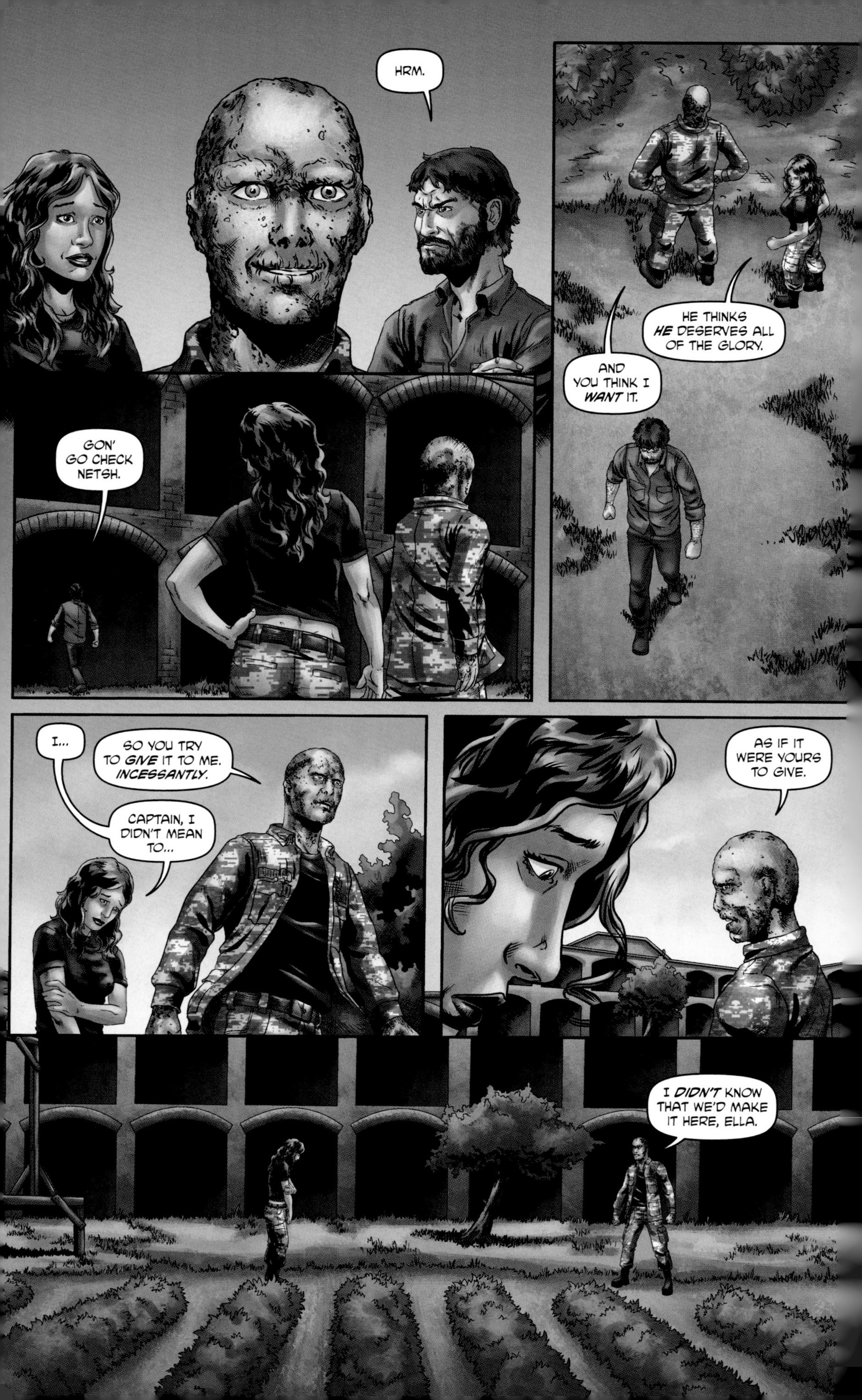
HRM.
HE THINKS *HE* DESERVES ALL OF THE GLORY.
AND YOU THINK I *WANT* IT.
GON' GO CHECK NETSH.
I...
SO YOU TRY TO *GIVE* IT TO ME. *INCESSANTLY*.
CAPTAIN, I DIDN'T MEAN TO...
AS IF IT WERE YOURS TO GIVE.
I *DIDN'T* KNOW THAT WE'D MAKE IT HERE, ELLA.

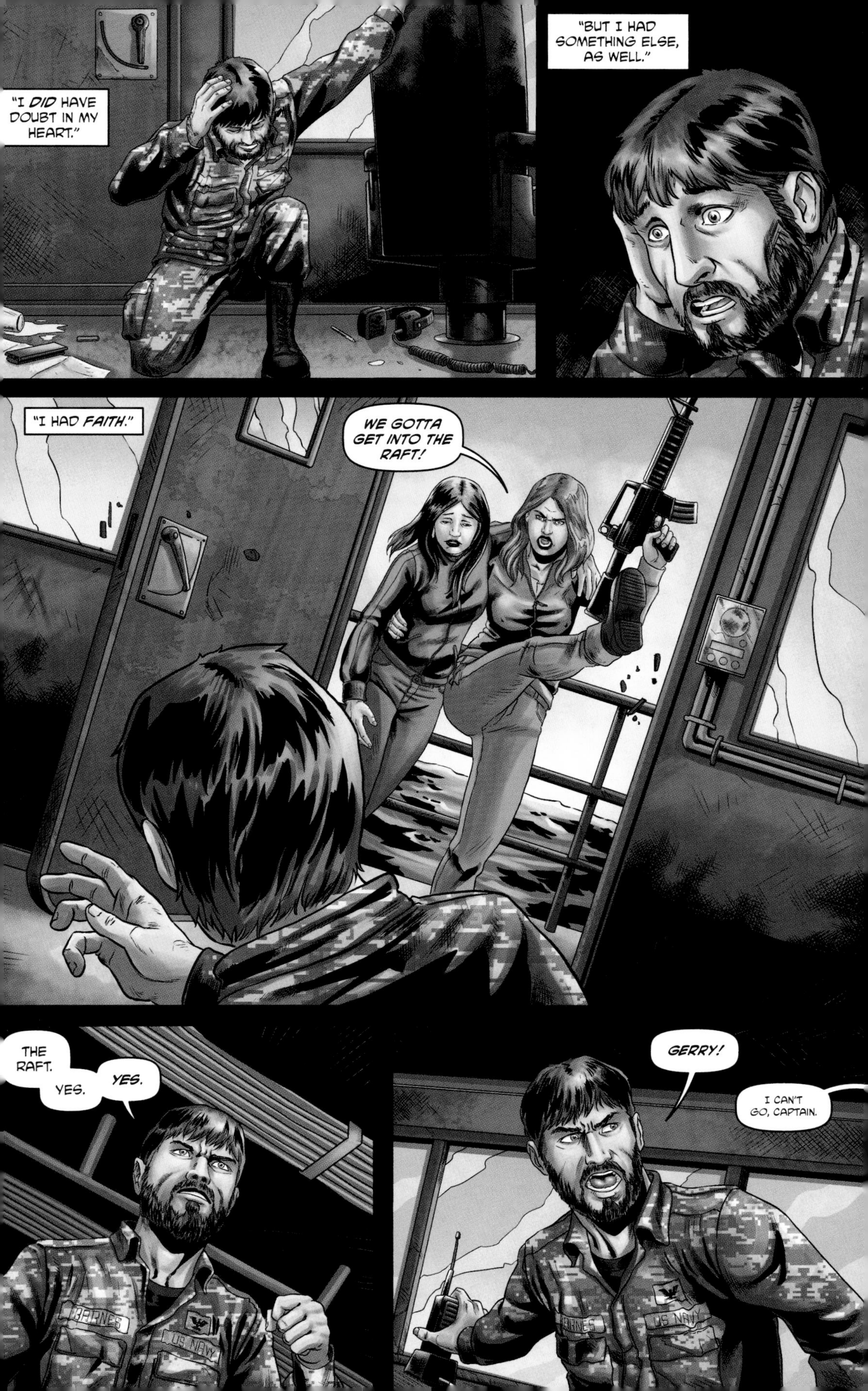
"I *DID* HAVE DOUBT IN MY HEART."
"BUT I HAD SOMETHING ELSE, AS WELL."
"I HAD *FAITH*."
WE GOTTA GET INTO THE RAFT!
THE RAFT.
YES.
YES.
GERRY!
I CAN'T GO, CAPTAIN.
BARNES
US NAVY

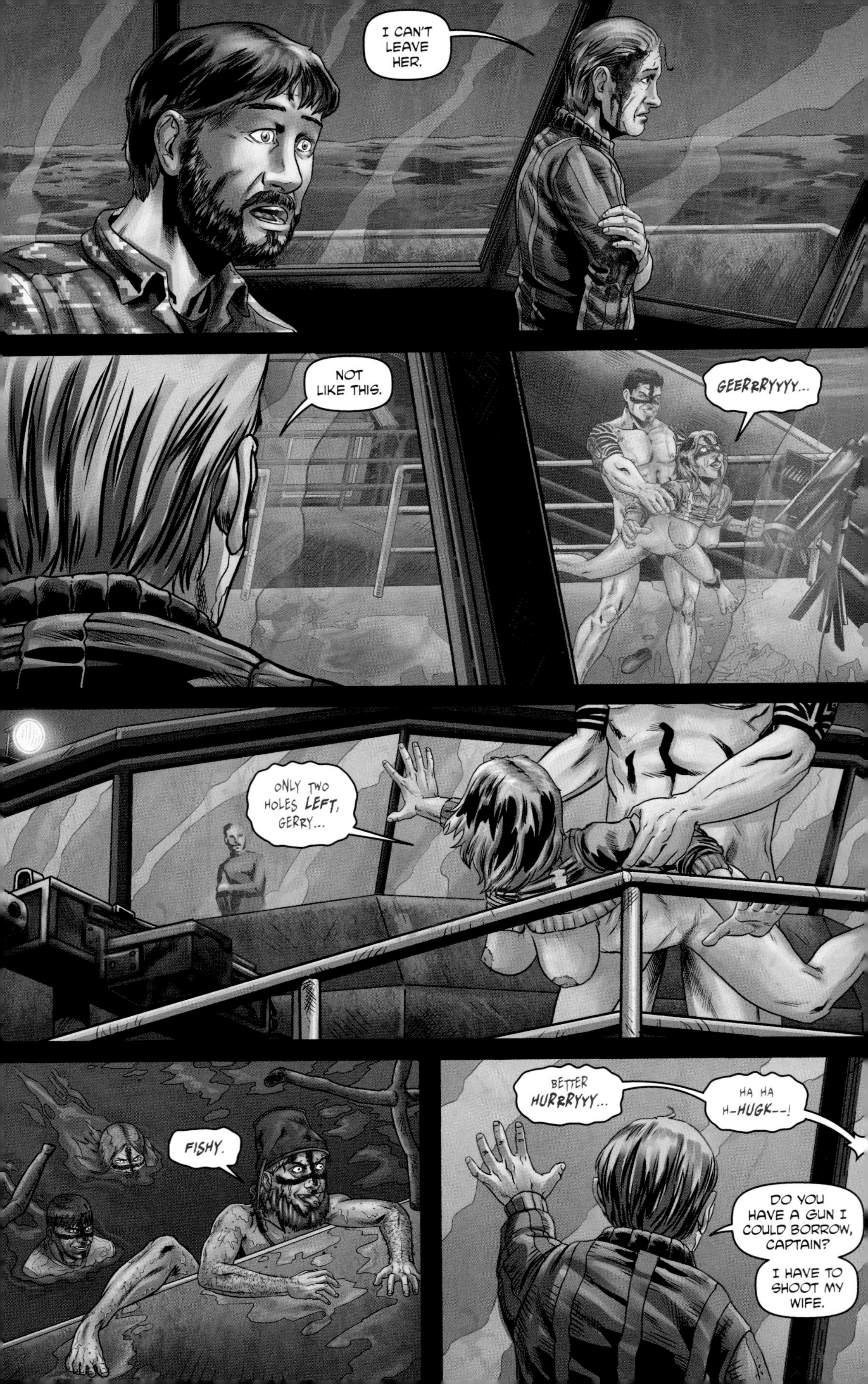
I CAN'T LEAVE HER.
NOT LIKE THIS.
GEERrRYYYY...
ONLY TWO HOLES LEFT, GERRY...
FISHY.
BETTER HURRRYYY...
HA HA H-HUGK--!
DO YOU HAVE A GUN I COULD BORROW, CAPTAIN?
I HAVE TO SHOOT MY WIFE.

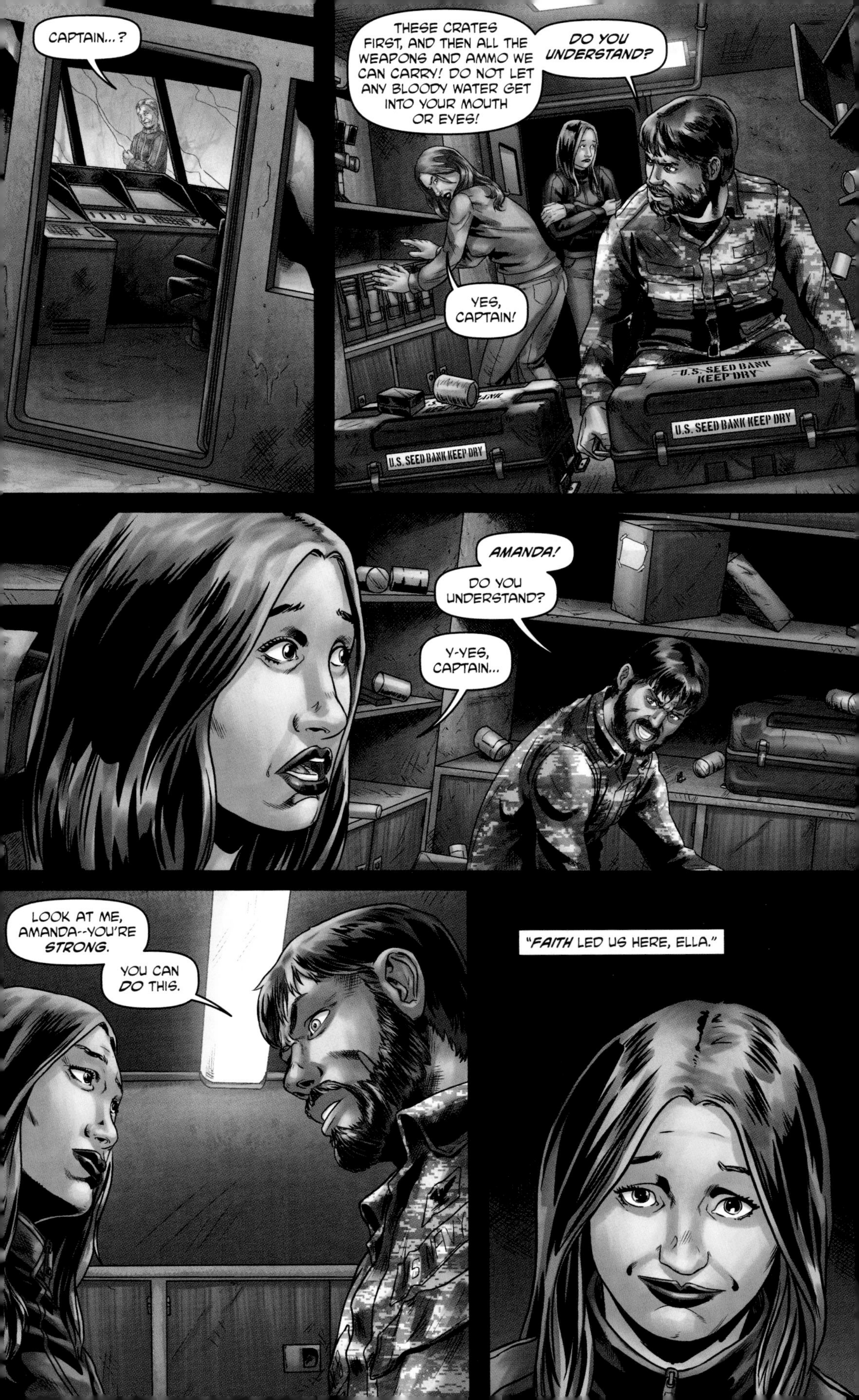

CAPTAIN...?
THESE CRATES FIRST, AND THEN ALL THE WEAPONS AND AMMO WE CAN CARRY! DO NOT LET ANY BLOODY WATER GET INTO YOUR MOUTH OR EYES!
DO YOU UNDERSTAND?
YES, CAPTAIN!
U.S. SEED BANK KEEP DRY
U.S. SEED BANK KEEP DRY
U.S. SEED BANK KEEP DRY
AMANDA!
DO YOU UNDERSTAND?
Y-YES, CAPTAIN...
LOOK AT ME, AMANDA--YOU'RE STRONG.
YOU CAN DO THIS.
"FAITH LED US HERE, ELLA."

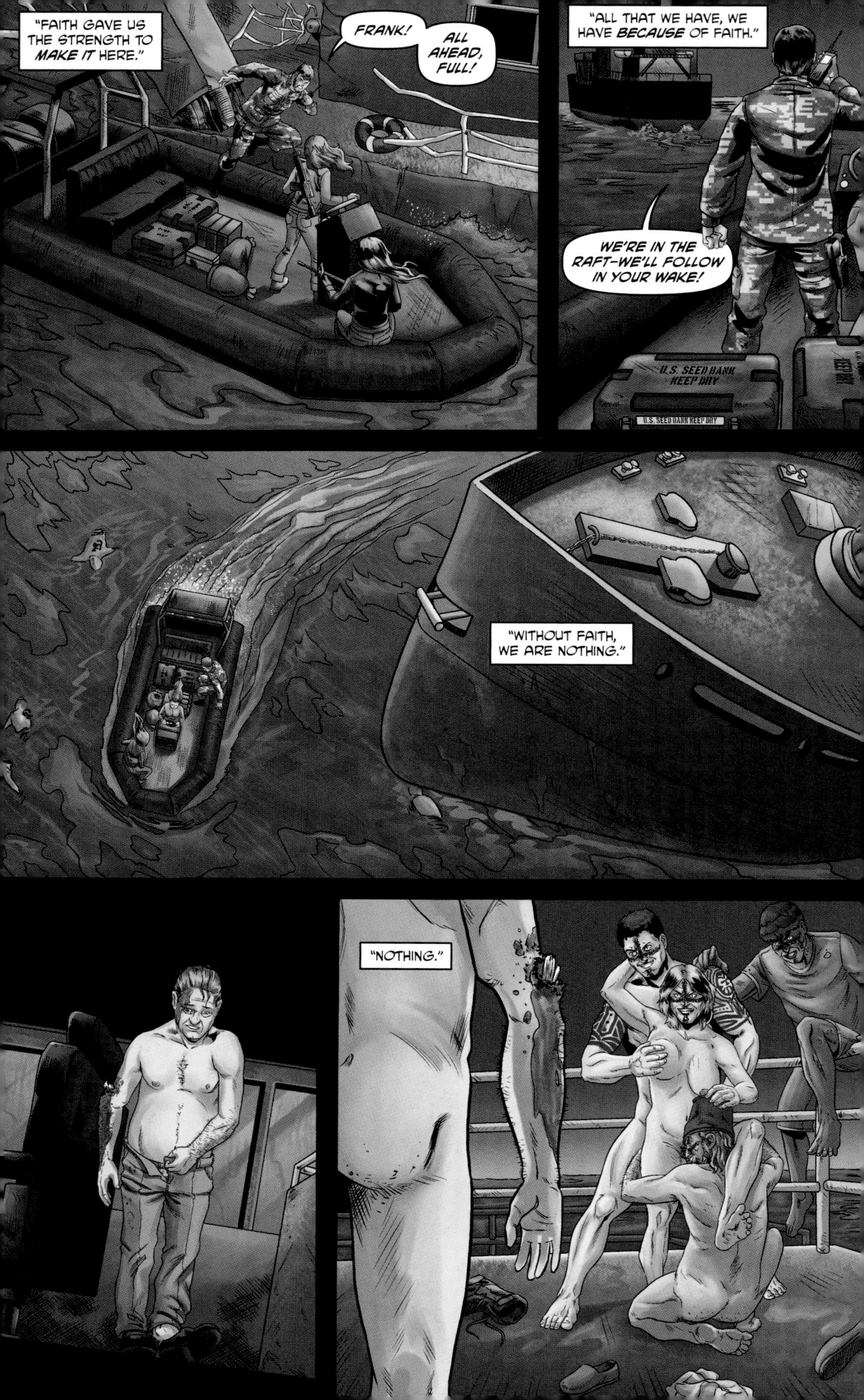
"FAITH GAVE US THE STRENGTH TO MAKE IT HERE."
FRANK!
ALL AHEAD, FULL!
"ALL THAT WE HAVE, WE HAVE BECAUSE OF FAITH."
WE'RE IN THE RAFT–WE'LL FOLLOW IN YOUR WAKE!
U.S. SEED BANK KEEP DRY
U.S. SEED BANK KEEP DRY
"WITHOUT FAITH, WE ARE NOTHING."
"NOTHING."

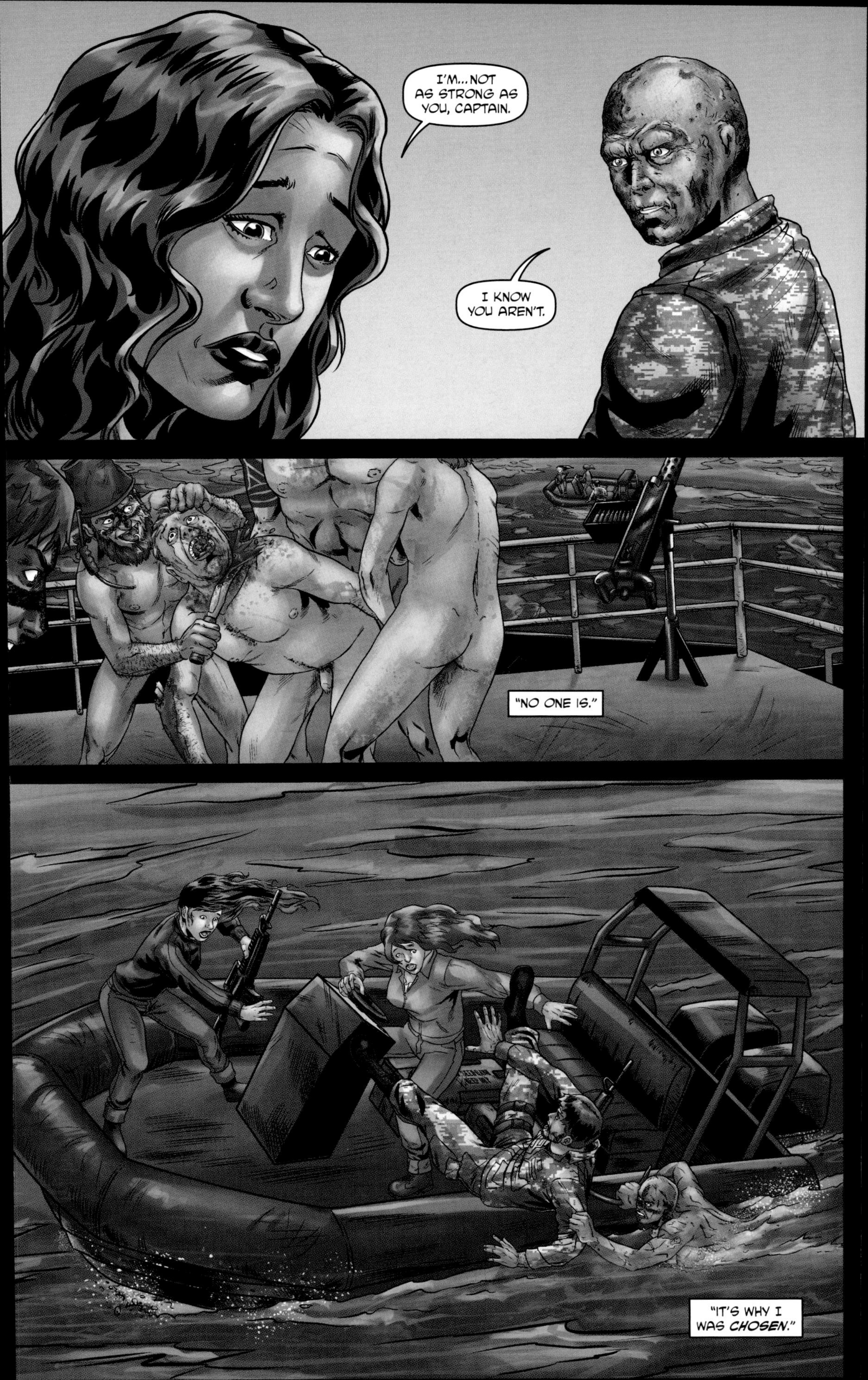

I'M...NOT AS STRONG AS YOU, CAPTAIN.
I KNOW YOU AREN'T.
"NO ONE IS."
"IT'S WHY I WAS *CHOSEN*."

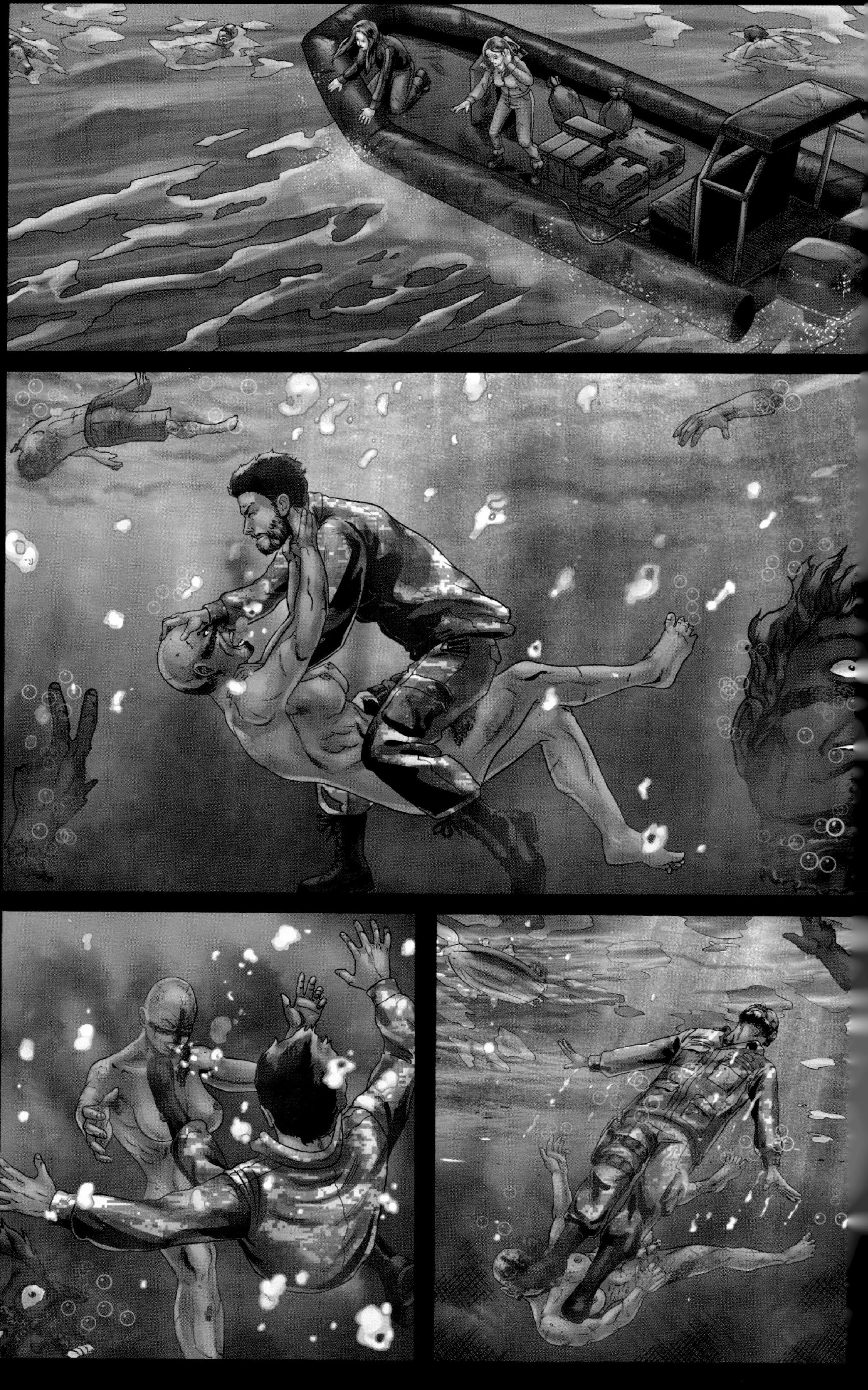

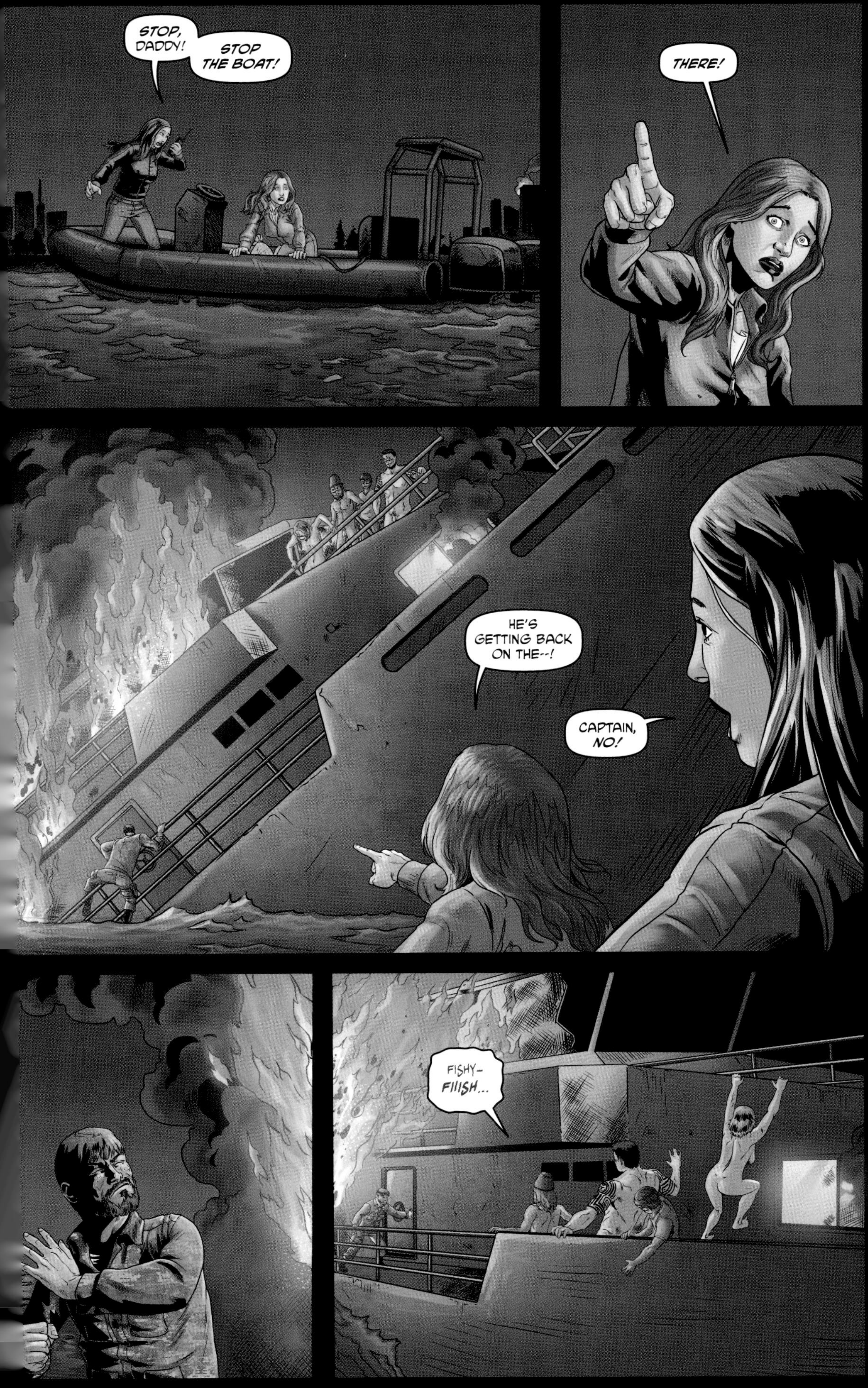
STOP, DADDY!
STOP THE BOAT!
THERE!
HE'S GETTING BACK ON THE--!
CAPTAIN, NO!
FISHY-
FIIISH...

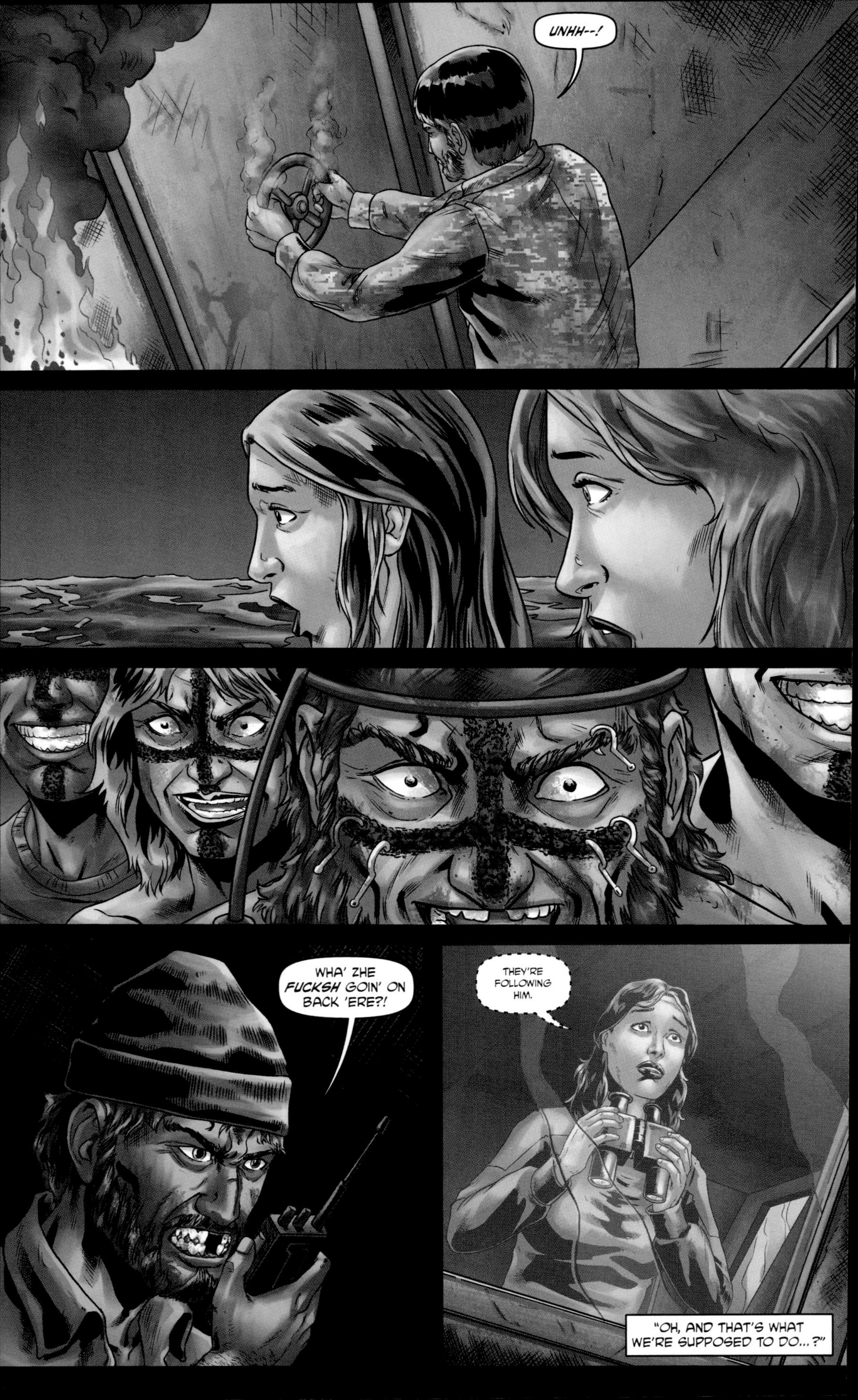
UNHH--!
WHA' ZHE FUCKSH GOIN' ON BACK 'ERE?!
THEY'RE FOLLOWING HIM.
"OH, AND THAT'S WHAT WE'RE SUPPOSED TO DO...?"

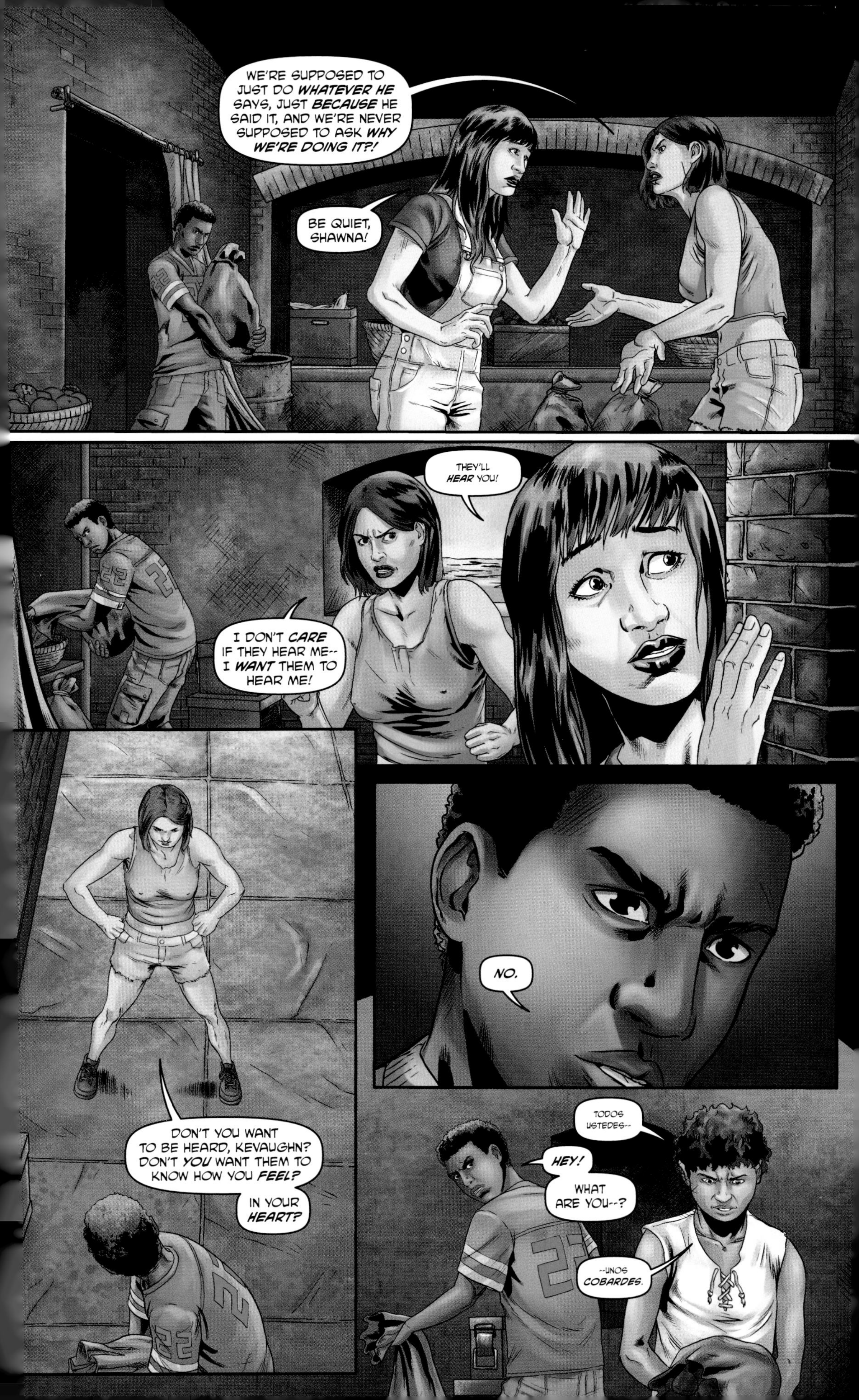
WE'RE SUPPOSED TO JUST DO WHATEVER HE SAYS, JUST BECAUSE HE SAID IT, AND WE'RE NEVER SUPPOSED TO ASK WHY WE'RE DOING IT?!
BE QUIET, SHAWNA!
THEY'LL HEAR YOU!
I DON'T CARE IF THEY HEAR ME-- I WANT THEM TO HEAR ME!
DON'T YOU WANT TO BE HEARD, KEVAUGHN? DON'T YOU WANT THEM TO KNOW HOW YOU FEEL?
IN YOUR HEART?
NO.
TODOS USTEDES--
HEY!
WHAT ARE YOU--?
--UNOS COBARDES.

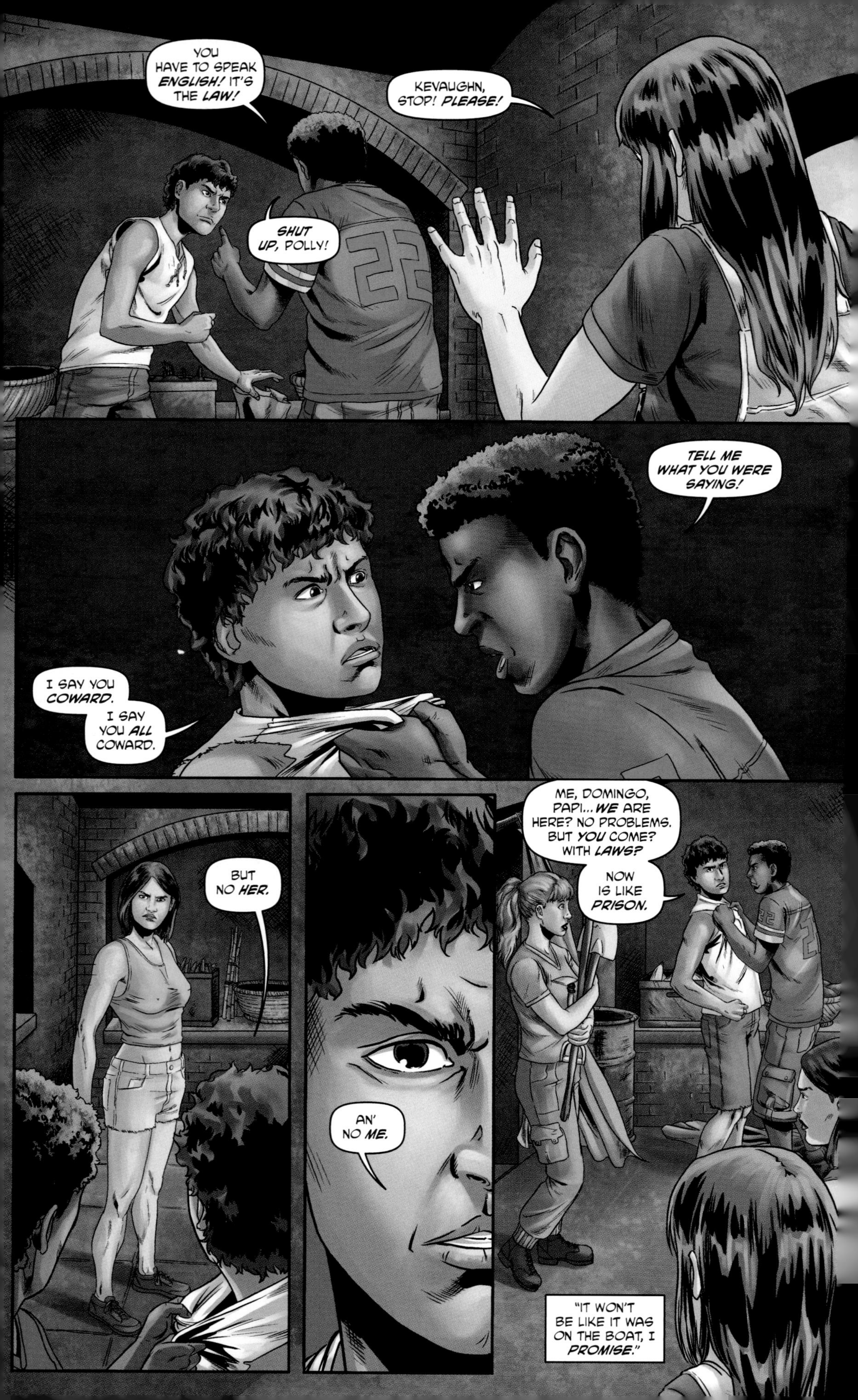
YOU HAVE TO SPEAK ENGLISH! IT'S THE LAW!
KEVAUGHN, STOP! PLEASE!
SHUT UP, POLLY!
TELL ME WHAT YOU WERE SAYING!
I SAY YOU COWARD.
I SAY YOU ALL COWARD.
BUT NO HER.
AN' NO ME.
ME, DOMINGO, PAPI... WE ARE HERE? NO PROBLEMS. BUT YOU COME? WITH LAWS?
NOW IS LIKE PRISON.
"IT WON'T BE LIKE IT WAS ON THE BOAT, I PROMISE."

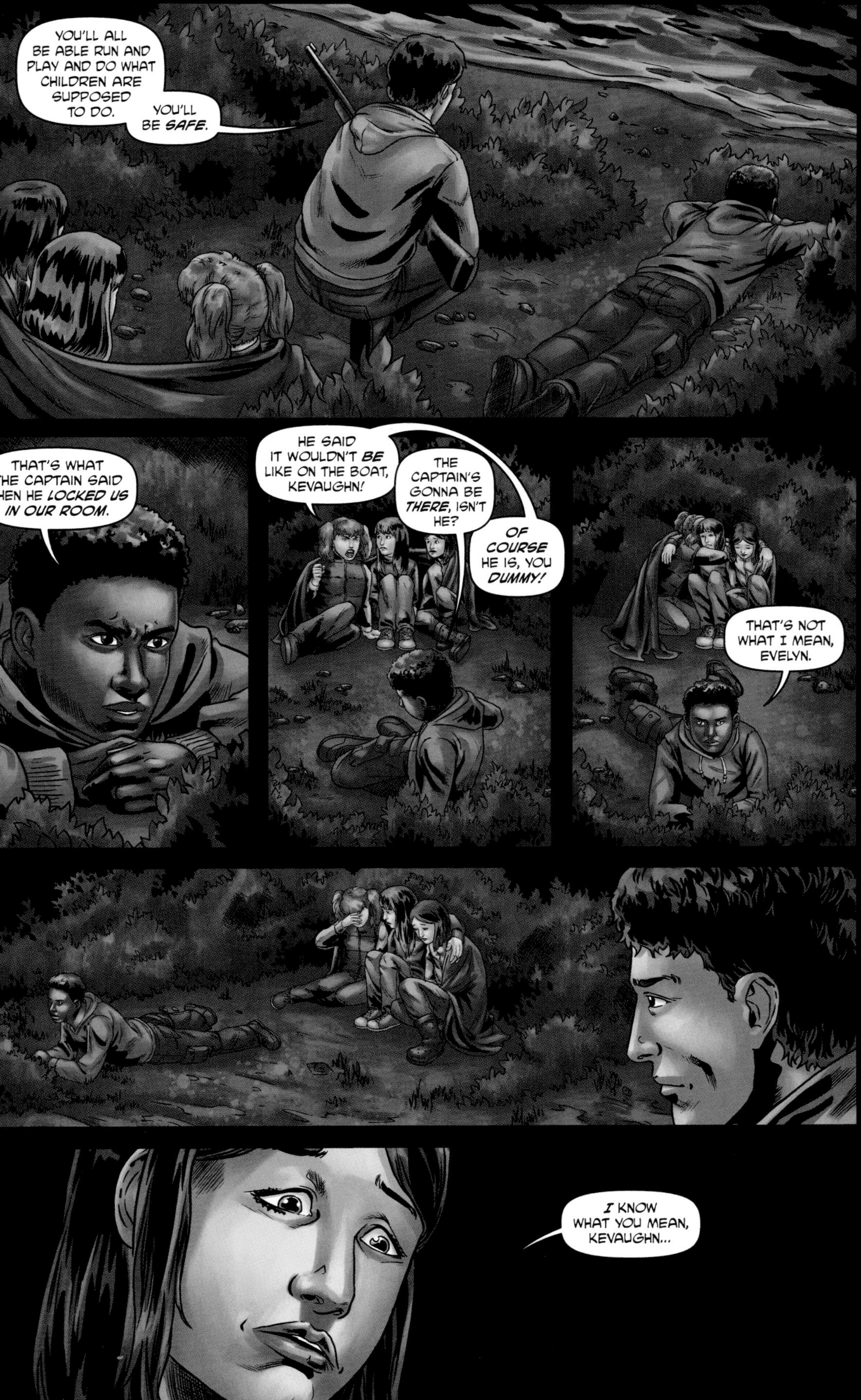
YOU'LL ALL BE ABLE RUN AND PLAY AND DO WHAT CHILDREN ARE SUPPOSED TO DO.
YOU'LL BE *SAFE*.
THAT'S WHAT THE CAPTAIN SAID WHEN HE *LOCKED US IN OUR ROOM*.
HE SAID IT WOULDN'T *BE* LIKE ON THE BOAT, KEVAUGHN!
THE CAPTAIN'S GONNA BE *THERE*, ISN'T HE?
OF COURSE HE IS, YOU *DUMMY!*
THAT'S NOT WHAT I MEAN, EVELYN.
I KNOW WHAT YOU MEAN, KEVAUGHN...

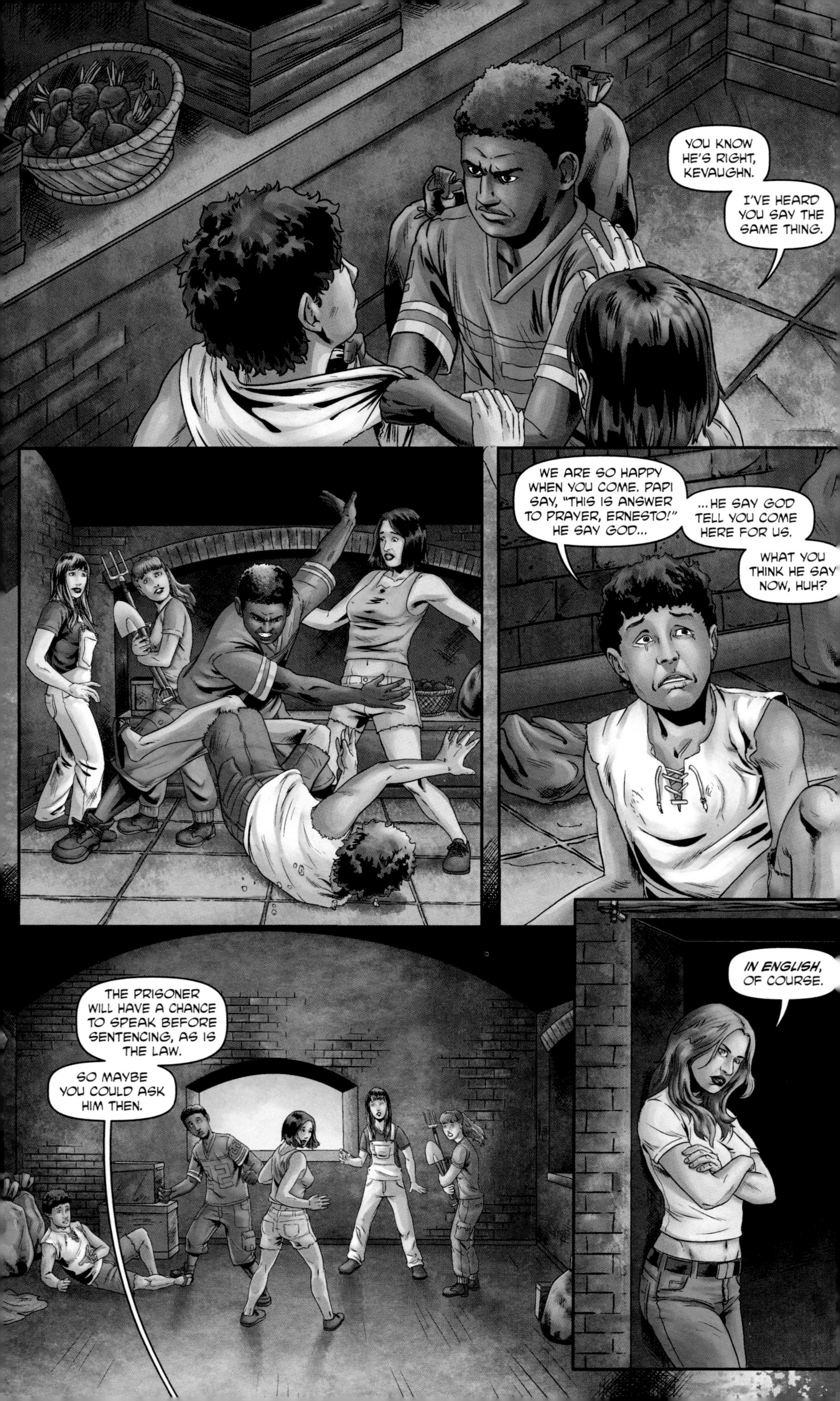
YOU KNOW HE'S RIGHT, KEVAUGHN.
I'VE HEARD YOU SAY THE SAME THING.
WE ARE SO HAPPY WHEN YOU COME. PAPI SAY, "THIS IS ANSWER TO PRAYER, ERNESTO!" HE SAY GOD...
...HE SAY GOD TELL YOU COME HERE FOR US.
WHAT YOU THINK HE SAY NOW, HUH?
THE PRISONER WILL HAVE A CHANCE TO SPEAK BEFORE SENTENCING, AS IS THE LAW.
SO MAYBE YOU COULD ASK HIM THEN.
IN ENGLISH, OF COURSE.

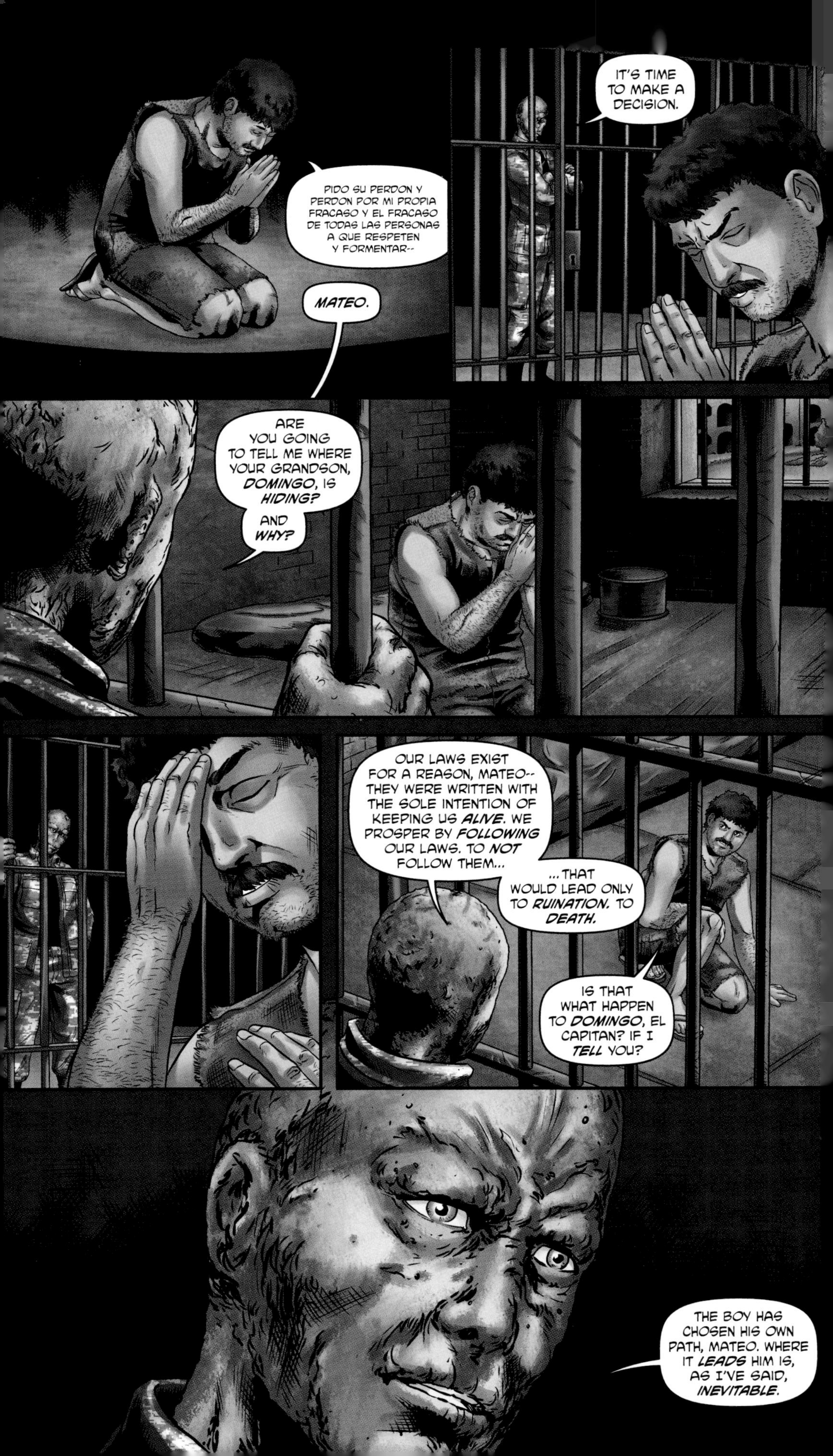
PIDO SU PERDON Y PERDON POR MI PROPIA FRACASO Y EL FRACASO DE TODAS LAS PERSONAS A QUE RESPETEN Y FORMENTAR--
MATEO.
IT'S TIME TO MAKE A DECISION.
ARE YOU GOING TO TELL ME WHERE YOUR GRANDSON, DOMINGO, IS HIDING?
AND WHY?
OUR LAWS EXIST FOR A REASON, MATEO-- THEY WERE WRITTEN WITH THE SOLE INTENTION OF KEEPING US ALIVE. WE PROSPER BY FOLLOWING OUR LAWS. TO NOT FOLLOW THEM...
...THAT WOULD LEAD ONLY TO RUINATION. TO DEATH.
IS THAT WHAT HAPPEN TO DOMINGO, EL CAPITAN? IF I TELL YOU?
THE BOY HAS CHOSEN HIS OWN PATH, MATEO. WHERE IT LEADS HIM IS, AS I'VE SAID, INEVITABLE.

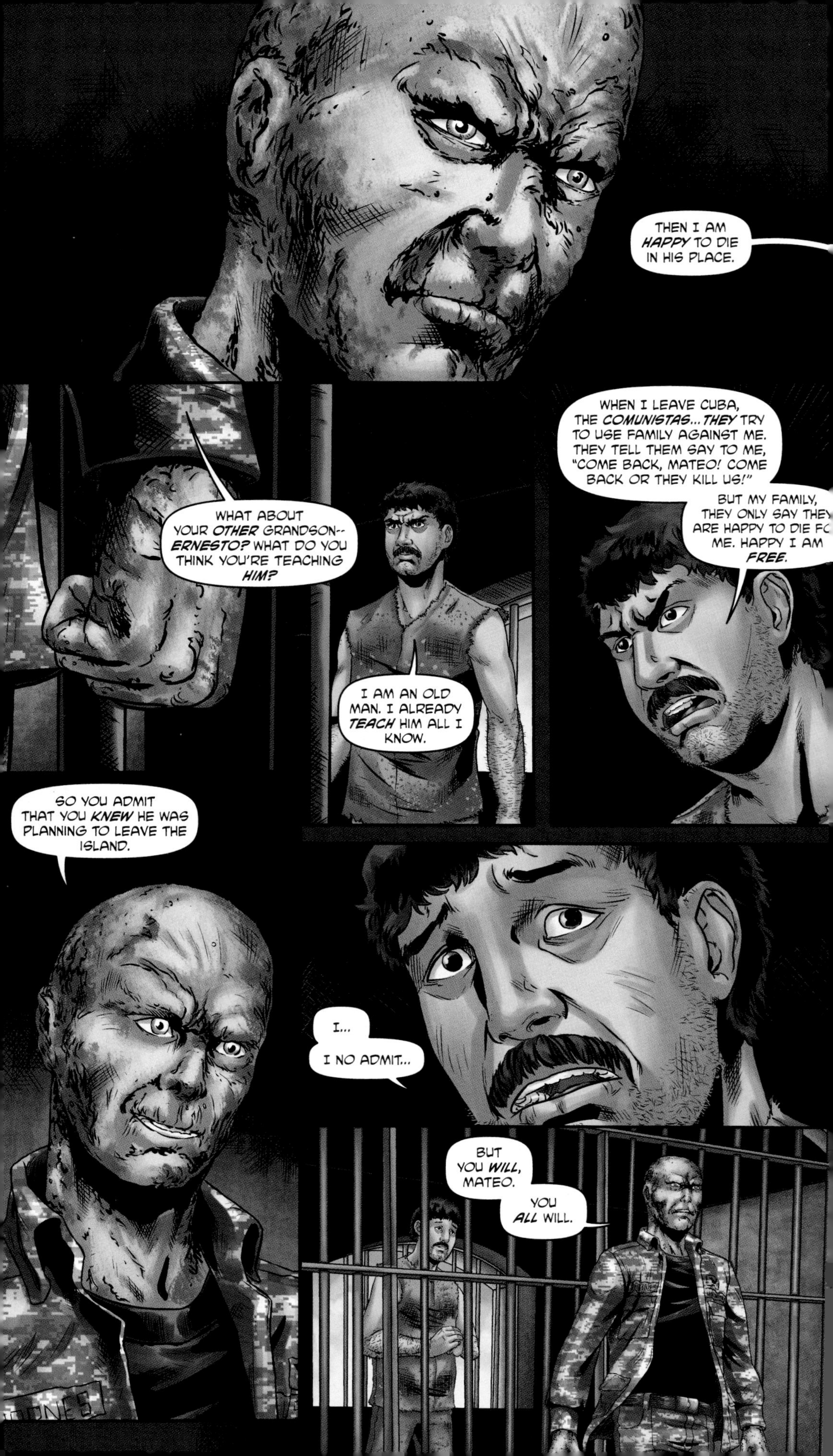
THEN I AM HAPPY TO DIE IN HIS PLACE.
WHAT ABOUT YOUR OTHER GRANDSON-- ERNESTO? WHAT DO YOU THINK YOU'RE TEACHING HIM?
I AM AN OLD MAN. I ALREADY TEACH HIM ALL I KNOW.
WHEN I LEAVE CUBA, THE COMUNISTAS... THEY TRY TO USE FAMILY AGAINST ME. THEY TELL THEM SAY TO ME, "COME BACK, MATEO! COME BACK OR THEY KILL US!"
BUT MY FAMILY, THEY ONLY SAY THEY ARE HAPPY TO DIE FO ME. HAPPY I AM FREE.
SO YOU ADMIT THAT YOU KNEW HE WAS PLANNING TO LEAVE THE ISLAND.
I...
I NO ADMIT...
BUT YOU WILL, MATEO.
YOU ALL WILL.

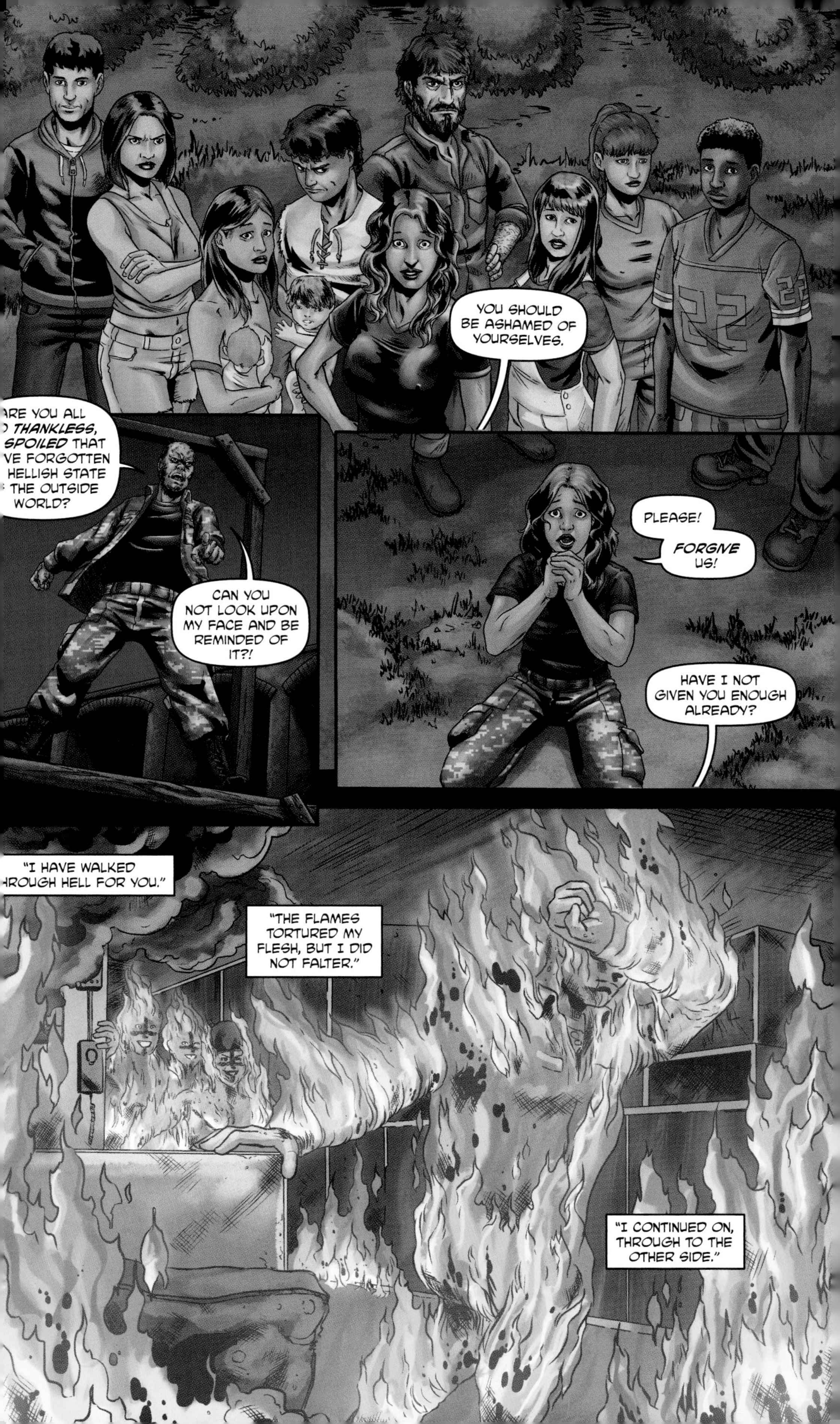
YOU SHOULD BE ASHAMED OF YOURSELVES.
ARE YOU ALL SO THANKLESS, SO SPOILED THAT YOU'VE FORGOTTEN THE HELLISH STATE OF THE OUTSIDE WORLD?
CAN YOU NOT LOOK UPON MY FACE AND BE REMINDED OF IT?!
PLEASE!
FORGIVE US!
HAVE I NOT GIVEN YOU ENOUGH ALREADY?
"I HAVE WALKED THROUGH HELL FOR YOU."
"THE FLAMES TORTURED MY FLESH, BUT I DID NOT FALTER."
"I CONTINUED ON, THROUGH TO THE OTHER SIDE."

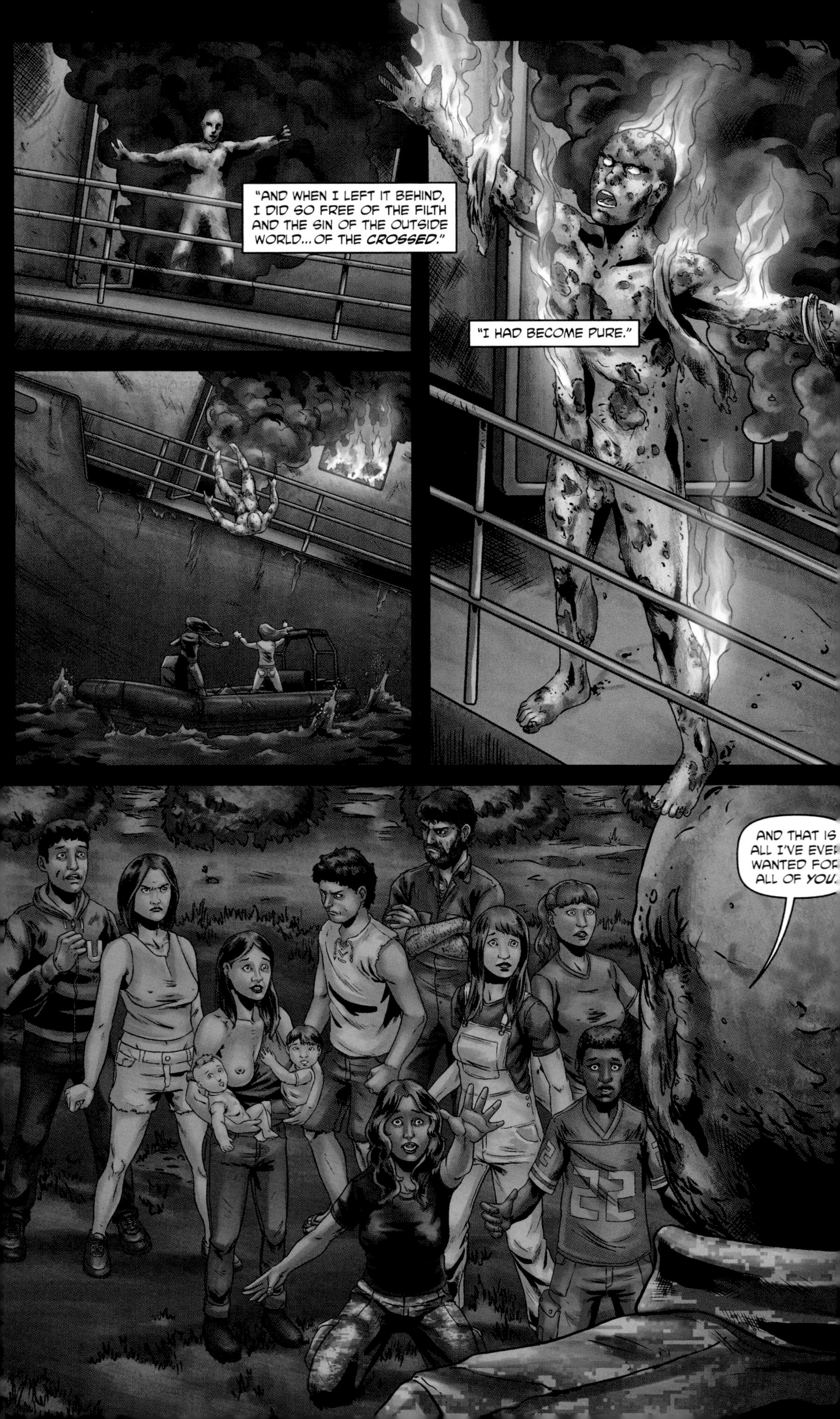
"AND WHEN I LEFT IT BEHIND, I DID SO FREE OF THE FILTH AND THE SIN OF THE OUTSIDE WORLD... OF THE *CROSSED*."
"I HAD BECOME PURE."
AND THAT IS ALL I'VE EVER WANTED FOR ALL OF *YOU*.

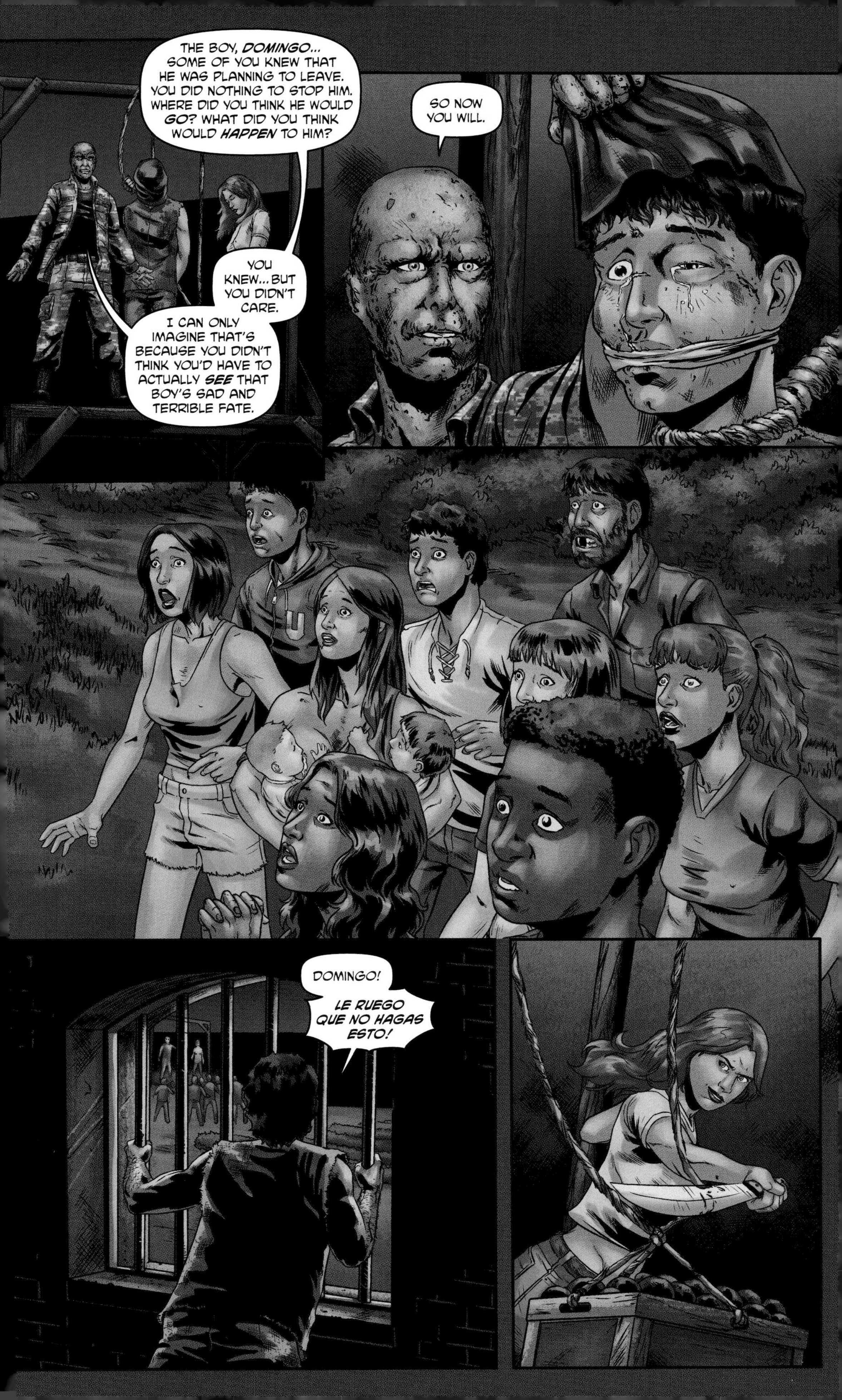
THE BOY, *DOMINGO*... SOME OF YOU KNEW THAT HE WAS PLANNING TO LEAVE. YOU DID NOTHING TO STOP HIM. WHERE DID YOU THINK HE WOULD *GO*? WHAT DID YOU THINK WOULD *HAPPEN* TO HIM?
YOU KNEW...BUT YOU DIDN'T CARE.
I CAN ONLY IMAGINE THAT'S BECAUSE YOU DIDN'T THINK YOU'D HAVE TO ACTUALLY *SEE* THAT BOY'S SAD AND TERRIBLE FATE.
SO NOW YOU WILL.
DOMINGO!
LE RUEGO QUE NO HAGAS ESTO!

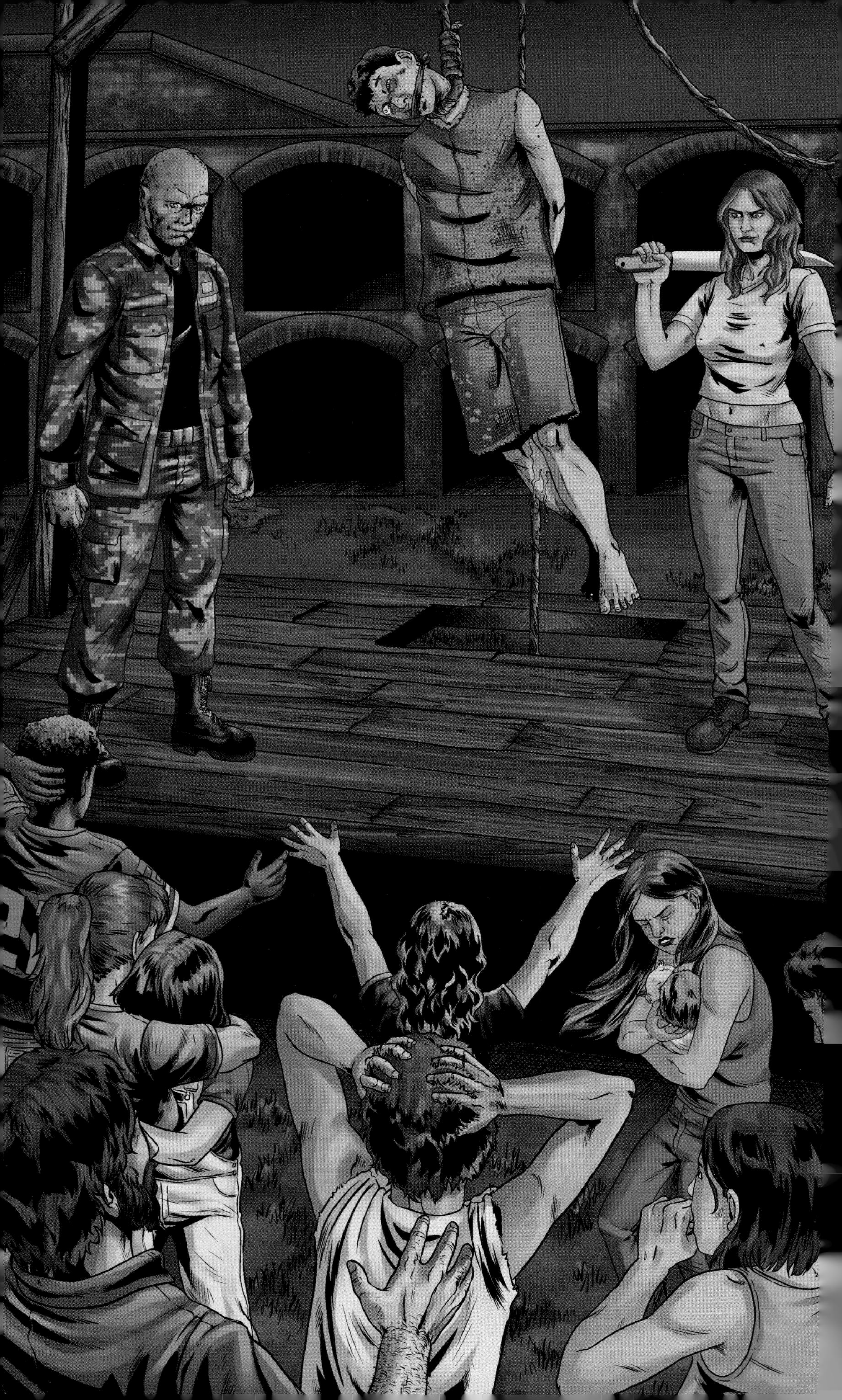

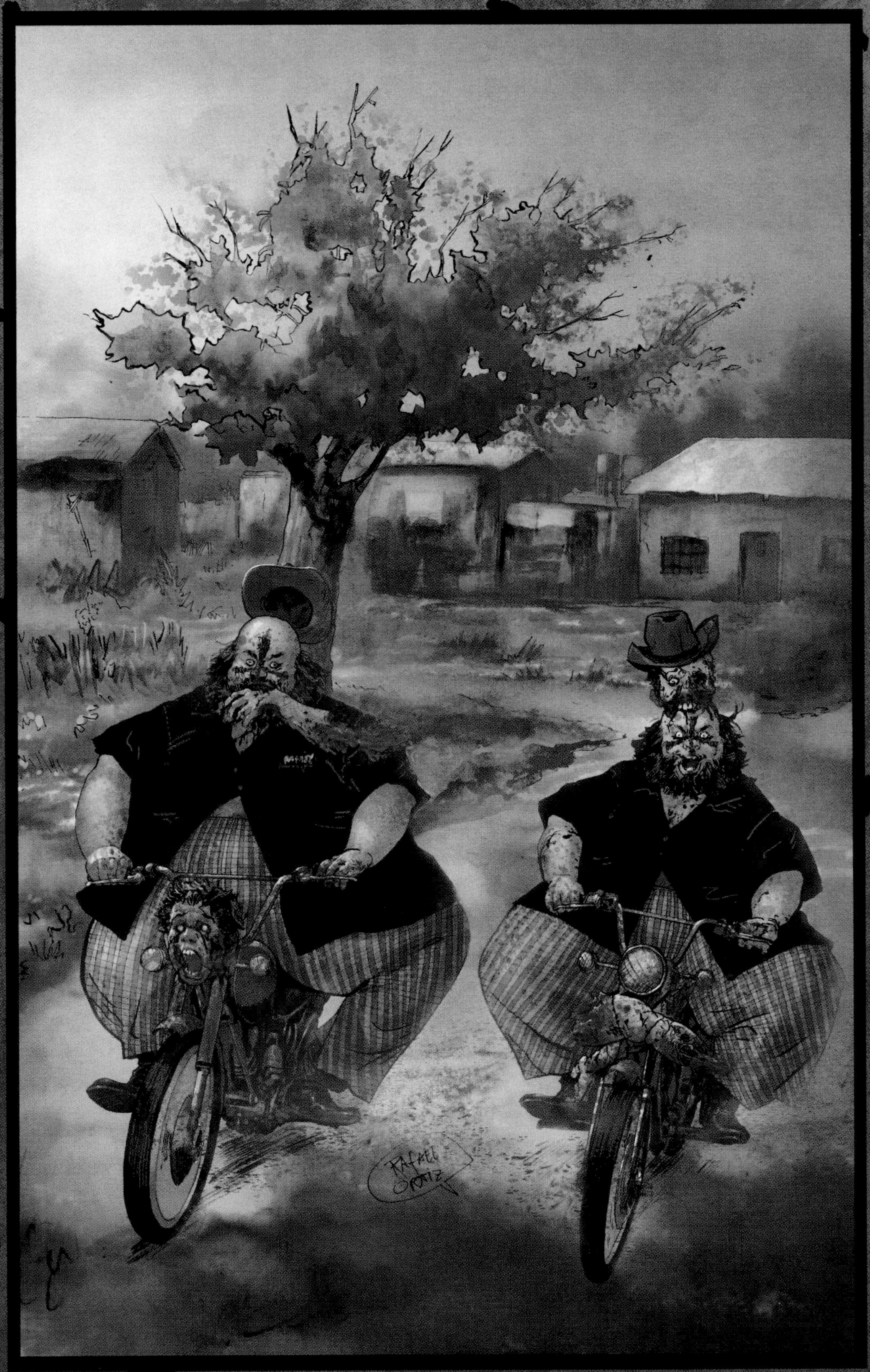

PART 5

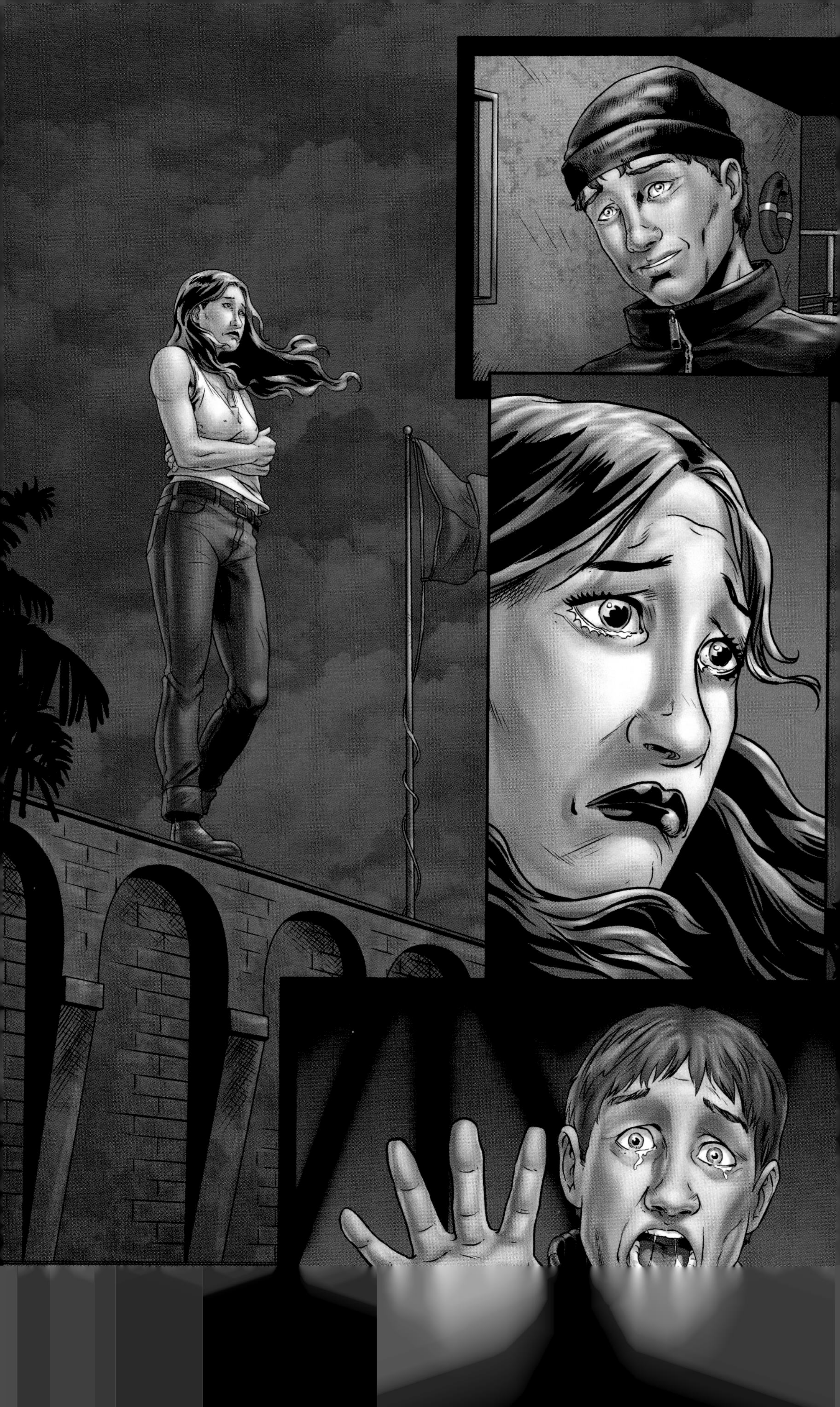

CROSSED: GRAVE NEW WORLD

PART 5: THE DUST OF HOPE

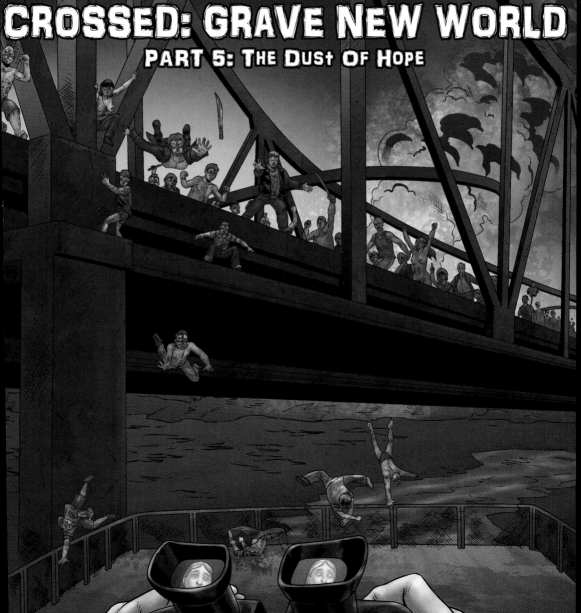

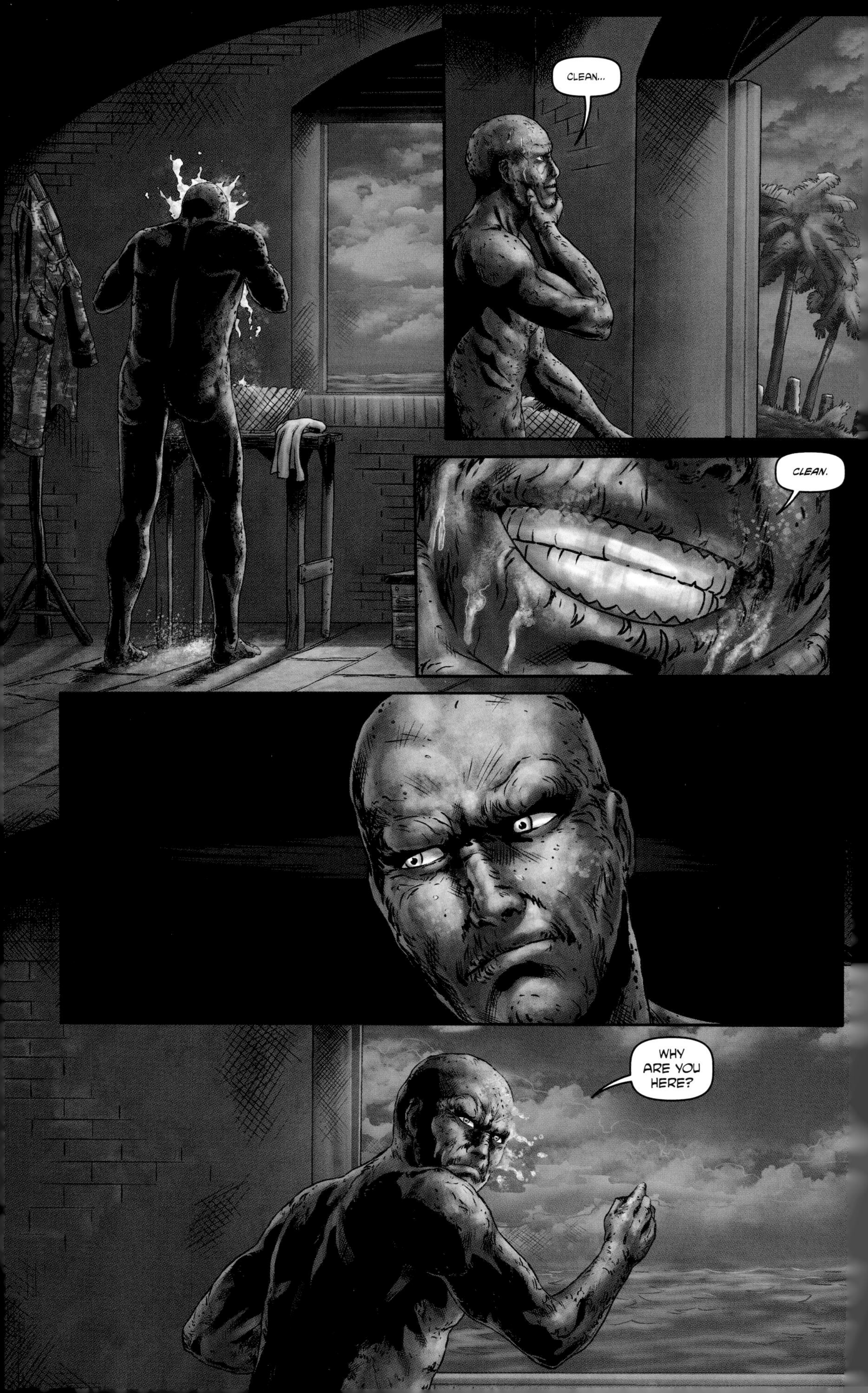
CLEAN...
CLEAN.
WHY ARE YOU HERE?

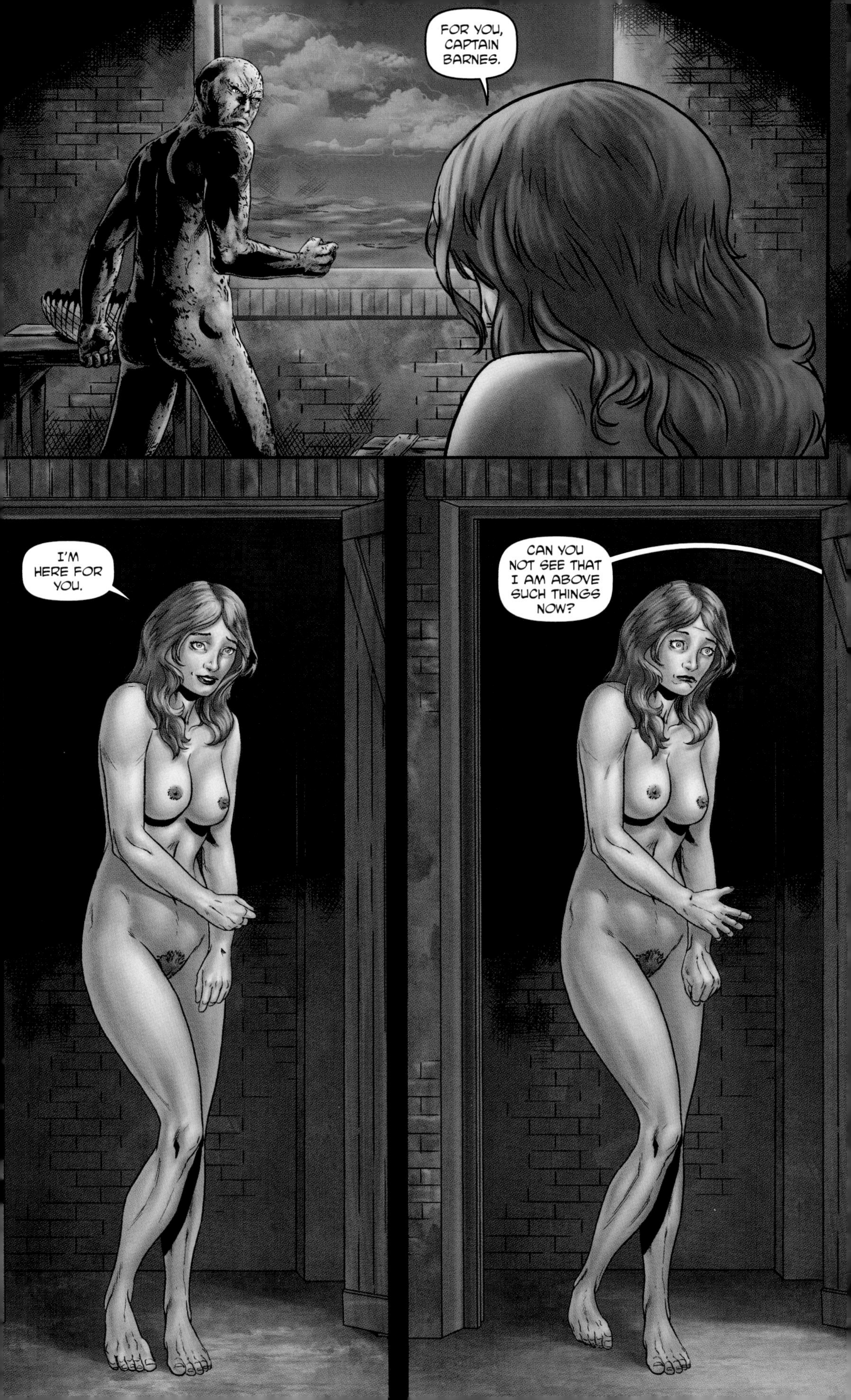
FOR YOU, CAPTAIN BARNES.
I'M HERE FOR YOU.
CAN YOU NOT SEE THAT I AM ABOVE SUCH THINGS NOW?

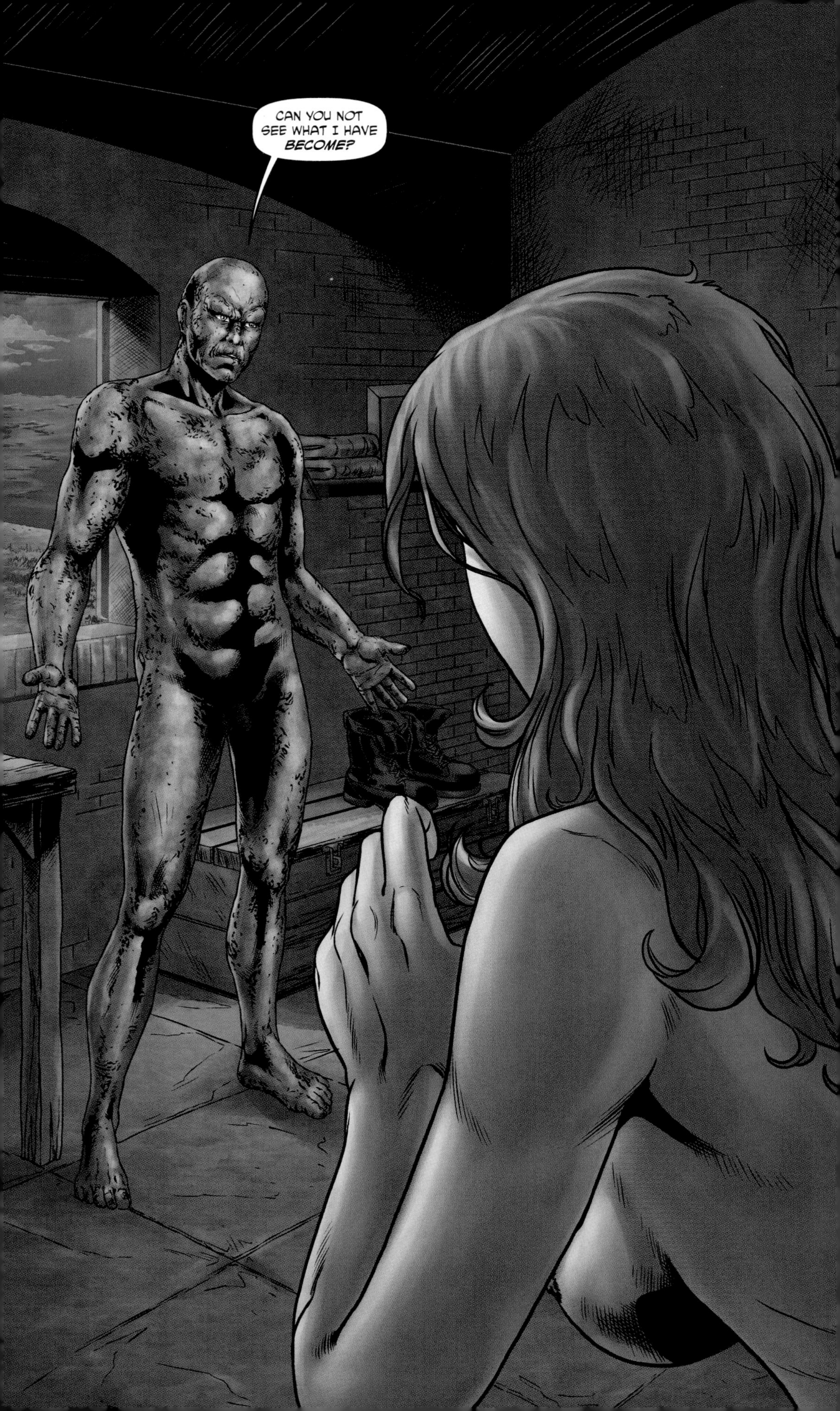
CAN YOU NOT SEE WHAT I HAVE *BECOME?*

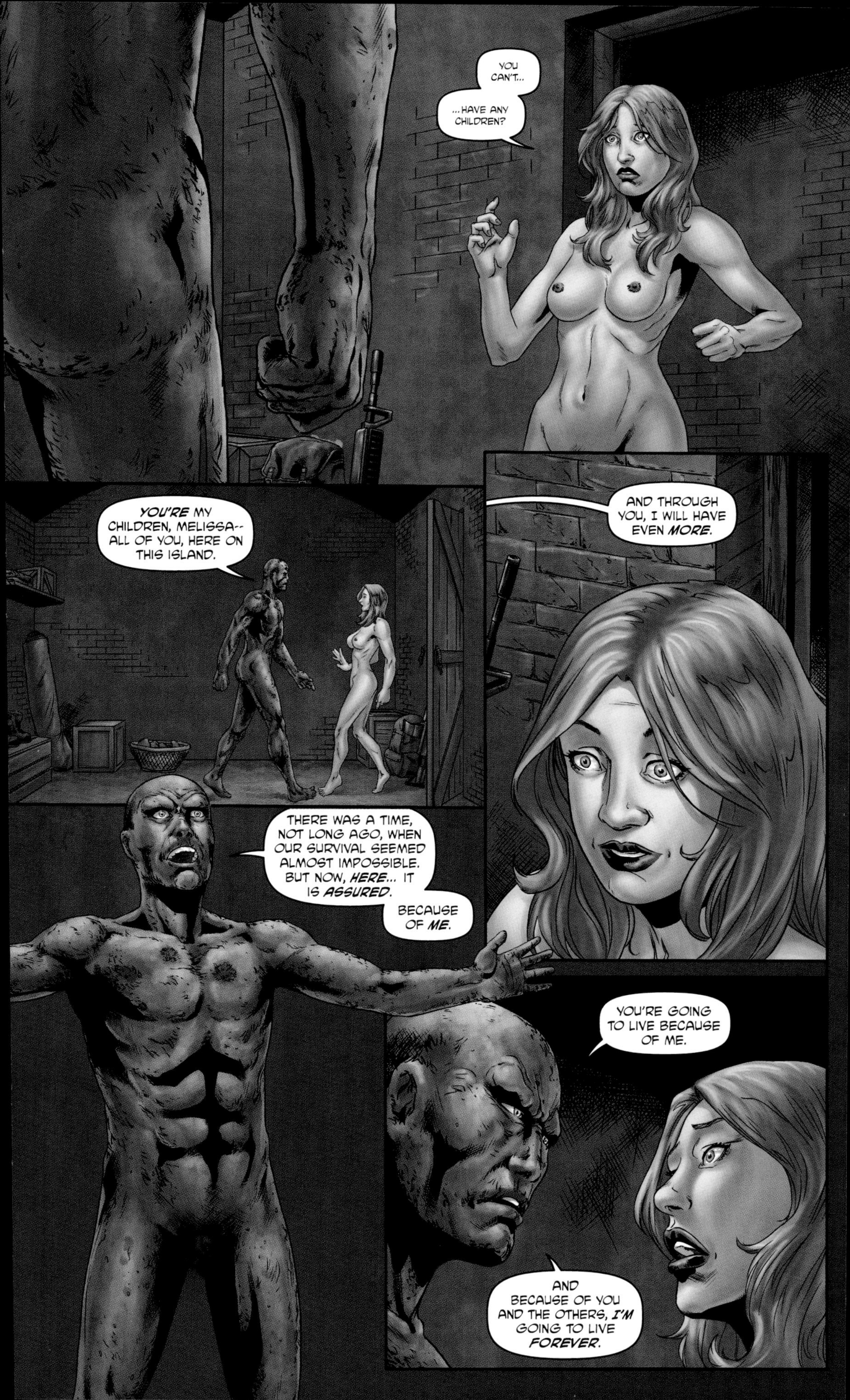
YOU CAN'T...
...HAVE ANY CHILDREN?
YOU'RE MY CHILDREN, MELISSA-- ALL OF YOU, HERE ON THIS ISLAND.
AND THROUGH YOU, I WILL HAVE EVEN MORE.
THERE WAS A TIME, NOT LONG AGO, WHEN OUR SURVIVAL SEEMED ALMOST IMPOSSIBLE. BUT NOW, HERE... IT IS ASSURED.
BECAUSE OF ME.
YOU'RE GOING TO LIVE BECAUSE OF ME.
AND BECAUSE OF YOU AND THE OTHERS, I'M GOING TO LIVE FOREVER.

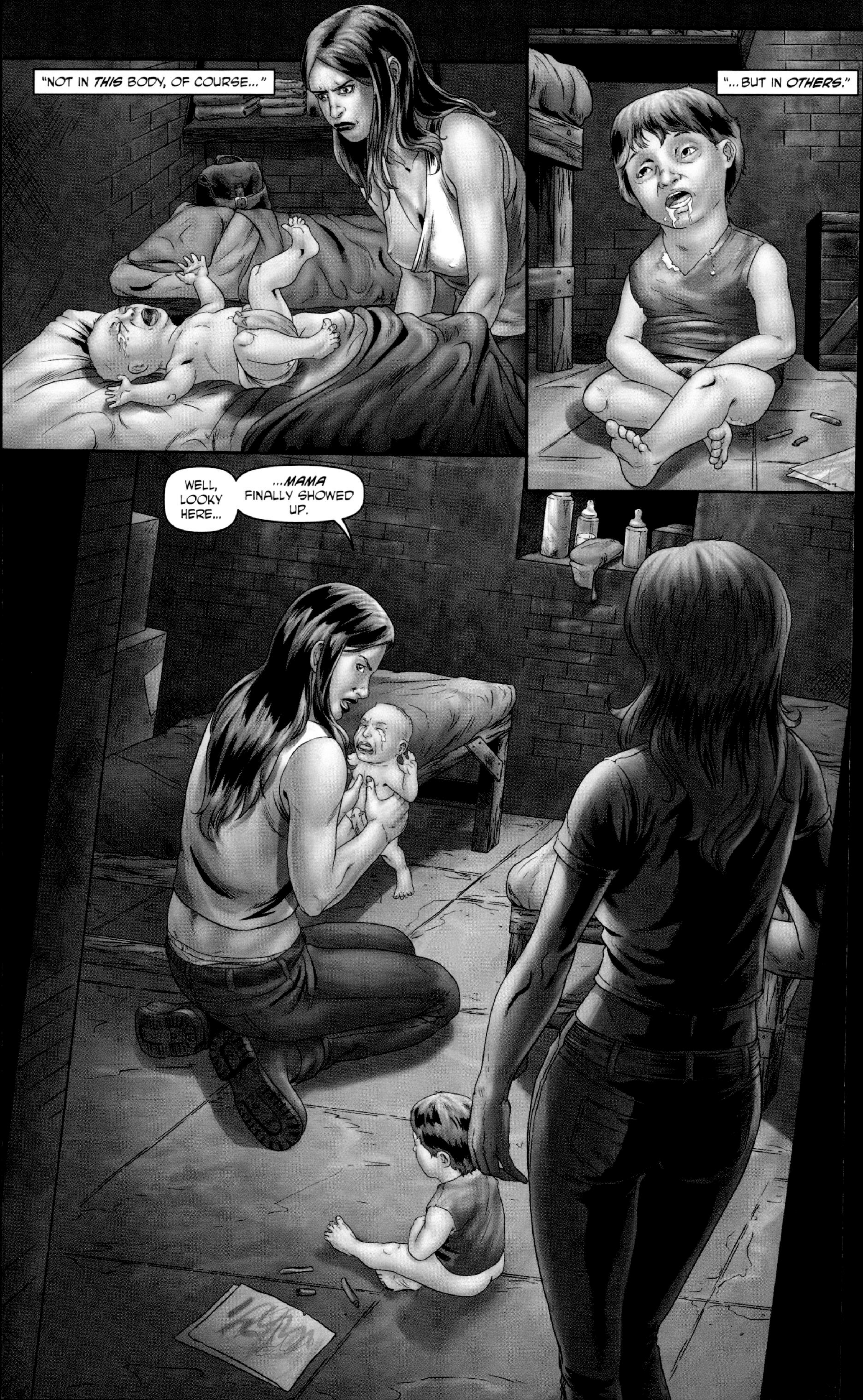
"NOT IN THIS BODY, OF COURSE..."
"...BUT IN OTHERS."
WELL, LOOKY HERE...
...MAMA FINALLY SHOWED UP.

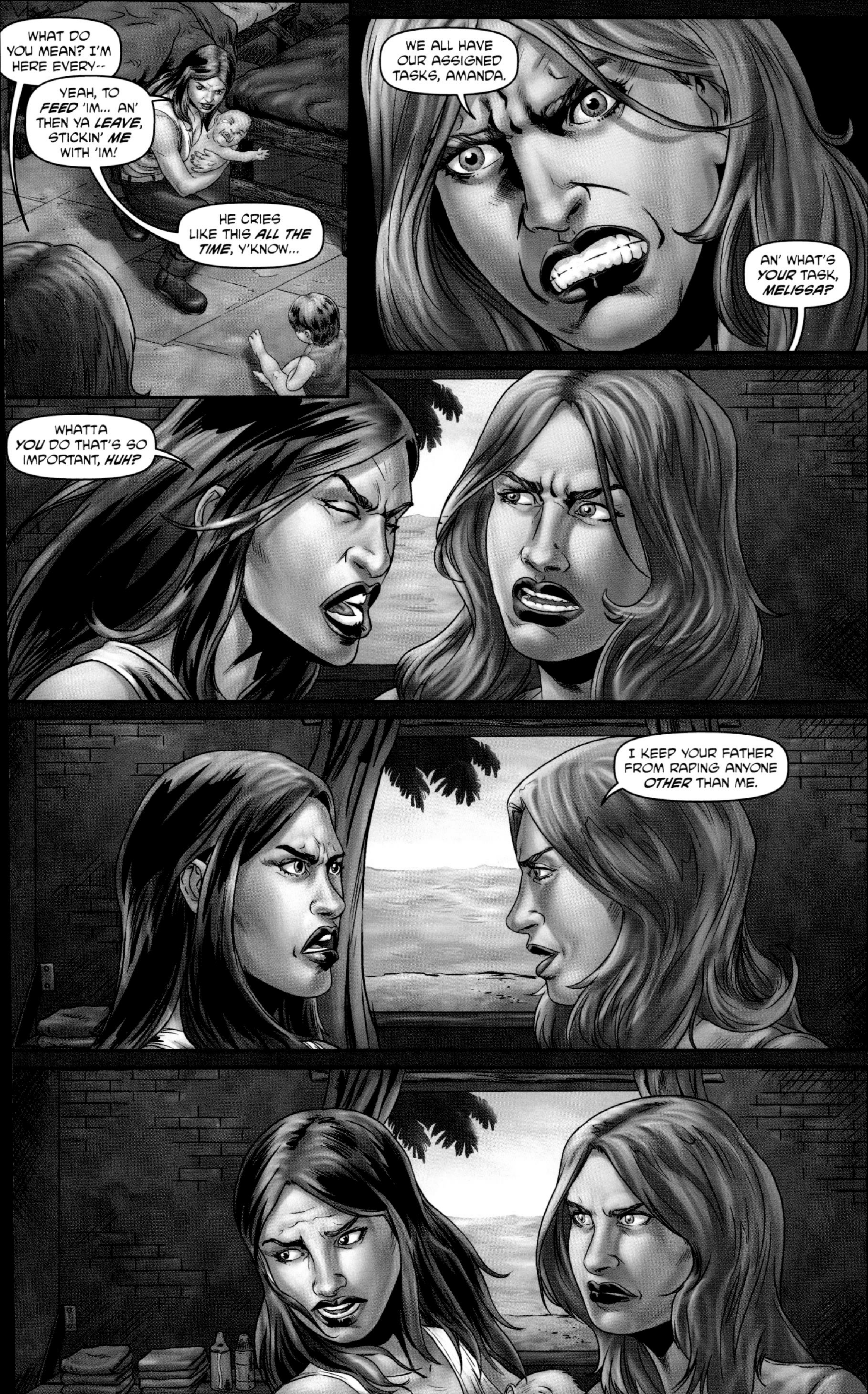
WHAT DO YOU MEAN? I'M HERE EVERY--
YEAH, TO FEED 'IM... AN' THEN YA LEAVE, STICKIN' ME WITH 'IM!
HE CRIES LIKE THIS ALL THE TIME, Y'KNOW...
WE ALL HAVE OUR ASSIGNED TASKS, AMANDA.
AN' WHAT'S YOUR TASK, MELISSA?
WHATTA YOU DO THAT'S SO IMPORTANT, HUH?
I KEEP YOUR FATHER FROM RAPING ANYONE OTHER THAN ME.

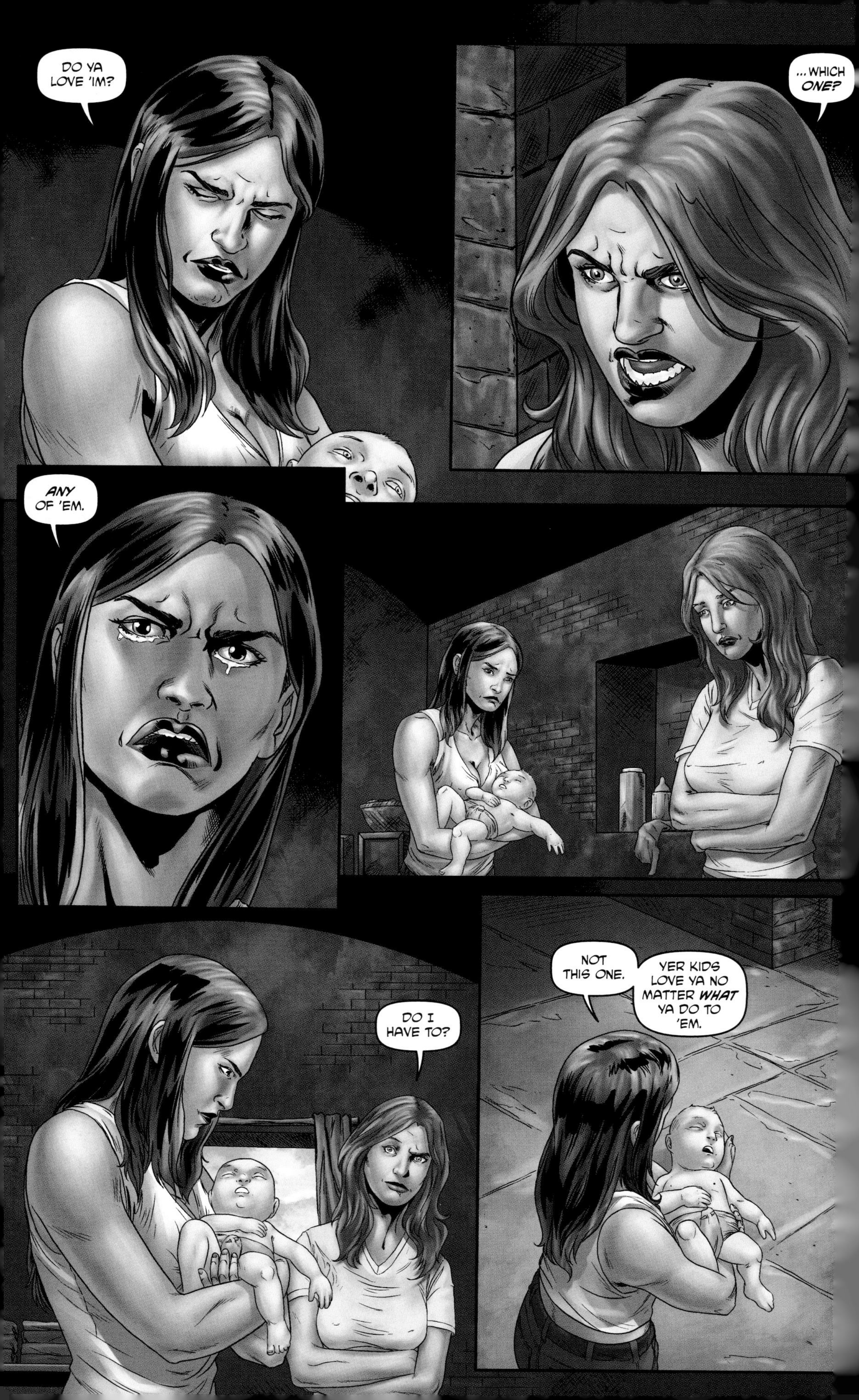
DO YA LOVE 'IM?
...WHICH ONE?
ANY OF 'EM.
DO I HAVE TO?
NOT THIS ONE.
YER KIDS LOVE YA NO MATTER WHAT YA DO TO 'EM.

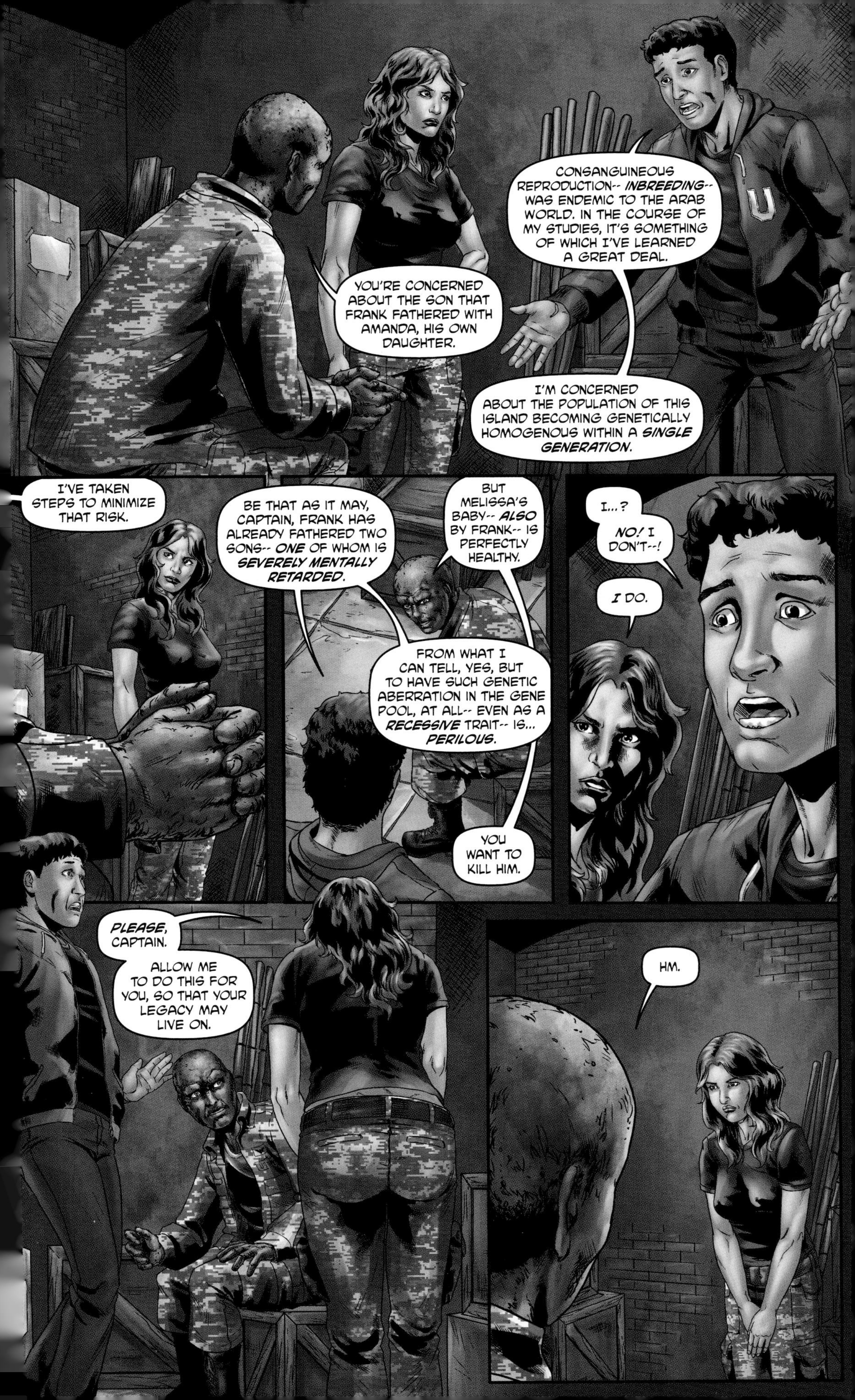
CONSANGUINEOUS REPRODUCTION-- INBREEDING-- WAS ENDEMIC TO THE ARAB WORLD. IN THE COURSE OF MY STUDIES, IT'S SOMETHING OF WHICH I'VE LEARNED A GREAT DEAL.
YOU'RE CONCERNED ABOUT THE SON THAT FRANK FATHERED WITH AMANDA, HIS OWN DAUGHTER.
I'M CONCERNED ABOUT THE POPULATION OF THIS ISLAND BECOMING GENETICALLY HOMOGENOUS WITHIN A SINGLE GENERATION.
I'VE TAKEN STEPS TO MINIMIZE THAT RISK.
BE THAT AS IT MAY, CAPTAIN, FRANK HAS ALREADY FATHERED TWO SONS-- ONE OF WHOM IS SEVERELY MENTALLY RETARDED.
BUT MELISSA'S BABY-- ALSO BY FRANK-- IS PERFECTLY HEALTHY.
FROM WHAT I CAN TELL, YES, BUT TO HAVE SUCH GENETIC ABERRATION IN THE GENE POOL, AT ALL-- EVEN AS A RECESSIVE TRAIT-- IS... PERILOUS.
YOU WANT TO KILL HIM.
I...?
NO! I DON'T--!
I DO.
PLEASE, CAPTAIN.
ALLOW ME TO DO THIS FOR YOU, SO THAT YOUR LEGACY MAY LIVE ON.
HM.

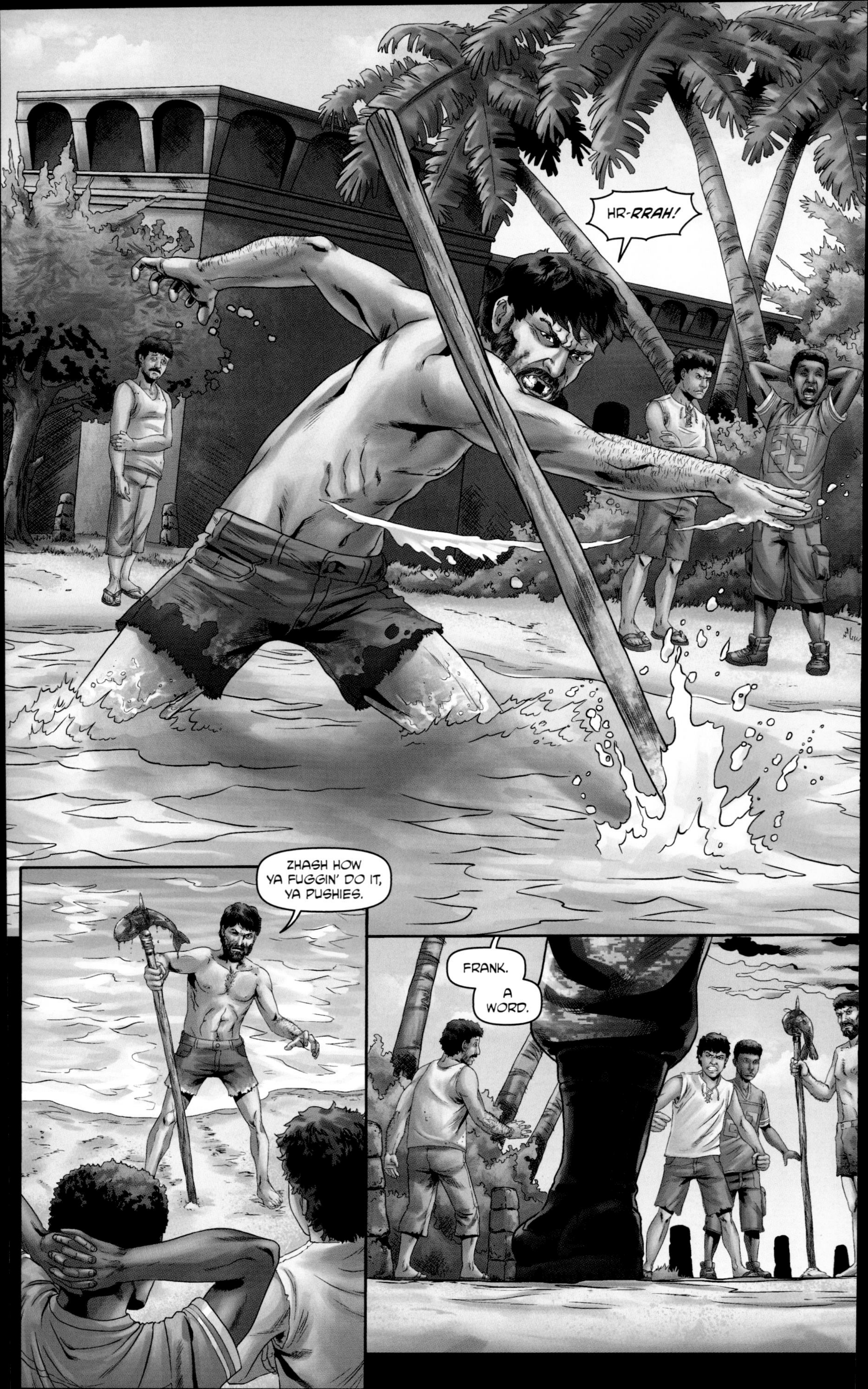
HR-RRAH!
ZHASH HOW YA FUGGIN' DO IT, YA PUSHIES.
FRANK.
A WORD.

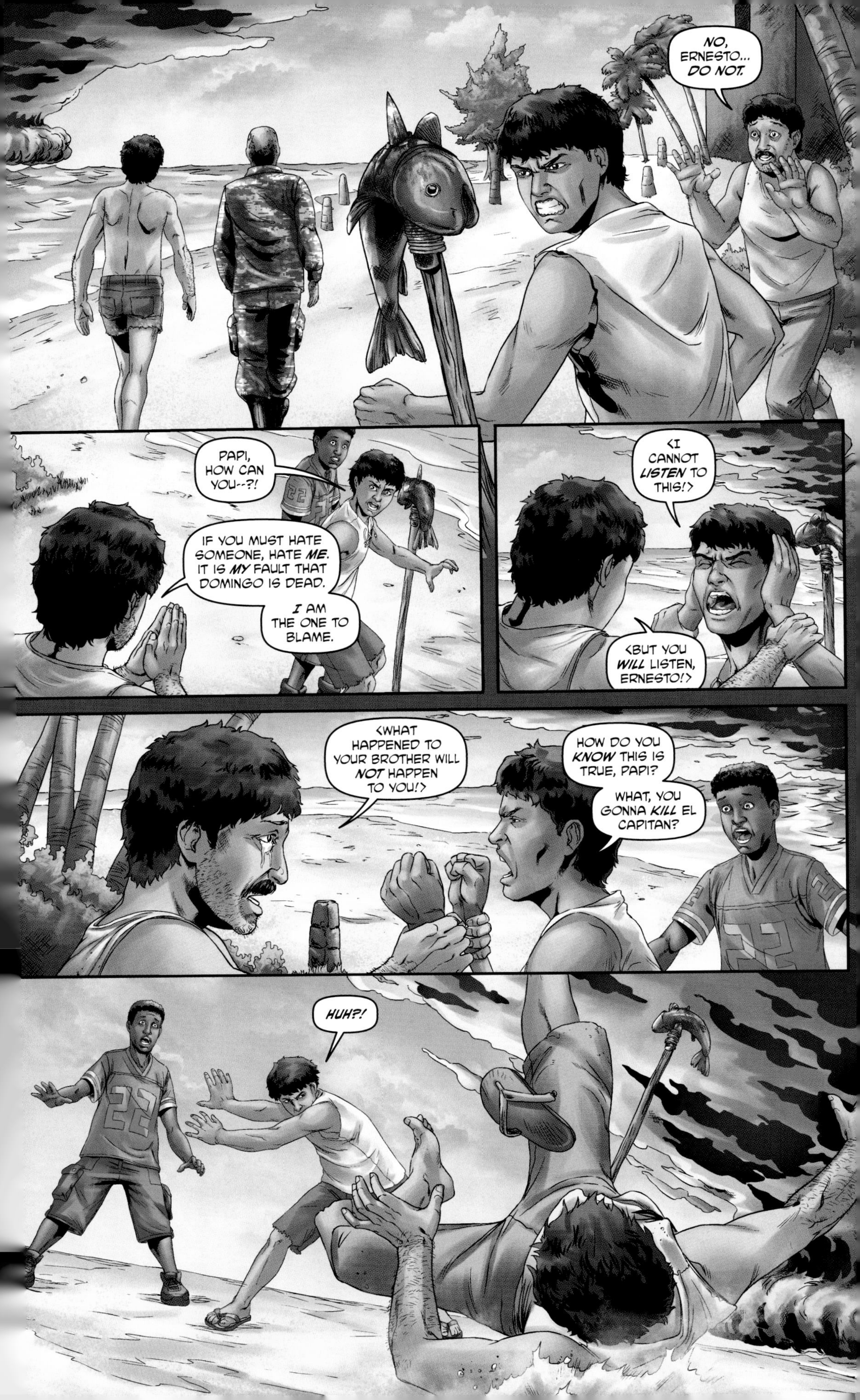
NO, ERNESTO... DO NOT.
PAPI, HOW CAN YOU--?!
IF YOU MUST HATE SOMEONE, HATE ME. IT IS MY FAULT THAT DOMINGO IS DEAD.
I AM THE ONE TO BLAME.
<I CANNOT LISTEN TO THIS!>
<BUT YOU WILL LISTEN, ERNESTO!>
<WHAT HAPPENED TO YOUR BROTHER WILL NOT HAPPEN TO YOU!>
HOW DO YOU KNOW THIS IS TRUE, PAPI?
WHAT, YOU GONNA KILL EL CAPITAN?
HUH?!

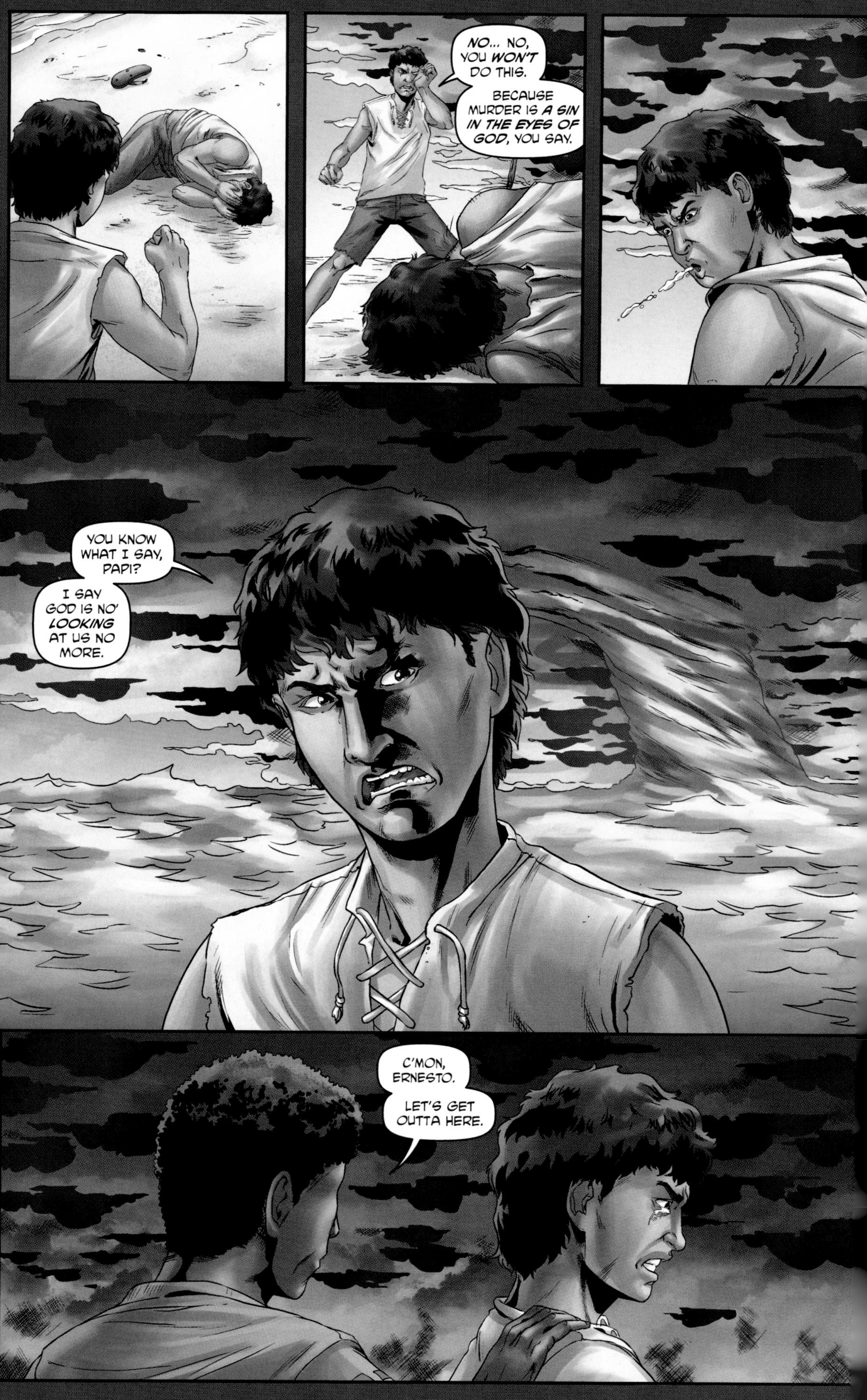
NO... NO, YOU WON'T DO THIS.
BECAUSE MURDER IS A SIN IN THE EYES OF GOD, YOU SAY.
YOU KNOW WHAT I SAY, PAPI?
I SAY GOD IS NO' LOOKING AT US NO MORE.
C'MON, ERNESTO.
LET'S GET OUTTA HERE.

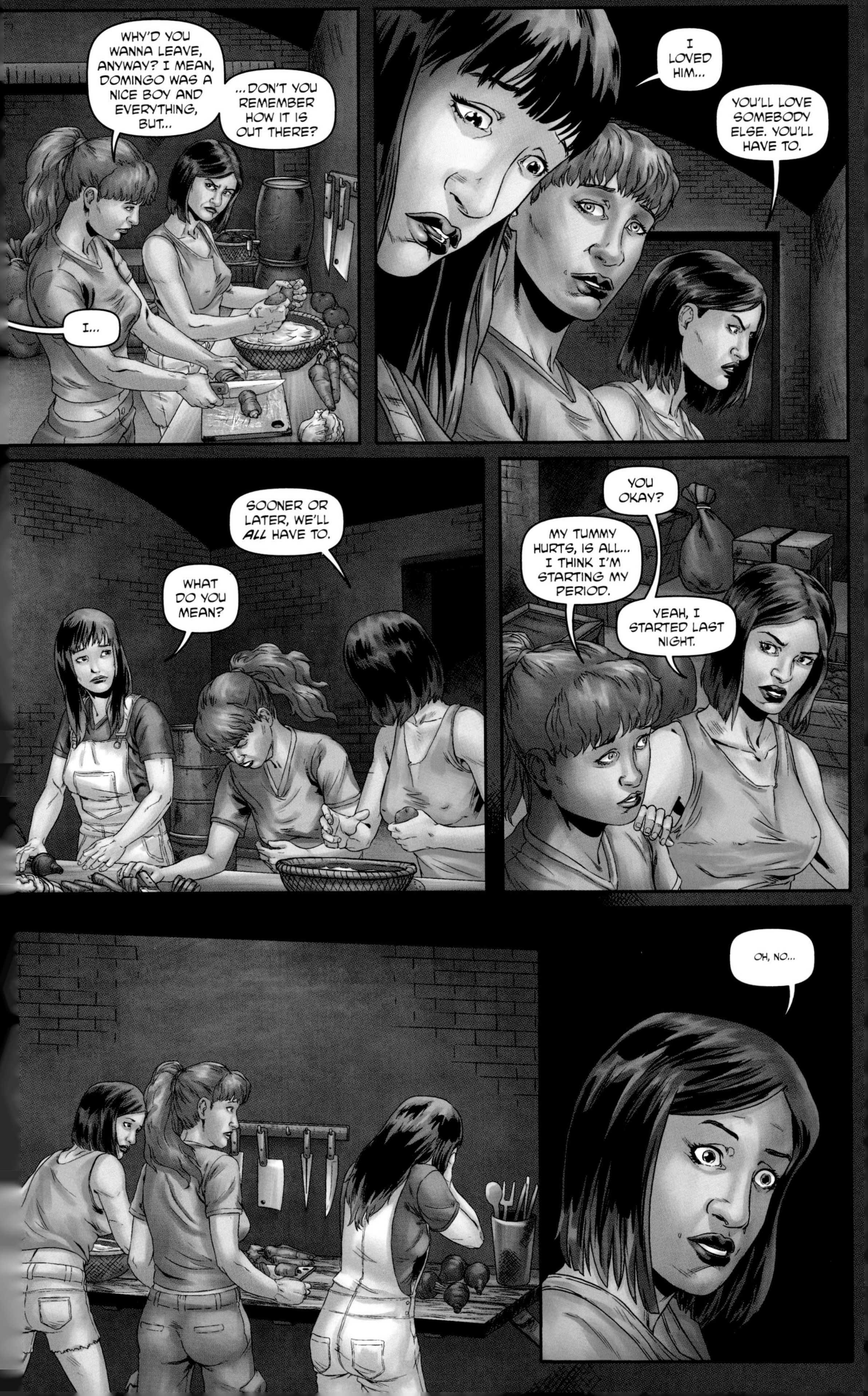
WHY'D YOU WANNA LEAVE, ANYWAY? I MEAN, DOMINGO WAS A NICE BOY AND EVERYTHING, BUT...
...DON'T YOU REMEMBER HOW IT IS OUT THERE?
I...
I LOVED HIM...
YOU'LL LOVE SOMEBODY ELSE. YOU'LL HAVE TO.
SOONER OR LATER, WE'LL ALL HAVE TO.
WHAT DO YOU MEAN?
YOU OKAY?
MY TUMMY HURTS, IS ALL... I THINK I'M STARTING MY PERIOD.
YEAH, I STARTED LAST NIGHT.
OH, NO...

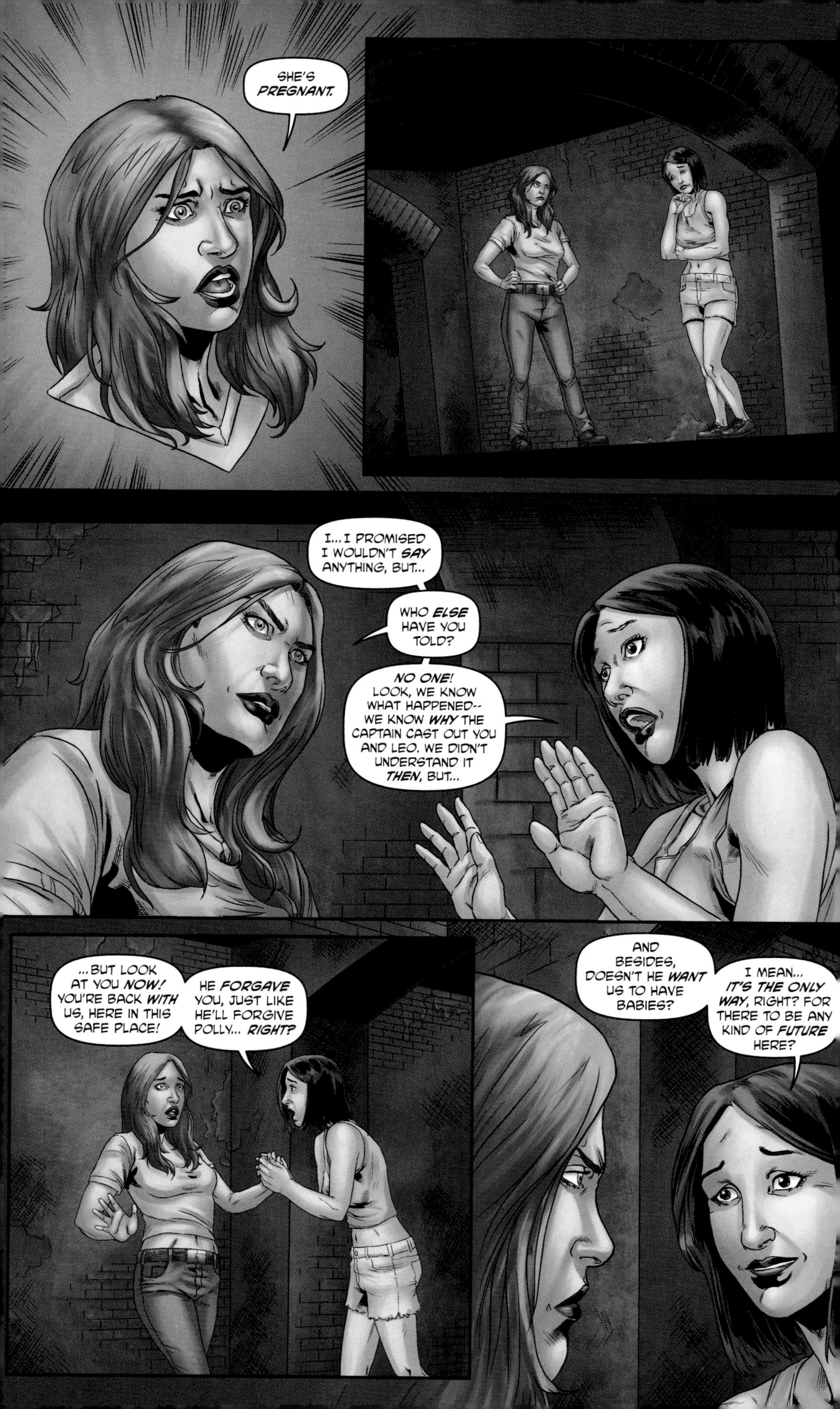
SHE'S PREGNANT.
I... I PROMISED I WOULDN'T SAY ANYTHING, BUT...
WHO ELSE HAVE YOU TOLD?
NO ONE! LOOK, WE KNOW WHAT HAPPENED-- WE KNOW WHY THE CAPTAIN CAST OUT YOU AND LEO. WE DIDN'T UNDERSTAND IT THEN, BUT...
...BUT LOOK AT YOU NOW! YOU'RE BACK WITH US, HERE IN THIS SAFE PLACE!
HE FORGAVE YOU, JUST LIKE HE'LL FORGIVE POLLY... RIGHT?
AND BESIDES, DOESN'T HE WANT US TO HAVE BABIES?
I MEAN... IT'S THE ONLY WAY, RIGHT? FOR THERE TO BE ANY KIND OF FUTURE HERE?

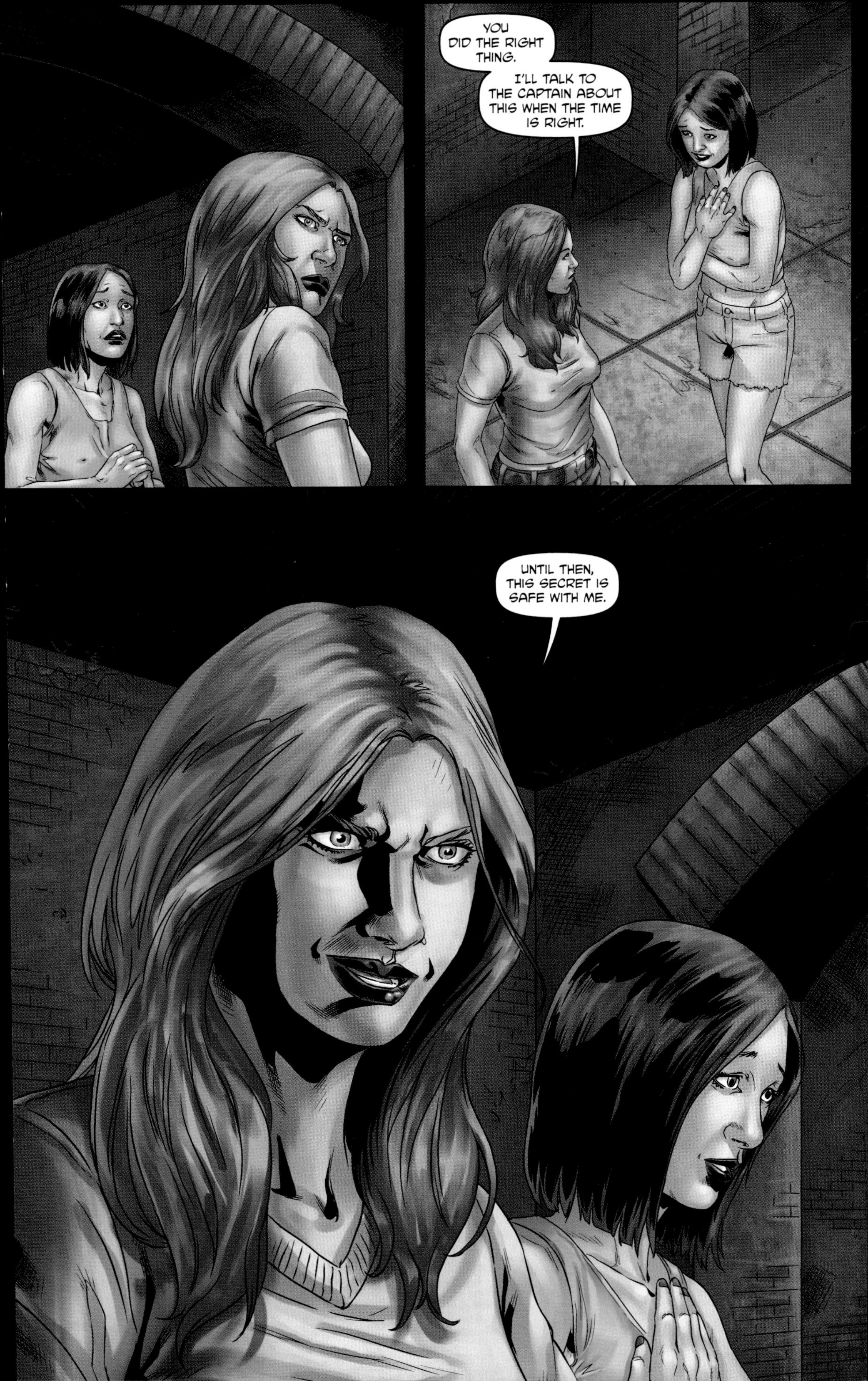
YOU DID THE RIGHT THING.
I'LL TALK TO THE CAPTAIN ABOUT THIS WHEN THE TIME IS RIGHT.
UNTIL THEN, THIS SECRET IS SAFE WITH ME.

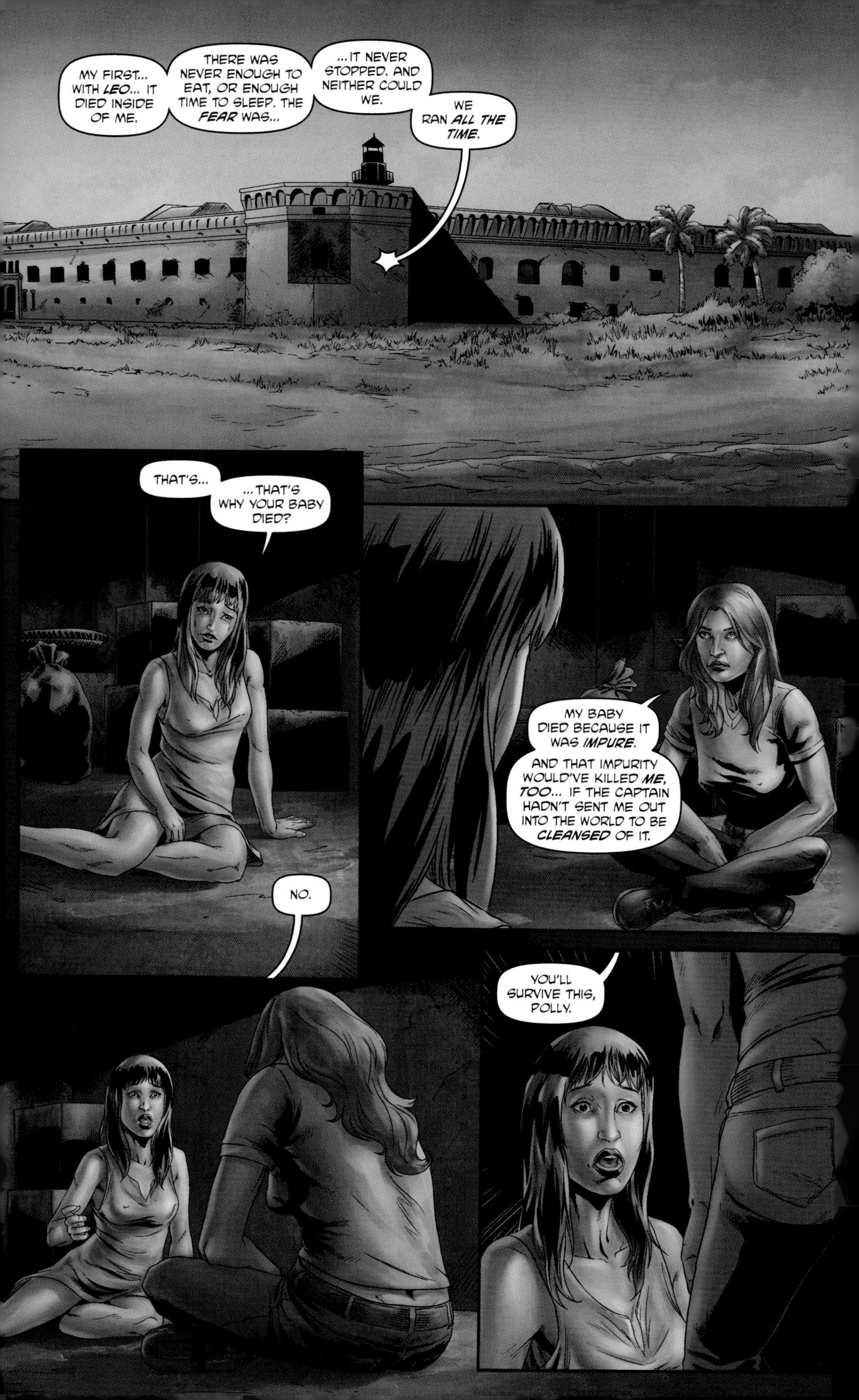
MY FIRST... WITH LEO... IT DIED INSIDE OF ME.
THERE WAS NEVER ENOUGH TO EAT, OR ENOUGH TIME TO SLEEP. THE FEAR WAS...
...IT NEVER STOPPED. AND NEITHER COULD WE.
WE RAN ALL THE TIME.
THAT'S...
...THAT'S WHY YOUR BABY DIED?
MY BABY DIED BECAUSE IT WAS IMPURE.
AND THAT IMPURITY WOULD'VE KILLED ME, TOO... IF THE CAPTAIN HADN'T SENT ME OUT INTO THE WORLD TO BE CLEANSED OF IT.
NO.
YOU'LL SURVIVE THIS, POLLY.

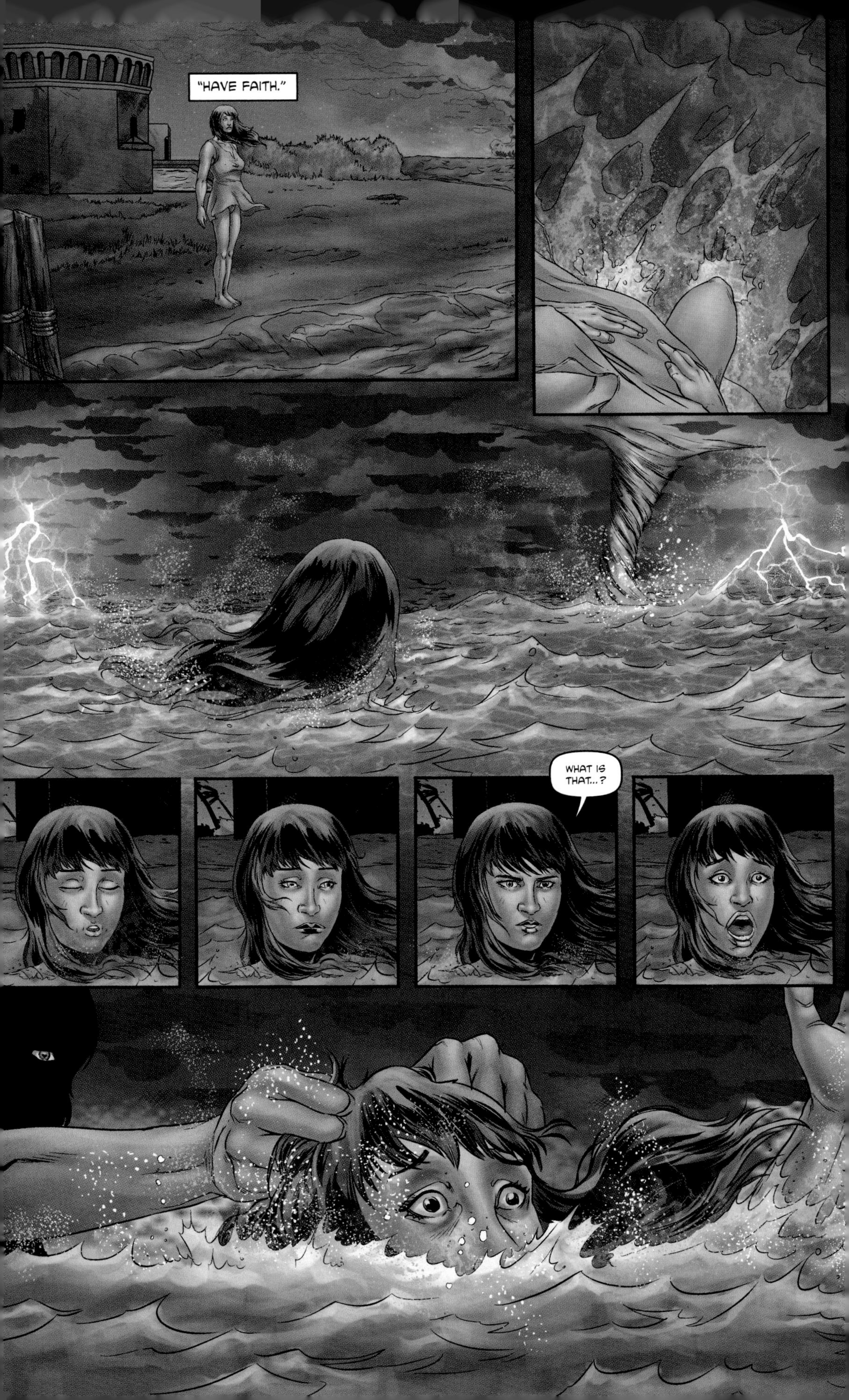
"HAVE FAITH."
WHAT IS THAT...?

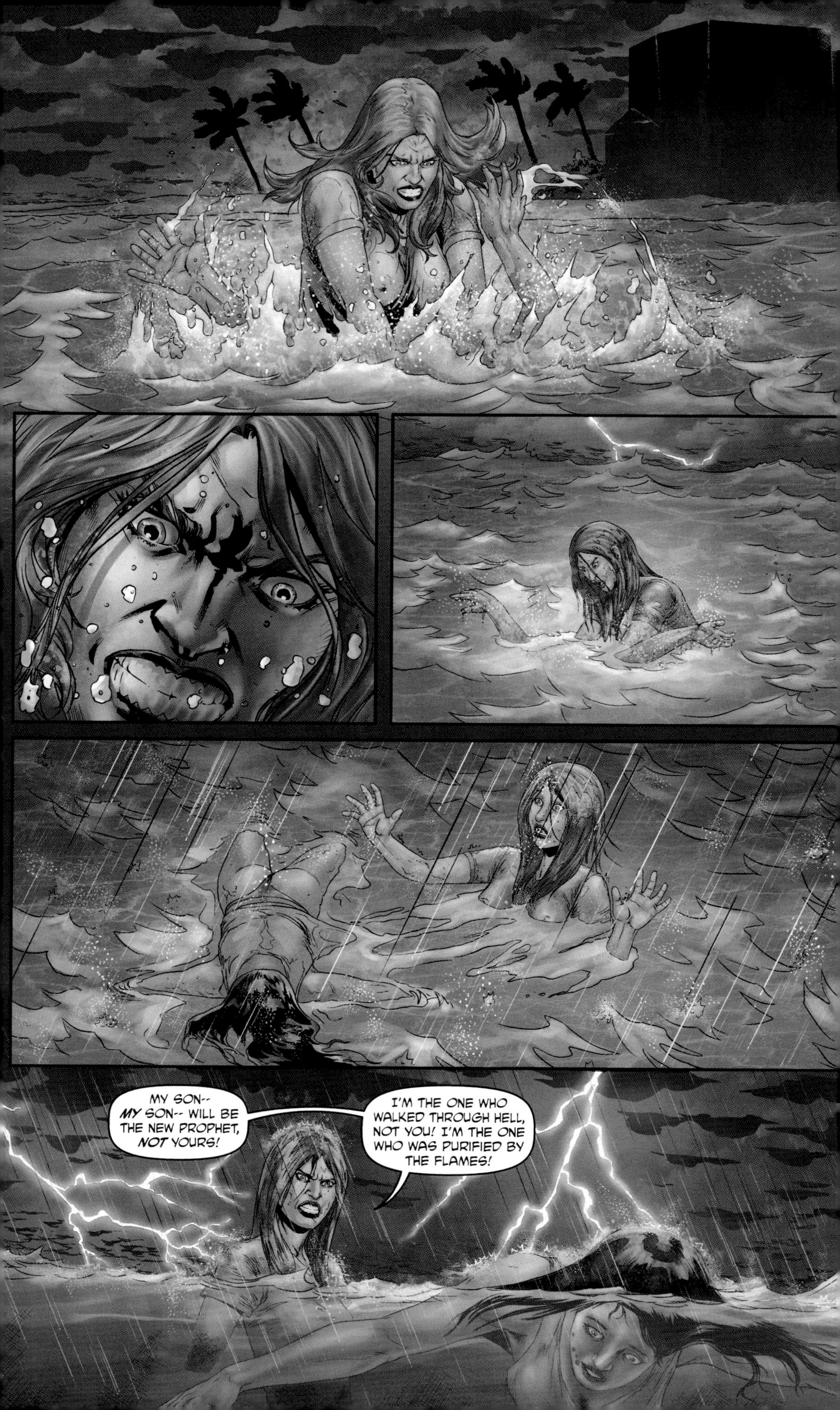
MY SON-- MY SON-- WILL BE THE NEW PROPHET, NOT YOURS!
I'M THE ONE WHO WALKED THROUGH HELL, NOT YOU! I'M THE ONE WHO WAS PURIFIED BY THE FLAMES!

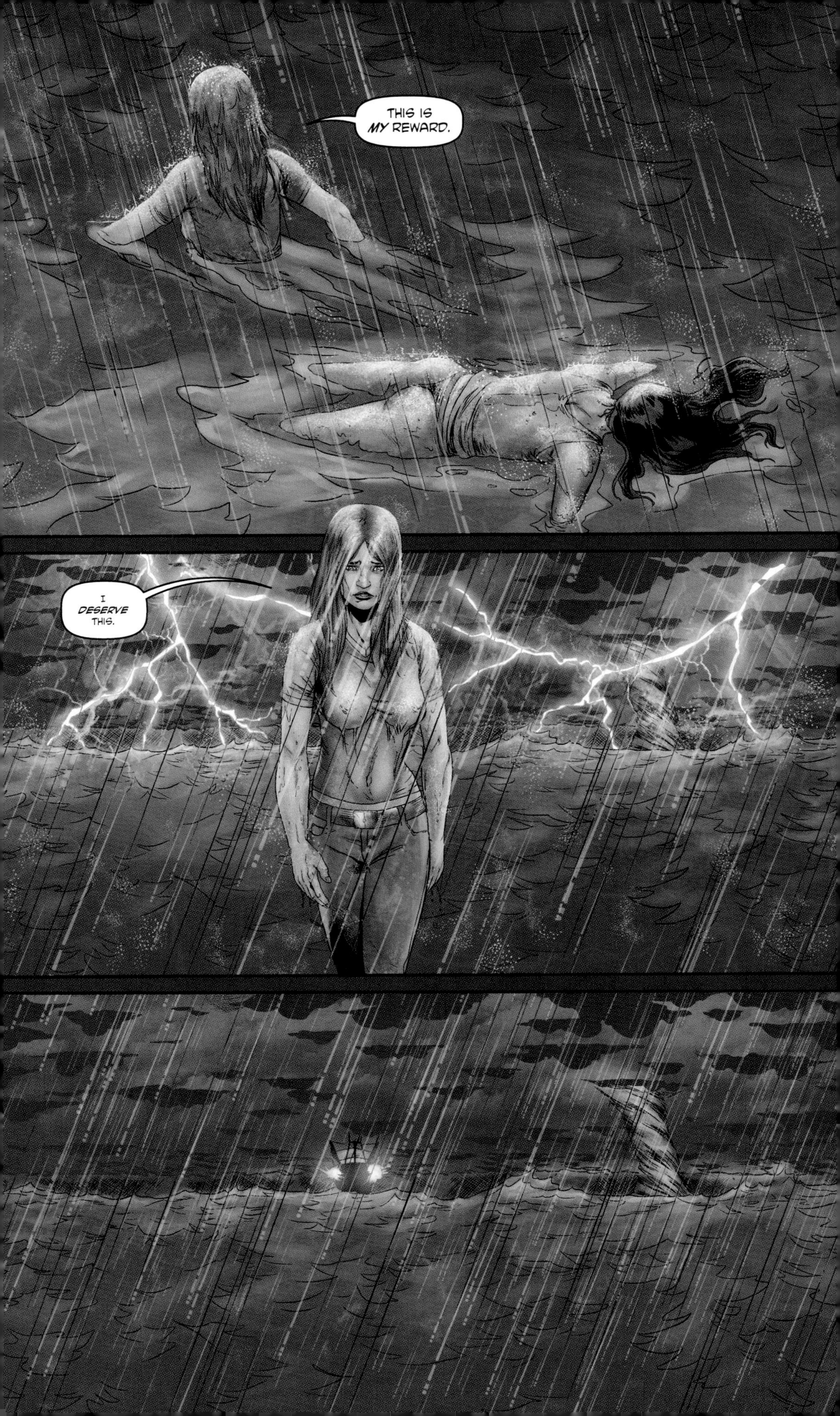
THIS IS *MY* REWARD.
I *DESERVE* THIS.

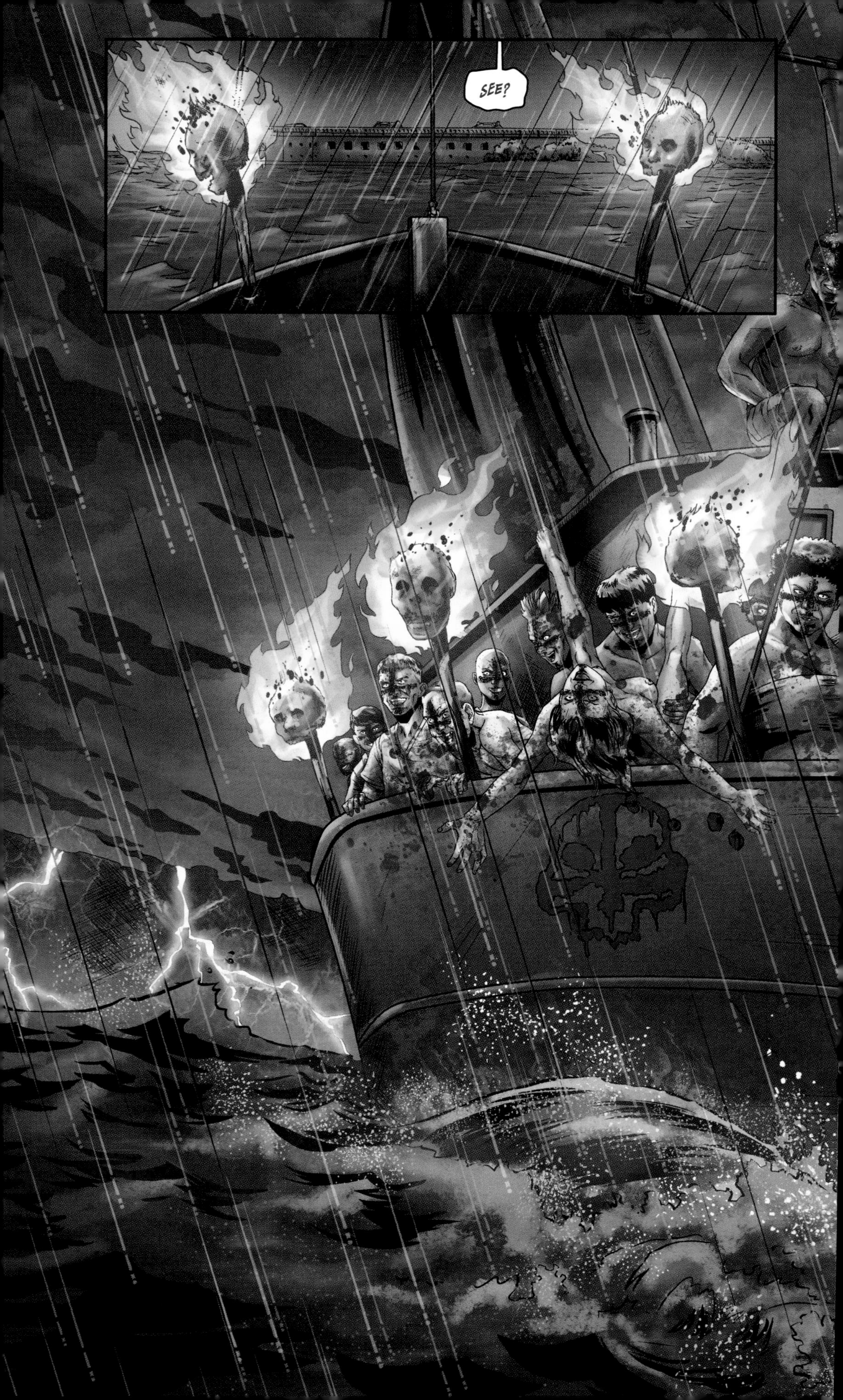
SEE?

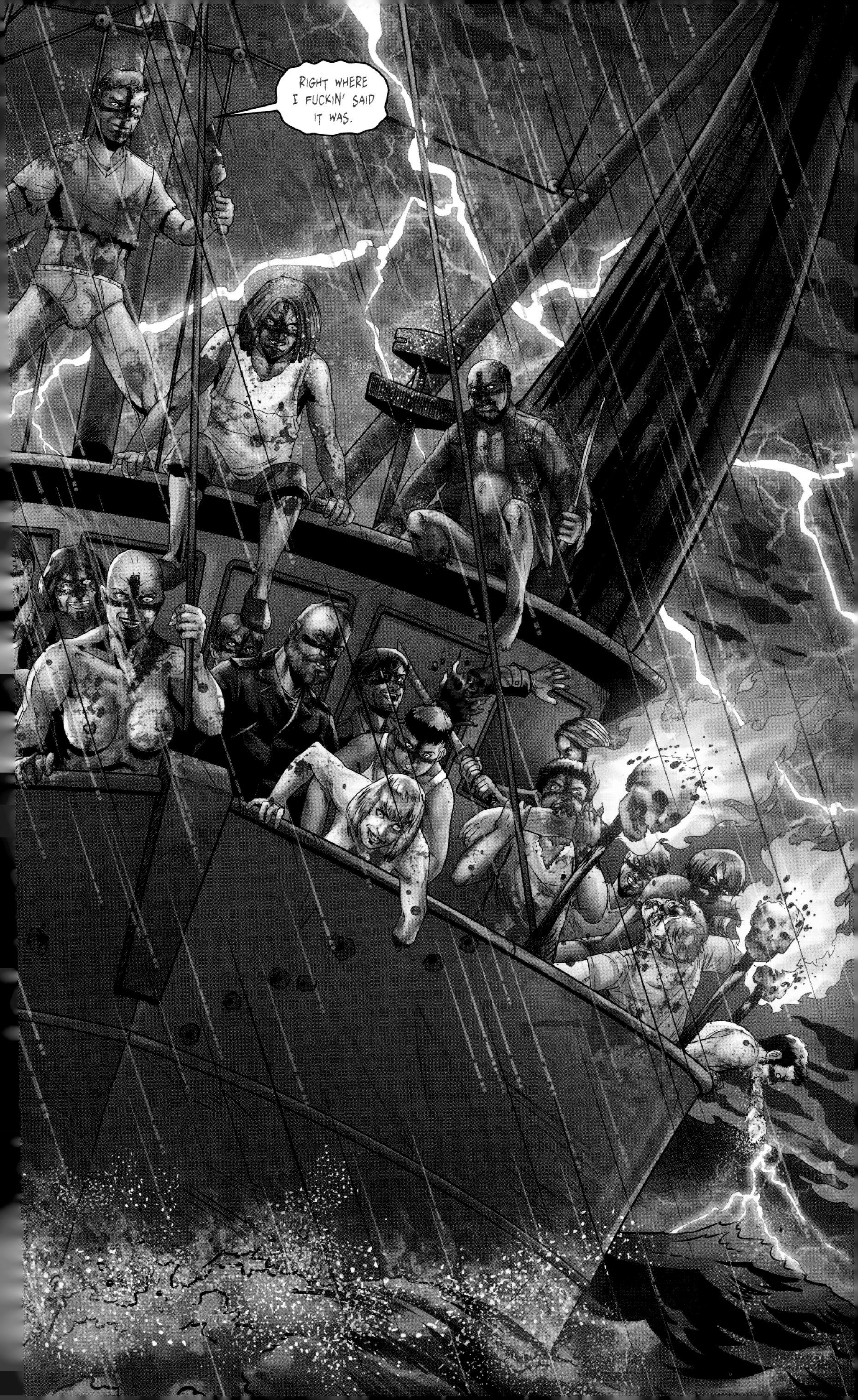
RIGHT WHERE I FUCKIN' SAID IT WAS.

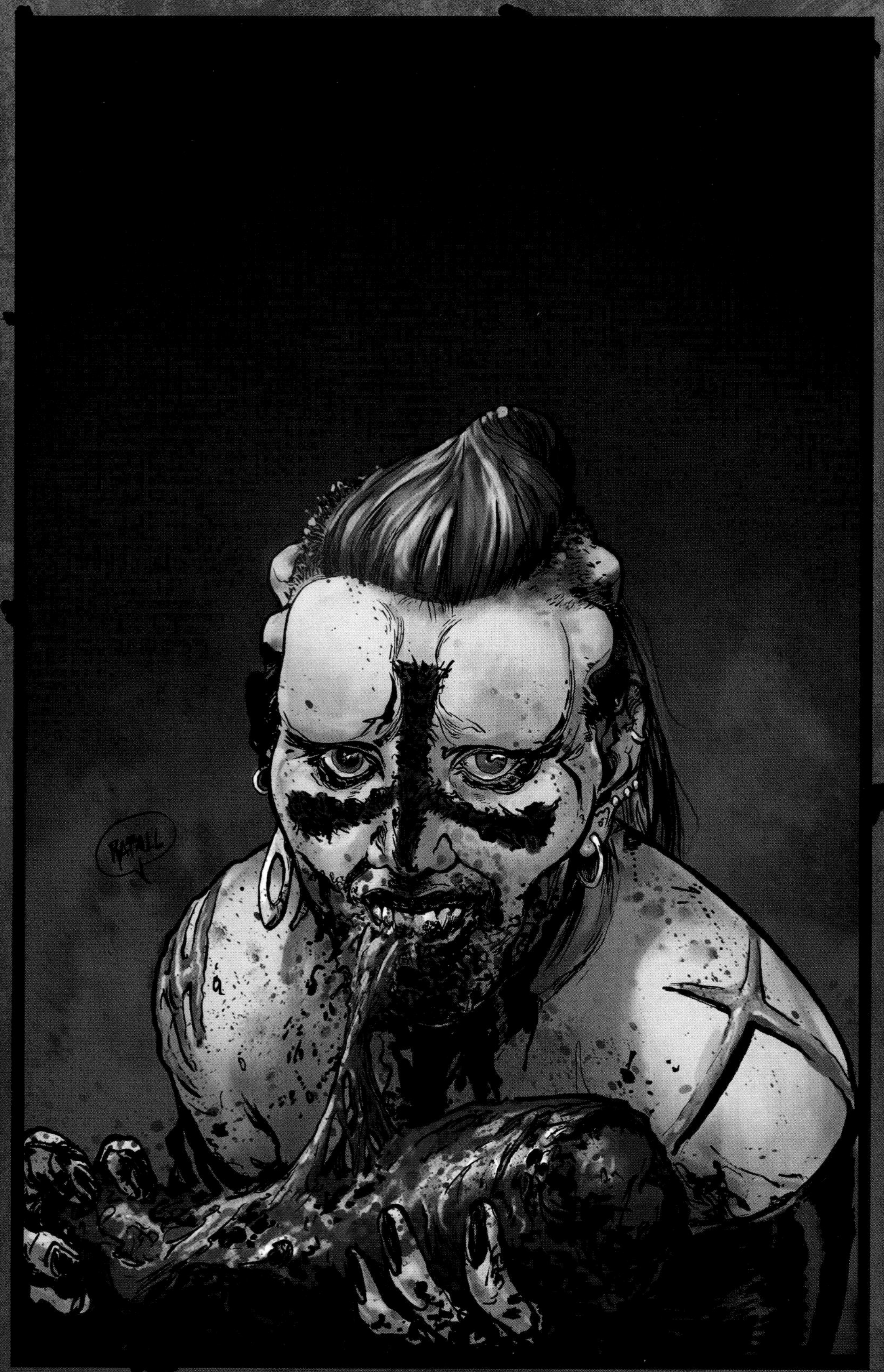

PART 6

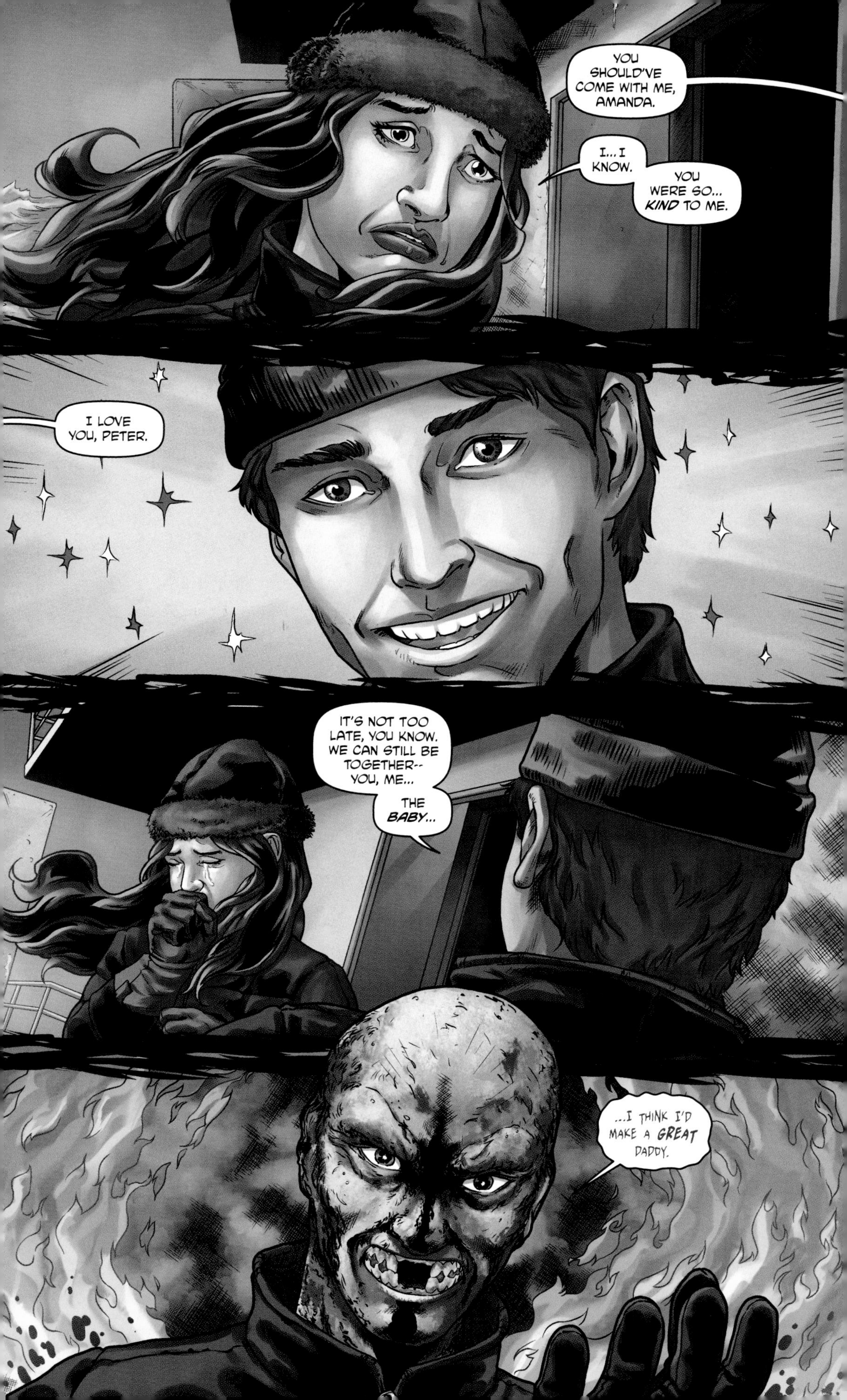
YOU SHOULD'VE COME WITH ME, AMANDA.
I... I KNOW.
YOU WERE SO... *KIND* TO ME.
I LOVE YOU, PETER.
IT'S NOT TOO LATE, YOU KNOW. WE CAN STILL BE TOGETHER-- YOU, ME...
THE *BABY*...
...I THINK I'D MAKE A *GREAT* DADDY.

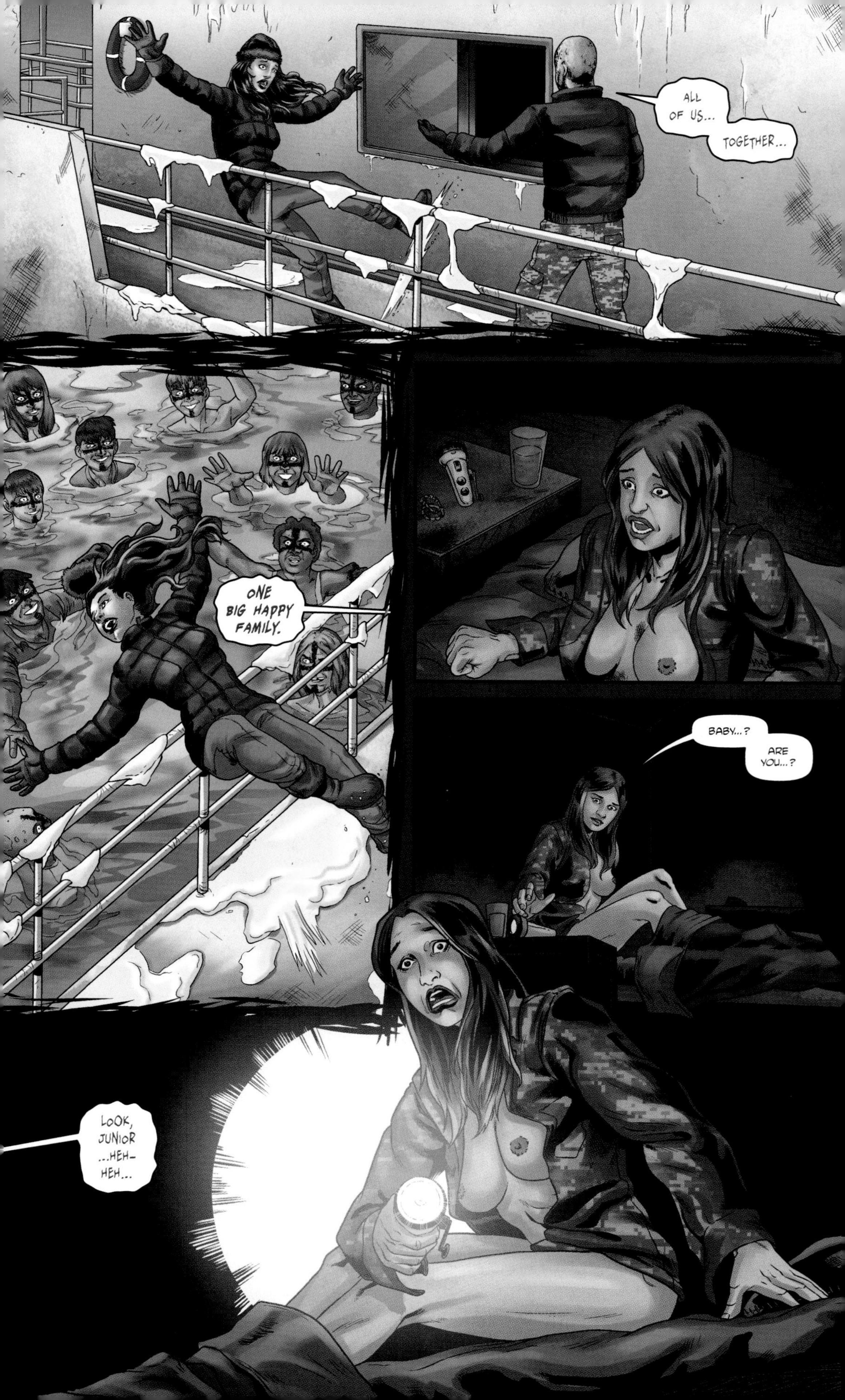
ALL OF US...
TOGETHER...
ONE BIG HAPPY FAMILY.
BABY...?
ARE YOU...?
LOOK, JUNIOR ...HEH-HEH...

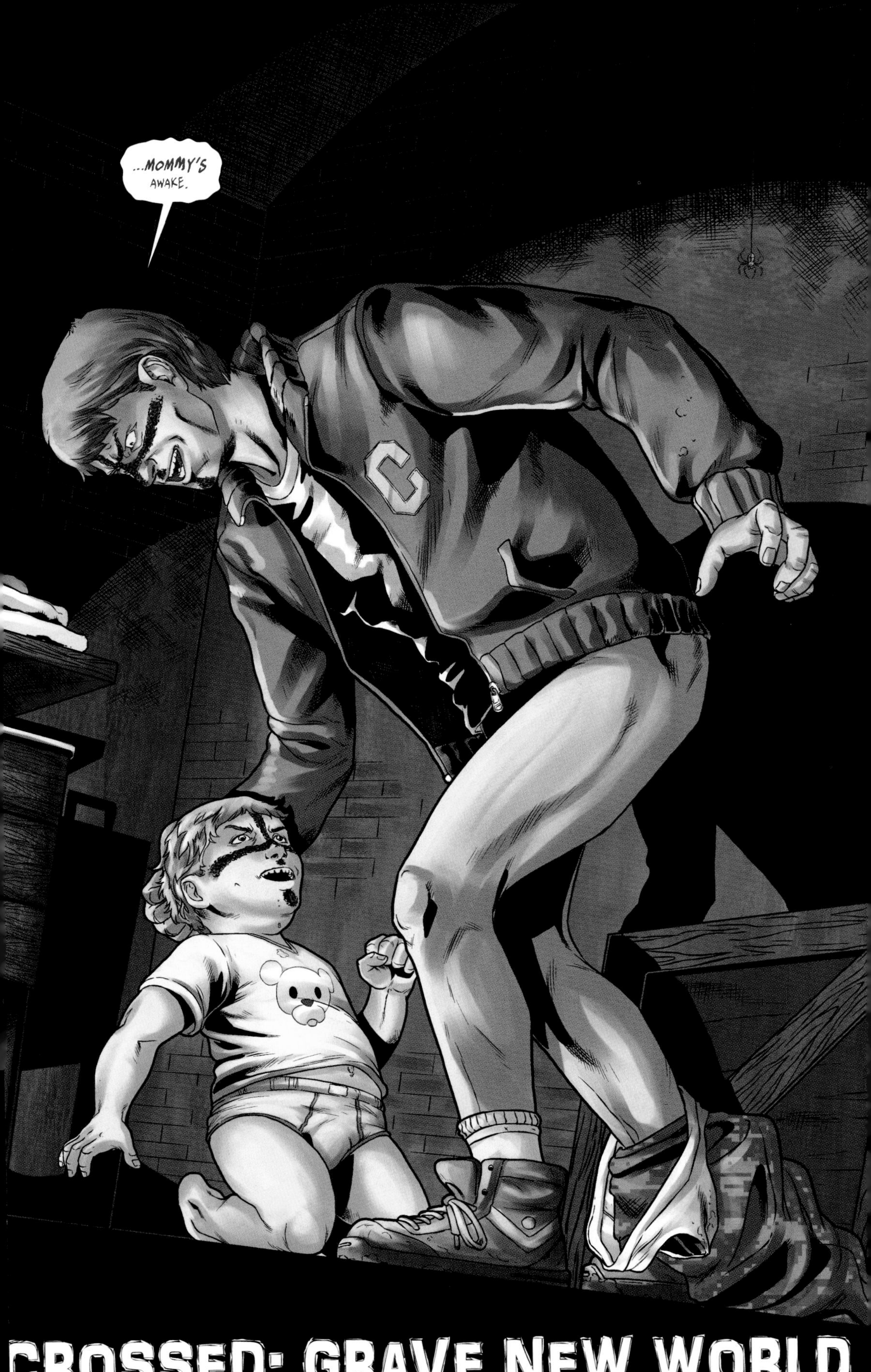
...MOMMY'S AWAKE.

CROSSED: GRAVE NEW WORLD

PART 6: THE THREE CRIES OF HISTORY

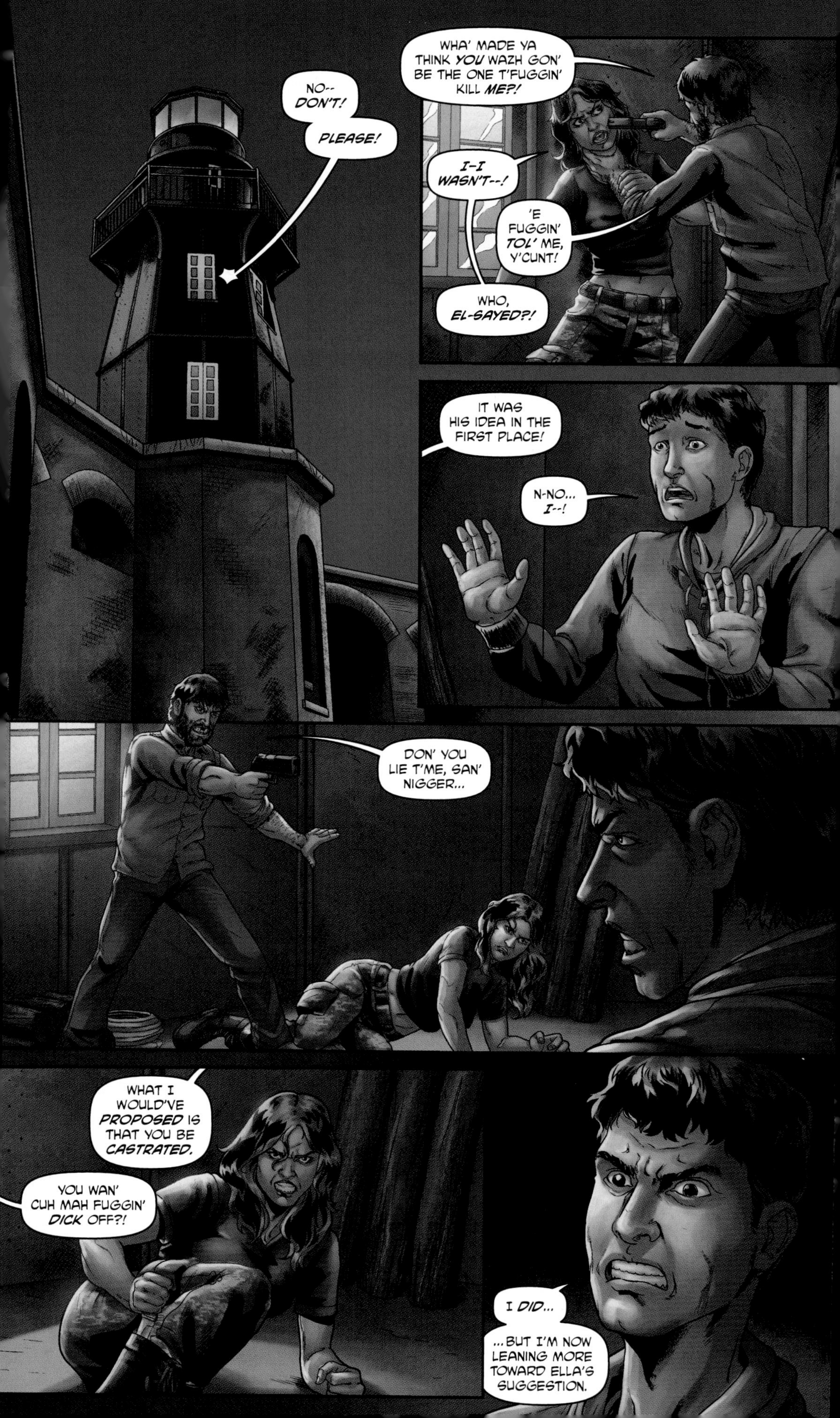
NO-- DON'T!
PLEASE!
WHA' MADE YA THINK YOU WAZH GON' BE THE ONE T'FUGGIN' KILL ME?!
I--I WASN'T--!
'E FUGGIN' TOL' ME, Y'CUNT!
WHO, EL-SAYED?!
IT WAS HIS IDEA IN THE FIRST PLACE!
N-NO... I--!
DON' YOU LIE T'ME, SAN' NIGGER...
WHAT I WOULD'VE PROPOSED IS THAT YOU BE CASTRATED.
YOU WAN' CUH MAH FUGGIN' DICK OFF?!
I DID...
...BUT I'M NOW LEANING MORE TOWARD ELLA'S SUGGESTION.

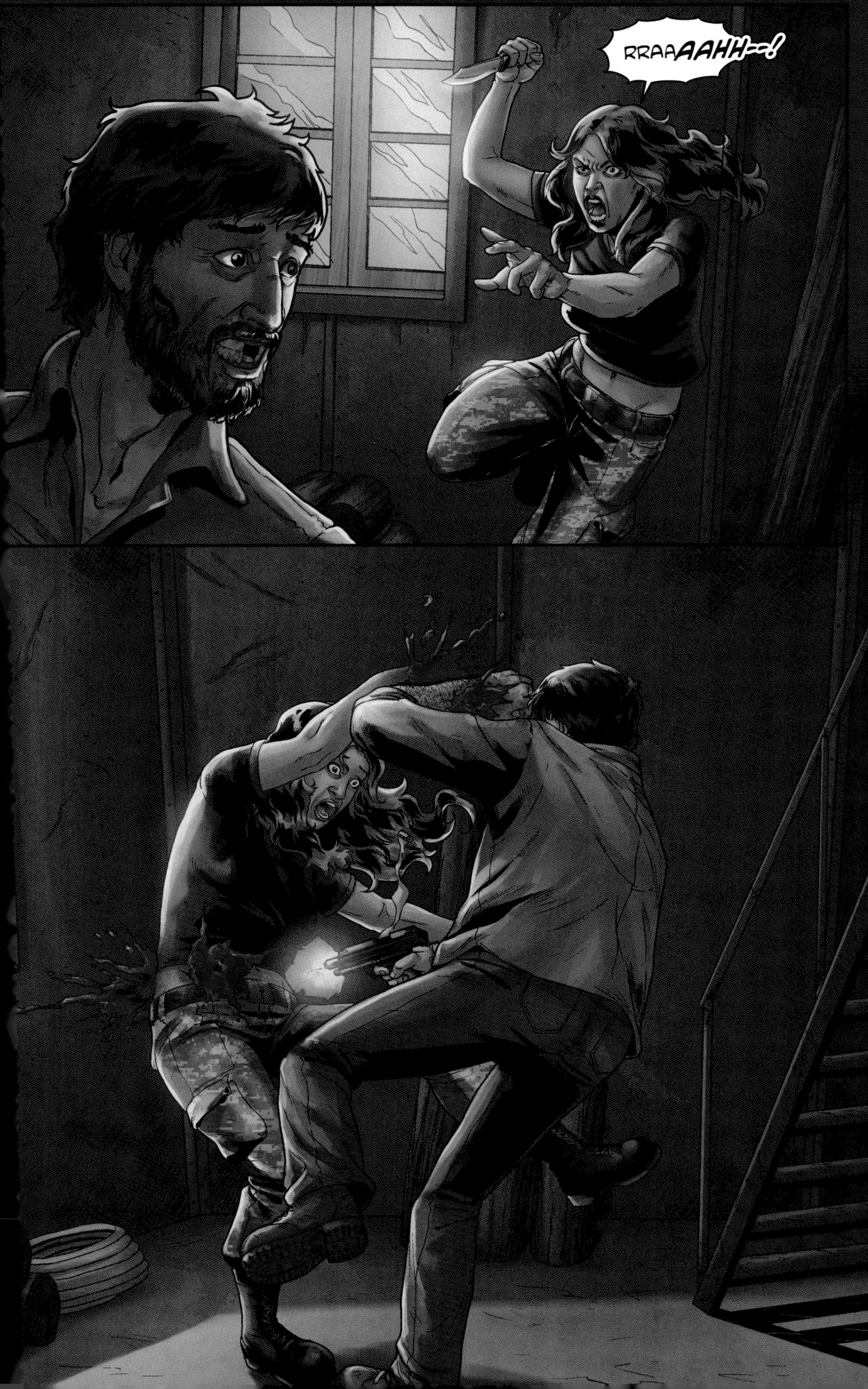
RRAAAAHH--!

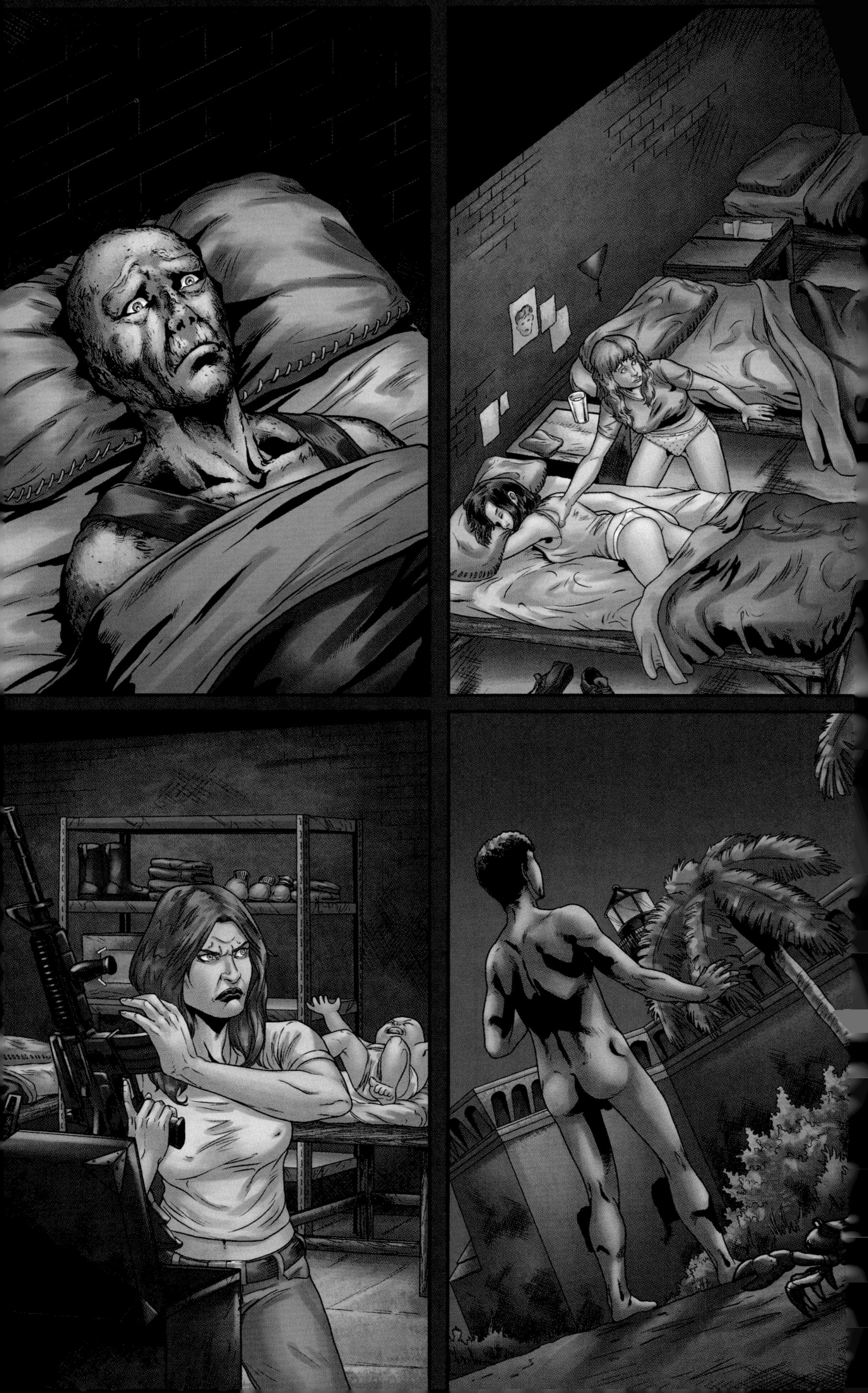

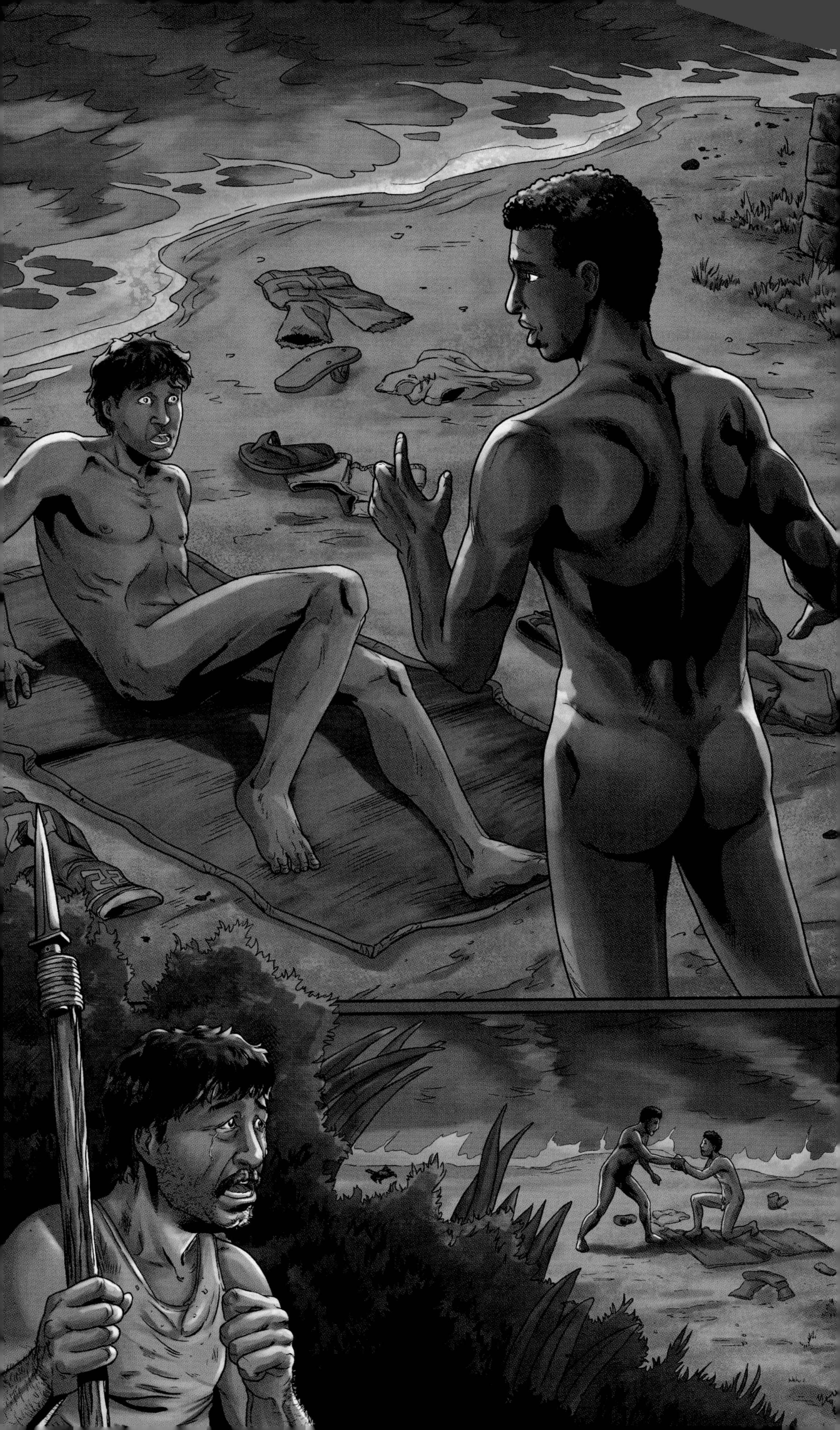

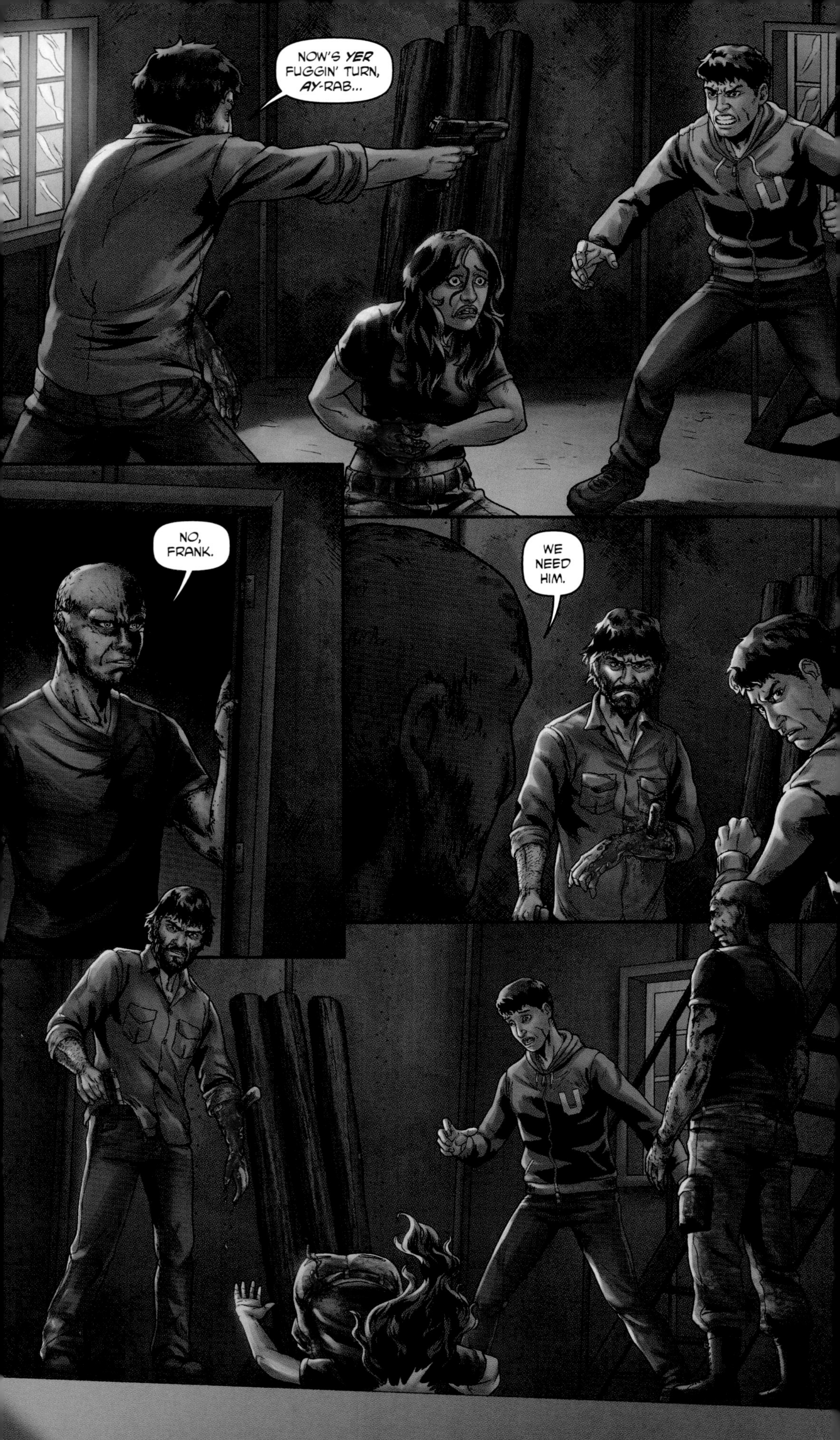
NOW'S *YER* FUGGIN' TURN, *AY*-RAB...
NO, FRANK.
WE NEED HIM.

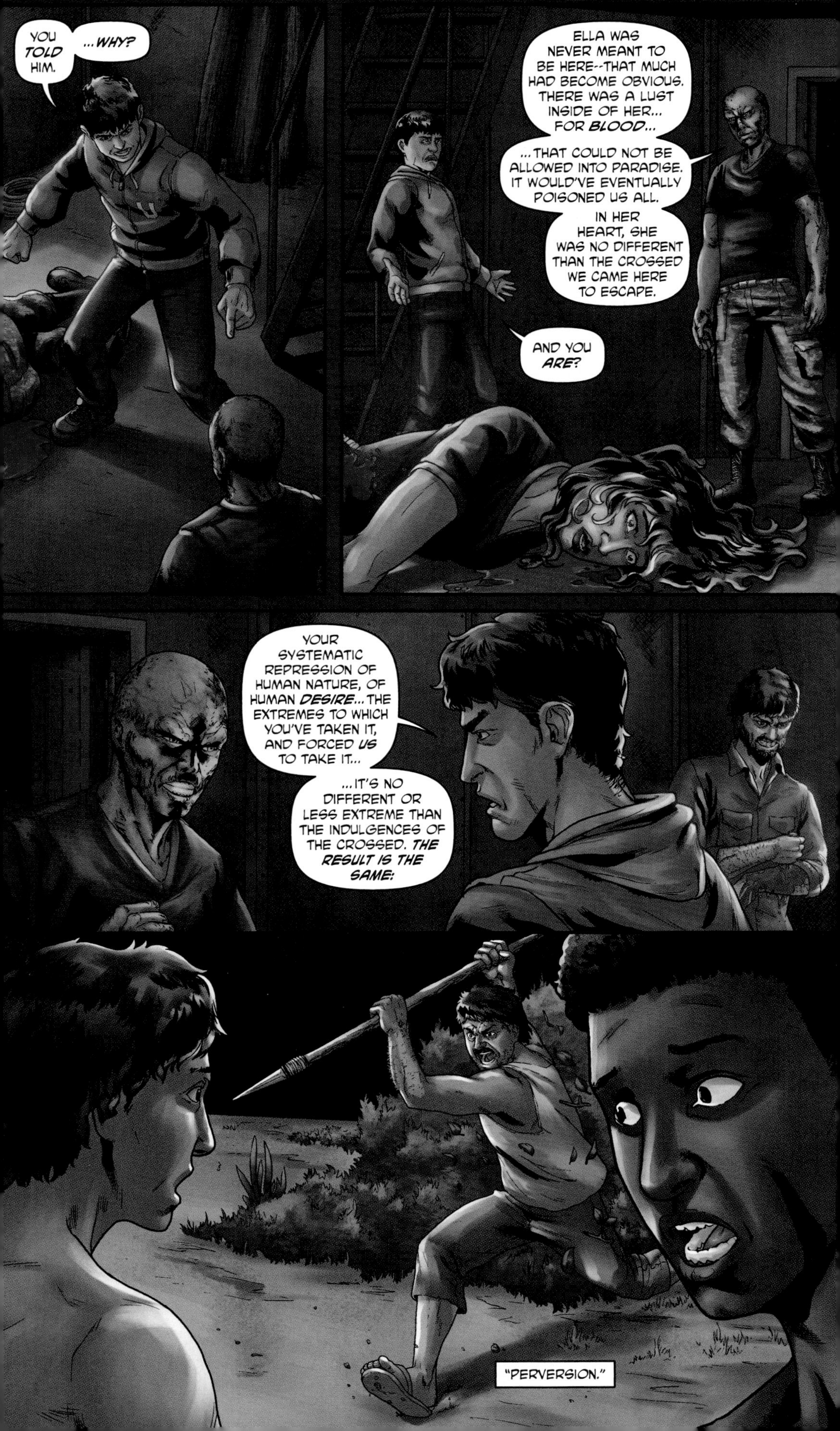
YOU *TOLD* HIM.
...*WHY?*
ELLA WAS NEVER MEANT TO BE HERE--THAT MUCH HAD BECOME OBVIOUS. THERE WAS A LUST INSIDE OF HER... FOR *BLOOD*...
...THAT COULD NOT BE ALLOWED INTO PARADISE. IT WOULD'VE EVENTUALLY POISONED US ALL.
IN HER HEART, SHE WAS NO DIFFERENT THAN THE CROSSED WE CAME HERE TO ESCAPE.
AND YOU *ARE?*
YOUR SYSTEMATIC REPRESSION OF HUMAN NATURE, OF HUMAN *DESIRE*... THE EXTREMES TO WHICH YOU'VE TAKEN IT, AND FORCED *US* TO TAKE IT...
...IT'S NO DIFFERENT OR LESS EXTREME THAN THE INDULGENCES OF THE CROSSED. *THE RESULT IS THE SAME:*
"PERVERSION."

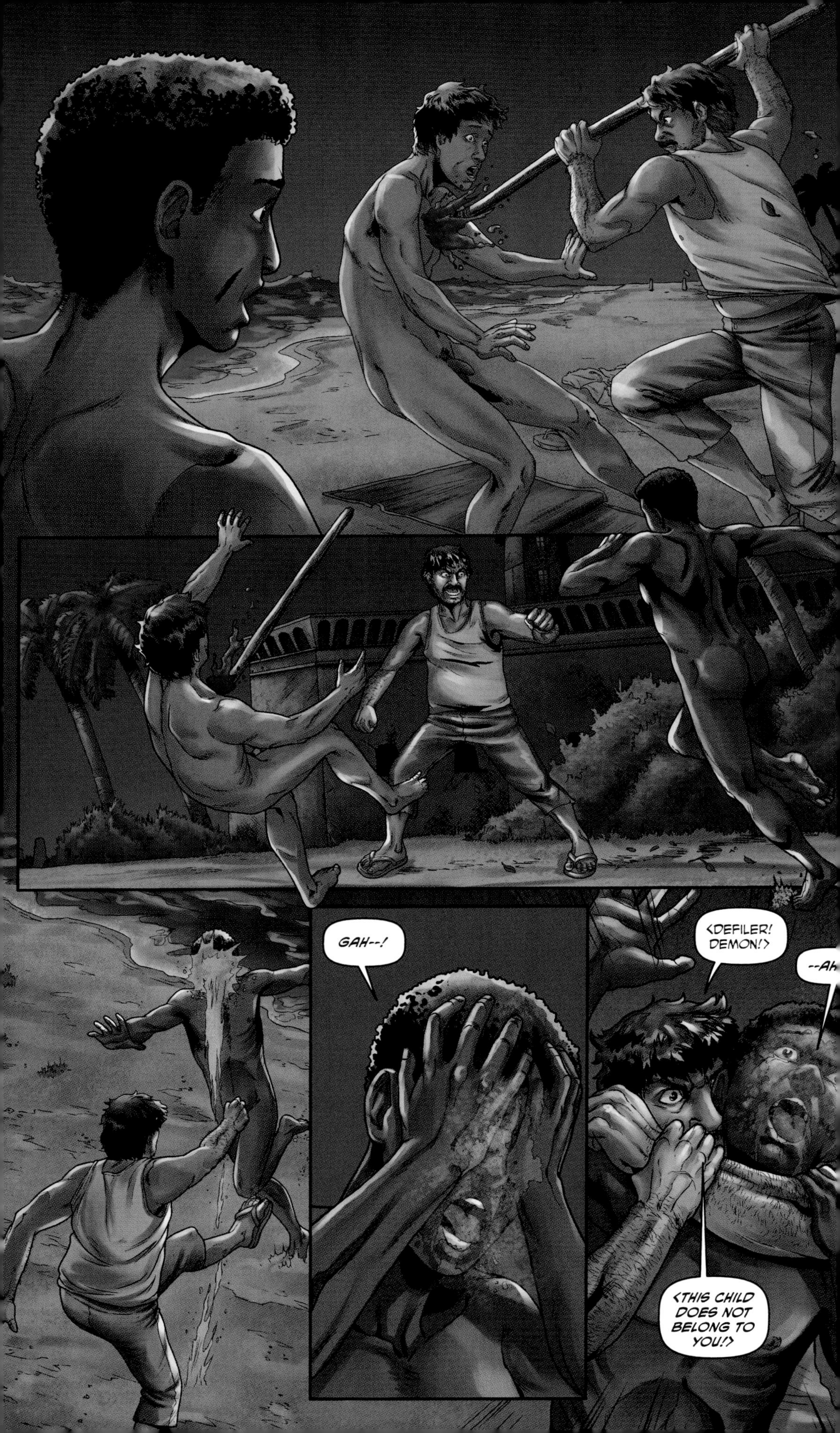
GAH--!
<DEFILER! DEMON!>
--Ah
<THIS CHILD DOES NOT BELONG TO YOU!>

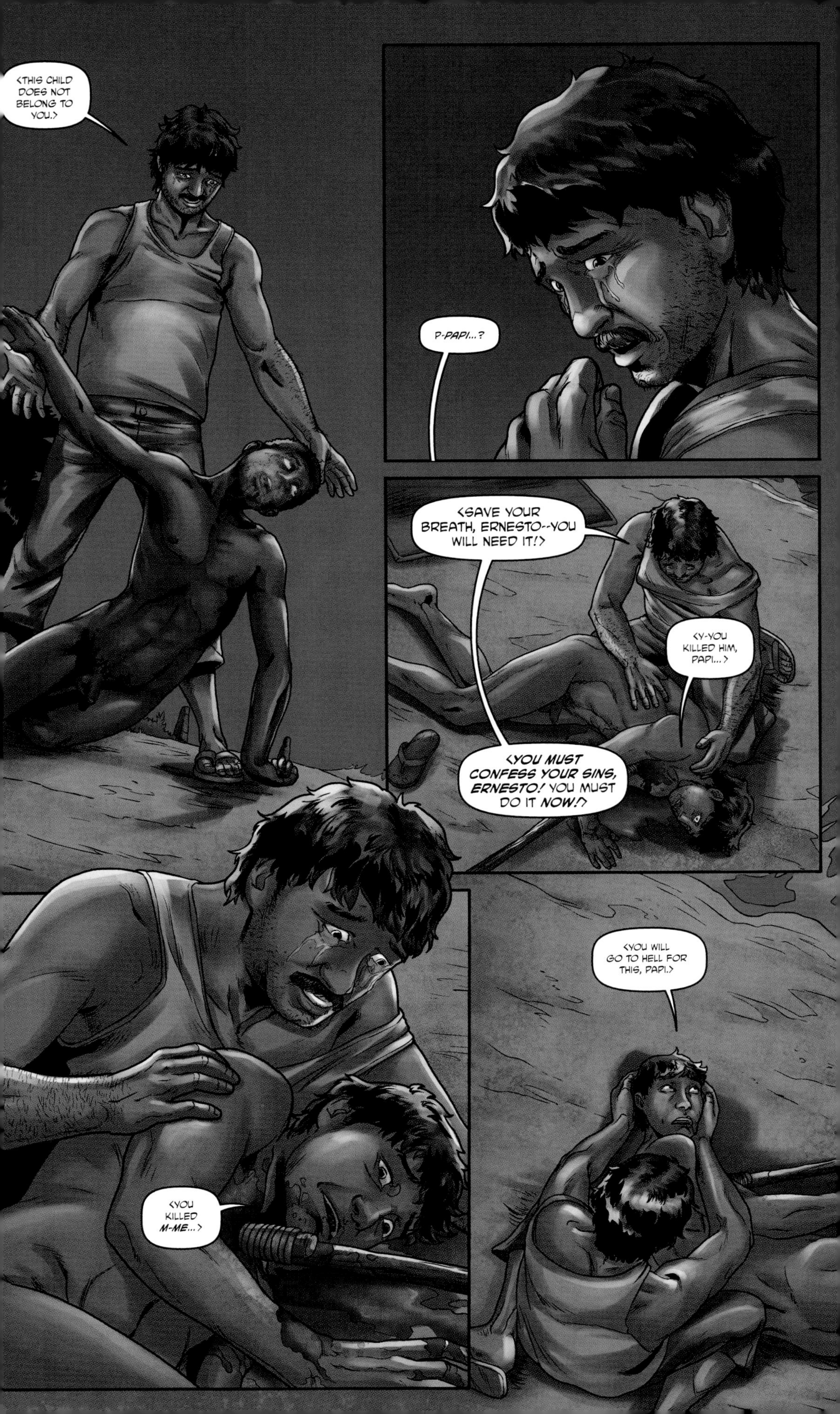

<THIS CHILD DOES NOT BELONG TO YOU.>
P-PAPI...?
<SAVE YOUR BREATH, ERNESTO--YOU WILL NEED IT!>
<Y-YOU KILLED HIM, PAPI...>
<YOU MUST CONFESS YOUR SINS, ERNESTO! YOU MUST DO IT NOW!>
<YOU KILLED M-ME...>
<YOU WILL GO TO HELL FOR THIS, PAPI.>

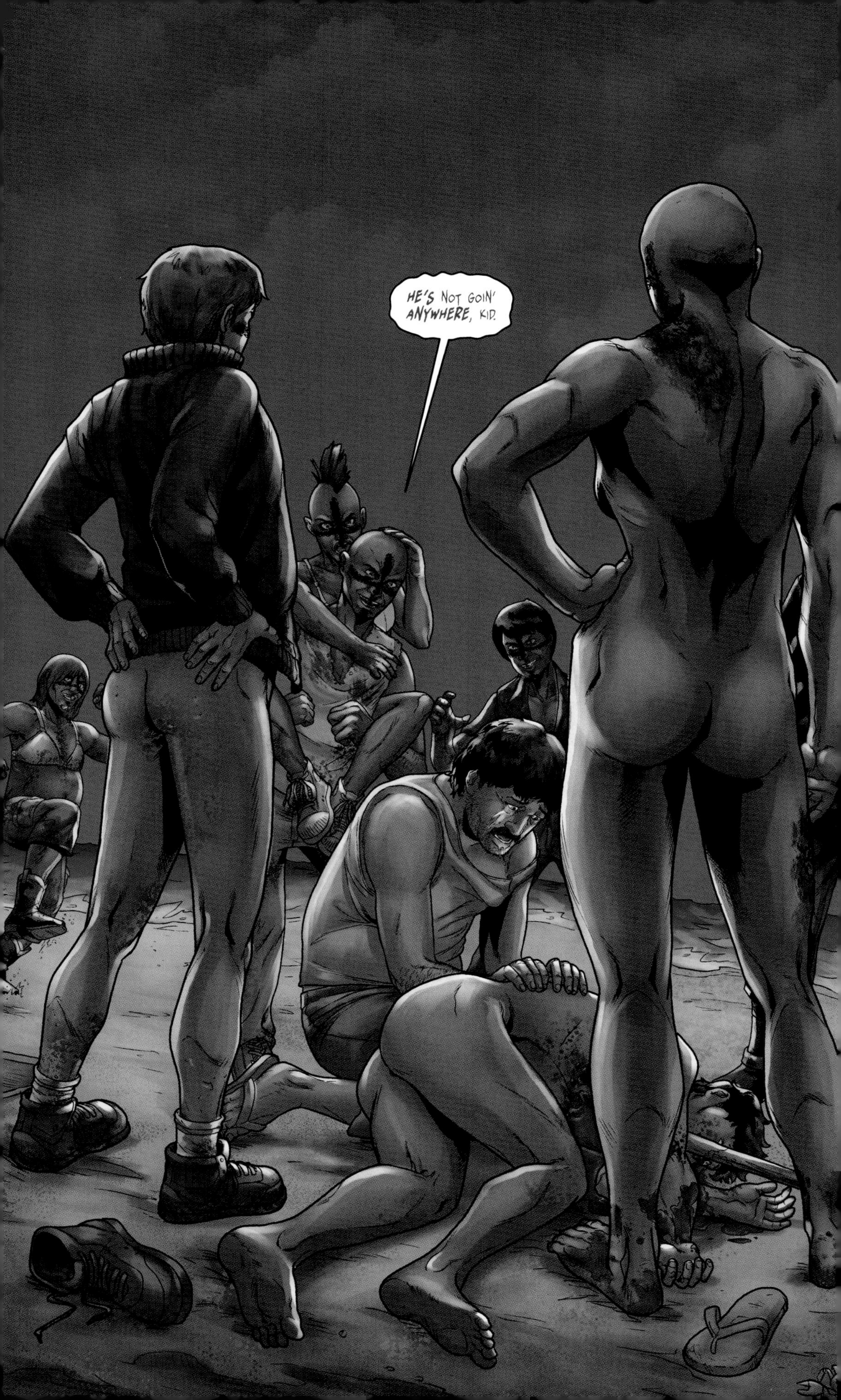
HE'S NOT GOIN' ANYWHERE, KID.

YOU HAVEN'T CREATED PARADISE, CAPTAIN BARNES... YOU'VE CREATED *A MIRROR IMAGE OF HELL.*

CAN'T YOU *SEE* THAT?

NO.

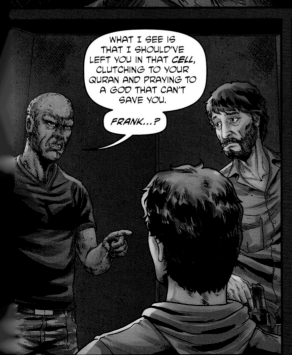

WHAT I SEE IS THAT I SHOULD'VE LEFT YOU IN THAT *CELL*, CLUTCHING TO YOUR QURAN AND PRAYING TO A GOD THAT CAN'T SAVE YOU.

FRANK...?

CAPTAIN!

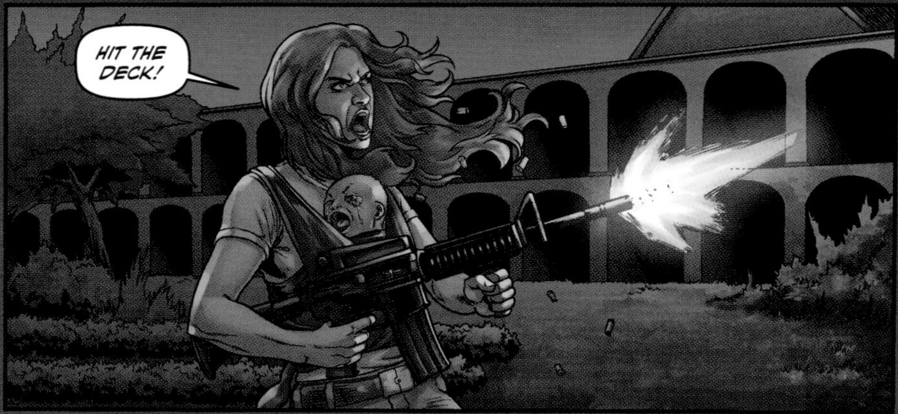
HIT THE DECK!

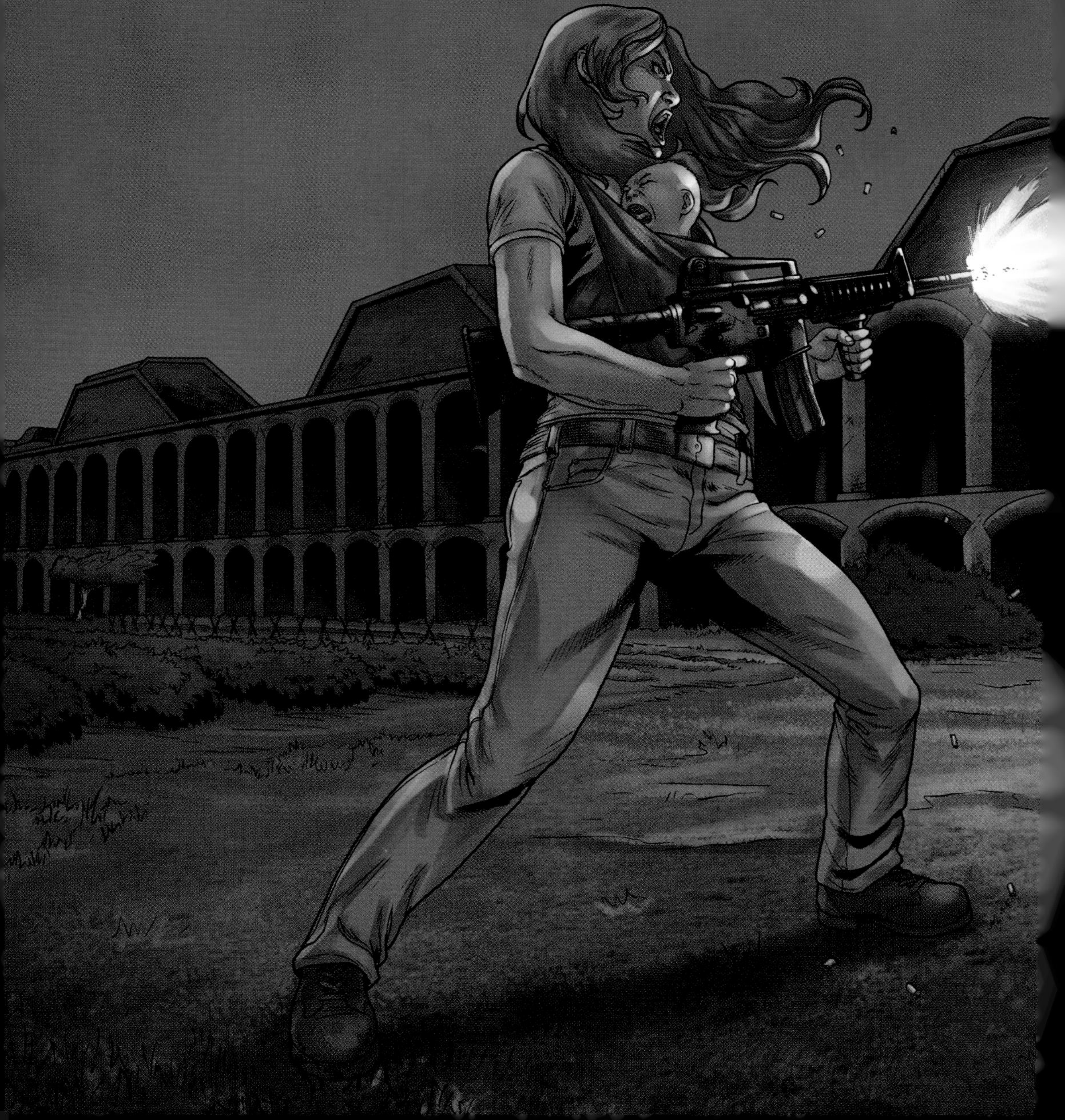

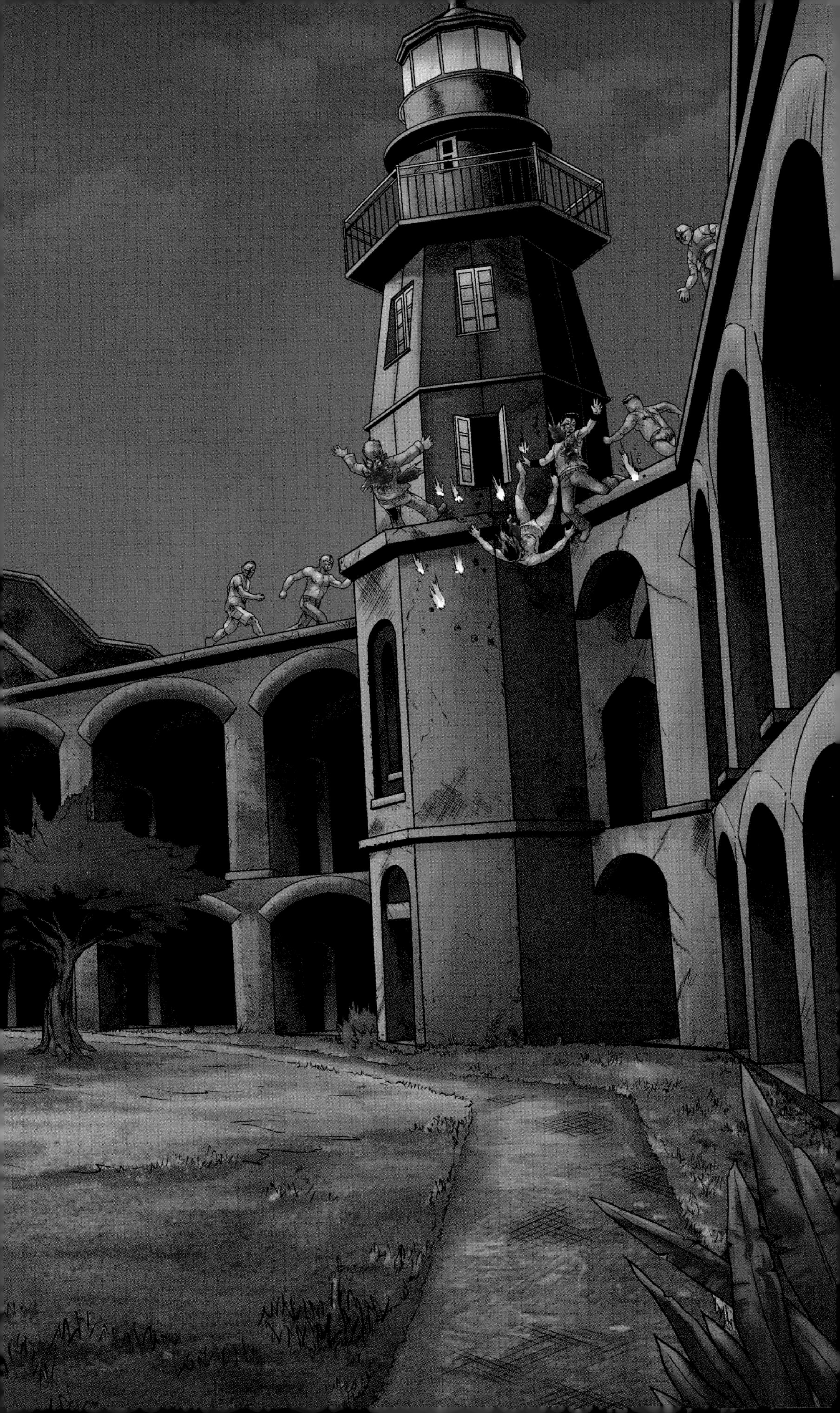

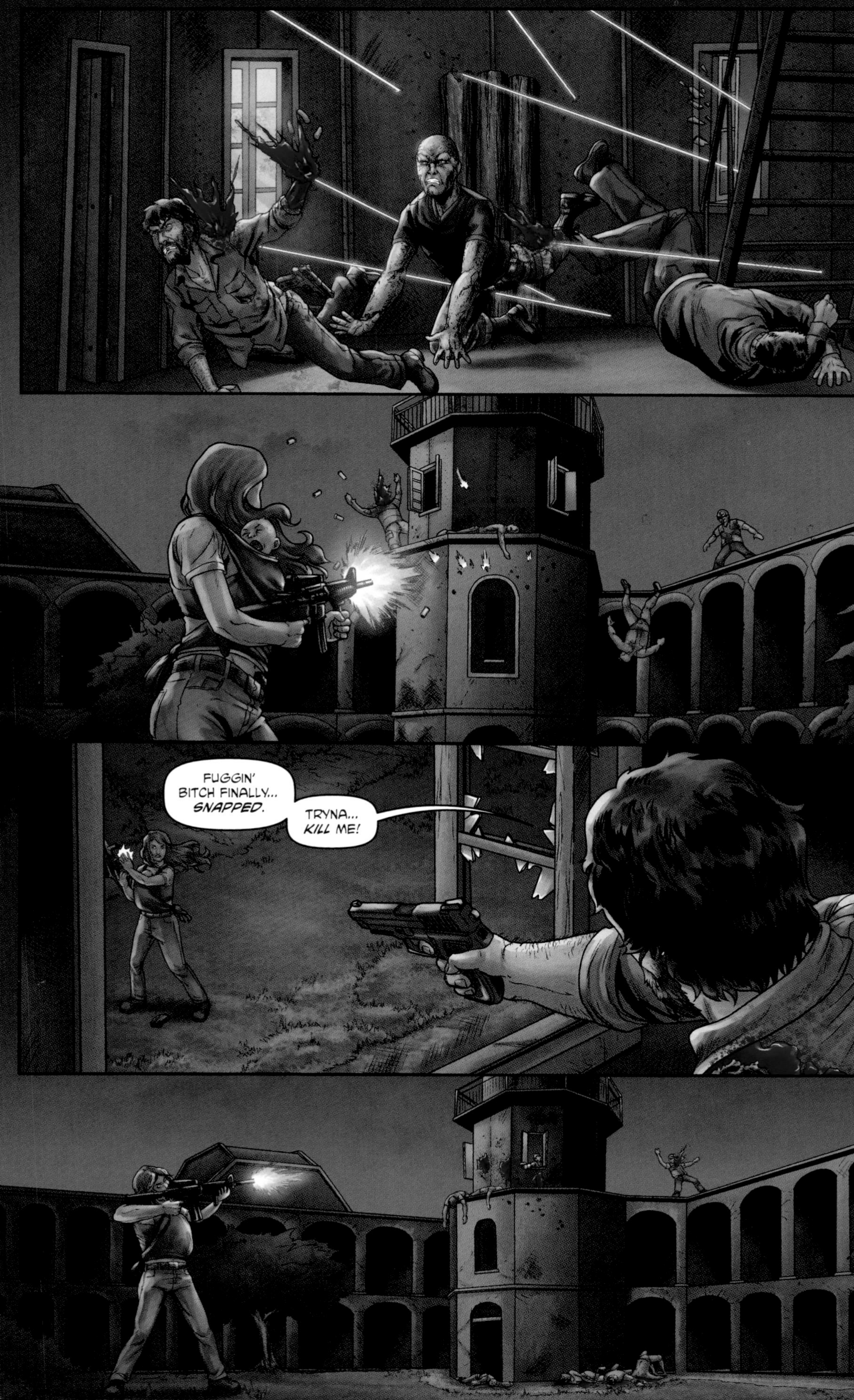
FUGGIN' BITCH FINALLY... SNAPPED.
TRYNA... KILL ME!

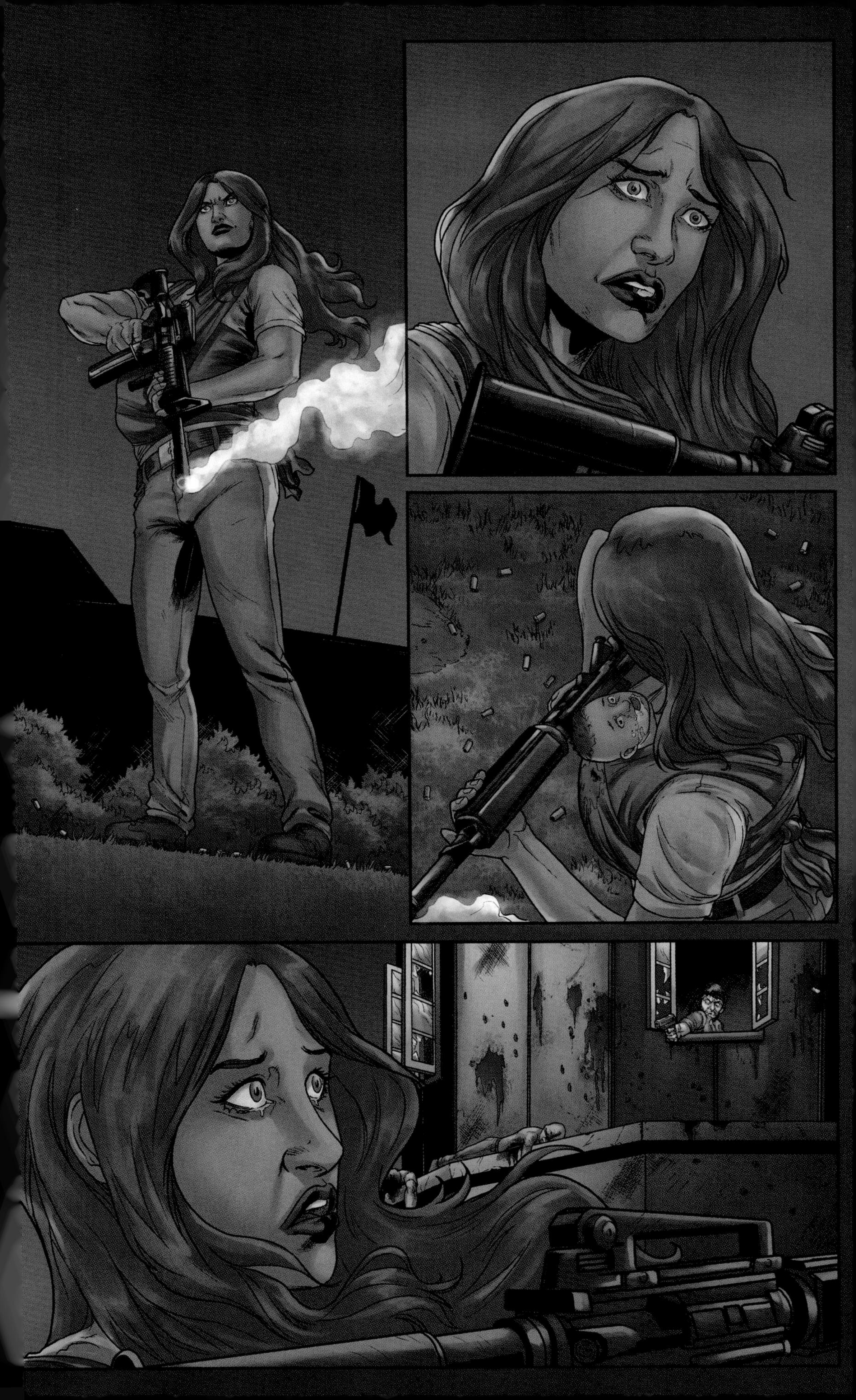

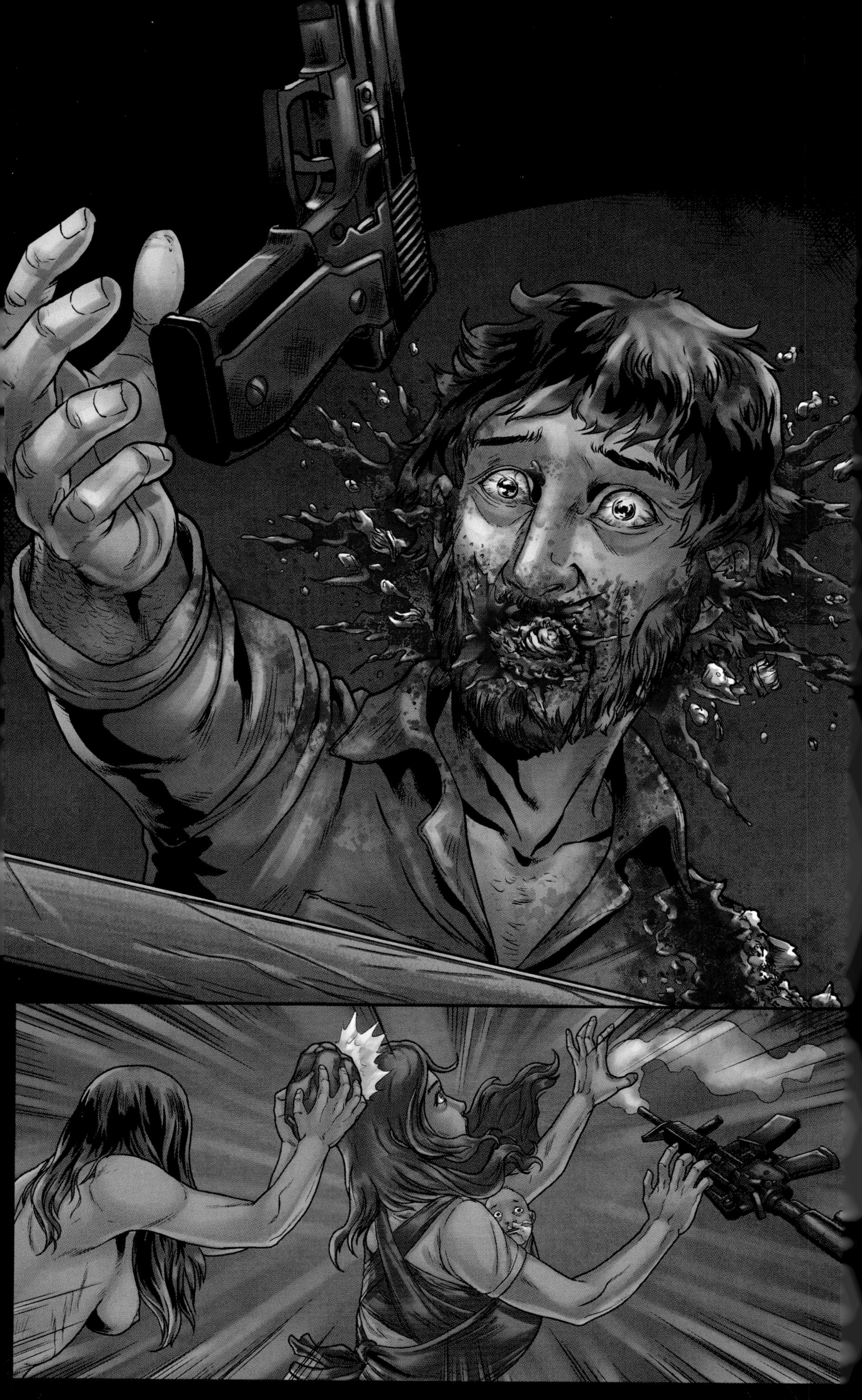

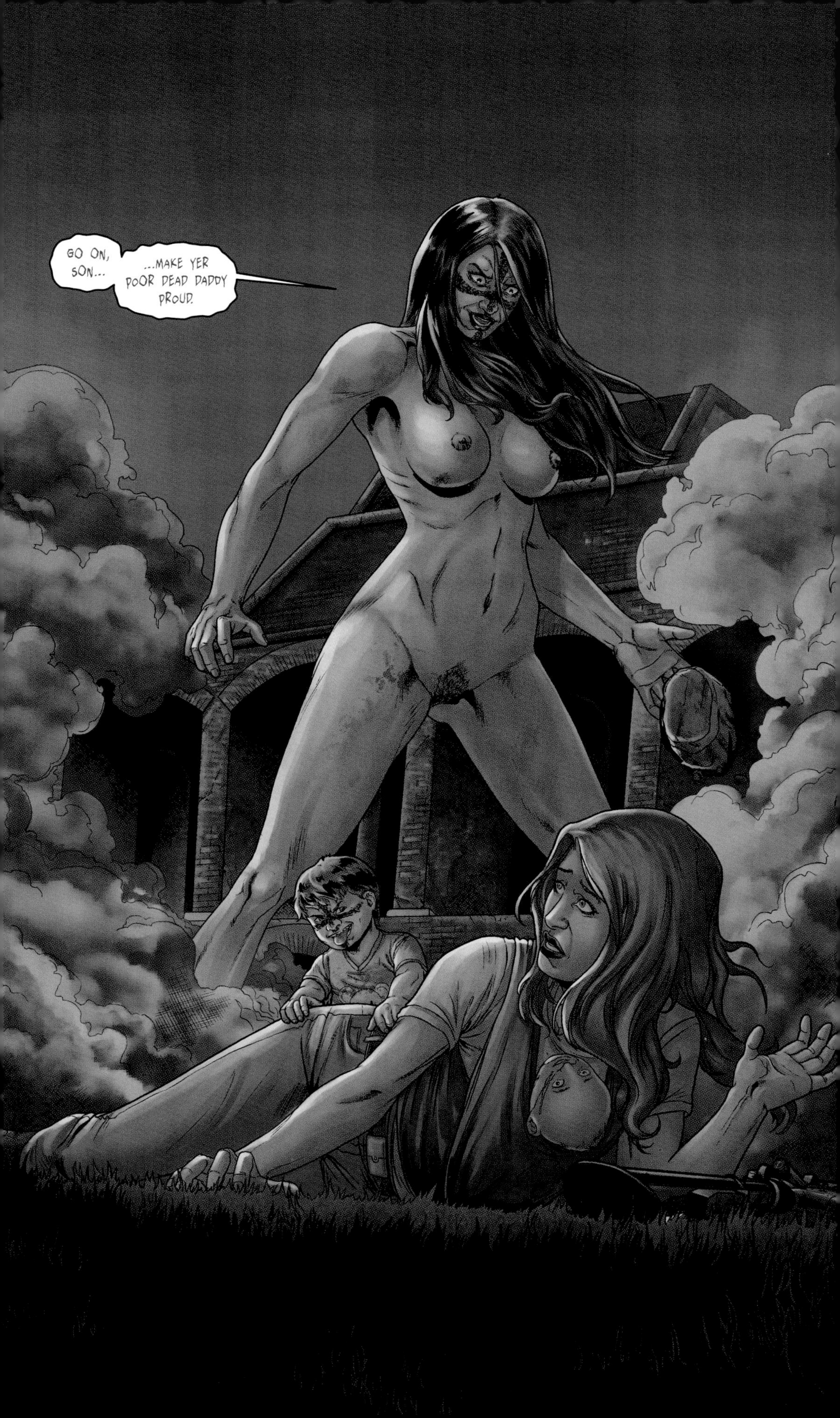
GO ON, SON...
...MAKE YER POOR DEAD DADDY PROUD.

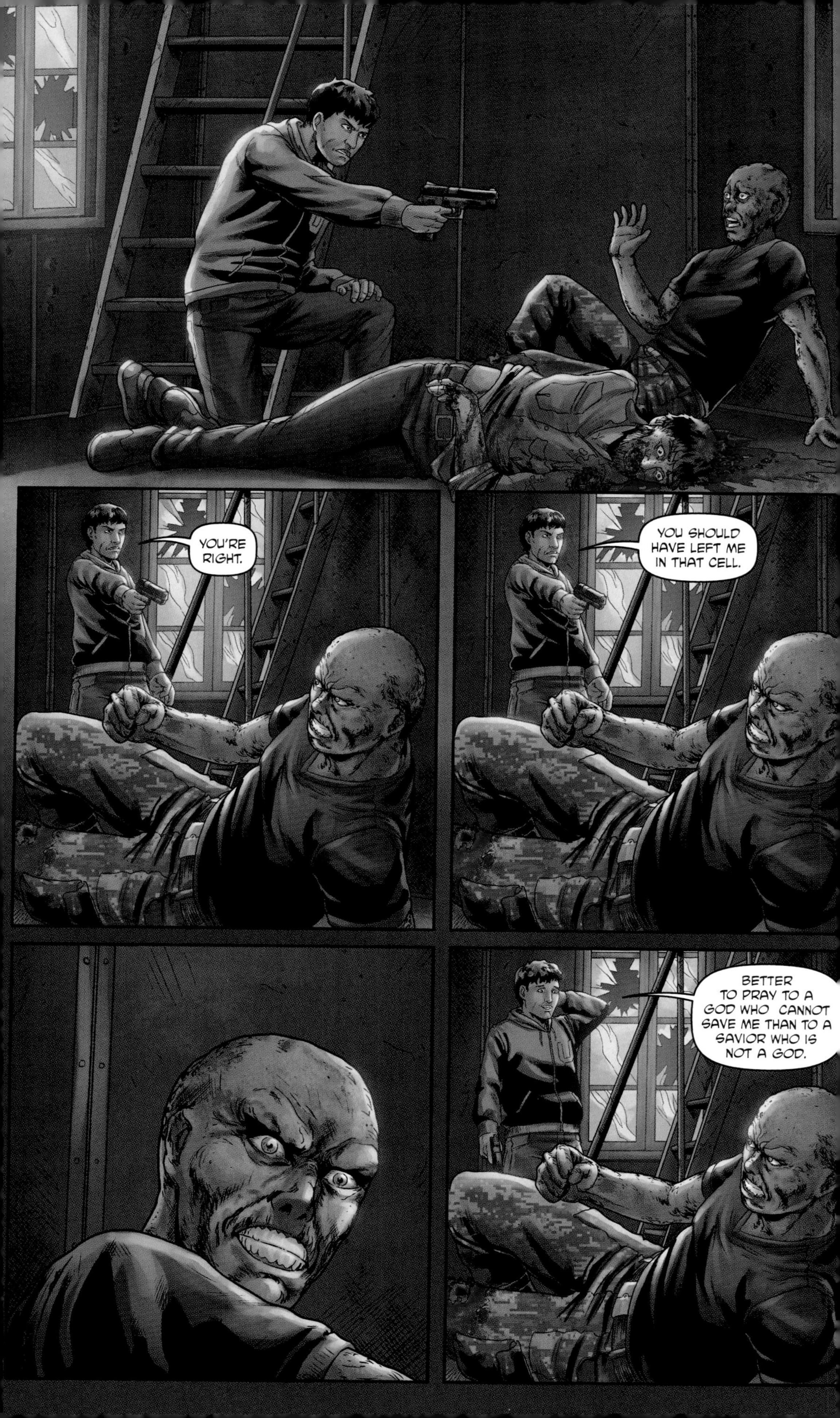
YOU'RE RIGHT.
YOU SHOULD HAVE LEFT ME IN THAT CELL.
BETTER TO PRAY TO A GOD WHO CANNOT SAVE ME THAN TO A SAVIOR WHO IS NOT A GOD.

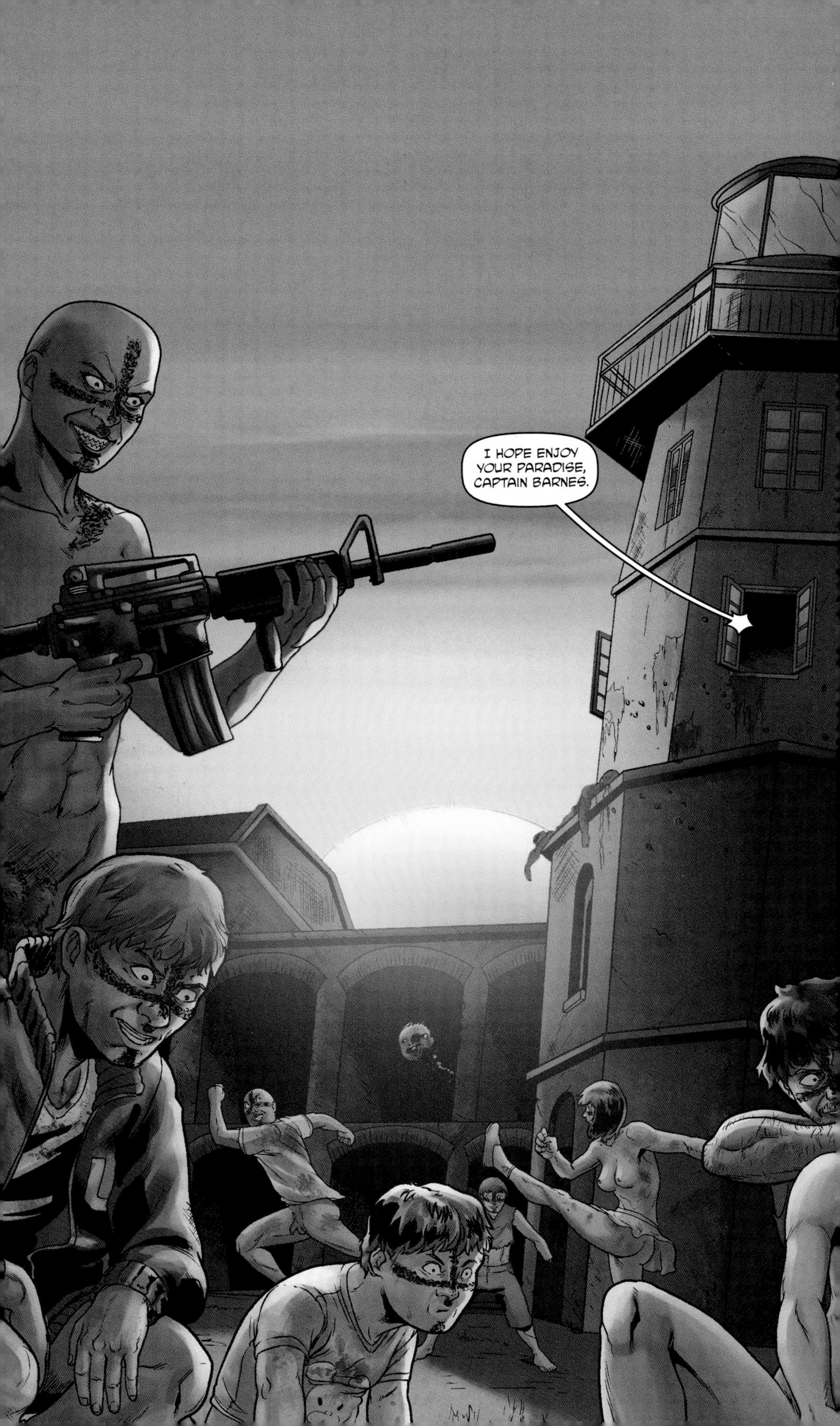
I HOPE ENJOY YOUR PARADISE, CAPTAIN BARNES.

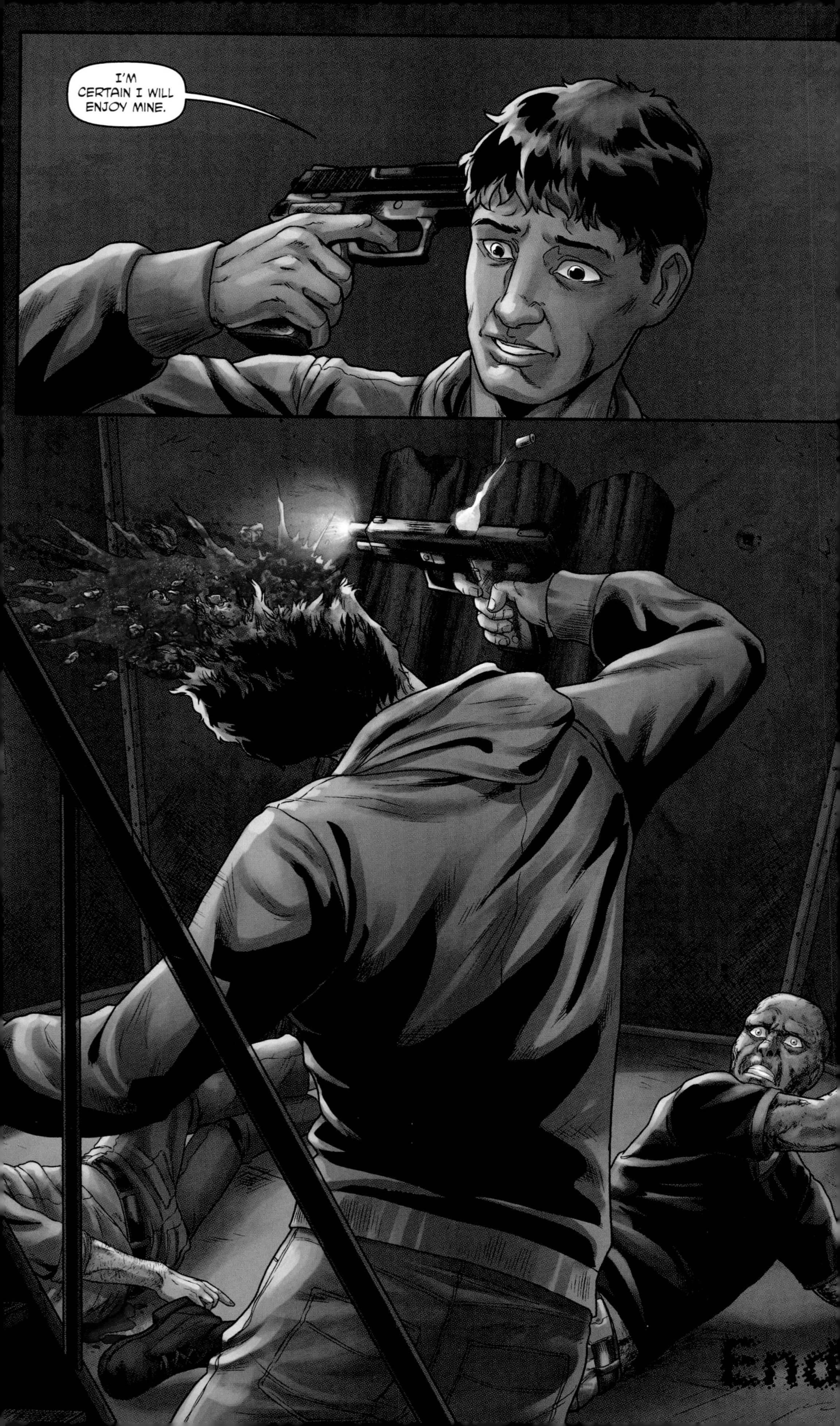
I'M CERTAIN I WILL ENJOY MINE.
End

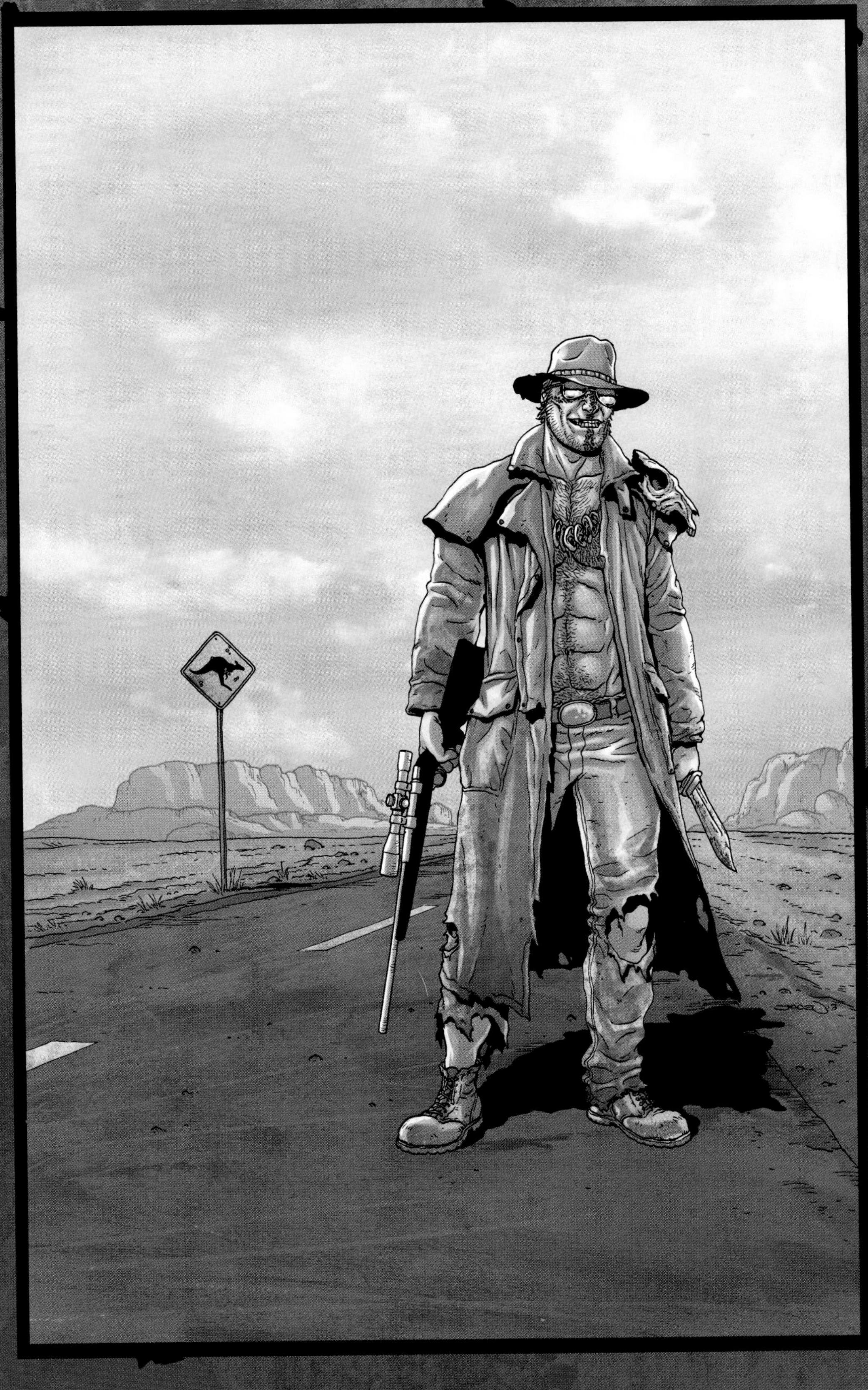

PART 7

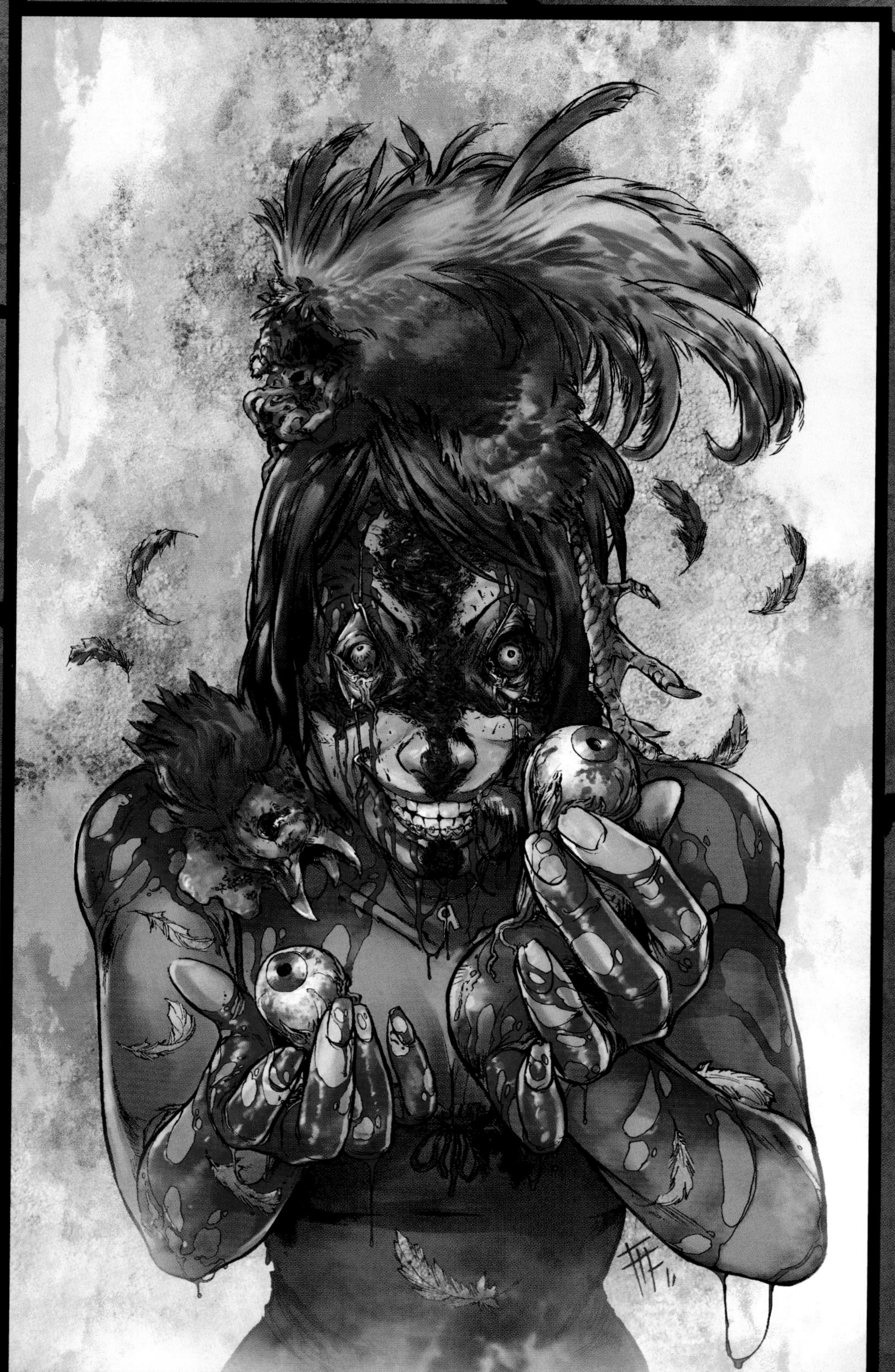

THE WIZARD OF AUS

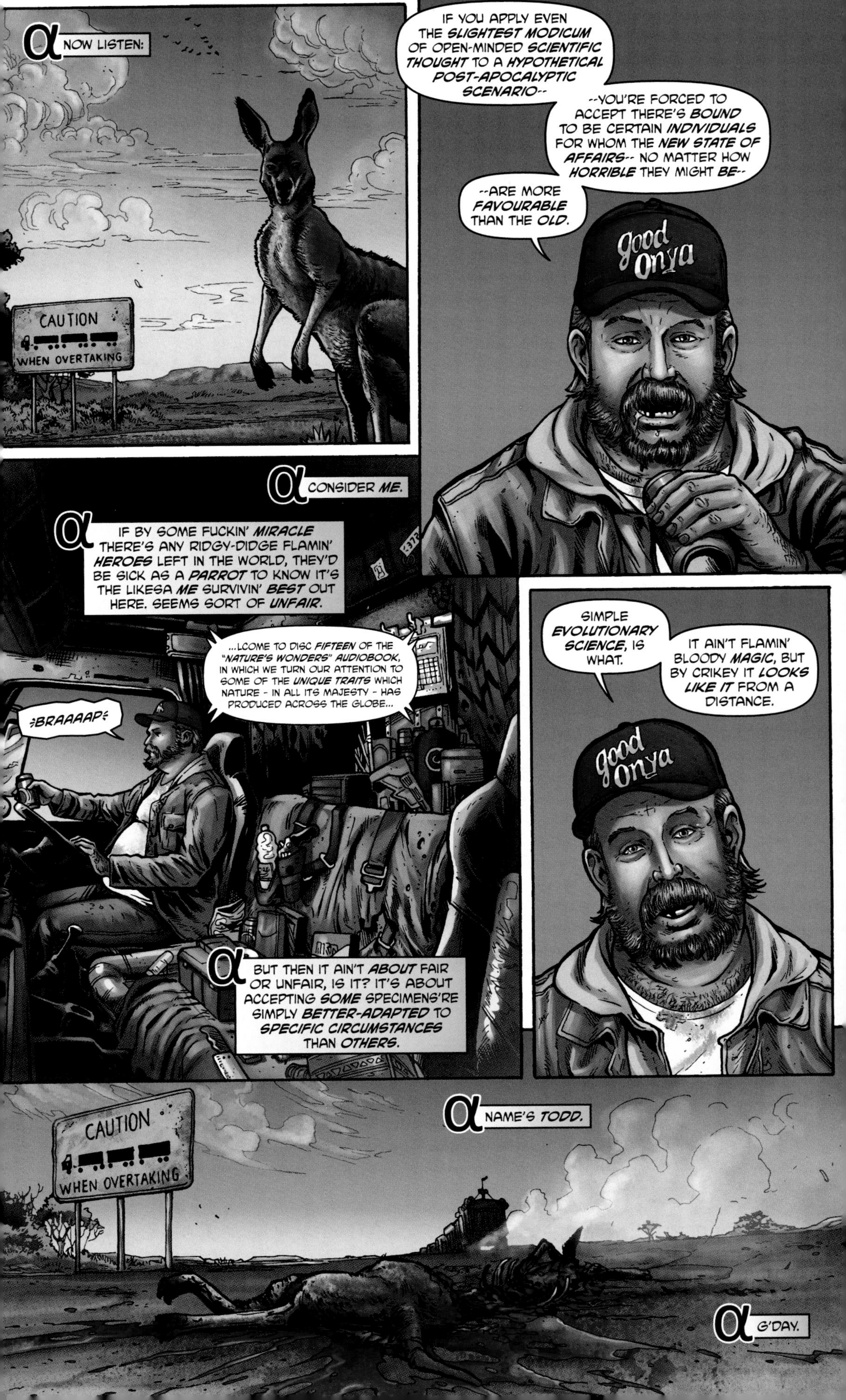
NOW LISTEN:
CAUTION
WHEN OVERTAKING
IF YOU APPLY EVEN THE SLIGHTEST MODICUM OF OPEN-MINDED SCIENTIFIC THOUGHT TO A HYPOTHETICAL POST-APOCALYPTIC SCENARIO--
--YOU'RE FORCED TO ACCEPT THERE'S BOUND TO BE CERTAIN INDIVIDUALS FOR WHOM THE NEW STATE OF AFFAIRS-- NO MATTER HOW HORRIBLE THEY MIGHT BE--
--ARE MORE FAVOURABLE THAN THE OLD.
good onya
CONSIDER ME.
IF BY SOME FUCKIN' MIRACLE THERE'S ANY RIDGY-DIDGE FLAMIN' HEROES LEFT IN THE WORLD, THEY'D BE SICK AS A PARROT TO KNOW IT'S THE LIKESA ME SURVIVIN' BEST OUT HERE. SEEMS SORT OF UNFAIR.
...LCOME TO DISC FIFTEEN OF THE "NATURE'S WONDERS" AUDIOBOOK, IN WHICH WE TURN OUR ATTENTION TO SOME OF THE UNIQUE TRAITS WHICH NATURE - IN ALL ITS MAJESTY - HAS PRODUCED ACROSS THE GLOBE...
BRAAAAP
BUT THEN IT AIN'T ABOUT FAIR OR UNFAIR, IS IT? IT'S ABOUT ACCEPTING SOME SPECIMENS'RE SIMPLY BETTER-ADAPTED TO SPECIFIC CIRCUMSTANCES THAN OTHERS.
SIMPLE EVOLUTIONARY SCIENCE, IS WHAT.
IT AIN'T FLAMIN' BLOODY MAGIC, BUT BY CRIKEY IT LOOKS LIKE IT FROM A DISTANCE.
good onya
CAUTION
WHEN OVERTAKING
NAME'S TODD.
G'DAY.

Ten miles outside Kalgoorlie-Boulder
Western Australia
The arse-cleft of nowhere

OHNO.

OH. OH SHITCRAPFUCK. *REXY*. SHITCRAP.

THE *DOG*. THEY GOT THE DOOOOOG--

FUCKEM.

β NAME'S DAVID BAERST.

SITE-PROSPECTOR FOR THE LOCAL *MINING CORPS*, THESE PAST SIX YEARS.

SPENT A LOT OF TIME IN THE *WILD*, YA KNOW? FELLER LEARNS TO TAKE *CARE* OF HIMSELF. TO *TAKE NO SHIT* AN' TAME WHATEVER *FELLER, CRITTER* OR *NATURAL-FUCKIN'-FEATURE* DARES TA *TROUBLE HIM.*

β I AM A *SURVIVOR.*

β I AM A *PROTECTOR.*

β ON THE OTHER HAND I ENJOY *VICTORIAN LITERATURE*, CONSTRUCTING MODEL AIRPLANES AND MAINTAINING A HOBBYIST'S *FACEBOOK PAGE* ON *METAL-DETECTIN'* IN THE *OUTBACK.*

β I'M A PRETTY MODERN SORTA BLOKE, ALL IN ALL.

C'MON.

β GUESS WHAT I'M ACTUALLY *SAYIN'* IS:

THIS AIN'T THE *CROCODILE DUNDEE* YOU'RE LOOKIN' FOR.

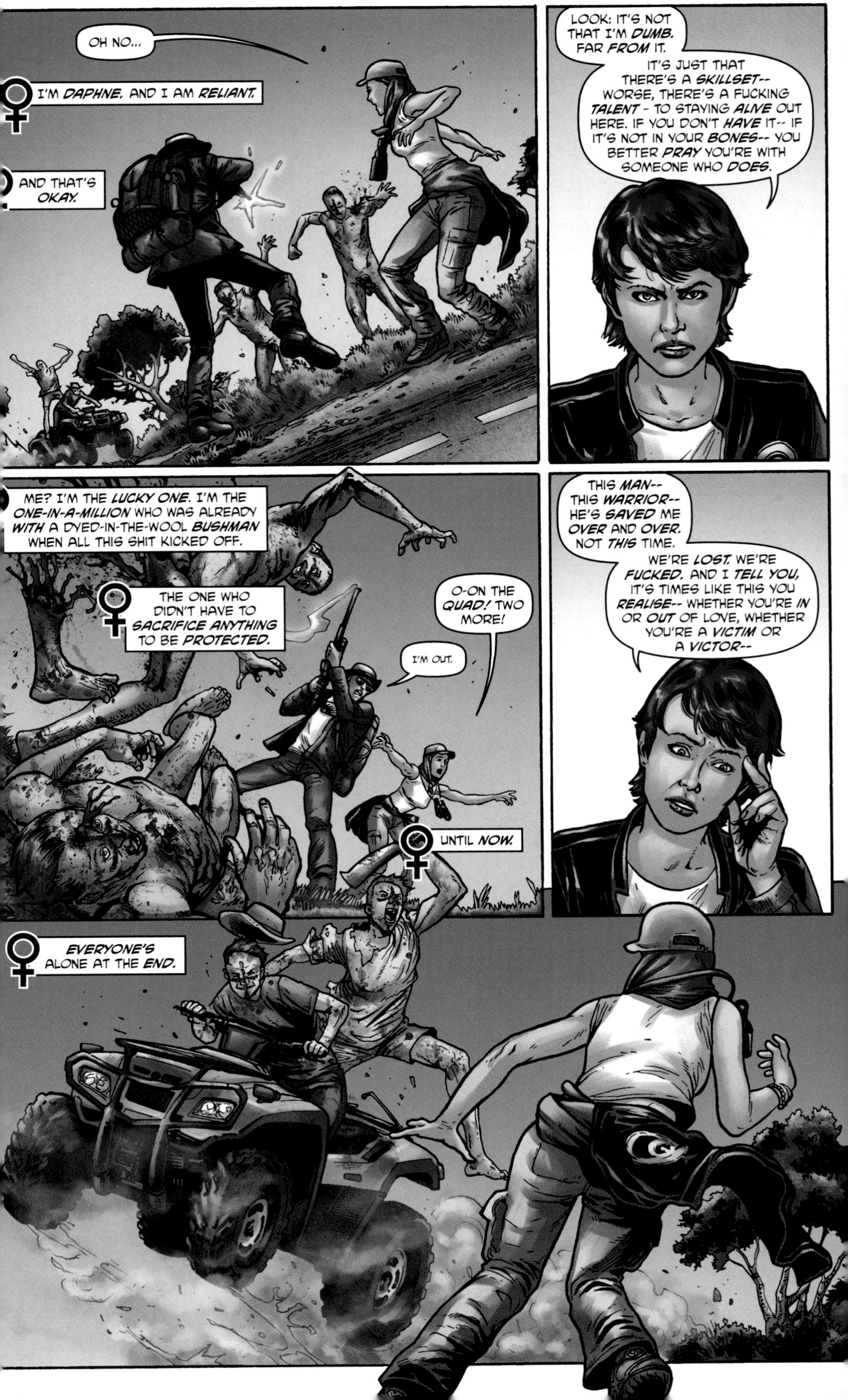
OH NO...
I'M DAPHNE. AND I AM RELIANT.
AND THAT'S OKAY.
LOOK: IT'S NOT THAT I'M DUMB. FAR FROM IT.
IT'S JUST THAT THERE'S A SKILLSET-- WORSE, THERE'S A FUCKING TALENT - TO STAYING ALIVE OUT HERE. IF YOU DON'T HAVE IT-- IF IT'S NOT IN YOUR BONES-- YOU BETTER PRAY YOU'RE WITH SOMEONE WHO DOES.
ME? I'M THE LUCKY ONE. I'M THE ONE-IN-A-MILLION WHO WAS ALREADY WITH A DYED-IN-THE-WOOL BUSHMAN WHEN ALL THIS SHIT KICKED OFF.
THE ONE WHO DIDN'T HAVE TO SACRIFICE ANYTHING TO BE PROTECTED.
O-ON THE QUAD! TWO MORE!
I'M OUT.
UNTIL NOW.
THIS MAN-- THIS WARRIOR-- HE'S SAVED ME OVER AND OVER. NOT THIS TIME.
WE'RE LOST. WE'RE FUCKED. AND I TELL YOU, IT'S TIMES LIKE THIS YOU REALISE-- WHETHER YOU'RE IN OR OUT OF LOVE, WHETHER YOU'RE A VICTIM OR A VICTOR--
EVERYONE'S ALONE AT THE END.

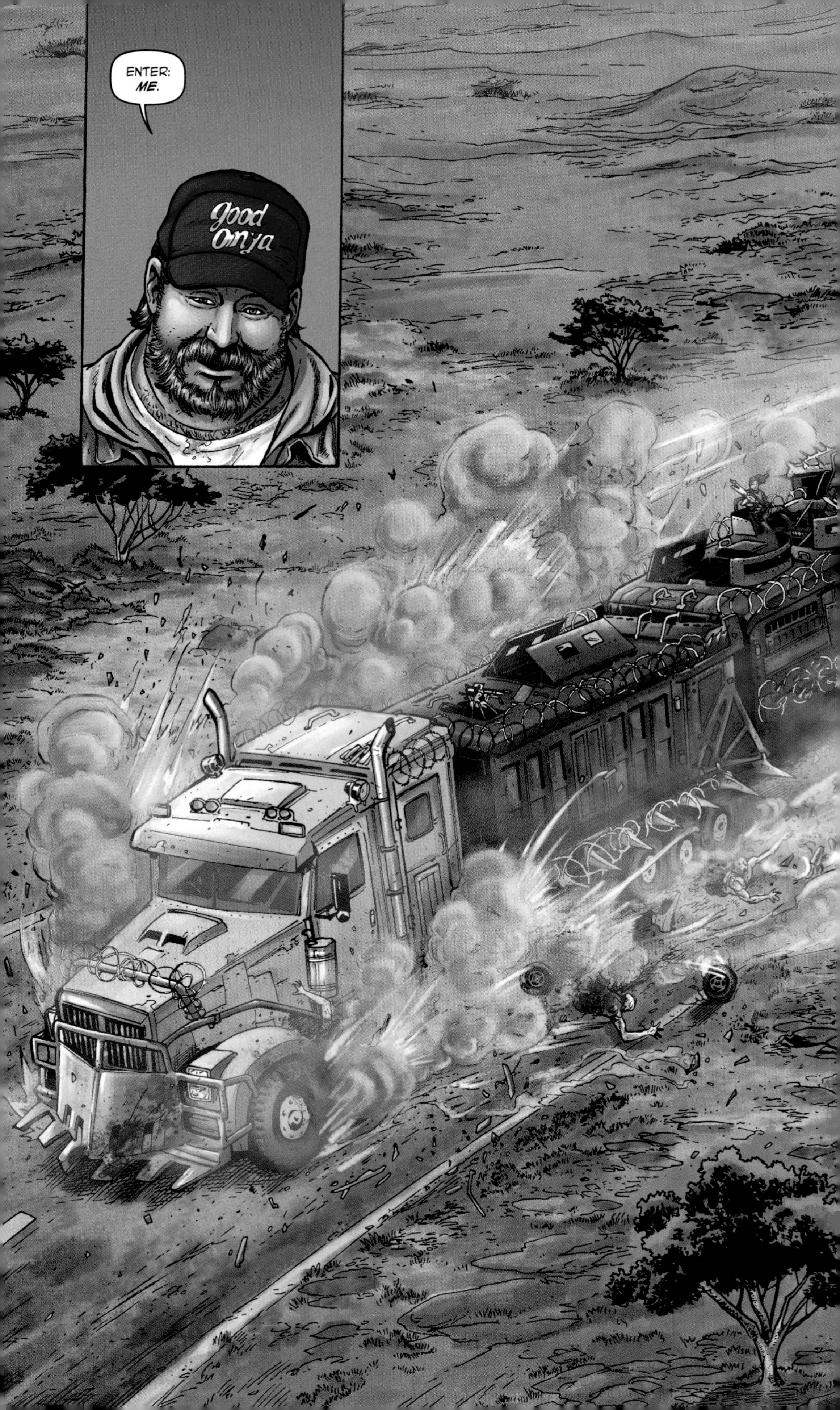
ENTER: ME.
Good Onya

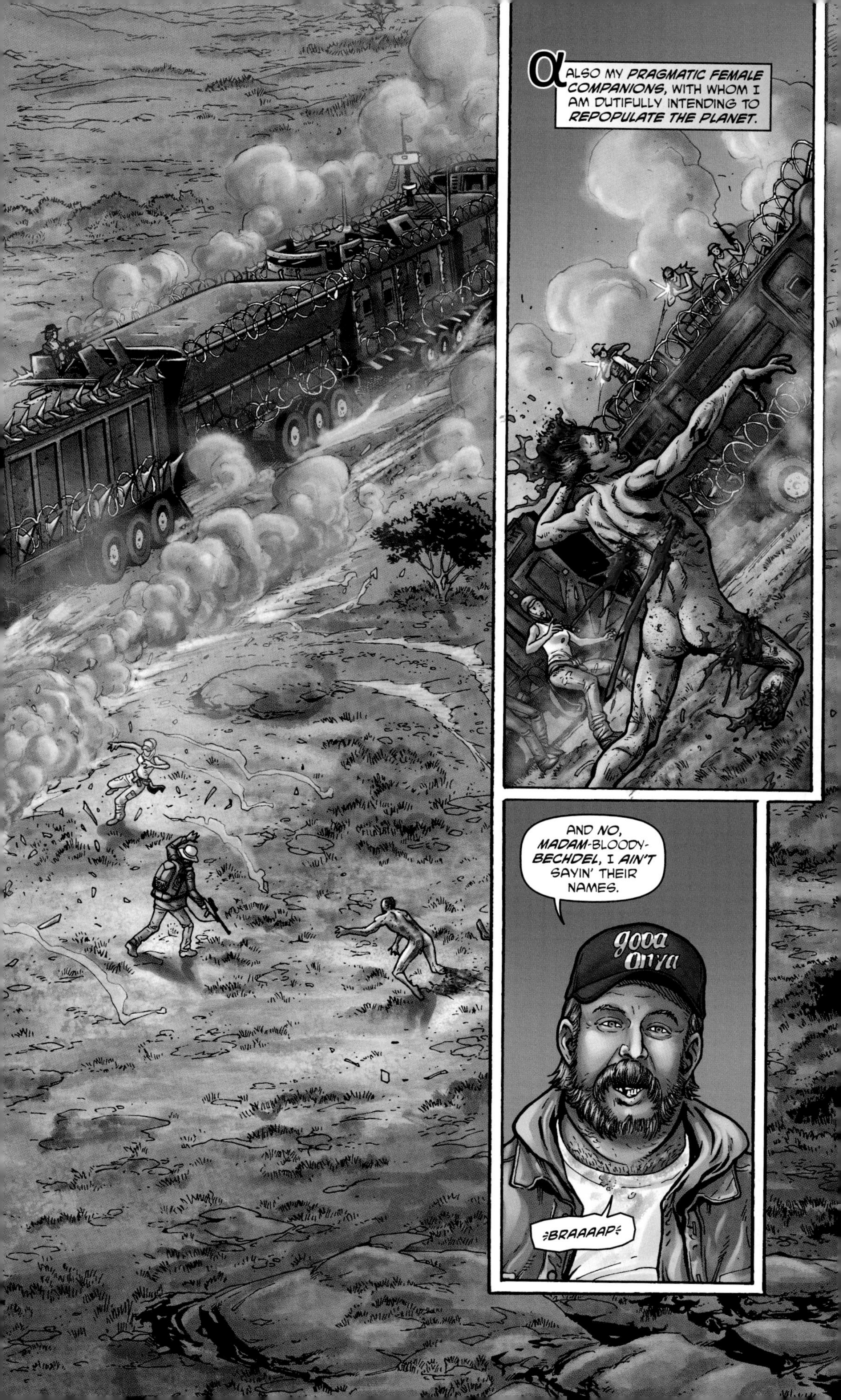
ALSO MY PRAGMATIC FEMALE COMPANIONS, WITH WHOM I AM DUTIFULLY INTENDING TO REPOPULATE THE PLANET.
AND NO, MADAM-BLOODY-BECHDEL, I AIN'T SAYIN' THEIR NAMES.
gooa onya
BRAAAAP

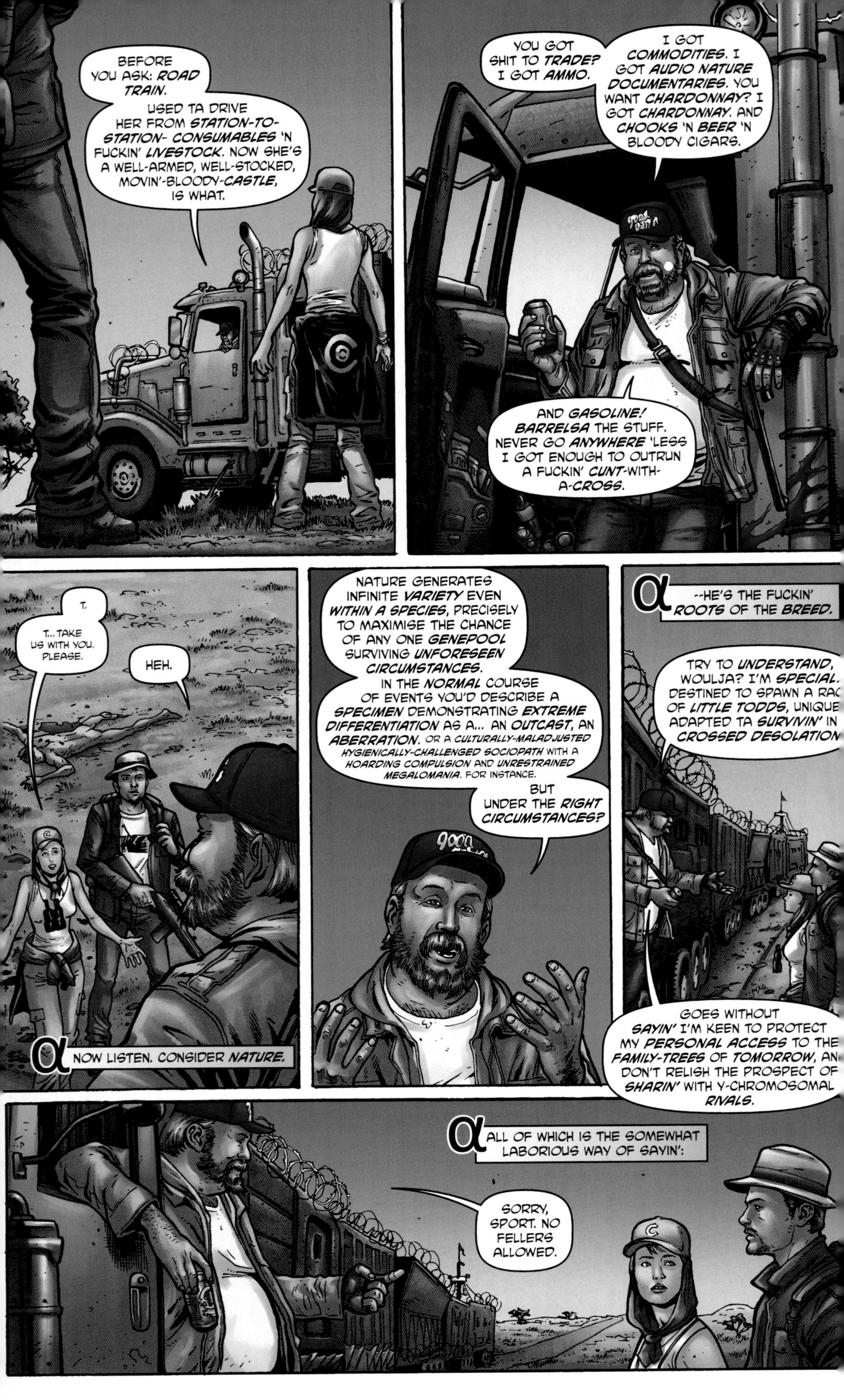

BEFORE YOU ASK: ROAD TRAIN.
USED TA DRIVE HER FROM STATION-TO-STATION- CONSUMABLES 'N FUCKIN' LIVESTOCK. NOW SHE'S A WELL-ARMED, WELL-STOCKED, MOVIN'-BLOODY-CASTLE, IS WHAT.
YOU GOT SHIT TO TRADE? I GOT AMMO.
I GOT COMMODITIES. I GOT AUDIO NATURE DOCUMENTARIES. YOU WANT CHARDONNAY? I GOT CHARDONNAY. AND CHOOKS 'N BEER 'N BLOODY CIGARS.
AND GASOLINE! BARRELSA THE STUFF. NEVER GO ANYWHERE 'LESS I GOT ENOUGH TO OUTRUN A FUCKIN' CUNT-WITH-A-CROSS.
T.
T...TAKE US WITH YOU. PLEASE.
HEH.
NOW LISTEN. CONSIDER NATURE.
NATURE GENERATES INFINITE VARIETY EVEN WITHIN A SPECIES, PRECISELY TO MAXIMISE THE CHANCE OF ANY ONE GENEPOOL SURVIVING UNFORESEEN CIRCUMSTANCES.
IN THE NORMAL COURSE OF EVENTS YOU'D DESCRIBE A SPECIMEN DEMONSTRATING EXTREME DIFFERENTIATION AS A... AN OUTCAST, AN ABERRATION. OR A CULTURALLY-MALADJUSTED HYGIENICALLY-CHALLENGED SOCIOPATH WITH A HOARDING COMPULSION AND UNRESTRAINED MEGALOMANIA. FOR INSTANCE.
BUT UNDER THE RIGHT CIRCUMSTANCES?
--HE'S THE FUCKIN' ROOTS OF THE BREED.
TRY TO UNDERSTAND, WOULJA? I'M SPECIAL. DESTINED TO SPAWN A RAC OF LITTLE TODDS, UNIQUE ADAPTED TA SURVIVIN' IN CROSSED DESOLATION
GOES WITHOUT SAYIN' I'M KEEN TO PROTECT MY PERSONAL ACCESS TO THE FAMILY-TREES OF TOMORROW, AN DON'T RELISH THE PROSPECT OF SHARIN' WITH Y-CHROMOSOMAL RIVALS.
ALL OF WHICH IS THE SOMEWHAT LABORIOUS WAY OF SAYIN':
SORRY, SPORT. NO FELLERS ALLOWED.

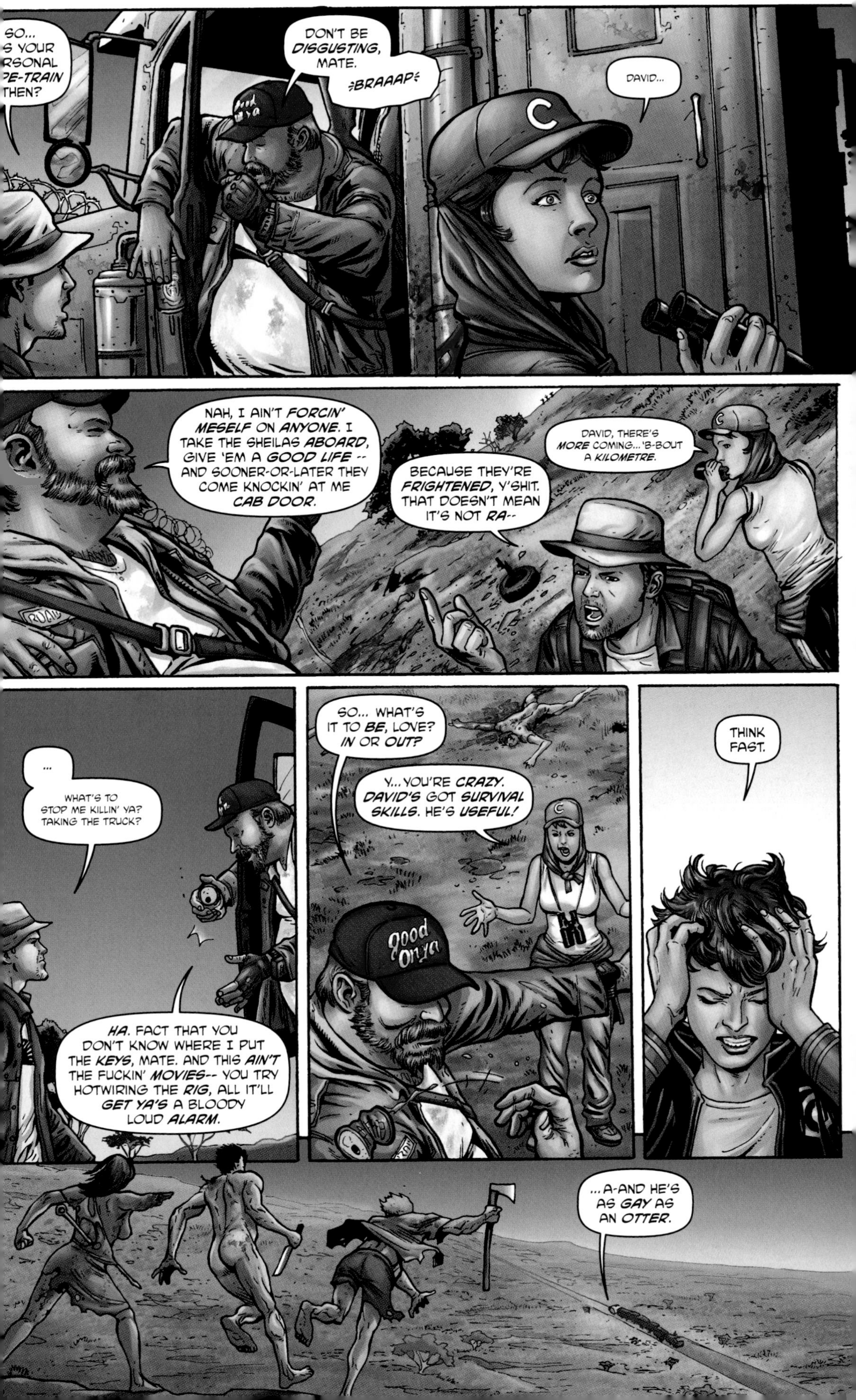
SO...
S YOUR
RSONAL
PE-TRAIN
THEN?
DON'T BE DISGUSTING, MATE.
BRAAAP
DAVID...
NAH, I AIN'T FORCIN' MESELF ON ANYONE. I TAKE THE SHEILAS ABOARD, GIVE 'EM A GOOD LIFE -- AND SOONER-OR-LATER THEY COME KNOCKIN' AT ME CAB DOOR.
BECAUSE THEY'RE FRIGHTENED, Y'SHIT. THAT DOESN'T MEAN IT'S NOT RA--
DAVID, THERE'S MORE COMING...'B-BOUT A KILOMETRE.
...
WHAT'S TO STOP ME KILLIN' YA? TAKING THE TRUCK?
HA. FACT THAT YOU DON'T KNOW WHERE I PUT THE KEYS, MATE. AND THIS AIN'T THE FUCKIN' MOVIES-- YOU TRY HOTWIRING THE RIG, ALL IT'LL GET YA'S A BLOODY LOUD ALARM.
SO... WHAT'S IT TO BE, LOVE? IN OR OUT?
Y...YOU'RE CRAZY. DAVID'S GOT SURVIVAL SKILLS. HE'S USEFUL!
THINK FAST.
...A-AND HE'S AS GAY AS AN OTTER.

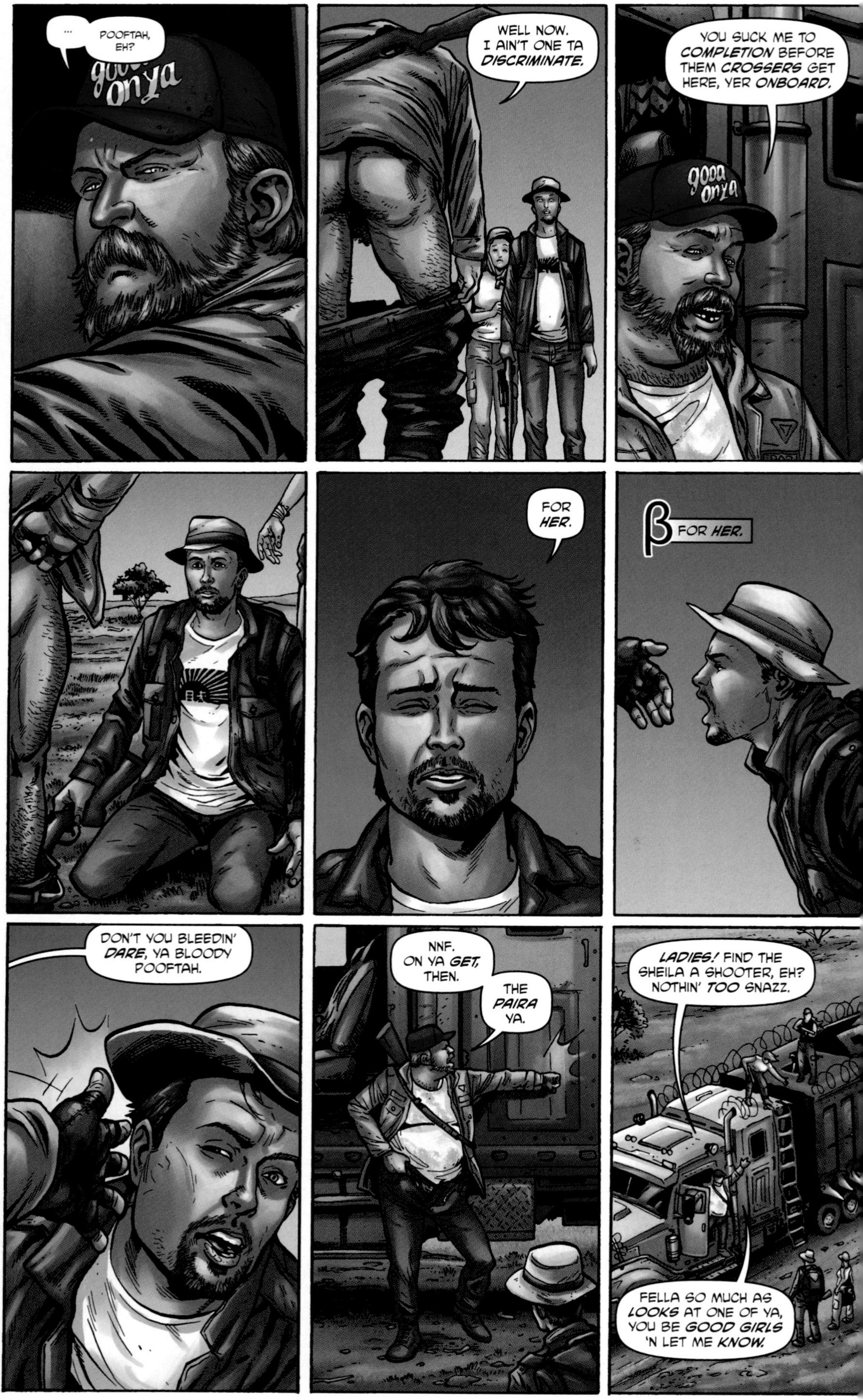
...
POOFTAH, EH?
goodonya
WELL NOW. I AIN'T ONE TA DISCRIMINATE.
YOU SUCK ME TO COMPLETION BEFORE THEM CROSSERS GET HERE, YER ONBOARD.
goodonya
FOR HER.
β FOR HER.
DON'T YOU BLEEDIN' DARE, YA BLOODY POOFTAH.
NNF. ON YA GET, THEN.
THE PAIRA YA.
LADIES! FIND THE SHEILA A SHOOTER, EH? NOTHIN' TOO SNAZZ.
FELLA SO MUCH AS LOOKS AT ONE OF YA, YOU BE GOOD GIRLS 'N LET ME KNOW.

NOW. I AIN'T A FLAMIN' *DUMMY.* I KNEW THEY WAS *TOGETHER*-- IN THE *BIBLICAL* SENSE-- THE SECOND I *SAW* 'EM.

BUT CALL IT A *CALCULATED* RISK ON THE PART OF THE *TOP DOG.*

α THEY KNOW THEY'RE ONTO A GOOD THING, RIGHT? THEY AIN'T GONNA ROCK THE BOAT TOO SOON.

α SO WITHIN A WEEK? WITHIN A WEEK THE PRETEND-POOFTAH'S *EARNIN'* HIS KEEP.

TWO WORDS:

BETA. MALE.

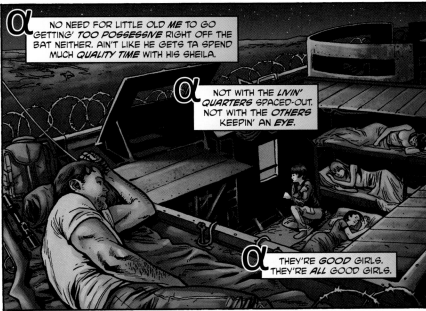

α NO NEED FOR LITTLE OLD *ME* TO GO GETTING' *TOO POSSESSIVE* RIGHT OFF THE BAT NEITHER. AIN'T LIKE HE GETS TA SPEND MUCH *QUALITY TIME* WITH HIS SHEILA.

α NOT WITH THE *LIVIN' QUARTERS* SPACED-OUT. NOT WITH THE *OTHERS* KEEPIN' AN *EYE.*

α THEY'RE *GOOD* GIRLS. THEY'RE *ALL* GOOD GIRLS.

α AND *HER...?* CRIKEY, WHAT A *SCORCHER...*

α WORTH HAVIN' A SUPERFLUOUS SET OF *BALLS ABOARD* FOR. JUST FOR A *MONTH* OR *TWO.* JUST 'TIL HE *FUCKS-UP* AND *EARNS* THE *KICKIN'* HE'S DUE.

α JUST 'TIL *SHE* COMES *ROUND.*

THEY ALWAYS *DO.*

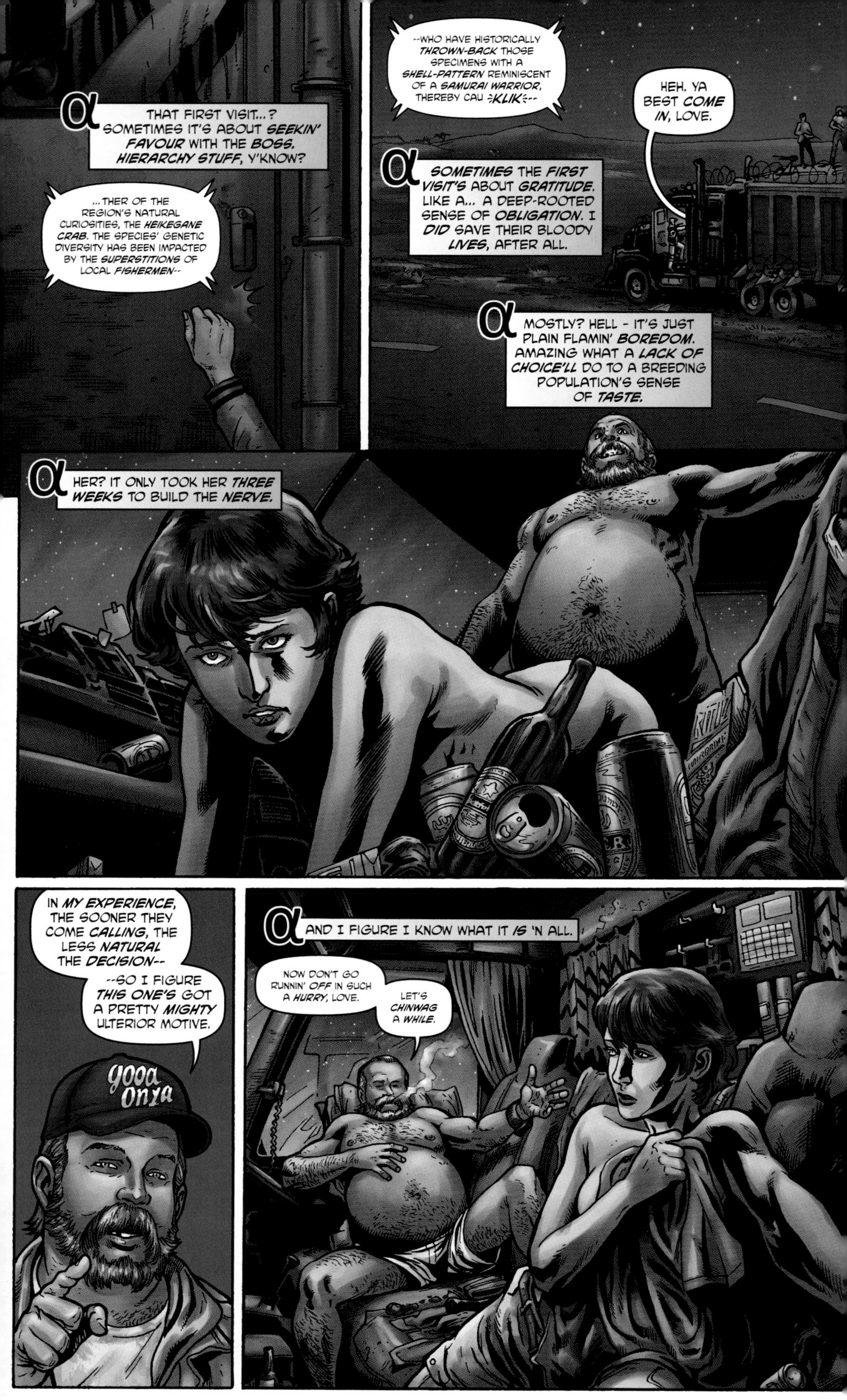
THAT FIRST VISIT...? SOMETIMES IT'S ABOUT SEEKIN' FAVOUR WITH THE BOSS. HIERARCHY STUFF, Y'KNOW?
...THER OF THE REGION'S NATURAL CURIOSITIES, THE HEIKEGANE CRAB. THE SPECIES' GENETIC DIVERSITY HAS BEEN IMPACTED BY THE SUPERSTITIONS OF LOCAL FISHERMEN--
--WHO HAVE HISTORICALLY THROWN-BACK THOSE SPECIMENS WITH A SHELL-PATTERN REMINISCENT OF A SAMURAI WARRIOR, THEREBY CAU -KLIK--
HEH. YA BEST COME IN, LOVE.
SOMETIMES THE FIRST VISIT'S ABOUT GRATITUDE. LIKE A... A DEEP-ROOTED SENSE OF OBLIGATION. I DID SAVE THEIR BLOODY LIVES, AFTER ALL.
MOSTLY? HELL - IT'S JUST PLAIN FLAMIN' BOREDOM. AMAZING WHAT A LACK OF CHOICE'LL DO TO A BREEDING POPULATION'S SENSE OF TASTE.
HER? IT ONLY TOOK HER THREE WEEKS TO BUILD THE NERVE.
IN MY EXPERIENCE, THE SOONER THEY COME CALLING, THE LESS NATURAL THE DECISION--
--SO I FIGURE THIS ONE'S GOT A PRETTY MIGHTY ULTERIOR MOTIVE.
yooa onya
AND I FIGURE I KNOW WHAT IT IS 'N ALL.
NOW DON'T GO RUNNIN' OFF IN SUCH A HURRY, LOVE.
LET'S CHINWAG A WHILE.

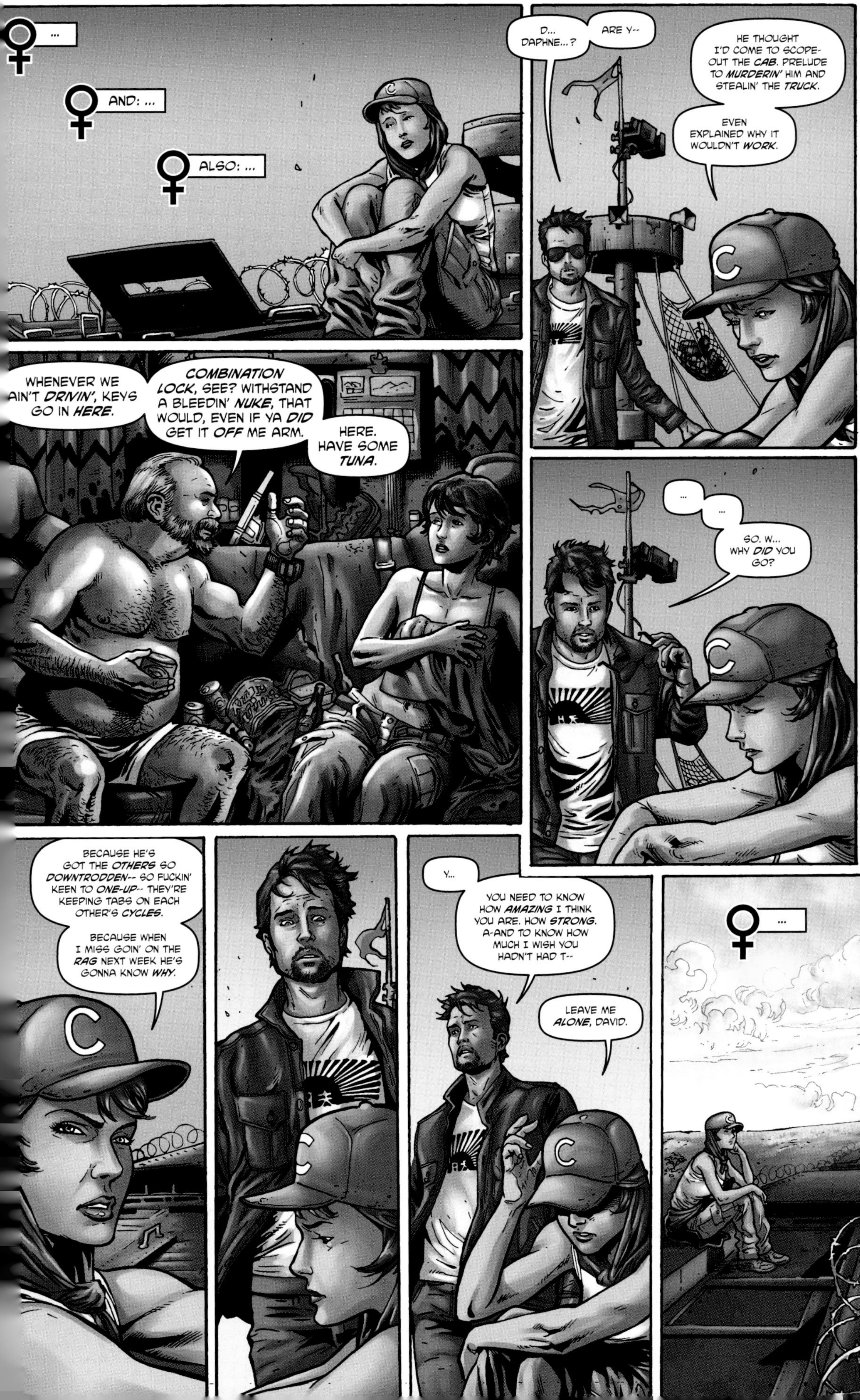
...
AND: ...
ALSO: ...
D... DAPHNE...?
ARE Y--
HE THOUGHT I'D COME TO SCOPE-OUT THE CAB. PRELUDE TO MURDERIN' HIM AND STEALIN' THE TRUCK.
EVEN EXPLAINED WHY IT WOULDN'T WORK.
WHENEVER WE AIN'T DRIVIN', KEYS GO IN HERE.
COMBINATION LOCK, SEE? WITHSTAND A BLEEDIN' NUKE, THAT WOULD, EVEN IF YA DID GET IT OFF ME ARM.
HERE. HAVE SOME TUNA.
...
...
SO. W... WHY DID YOU GO?
BECAUSE HE'S GOT THE OTHERS SO DOWNTRODDEN-- SO FUCKIN' KEEN TO ONE-UP-- THEY'RE KEEPING TABS ON EACH OTHER'S CYCLES.
BECAUSE WHEN I MISS GOIN' ON THE RAG NEXT WEEK HE'S GONNA KNOW WHY.
Y...
YOU NEED TO KNOW HOW AMAZING I THINK YOU ARE. HOW STRONG. A-AND TO KNOW HOW MUCH I WISH YOU HADN'T HAD T--
LEAVE ME ALONE, DAVID.
...

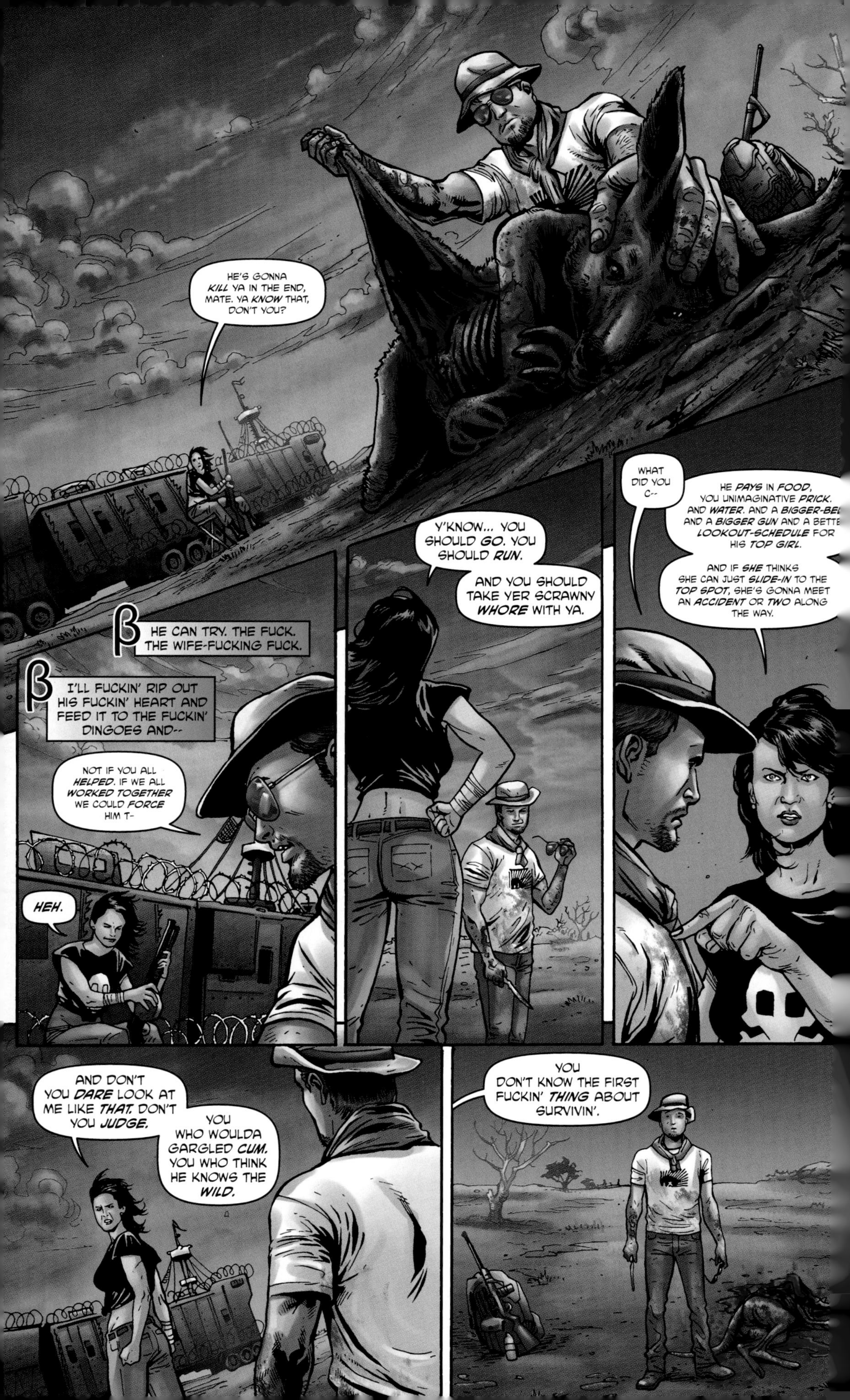
HE'S GONNA KILL YA IN THE END, MATE. YA KNOW THAT, DON'T YOU?
HE CAN TRY. THE FUCK. THE WIFE-FUCKING FUCK.
I'LL FUCKIN' RIP OUT HIS FUCKIN' HEART AND FEED IT TO THE FUCKIN' DINGOES AND--
NOT IF YOU ALL HELPED. IF WE ALL WORKED TOGETHER WE COULD FORCE HIM T-
HEH.
Y'KNOW... YOU SHOULD GO. YOU SHOULD RUN.
AND YOU SHOULD TAKE YER SCRAWNY WHORE WITH YA.
WHAT DID YOU C--
HE PAYS IN FOOD, YOU UNIMAGINATIVE PRICK. AND WATER. AND A BIGGER-BE AND A BIGGER GUN AND A BETTE LOOKOUT-SCHEDULE FOR HIS TOP GIRL.
AND IF SHE THINKS SHE CAN JUST SLIDE-IN TO THE TOP SPOT, SHE'S GONNA MEET AN ACCIDENT OR TWO ALONG THE WAY.
AND DON'T YOU DARE LOOK AT ME LIKE THAT. DON'T YOU JUDGE.
YOU WHO WOULDA GARGLED CUM. YOU WHO THINK HE KNOWS THE WILD.
YOU DON'T KNOW THE FIRST FUCKIN' THING ABOUT SURVIVIN'.

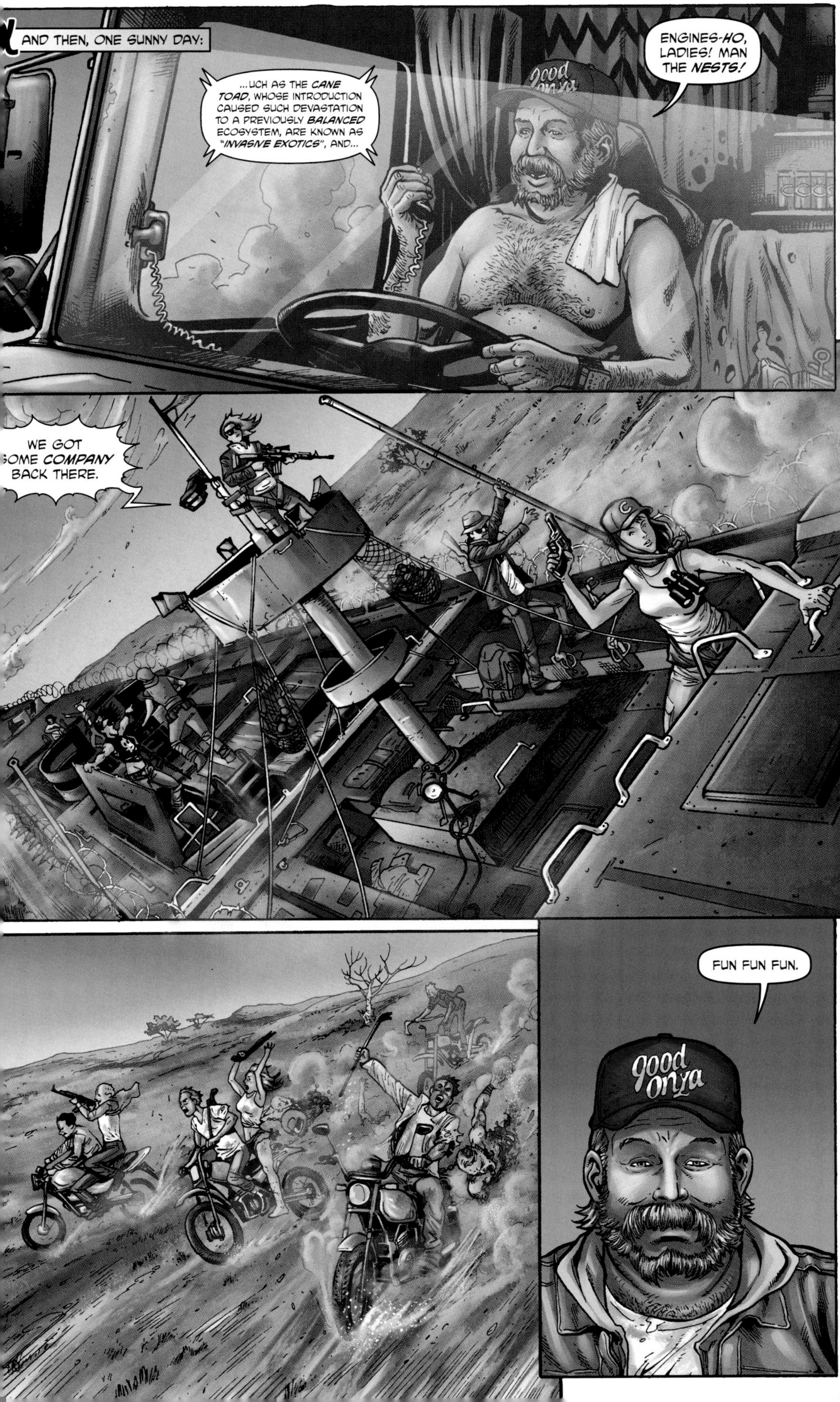
AND THEN, ONE SUNNY DAY:
...UCH AS THE CANE TOAD, WHOSE INTRODUCTION CAUSED SUCH DEVASTATION TO A PREVIOUSLY BALANCED ECOSYSTEM, ARE KNOWN AS "INVASIVE EXOTICS", AND...
ENGINES-HO, LADIES! MAN THE NESTS!
good onya
WE GOT SOME COMPANY BACK THERE.
FUN FUN FUN.
good onya

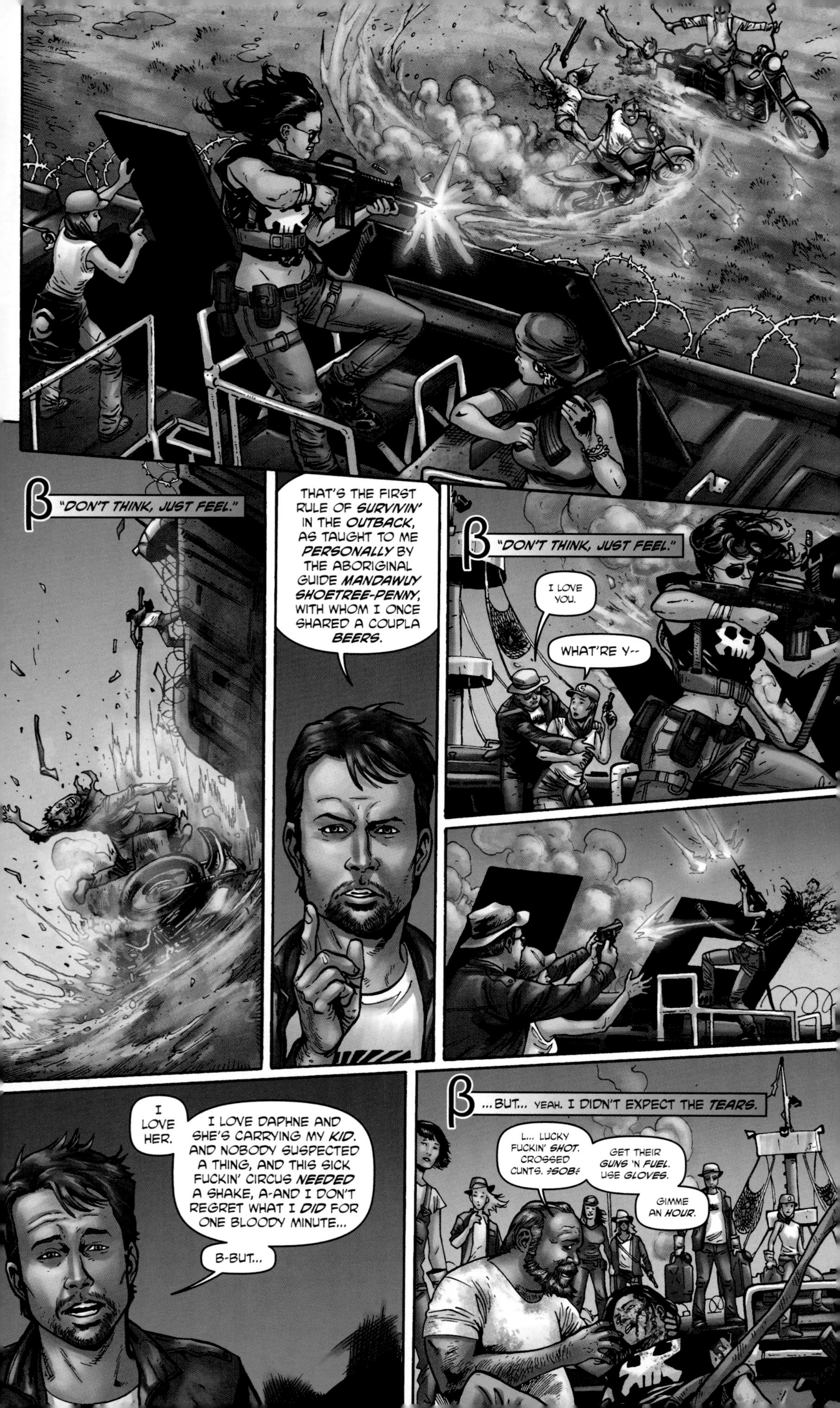
β "DON'T THINK, JUST FEEL."
THAT'S THE FIRST RULE OF SURVIVIN' IN THE OUTBACK, AS TAUGHT TO ME PERSONALLY BY THE ABORIGINAL GUIDE MANDAWUY SHOETREE-PENNY, WITH WHOM I ONCE SHARED A COUPLA BEERS.
β "DON'T THINK, JUST FEEL."
I LOVE YOU.
WHAT'RE Y--
I LOVE HER.
I LOVE DAPHNE AND SHE'S CARRYING MY KID. AND NOBODY SUSPECTED A THING, AND THIS SICK FUCKIN' CIRCUS NEEDED A SHAKE, A-AND I DON'T REGRET WHAT I DID FOR ONE BLOODY MINUTE...
B-BUT...
β ...BUT... YEAH. I DIDN'T EXPECT THE TEARS.
L... LUCKY FUCKIN' SHOT. CROSSED CUNTS. ≠SOB≠
GET THEIR GUNS 'N FUEL. USE GLOVES.
GIMME AN HOUR.

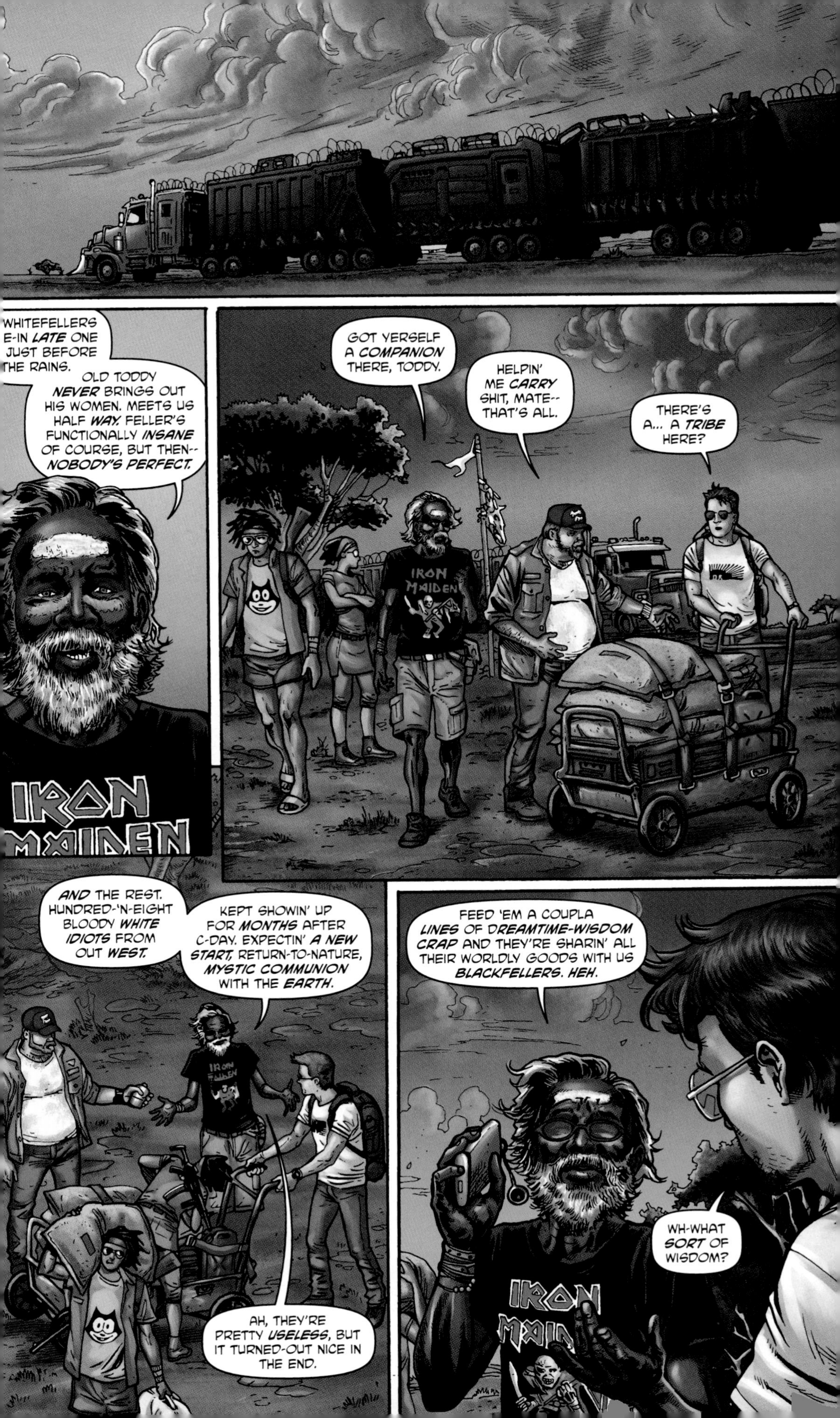
WHITEFELLERS E-IN LATE ONE JUST BEFORE THE RAINS.
OLD TODDY NEVER BRINGS OUT HIS WOMEN. MEETS US HALF WAY. FELLER'S FUNCTIONALLY INSANE OF COURSE, BUT THEN-- NOBODY'S PERFECT.
IRON MAIDEN
GOT YERSELF A COMPANION THERE, TODDY.
HELPIN' ME CARRY SHIT, MATE-- THAT'S ALL.
THERE'S A... A TRIBE HERE?
IRON MAIDEN
AND THE REST. HUNDRED-'N-EIGHT BLOODY WHITE IDIOTS FROM OUT WEST.
KEPT SHOWIN' UP FOR MONTHS AFTER C-DAY. EXPECTIN' A NEW START, RETURN-TO-NATURE, MYSTIC COMMUNION WITH THE EARTH.
AH, THEY'RE PRETTY USELESS, BUT IT TURNED-OUT NICE IN THE END.
FEED 'EM A COUPLA LINES OF DREAMTIME-WISDOM CRAP AND THEY'RE SHARIN' ALL THEIR WORLDLY GOODS WITH US BLACKFELLERS. HEH.
WH-WHAT SORT OF WISDOM?

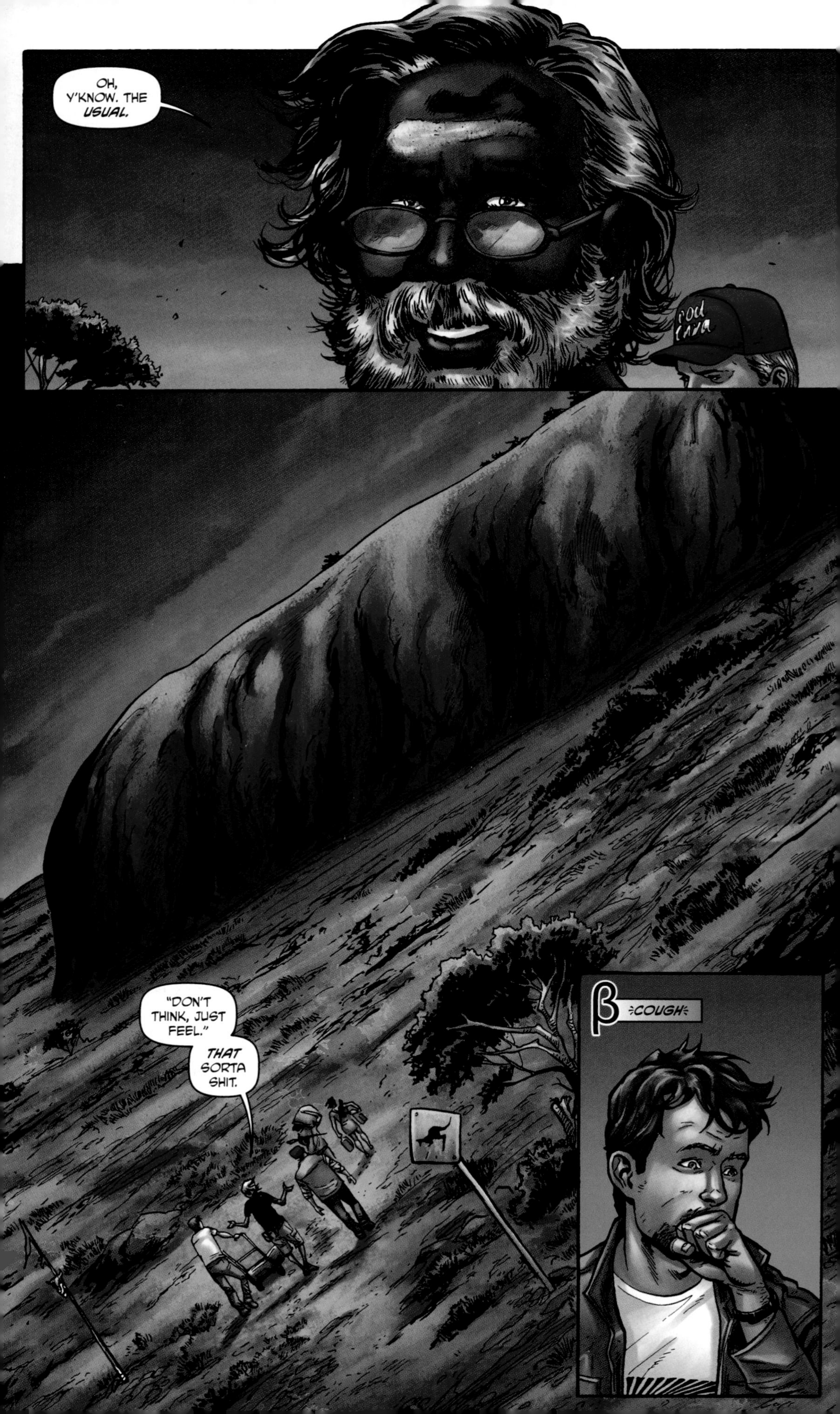
OH, Y'KNOW. THE USUAL.
"DON'T THINK, JUST FEEL."
THAT SORTA SHIT.
COUGH

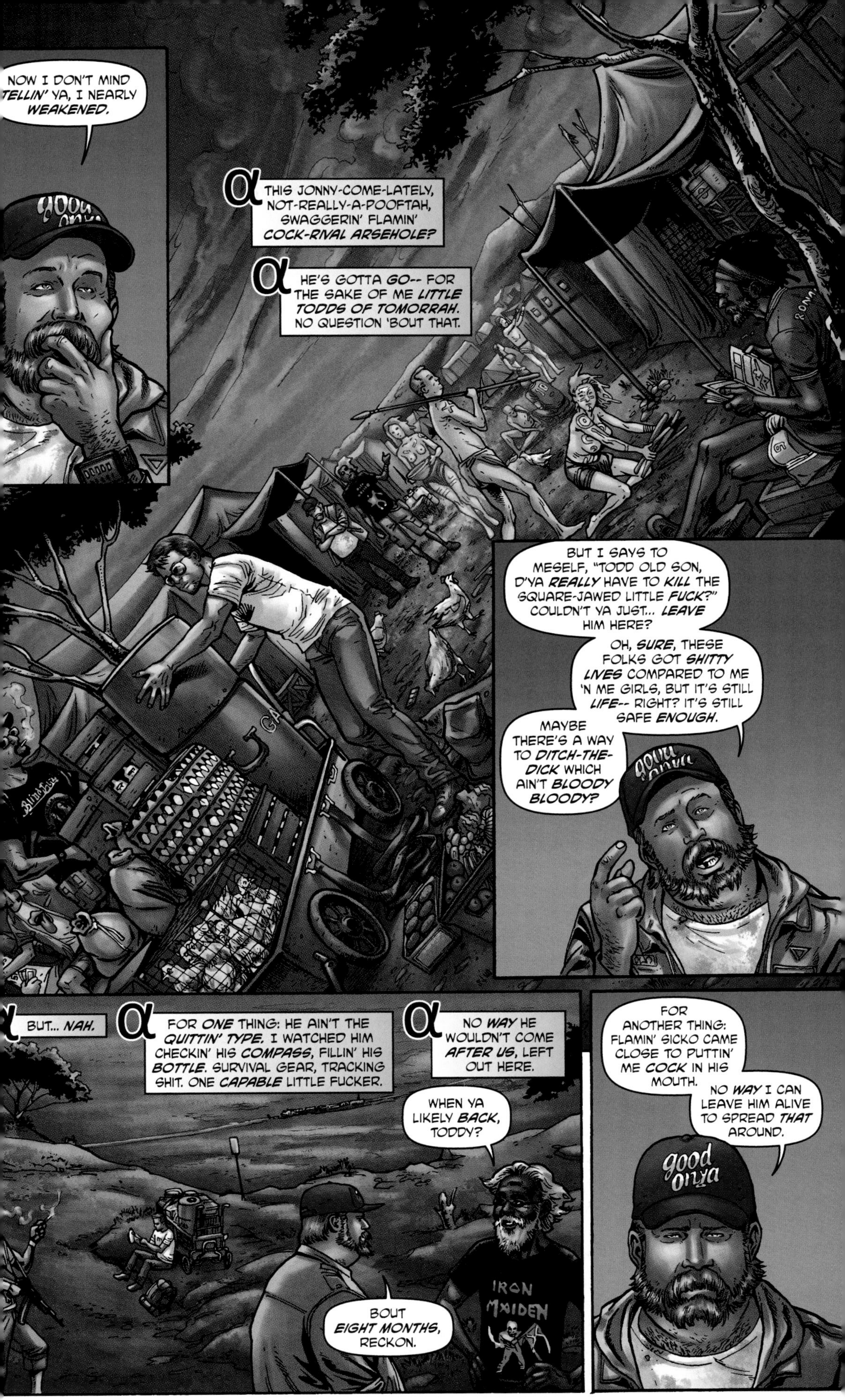
NOW I DON'T MIND TELLIN' YA, I NEARLY WEAKENED.
THIS JONNY-COME-LATELY, NOT-REALLY-A-POOFTAH, SWAGGERIN' FLAMIN' COCK-RIVAL ARSEHOLE?
HE'S GOTTA GO-- FOR THE SAKE OF ME LITTLE TODDS OF TOMORRAH. NO QUESTION 'BOUT THAT.
BUT I SAYS TO MESELF, "TODD OLD SON, D'YA REALLY HAVE TO KILL THE SQUARE-JAWED LITTLE FUCK?" COULDN'T YA JUST... LEAVE HIM HERE?
OH, SURE, THESE FOLKS GOT SHITTY LIVES COMPARED TO ME 'N ME GIRLS, BUT IT'S STILL LIFE-- RIGHT? IT'S STILL SAFE ENOUGH.
MAYBE THERE'S A WAY TO DITCH-THE-DICK WHICH AIN'T BLOODY BLOODY?
good onya
BUT... NAH.
FOR ONE THING: HE AIN'T THE QUITTIN' TYPE. I WATCHED HIM CHECKIN' HIS COMPASS, FILLIN' HIS BOTTLE. SURVIVAL GEAR, TRACKING SHIT. ONE CAPABLE LITTLE FUCKER.
NO WAY HE WOULDN'T COME AFTER US, LEFT OUT HERE.
WHEN YA LIKELY BACK, TODDY?
BOUT EIGHT MONTHS, RECKON.
IRON MAIDEN
FOR ANOTHER THING: FLAMIN' SICKO CAME CLOSE TO PUTTIN' ME COCK IN HIS MOUTH.
NO WAY I CAN LEAVE HIM ALIVE TO SPREAD THAT AROUND.
good onya

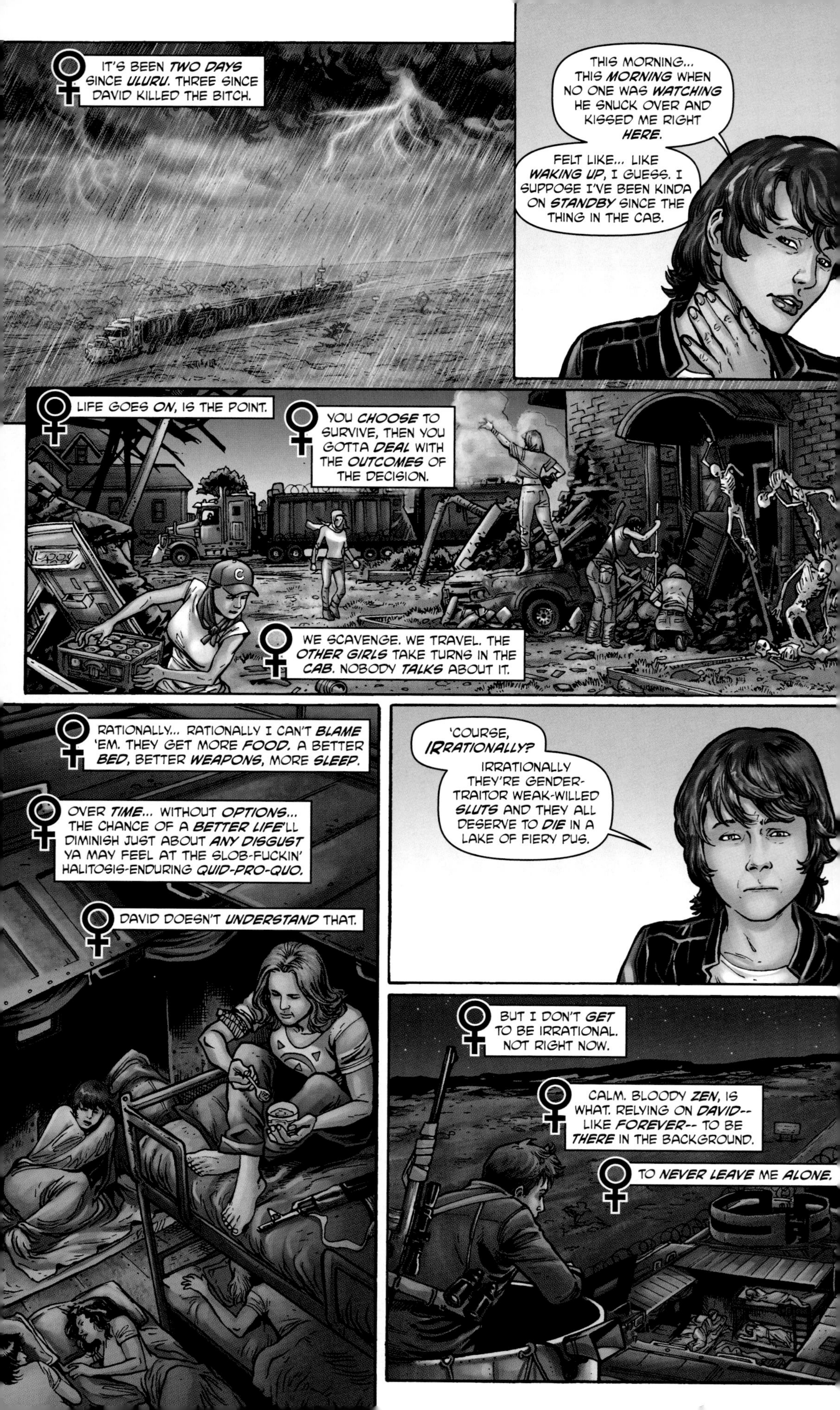
IT'S BEEN TWO DAYS SINCE ULURU. THREE SINCE DAVID KILLED THE BITCH.
THIS MORNING... THIS MORNING WHEN NO ONE WAS WATCHING HE SNUCK OVER AND KISSED ME RIGHT HERE.
FELT LIKE... LIKE WAKING UP, I GUESS. I SUPPOSE I'VE BEEN KINDA ON STANDBY SINCE THE THING IN THE CAB.
LIFE GOES ON, IS THE POINT.
YOU CHOOSE TO SURVIVE, THEN YOU GOTTA DEAL WITH THE OUTCOMES OF THE DECISION.
WE SCAVENGE. WE TRAVEL. THE OTHER GIRLS TAKE TURNS IN THE CAB. NOBODY TALKS ABOUT IT.
RATIONALLY... RATIONALLY I CAN'T BLAME 'EM. THEY GET MORE FOOD. A BETTER BED, BETTER WEAPONS, MORE SLEEP.
OVER TIME... WITHOUT OPTIONS... THE CHANCE OF A BETTER LIFE'LL DIMINISH JUST ABOUT ANY DISGUST YA MAY FEEL AT THE SLOB-FUCKIN' HALITOSIS-ENDURING QUID-PRO-QUO.
DAVID DOESN'T UNDERSTAND THAT.
'COURSE, IRRATIONALLY?
IRRATIONALLY THEY'RE GENDER-TRAITOR WEAK-WILLED SLUTS AND THEY ALL DESERVE TO DIE IN A LAKE OF FIERY PUS.
BUT I DON'T GET TO BE IRRATIONAL. NOT RIGHT NOW.
CALM. BLOODY ZEN, IS WHAT. RELYING ON DAVID-- LIKE FOREVER-- TO BE THERE IN THE BACKGROUND.
TO NEVER LEAVE ME ALONE.

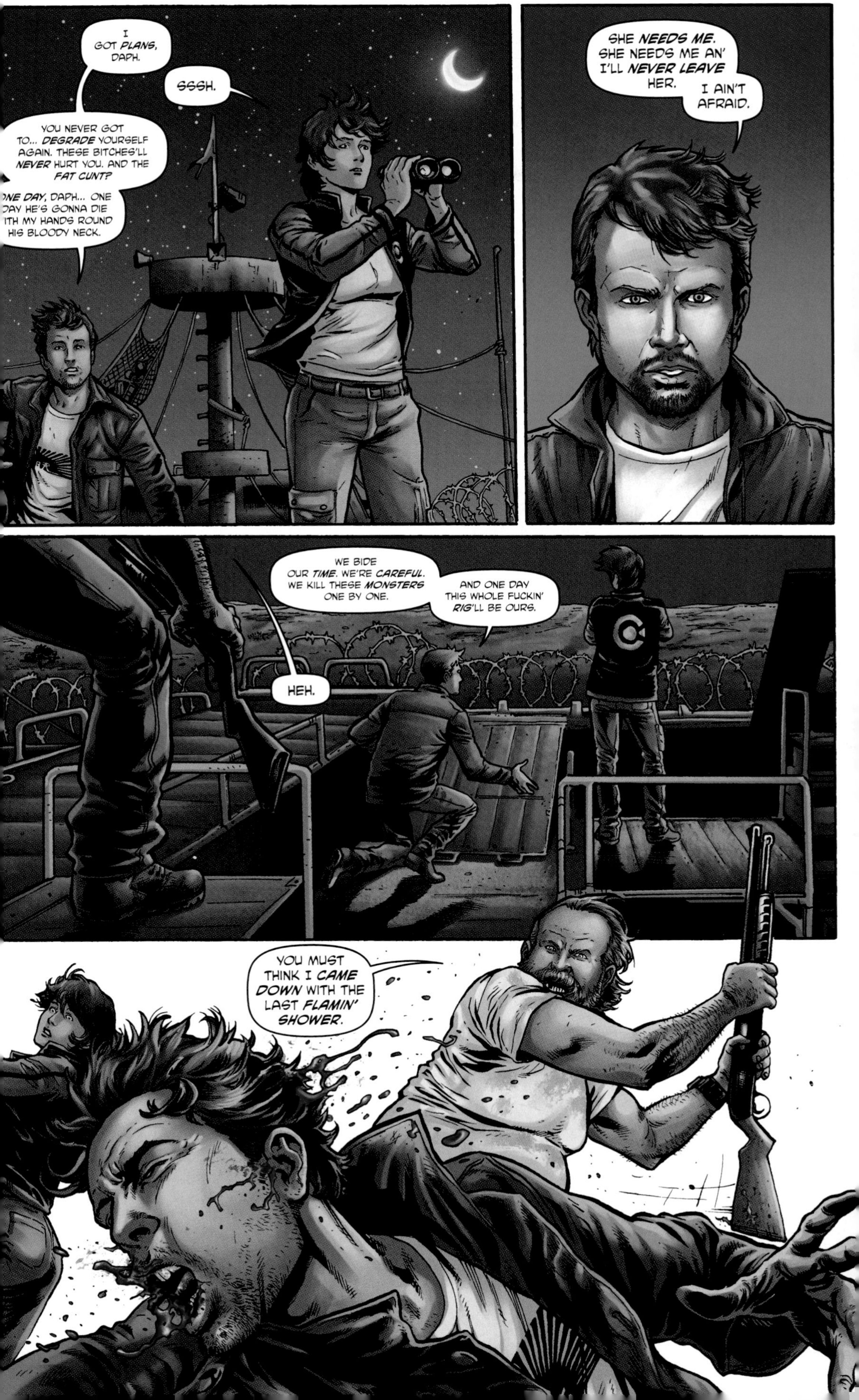
I GOT PLANS, DAPH.
SSSH.
YOU NEVER GOT TO... DEGRADE YOURSELF AGAIN. THESE BITCHES'LL NEVER HURT YOU. AND THE FAT CUNT?
ONE DAY, DAPH... ONE DAY HE'S GONNA DIE WITH MY HANDS ROUND HIS BLOODY NECK.
SHE NEEDS ME. SHE NEEDS ME AN' I'LL NEVER LEAVE HER.
I AIN'T AFRAID.
WE BIDE OUR TIME. WE'RE CAREFUL. WE KILL THESE MONSTERS ONE BY ONE.
AND ONE DAY THIS WHOLE FUCKIN' RIG'LL BE OURS.
HEH.
YOU MUST THINK I CAME DOWN WITH THE LAST FLAMIN' SHOWER.

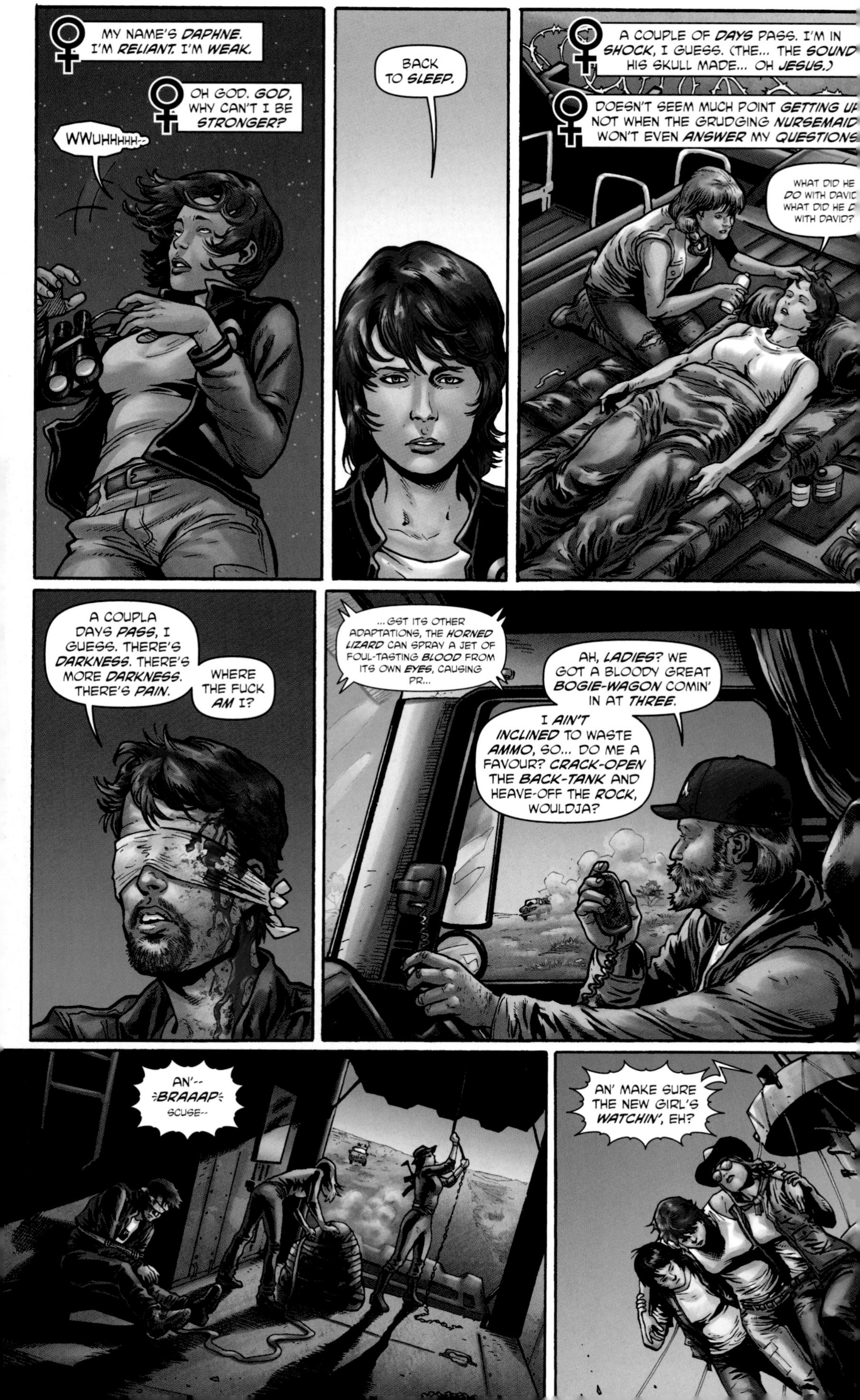

MY NAME'S *DAPHNE*. I'M *RELIANT*. I'M *WEAK*.
OH GOD. *GOD*, WHY CAN'T I BE *STRONGER?*
WWUHHHHH--
BACK TO *SLEEP*.
A COUPLE OF *DAYS* PASS. I'M IN *SHOCK*, I GUESS. (THE... THE *SOUND* HIS SKULL MADE... OH *JESUS*.)
DOESN'T SEEM MUCH POINT *GETTING U* NOT WHEN THE GRUDGING *NURSEMAID* WON'T EVEN *ANSWER* MY *QUESTIONS*
WHAT DID HE *DO* WITH DAVID WHAT DID HE *D* WITH DAVID?
A COUPLA DAYS *PASS*, I GUESS. THERE'S *DARKNESS*. THERE'S MORE *DARKNESS*. THERE'S *PAIN*.
WHERE THE FUCK *AM* I?
...GST ITS OTHER ADAPTATIONS, THE *HORNED LIZARD* CAN SPRAY A JET OF FOUL-TASTING *BLOOD* FROM ITS OWN *EYES*, CAUSING PR...
AH, *LADIES?* WE GOT A BLOODY GREAT *BOGIE-WAGON* COMIN' IN AT *THREE*.
I *AIN'T INCLINED* TO WASTE *AMMO*, SO... DO ME A FAVOUR? *CRACK-OPEN* THE *BACK-TANK* AND HEAVE-OFF THE *ROCK*, WOULDJA?
AN'--
BRAAAP
SCUSE--
AN' MAKE SURE THE NEW GIRL'S *WATCHIN'*, EH?

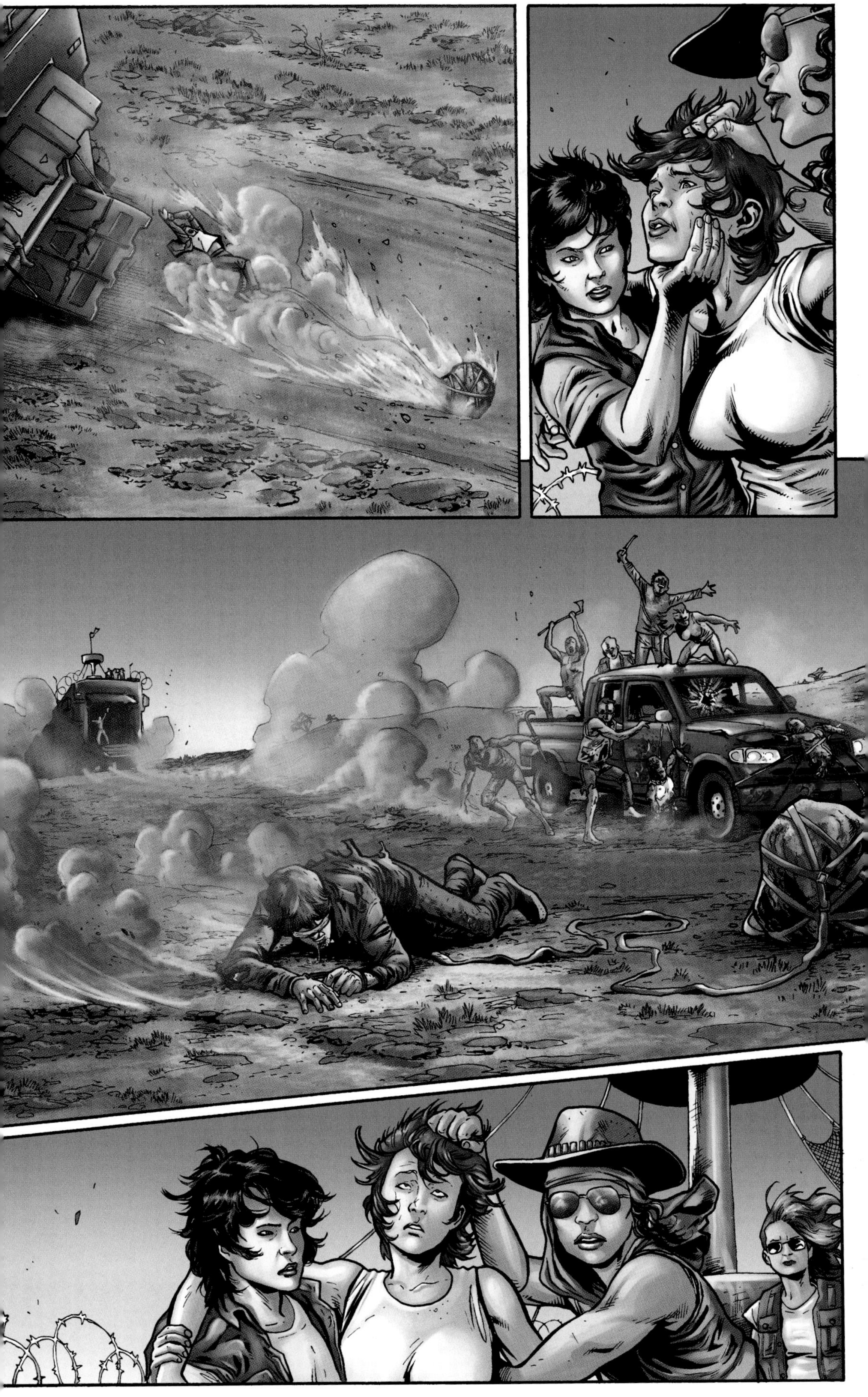

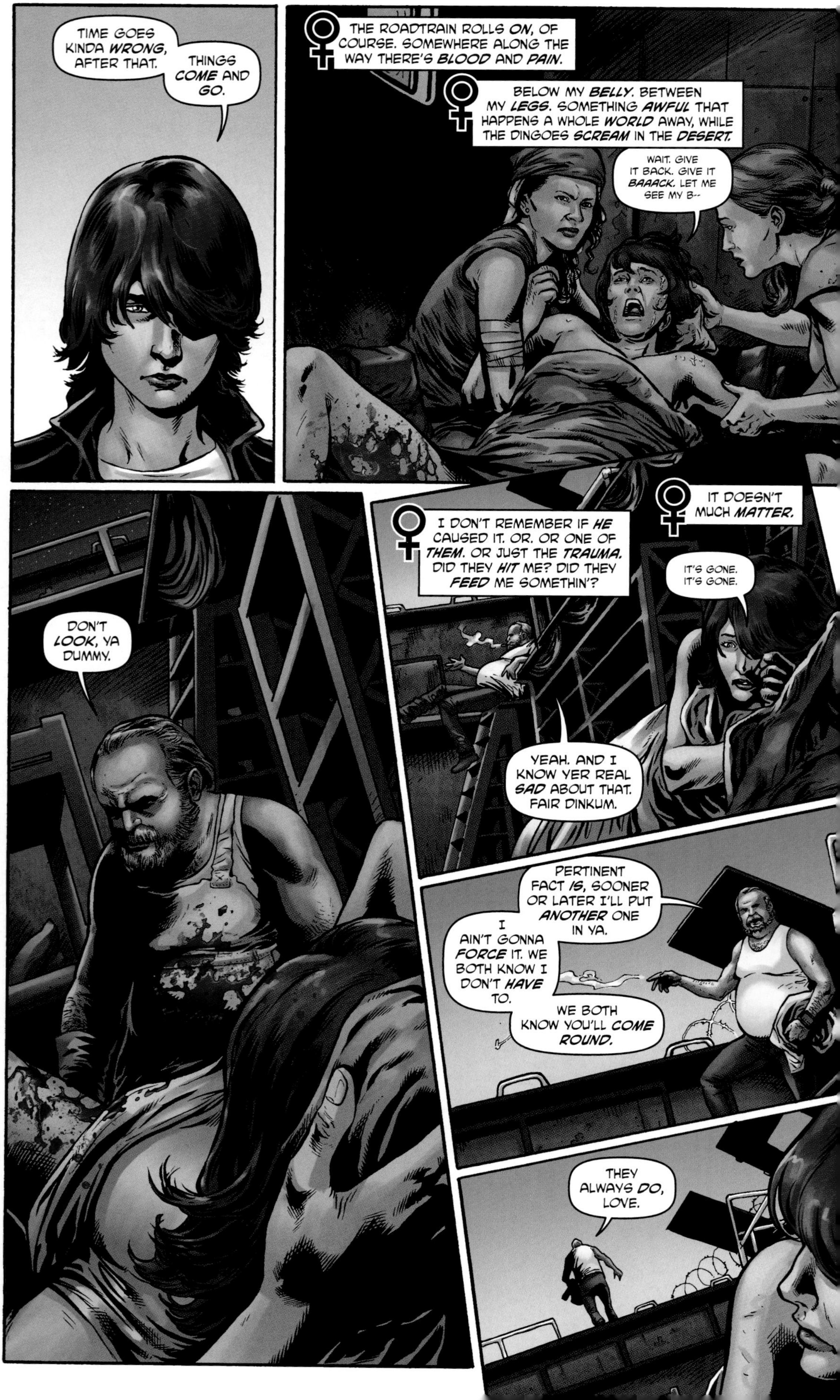
TIME GOES KINDA WRONG, AFTER THAT.
THINGS COME AND GO.
THE ROADTRAIN ROLLS ON, OF COURSE. SOMEWHERE ALONG THE WAY THERE'S BLOOD AND PAIN.
BELOW MY BELLY. BETWEEN MY LEGS. SOMETHING AWFUL THAT HAPPENS A WHOLE WORLD AWAY, WHILE THE DINGOES SCREAM IN THE DESERT.
WAIT. GIVE IT BACK. GIVE IT BAAACK. LET ME SEE MY B--
DON'T LOOK, YA DUMMY.
I DON'T REMEMBER IF HE CAUSED IT. OR. OR ONE OF THEM. OR JUST THE TRAUMA. DID THEY HIT ME? DID THEY FEED ME SOMETHIN'?
IT DOESN'T MUCH MATTER.
IT'S GONE. IT'S GONE.
YEAH. AND I KNOW YER REAL SAD ABOUT THAT. FAIR DINKUM.
PERTINENT FACT IS, SOONER OR LATER I'LL PUT ANOTHER ONE IN YA.
I AIN'T GONNA FORCE IT. WE BOTH KNOW I DON'T HAVE TO.
WE BOTH KNOW YOU'LL COME ROUND.
THEY ALWAYS DO, LOVE.

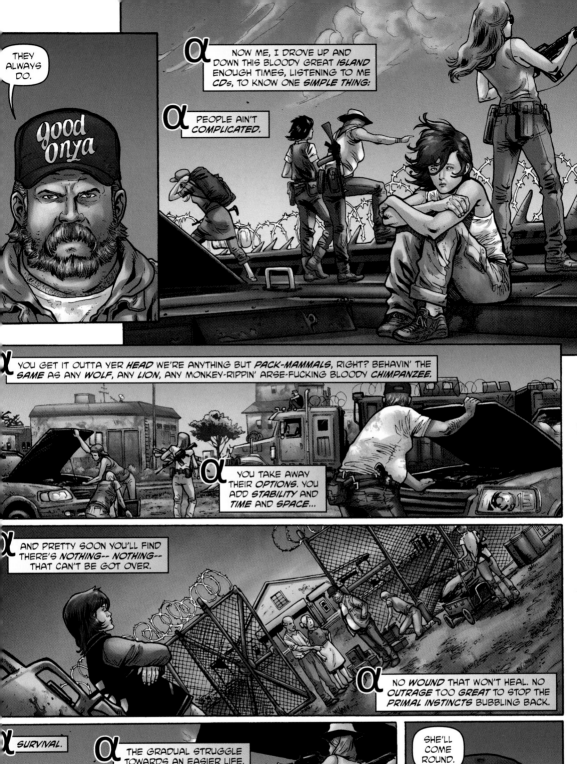

THEY ALWAYS DO.

good onya

α NOW ME, I DROVE UP AND DOWN THIS BLOODY GREAT *ISLAND* ENOUGH TIMES, LISTENING TO ME CDs, TO KNOW ONE *SIMPLE THING:*

α PEOPLE AIN'T *COMPLICATED.*

α YOU GET IT OUTTA YER *HEAD* WE'RE ANYTHING BUT *PACK-MAMMALS*, RIGHT? BEHAVIN' THE *SAME* AS ANY *WOLF*, ANY *LION*, ANY MONKEY-RIPPIN' ARSE-FUCKING BLOODY *CHIMPANZEE.*

α YOU TAKE AWAY THEIR *OPTIONS.* YOU ADD *STABILITY* AND *TIME* AND *SPACE...*

α AND PRETTY SOON YOU'LL FIND THERE'S *NOTHING-- NOTHING--* THAT CAN'T BE GOT OVER.

α NO *WOUND* THAT WON'T HEAL. NO *OUTRAGE* TOO *GREAT* TO STOP THE *PRIMAL INSTINCTS* BUBBLING BACK.

α SURVIVAL.

α THE GRADUAL STRUGGLE TOWARDS AN EASIER LIFE.

α COMPANIONSHIP. ACCEPTANCE. A HIGHER SPOT IN THE *HIERARCHY.*

SHE'LL COME ROUND.

good onya

... YOU OKAY, HUN?

LOOK, I... I KNOW YOU'RE *HURTIN'*. YOU BEEN THROUGH A *LOT*.

BUT IT GETS *EASIER*, OKAY? YOU JUST GOT TO LIVE *DAY TO DAY*. YC JUST GOT TO FOCUS *SMALL*.

YOU WANT A PIECE OF *CHOCOLATE?*

SHE'S BEING *NICE* TO ME. NO OTHER WAY OF *PUTTING IT*. SHE'S *REACHING OUT*, FORMING *BONDS*.

A *SHARED MOMENT*. A LITTLE REMINDER OF *HUMANITY*. A LITTLE *GLIMPSE* OF A BEARABLE FUTURE.

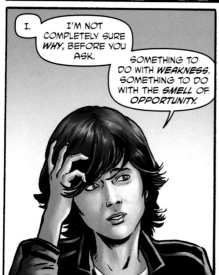

I. I'M NOT COMPLETELY SURE *WHY*, BEFORE YOU ASK.

SOMETHING TO DO WITH *WEAKNESS*. SOMETHING TO DO WITH THE *SMELL* OF *OPPORTUNITY*.

SOMETHING TO DO WITH *WAKING UP*.

SWAP.

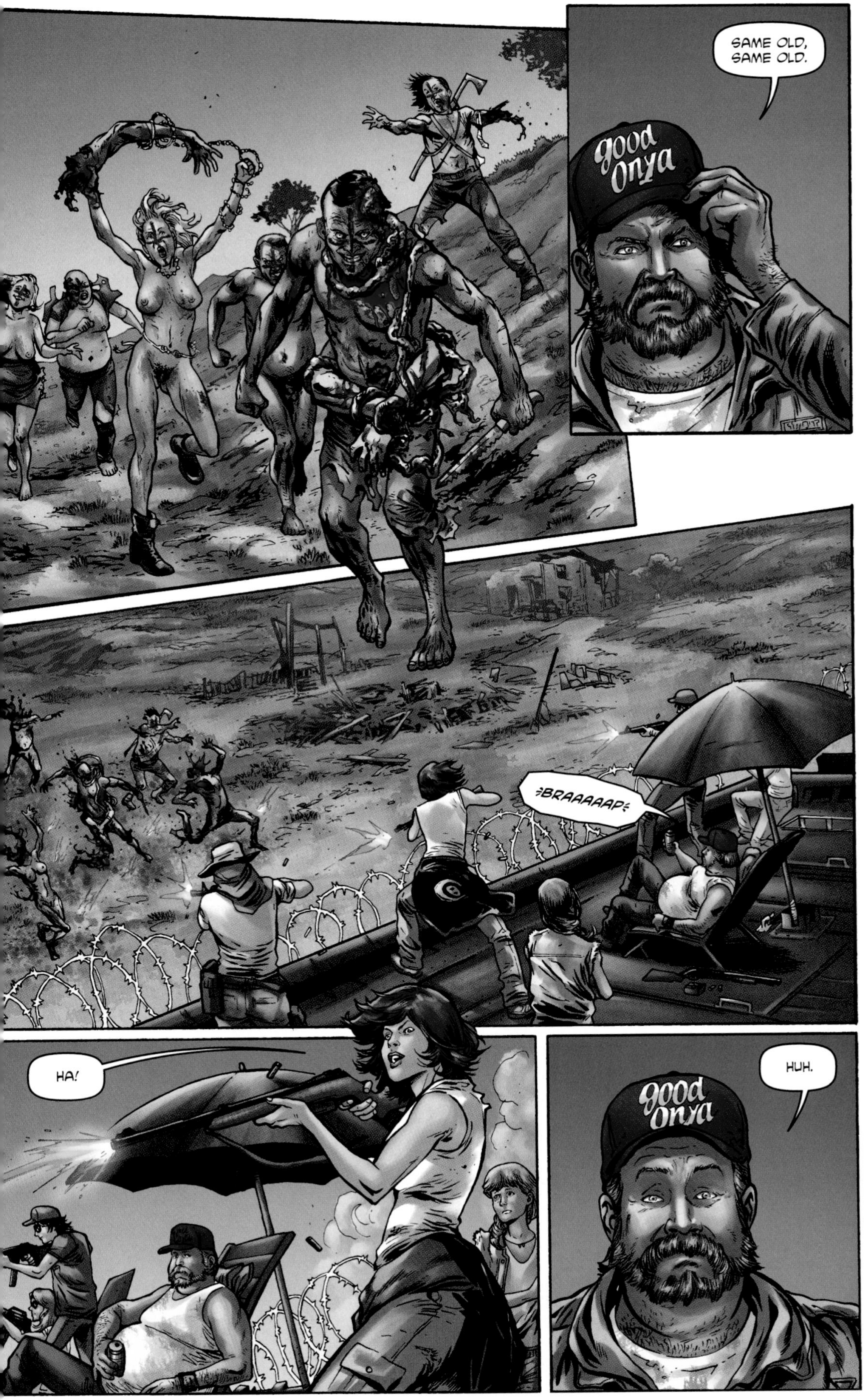
SAME OLD, SAME OLD.
good onya
BRAAAAAP
HA!
HUH.
good onya

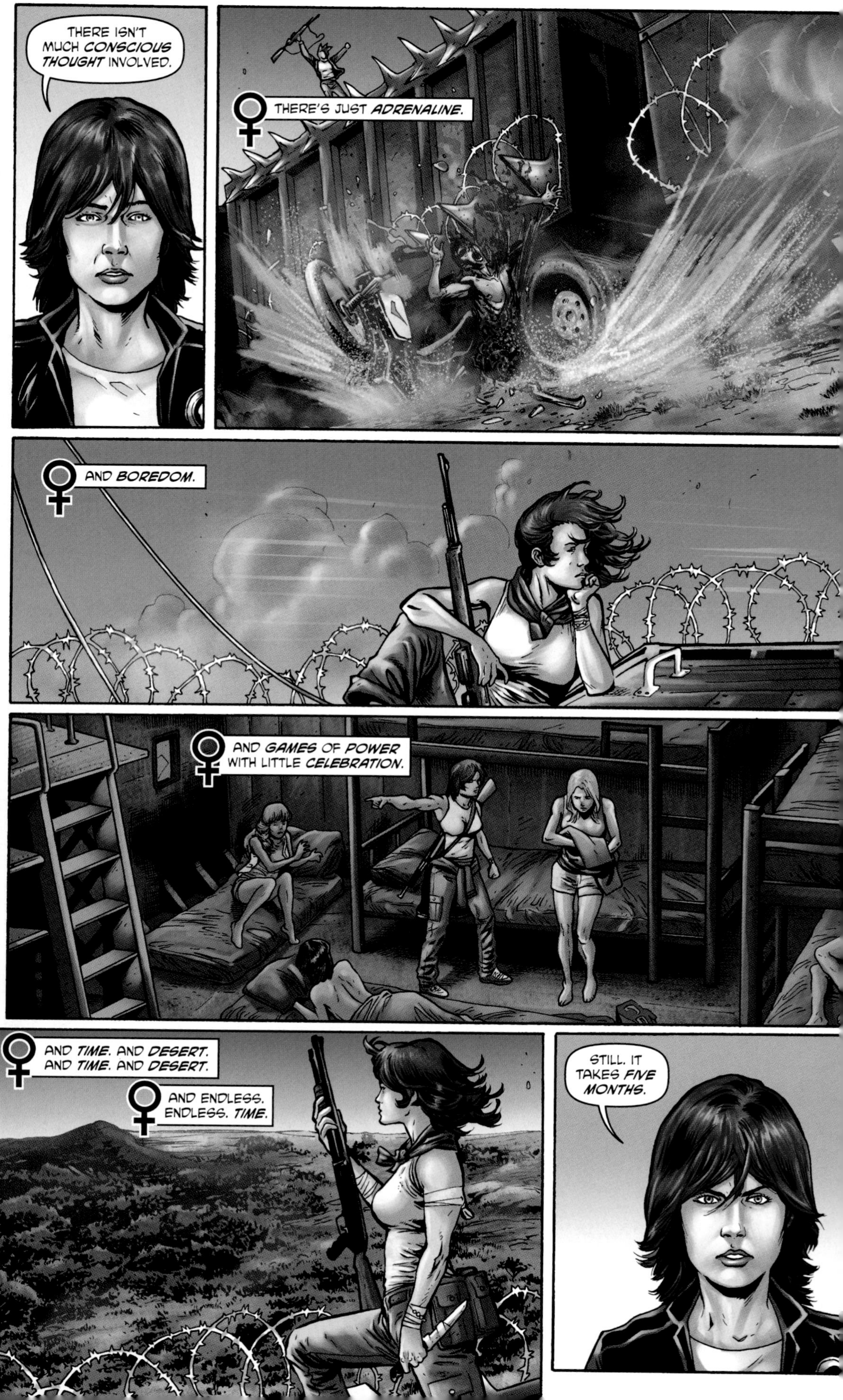
THERE ISN'T MUCH CONSCIOUS THOUGHT INVOLVED.
THERE'S JUST ADRENALINE.
AND BOREDOM.
AND GAMES OF POWER WITH LITTLE CELEBRATION.
AND TIME. AND DESERT. AND TIME. AND DESERT.
AND ENDLESS. ENDLESS. TIME.
STILL. IT TAKES FIVE MONTHS.

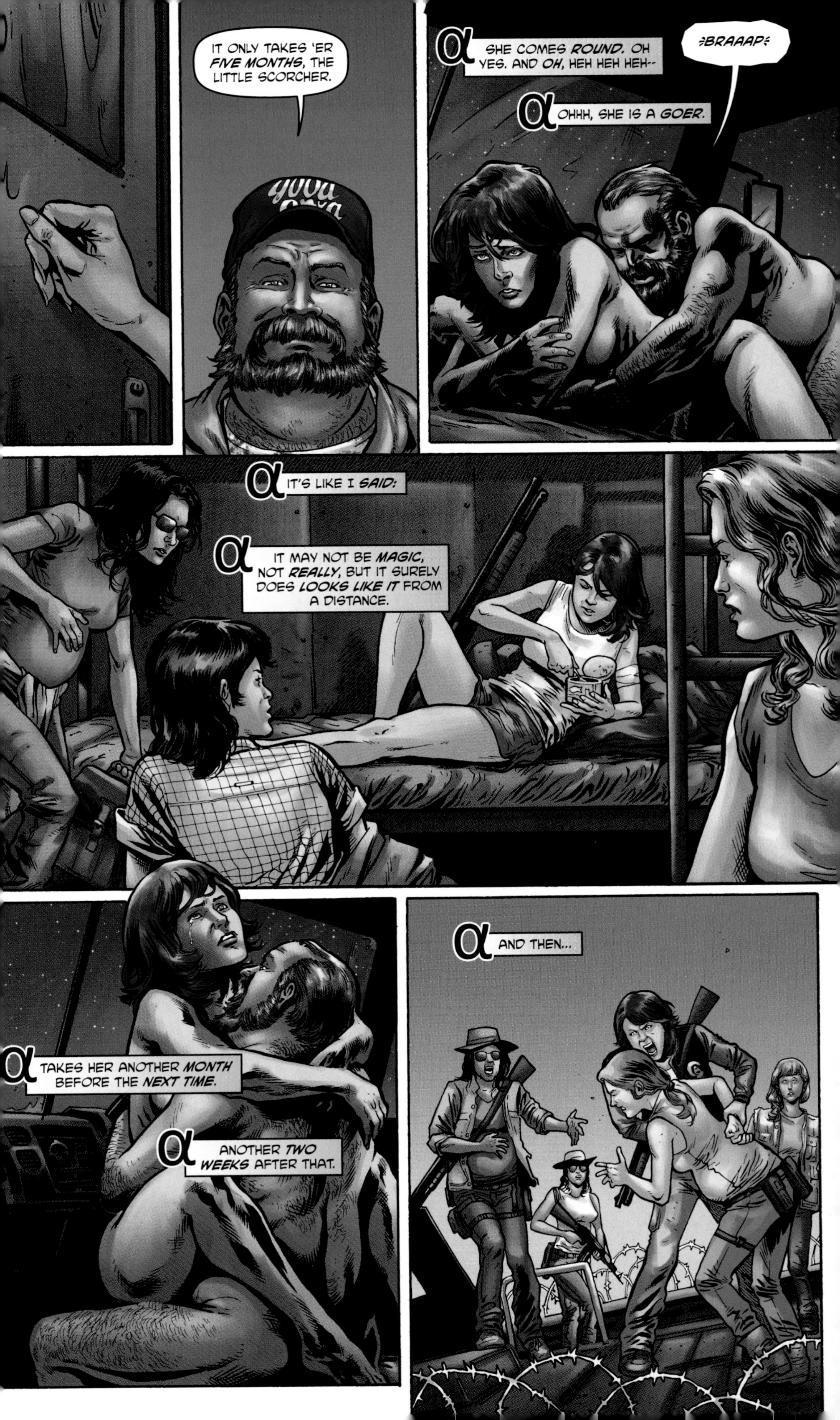
IT ONLY TAKES 'ER FIVE MONTHS, THE LITTLE SCORCHER.
SHE COMES ROUND. OH YES. AND OH, HEH HEH HEH--
OHHH, SHE IS A GOER.
BRAAAP
IT'S LIKE I SAID:
IT MAY NOT BE MAGIC, NOT REALLY, BUT IT SURELY DOES LOOKS LIKE IT FROM A DISTANCE.
TAKES HER ANOTHER MONTH BEFORE THE NEXT TIME.
ANOTHER TWO WEEKS AFTER THAT.
AND THEN...

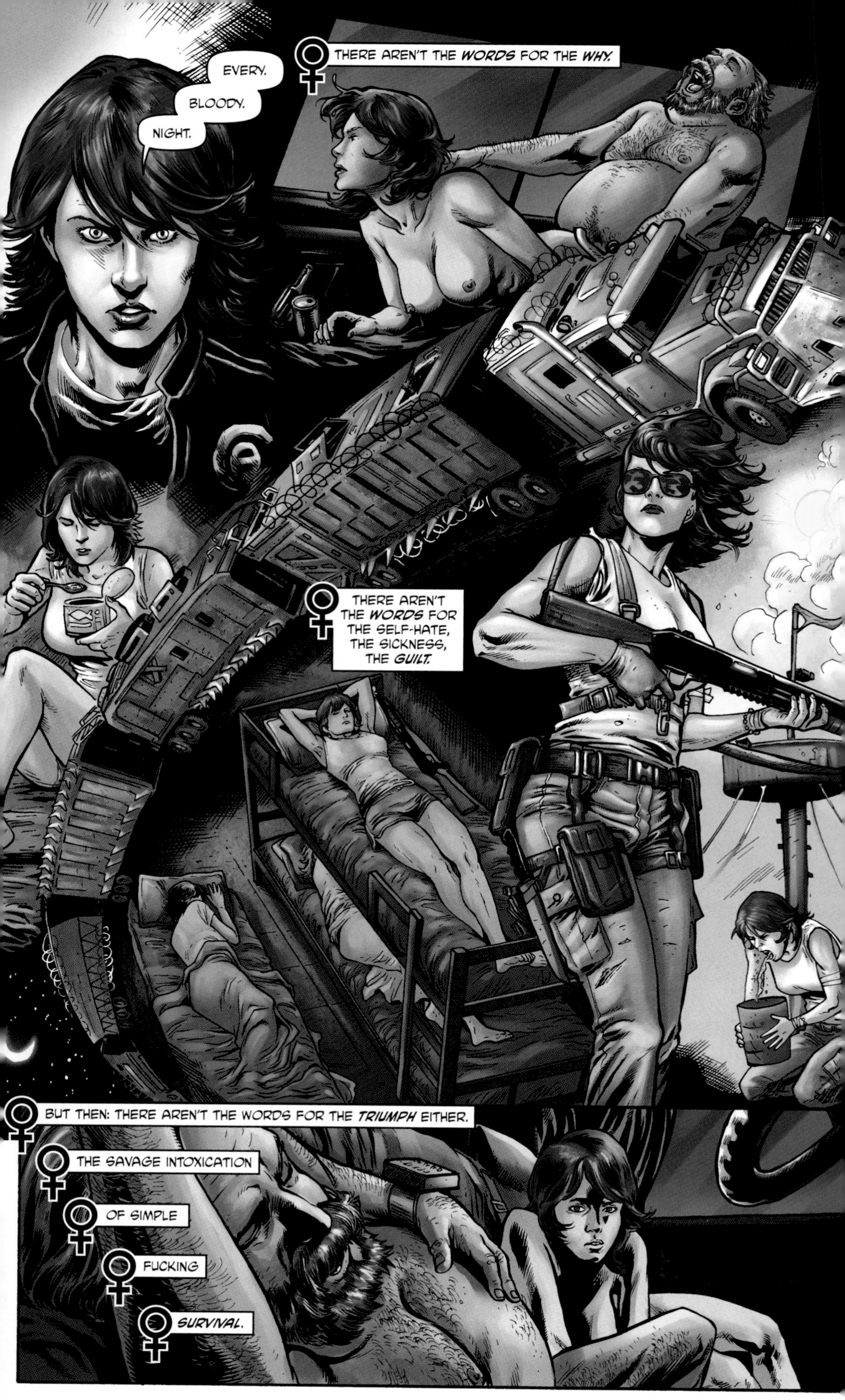
EVERY.
BLOODY.
NIGHT.
THERE AREN'T THE *WORDS* FOR THE *WHY.*
THERE AREN'T THE *WORDS* FOR THE SELF-HATE, THE SICKNESS, THE *GUILT.*
BUT THEN: THERE AREN'T THE WORDS FOR THE *TRIUMPH* EITHER.
THE SAVAGE INTOXICATION
OF SIMPLE
FUCKING
SURVIVAL.

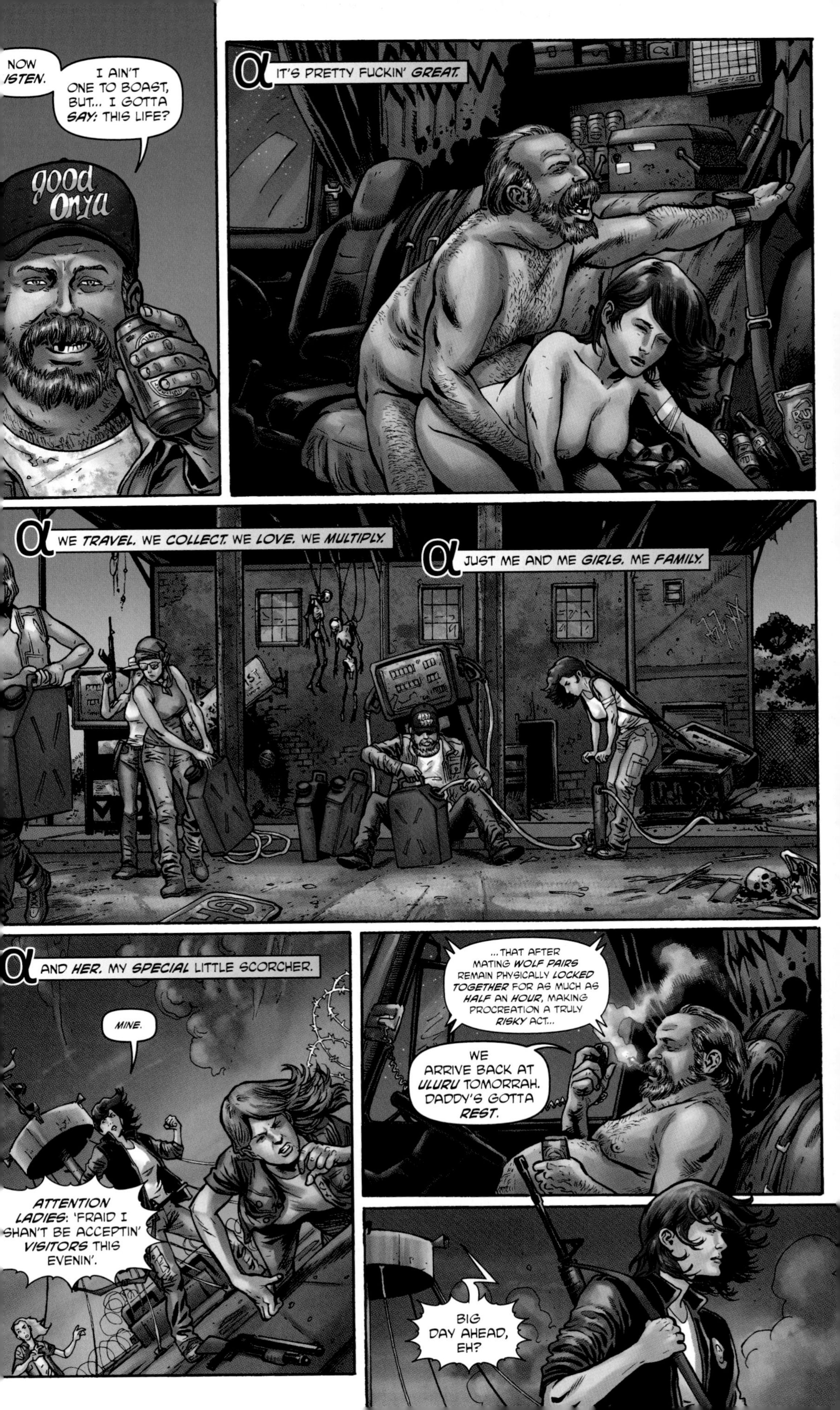
NOW ISTEN.
I AIN'T ONE TO BOAST, BUT... I GOTTA SAY: THIS LIFE?
good onya
IT'S PRETTY FUCKIN' GREAT.
WE TRAVEL. WE COLLECT. WE LOVE. WE MULTIPLY.
JUST ME AND ME GIRLS. ME FAMILY.
AND HER. MY SPECIAL LITTLE SCORCHER.
MINE.
ATTENTION LADIES: 'FRAID I SHAN'T BE ACCEPTIN' VISITORS THIS EVENIN'.
...THAT AFTER MATING WOLF PAIRS REMAIN PHYSICALLY LOCKED TOGETHER FOR AS MUCH AS HALF AN HOUR, MAKING PROCREATION A TRULY RISKY ACT...
WE ARRIVE BACK AT ULURU TOMORRAH. DADDY'S GOTTA REST.
BIG DAY AHEAD, EH?

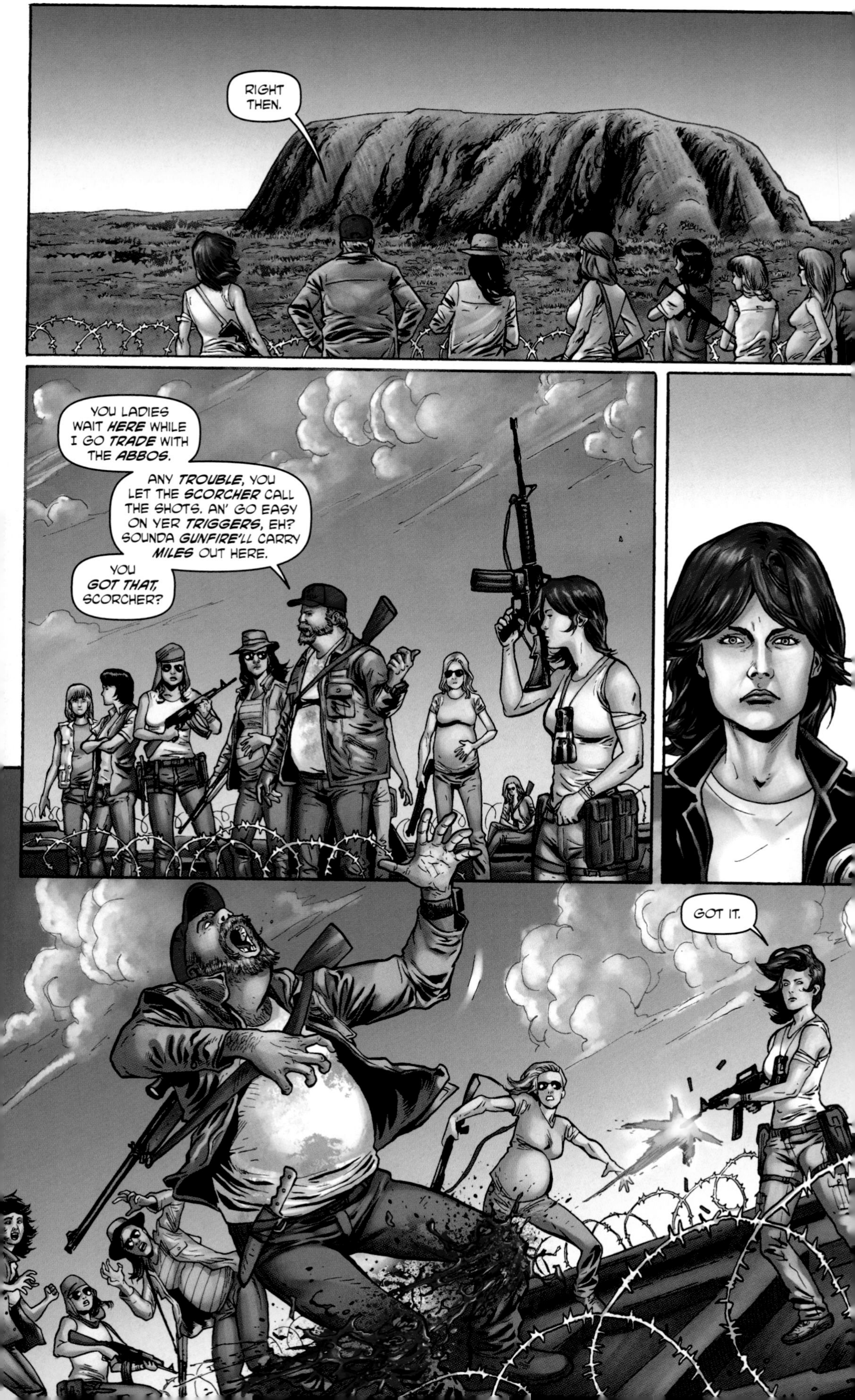
RIGHT THEN.
YOU LADIES WAIT HERE WHILE I GO TRADE WITH THE ABBOS.
ANY TROUBLE, YOU LET THE SCORCHER CALL THE SHOTS. AN' GO EASY ON YER TRIGGERS, EH? SOUNDA GUNFIRE'LL CARRY MILES OUT HERE.
YOU GOT THAT, SCORCHER?
GOT IT.

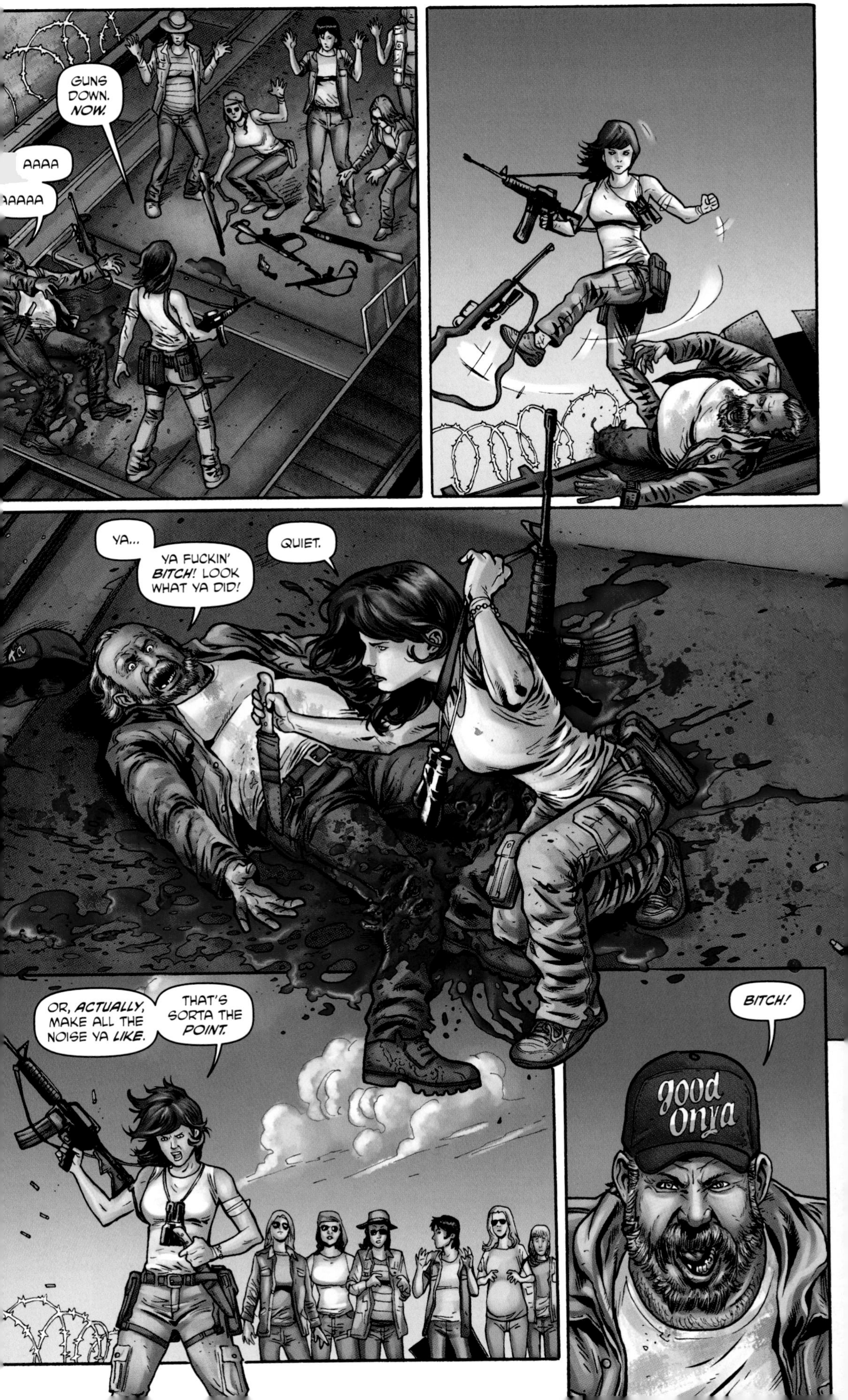
GUNS DOWN. NOW.
AAAA
AAAAA
YA...
YA FUCKIN' BITCH! LOOK WHAT YA DID!
QUIET.
OR, ACTUALLY, MAKE ALL THE NOISE YA LIKE.
THAT'S SORTA THE POINT.
BITCH!
good onya

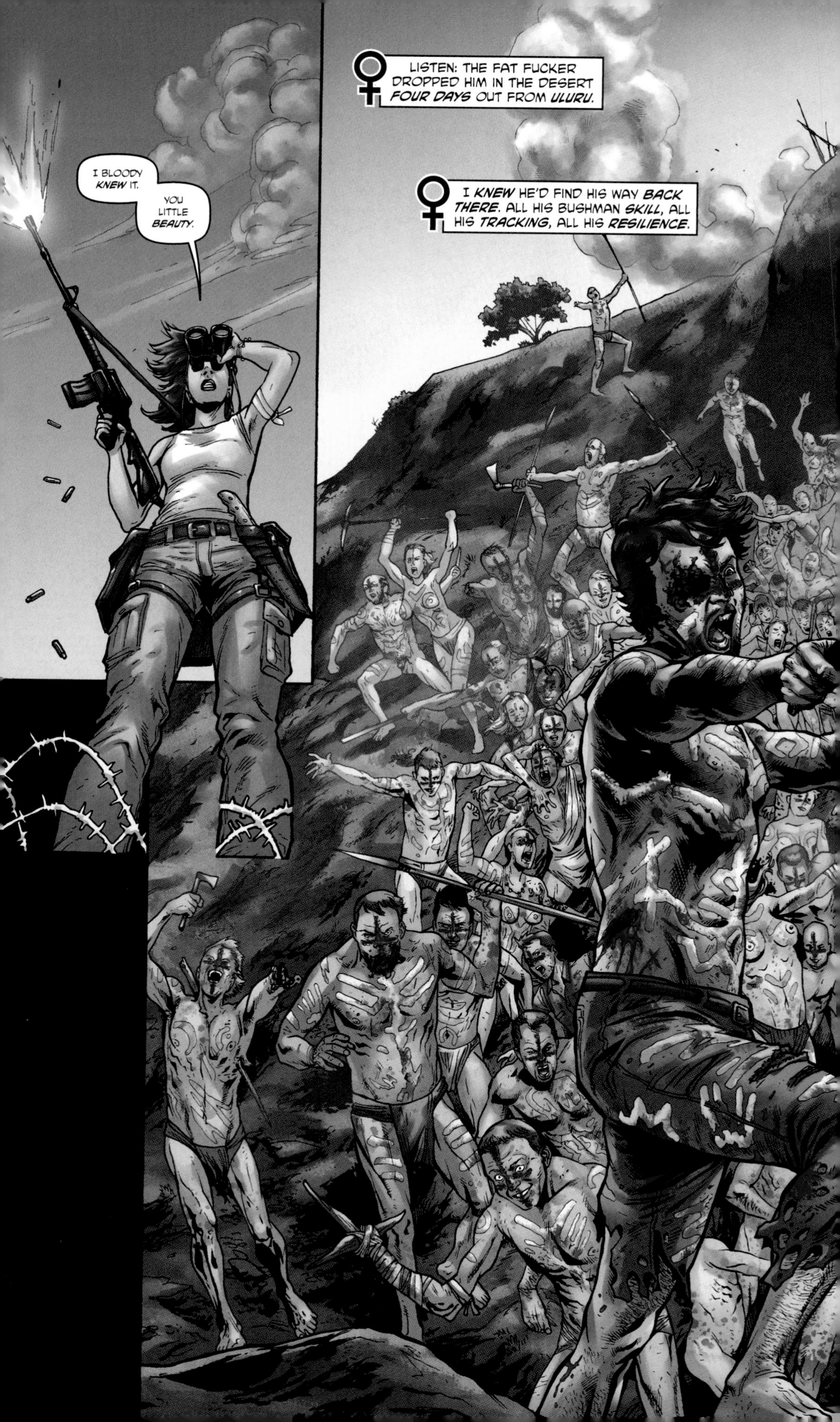
I BLOODY KNEW IT.
YOU LITTLE BEAUTY.
LISTEN: THE FAT FUCKER DROPPED HIM IN THE DESERT FOUR DAYS OUT FROM ULURU.
I KNEW HE'D FIND HIS WAY BACK THERE. ALL HIS BUSHMAN SKILL, ALL HIS TRACKING, ALL HIS RESILIENCE.

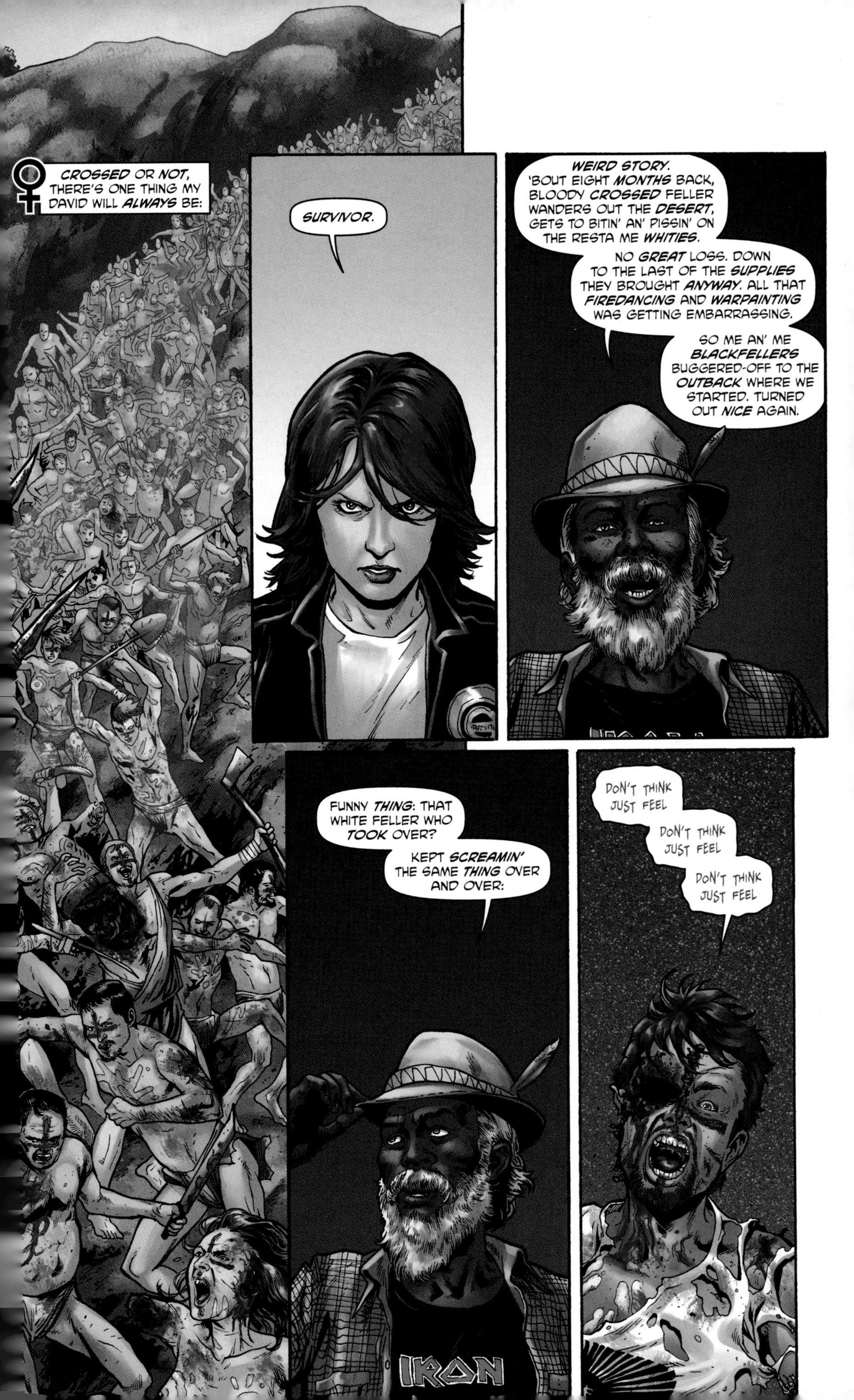

CROSSED OR NOT, THERE'S ONE THING MY DAVID WILL ALWAYS BE:
SURVIVOR.
WEIRD STORY. 'BOUT EIGHT MONTHS BACK, BLOODY CROSSED FELLER WANDERS OUT THE DESERT, GETS TO BITIN' AN' PISSIN' ON THE RESTA ME WHITIES.
NO GREAT LOSS. DOWN TO THE LAST OF THE SUPPLIES THEY BROUGHT ANYWAY. ALL THAT FIREDANCING AND WARPAINTING WAS GETTING EMBARRASSING.
SO ME AN' ME BLACKFELLERS BUGGERED-OFF TO THE OUTBACK WHERE WE STARTED. TURNED OUT NICE AGAIN.
FUNNY THING: THAT WHITE FELLER WHO TOOK OVER?
KEPT SCREAMIN' THE SAME THING OVER AND OVER:
DON'T THINK JUST FEEL
DON'T THINK JUST FEEL
DON'T THINK JUST FEEL
IRON

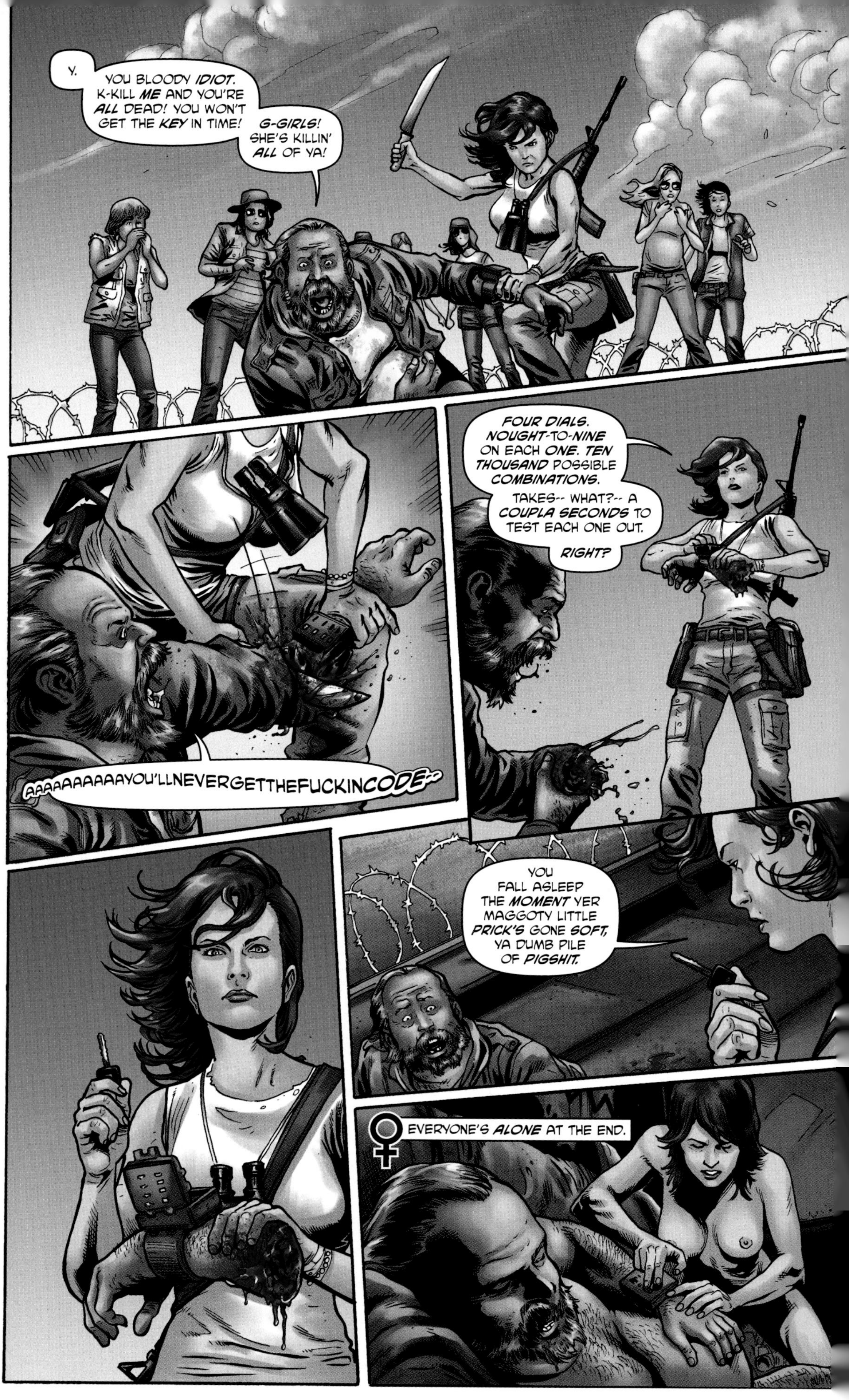
Y.
YOU BLOODY IDIOT. K-KILL ME AND YOU'RE ALL DEAD! YOU WON'T GET THE KEY IN TIME!
G-GIRLS! SHE'S KILLIN' ALL OF YA!
AAAAAAAAAAYOU'LLNEVERGETTHEFUCKINCODE--
FOUR DIALS. NOUGHT-TO-NINE ON EACH ONE. TEN THOUSAND POSSIBLE COMBINATIONS.
TAKES-- WHAT?-- A COUPLA SECONDS TO TEST EACH ONE OUT.
RIGHT?
YOU FALL ASLEEP THE MOMENT YER MAGGOTY LITTLE PRICK'S GONE SOFT, YA DUMB PILE OF PIGSHIT.
EVERYONE'S ALONE AT THE END.

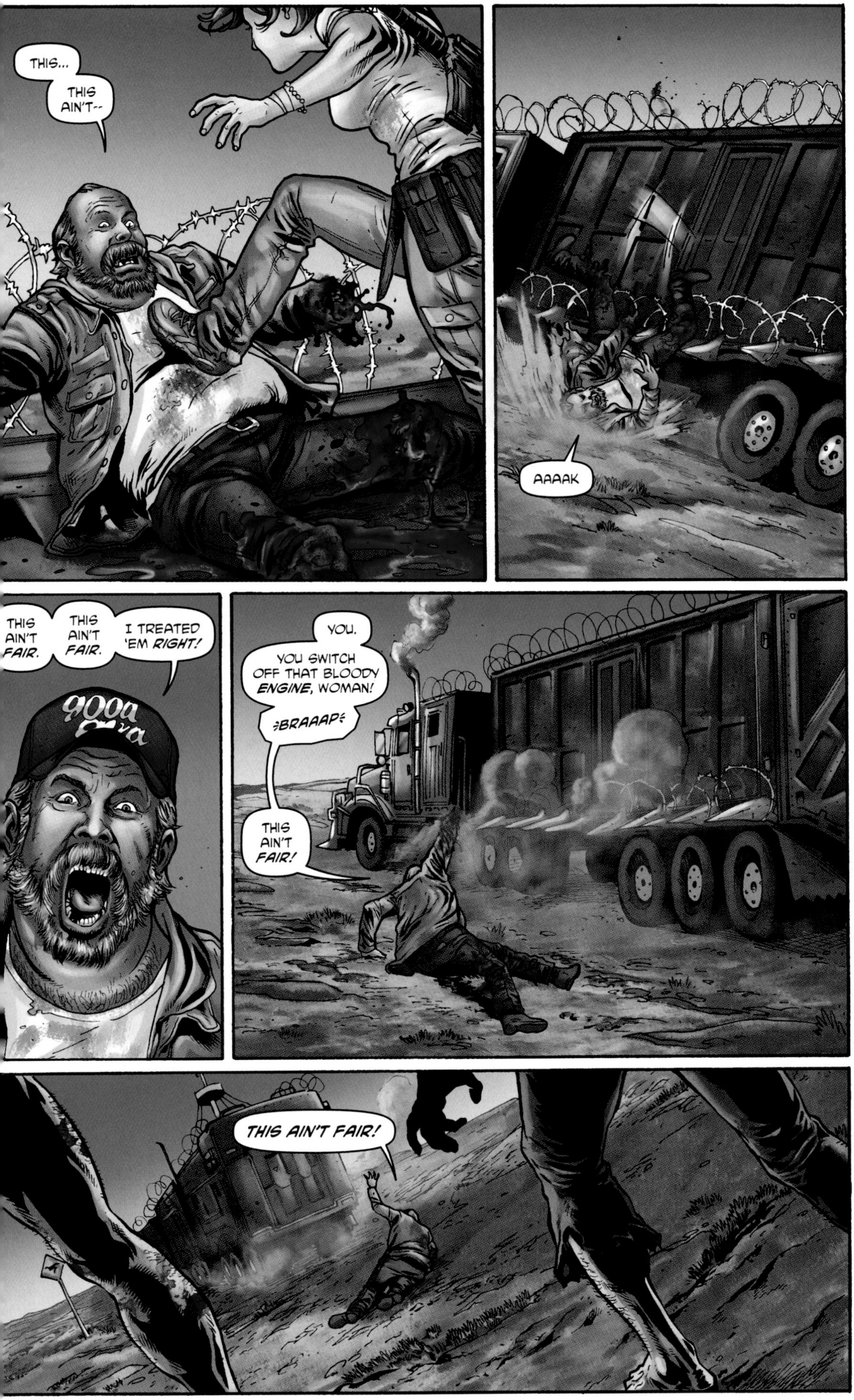
THIS...
THIS AIN'T--
AAAAK
THIS AIN'T *FAIR*.
THIS AIN'T *FAIR*.
I TREATED 'EM *RIGHT!*
YOU.
YOU SWITCH OFF THAT BLOODY *ENGINE*, WOMAN!
BRAAAP
THIS AIN'T *FAIR!*
THIS AIN'T FAIR!

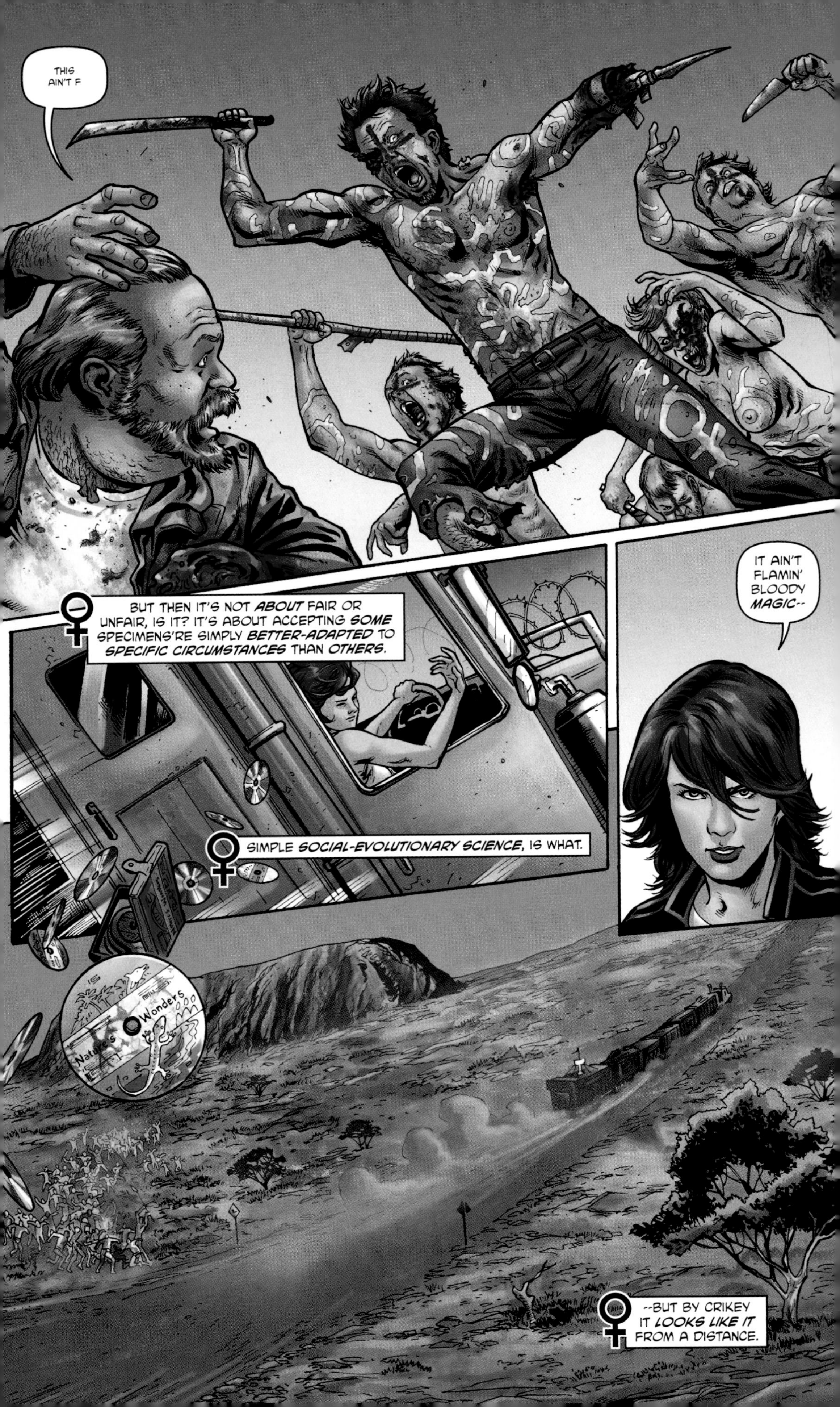
THIS AIN'T F
BUT THEN IT'S NOT ABOUT FAIR OR UNFAIR, IS IT? IT'S ABOUT ACCEPTING SOME SPECIMENS'RE SIMPLY BETTER-ADAPTED TO SPECIFIC CIRCUMSTANCES THAN OTHERS.
SIMPLE SOCIAL-EVOLUTIONARY SCIENCE, IS WHAT.
IT AIN'T FLAMIN' BLOODY MAGIC--
Nature's Wonders
--BUT BY CRIKEY IT LOOKS LIKE IT FROM A DISTANCE.

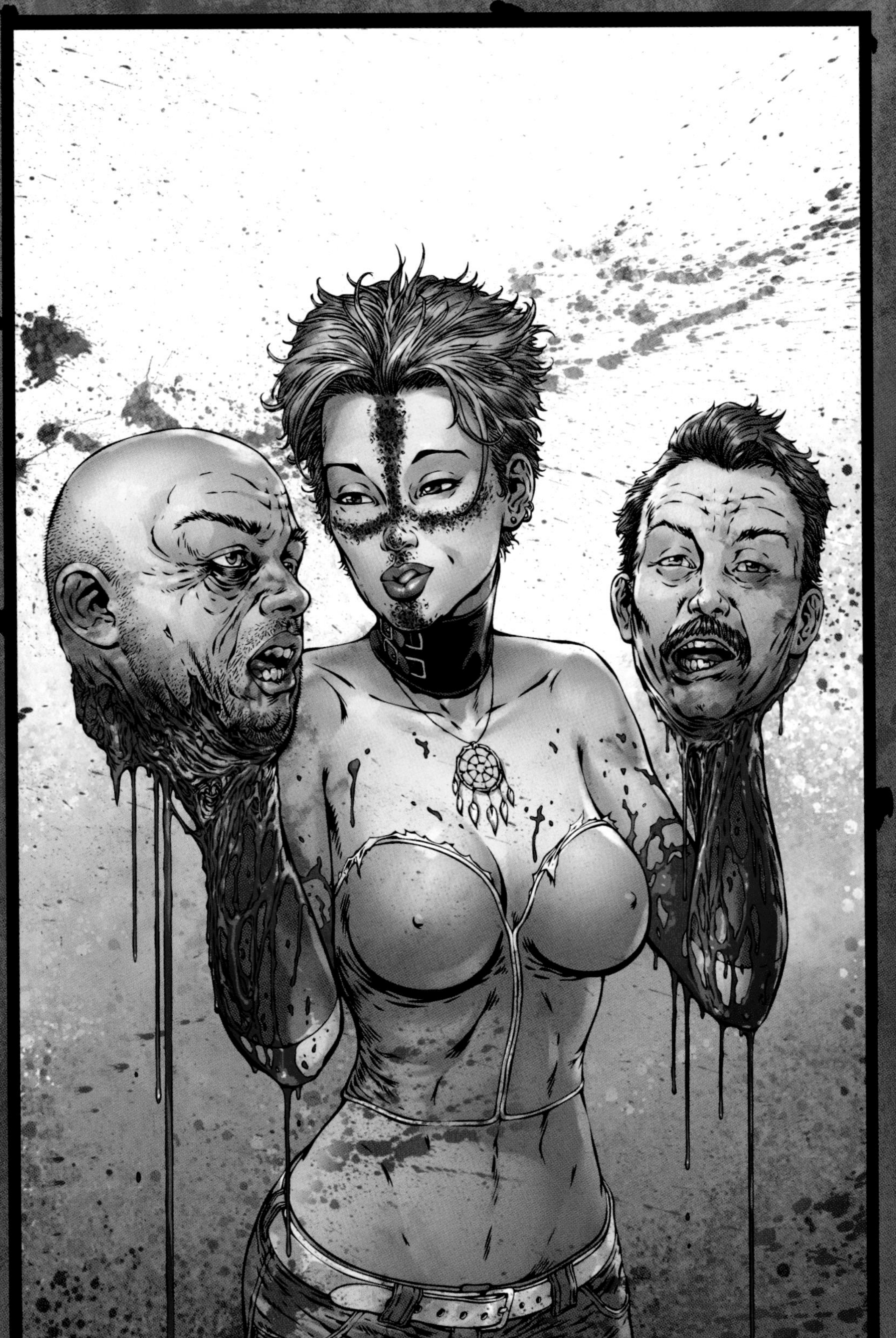

GALLERY

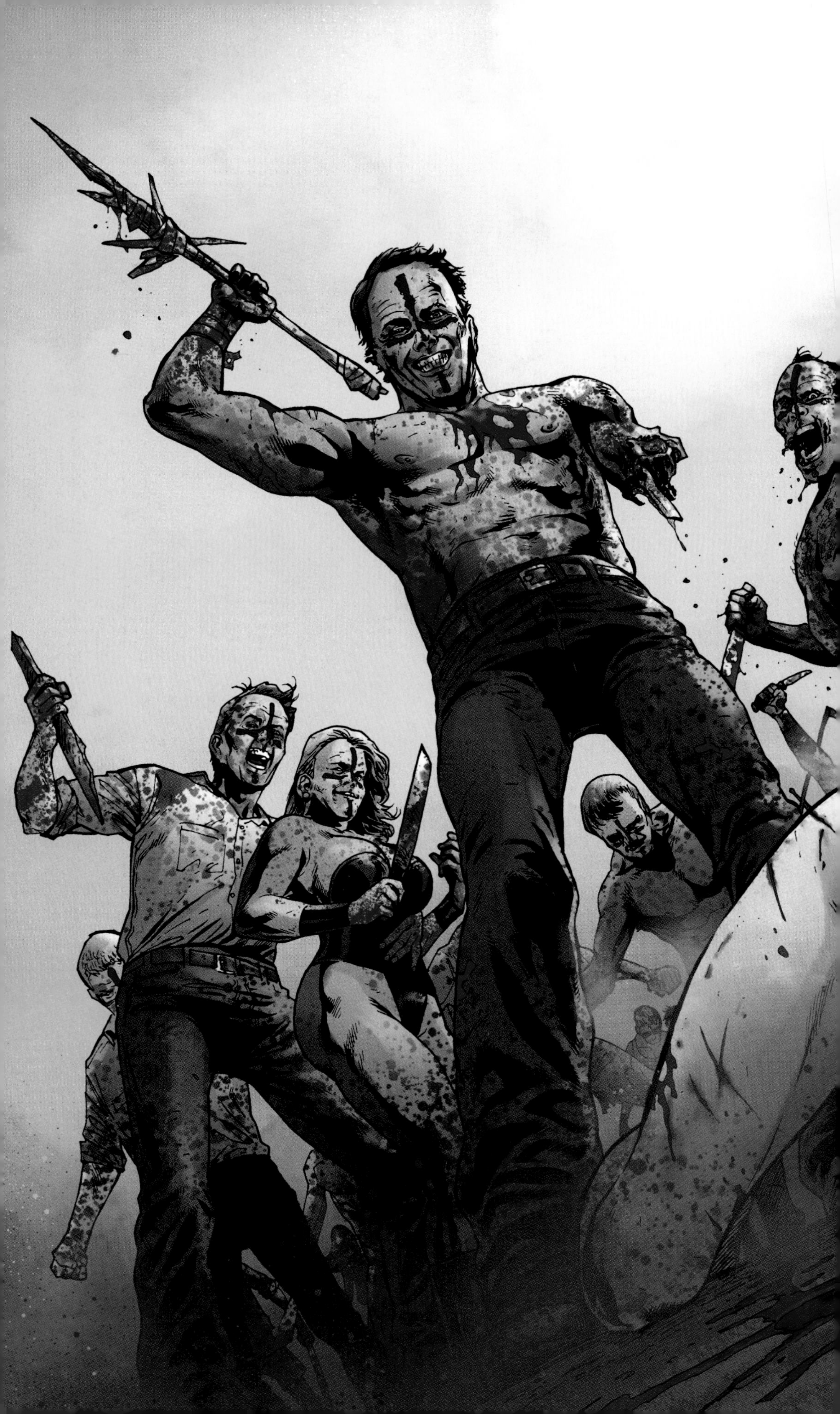

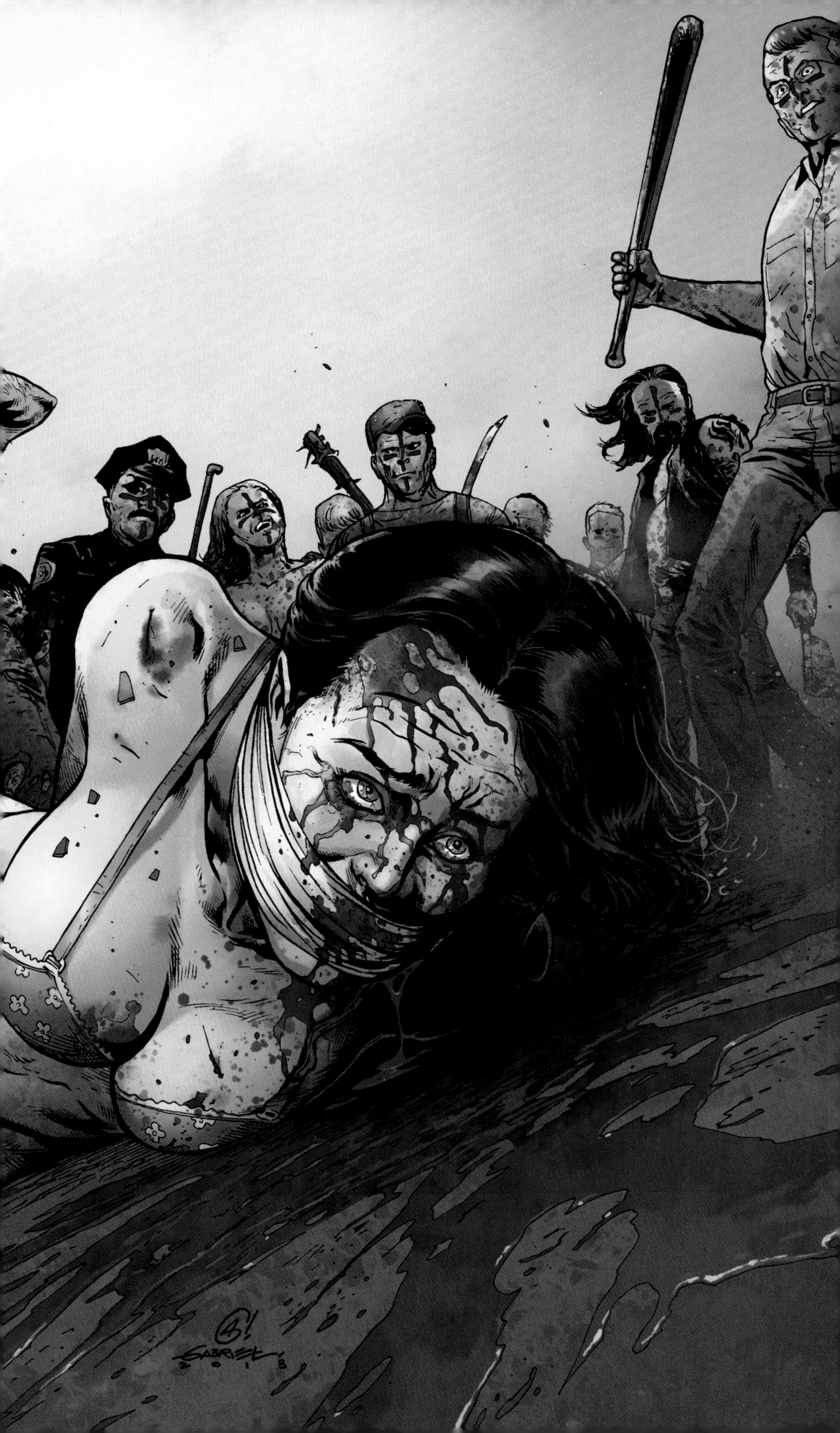

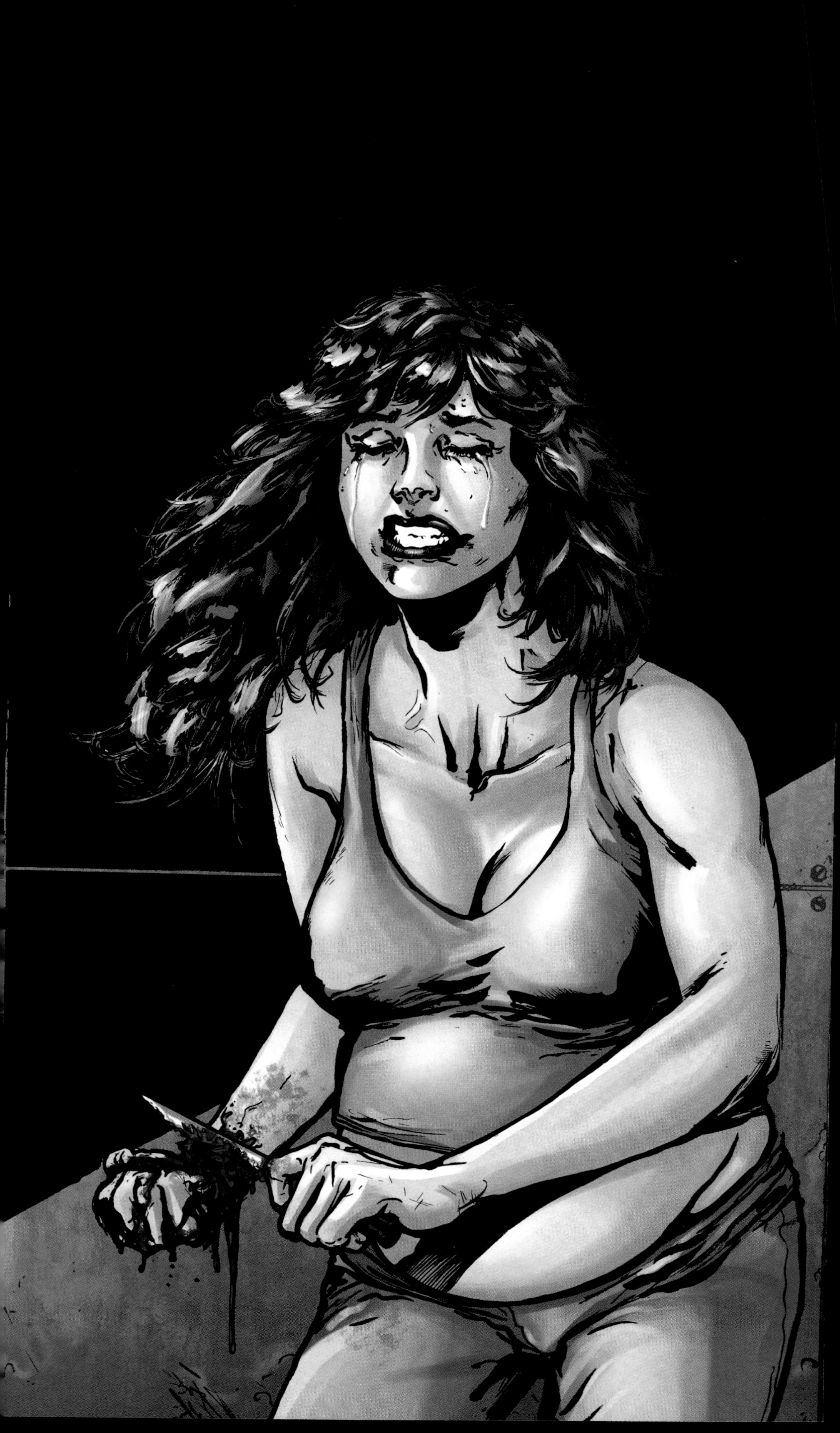

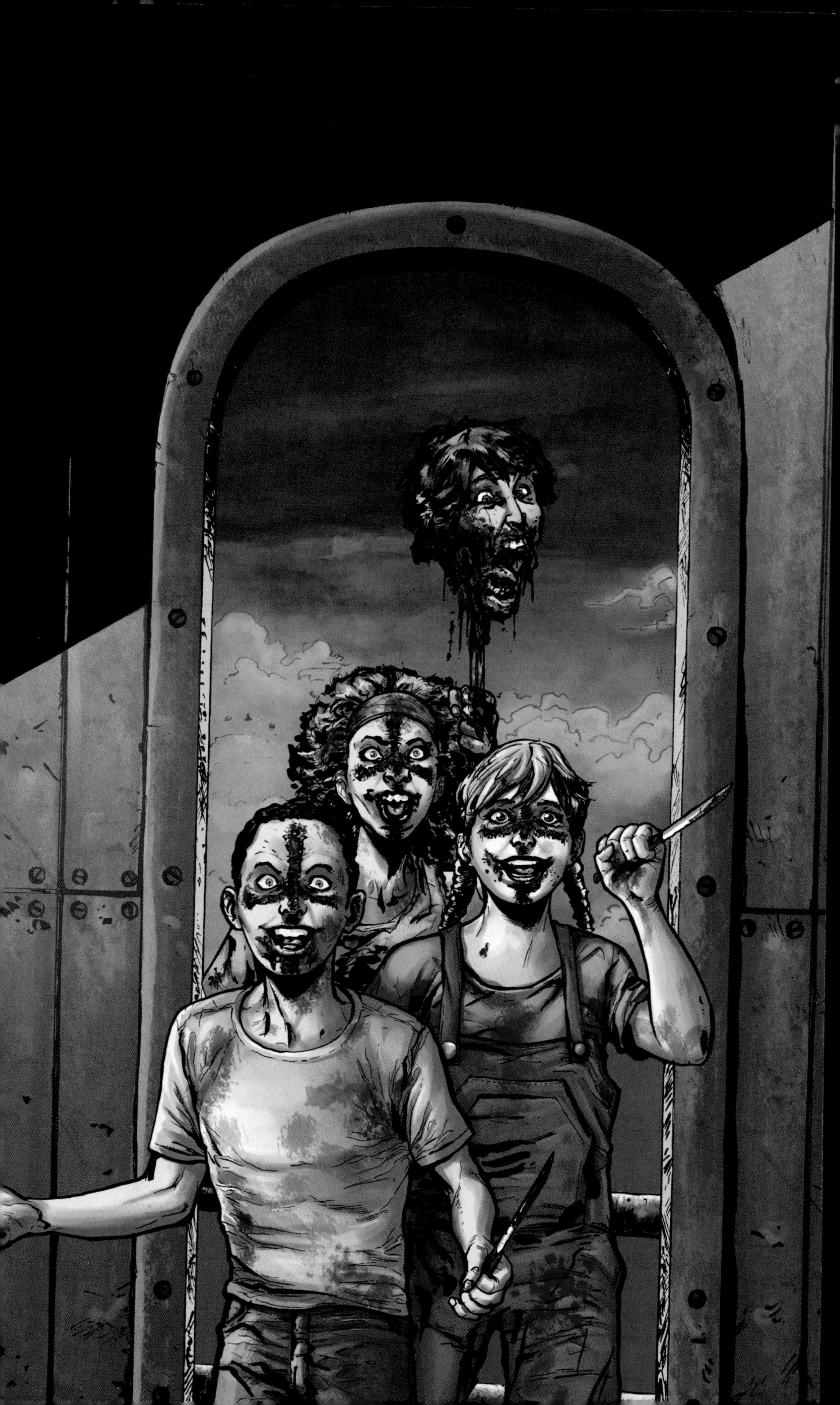

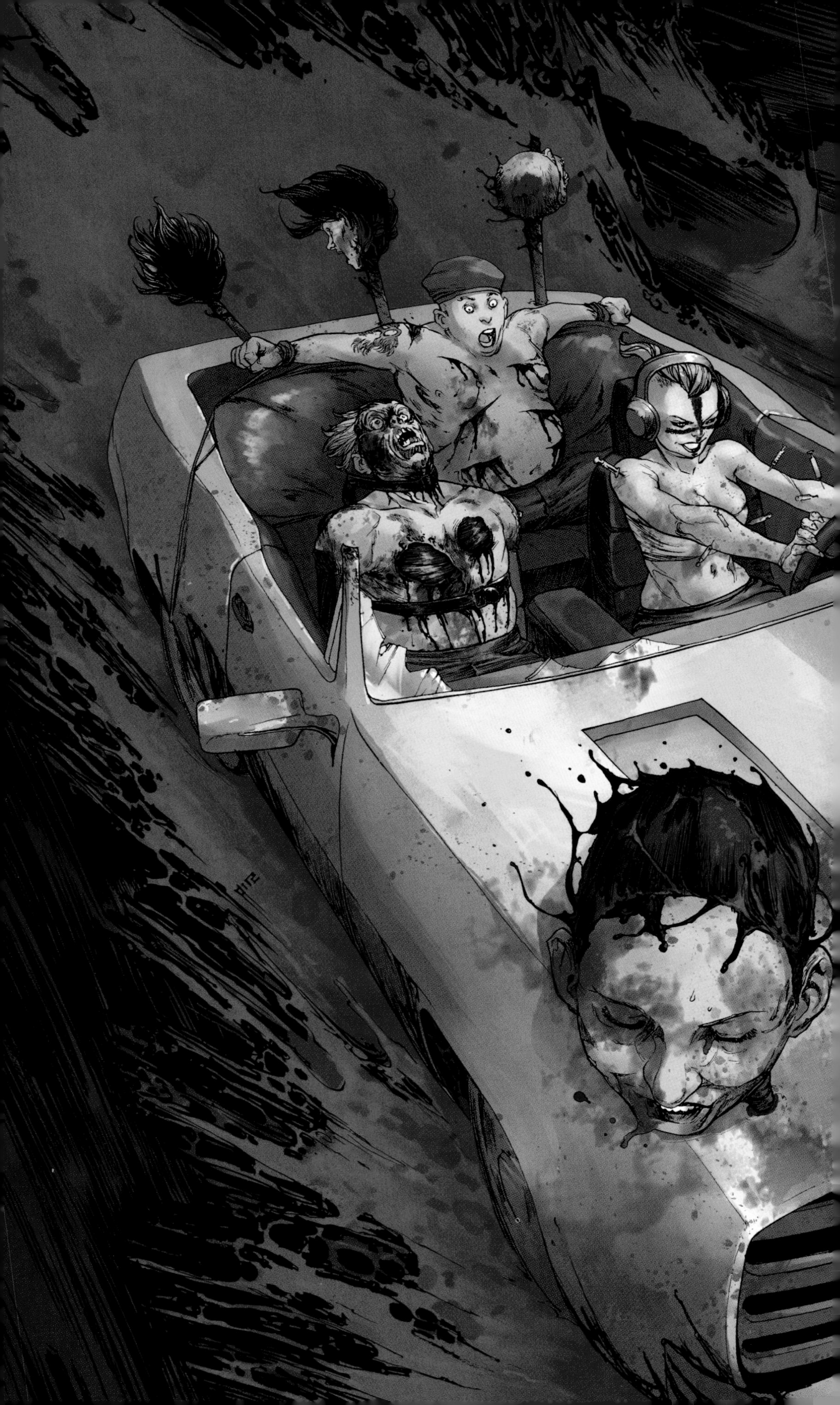

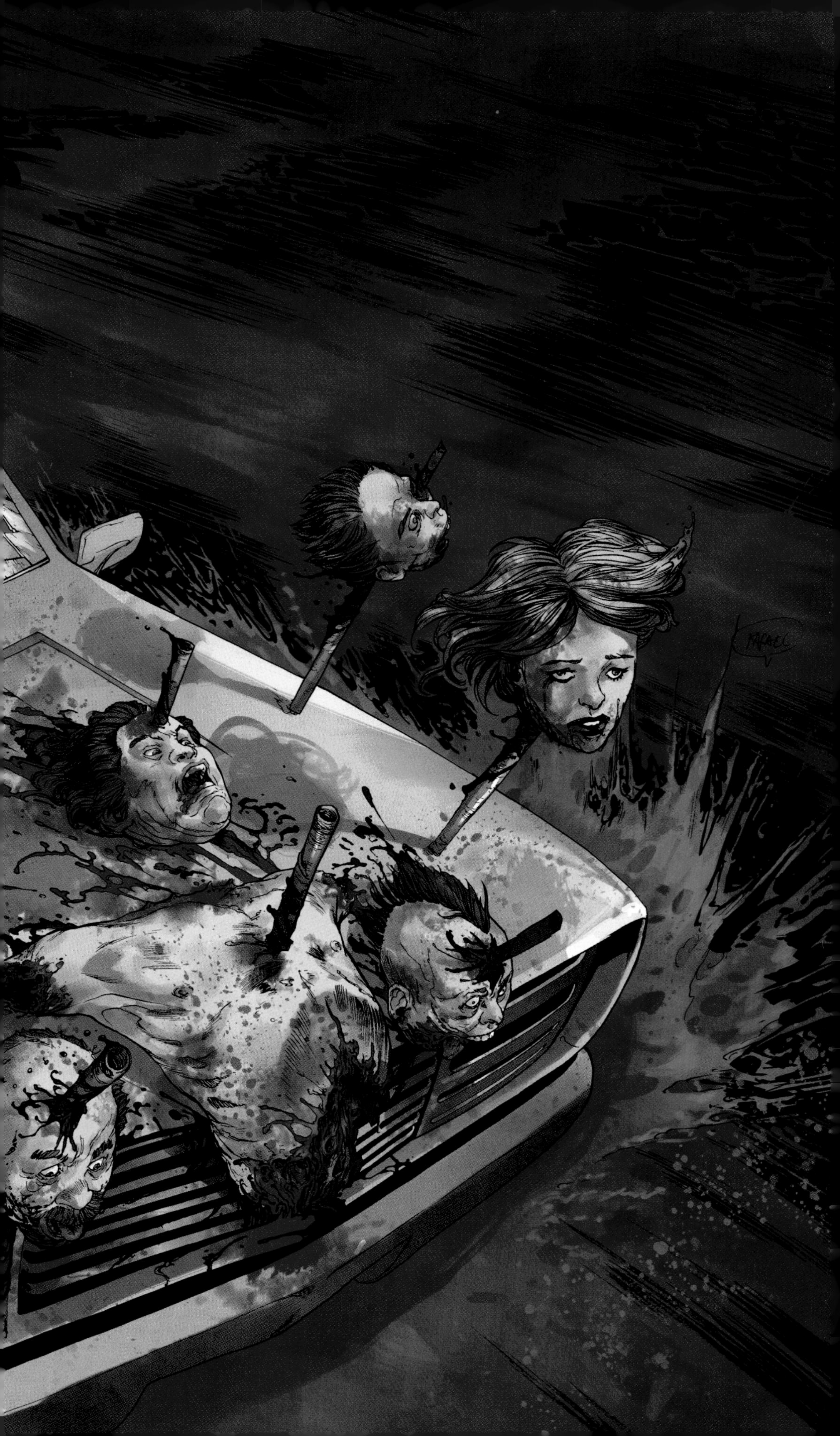

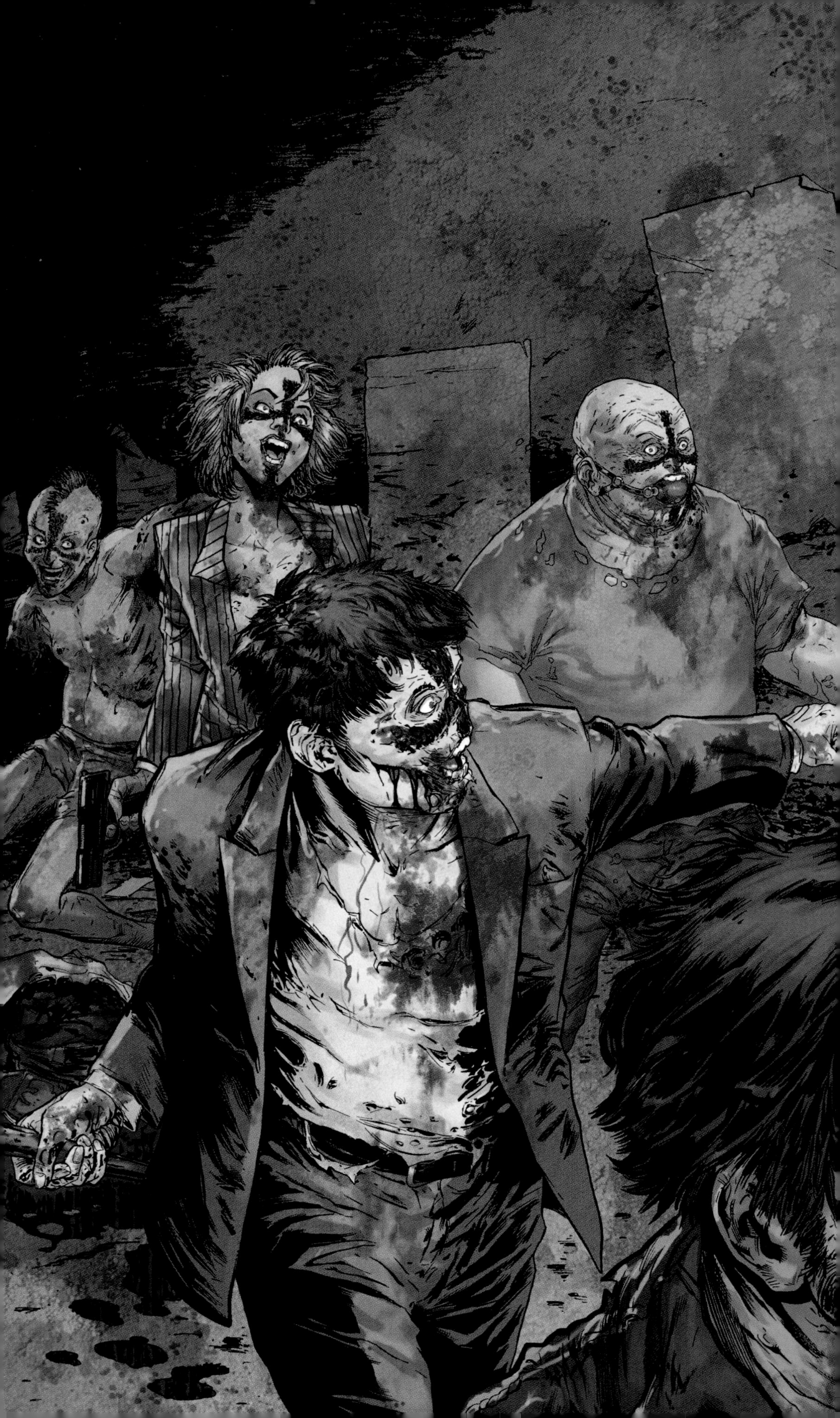

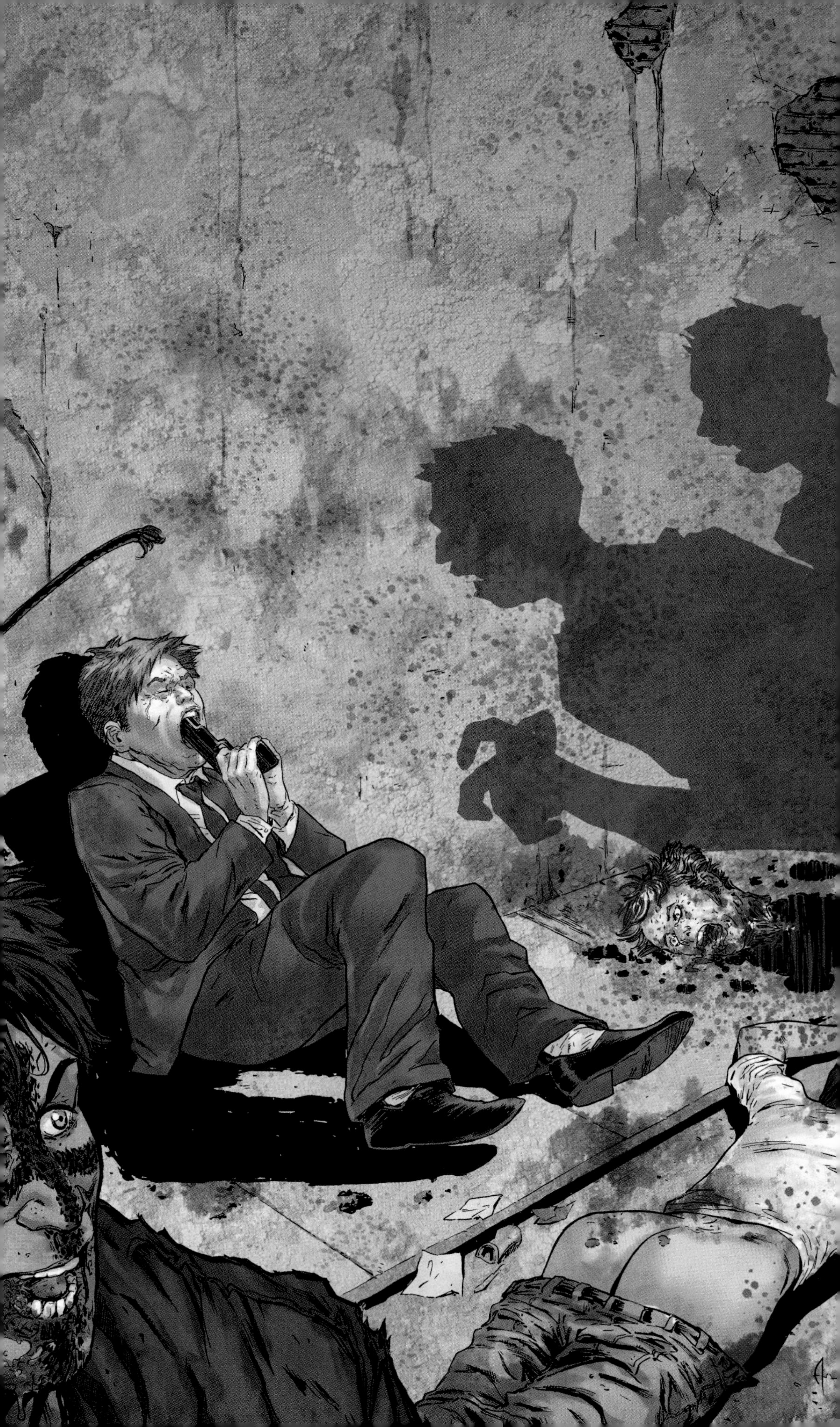

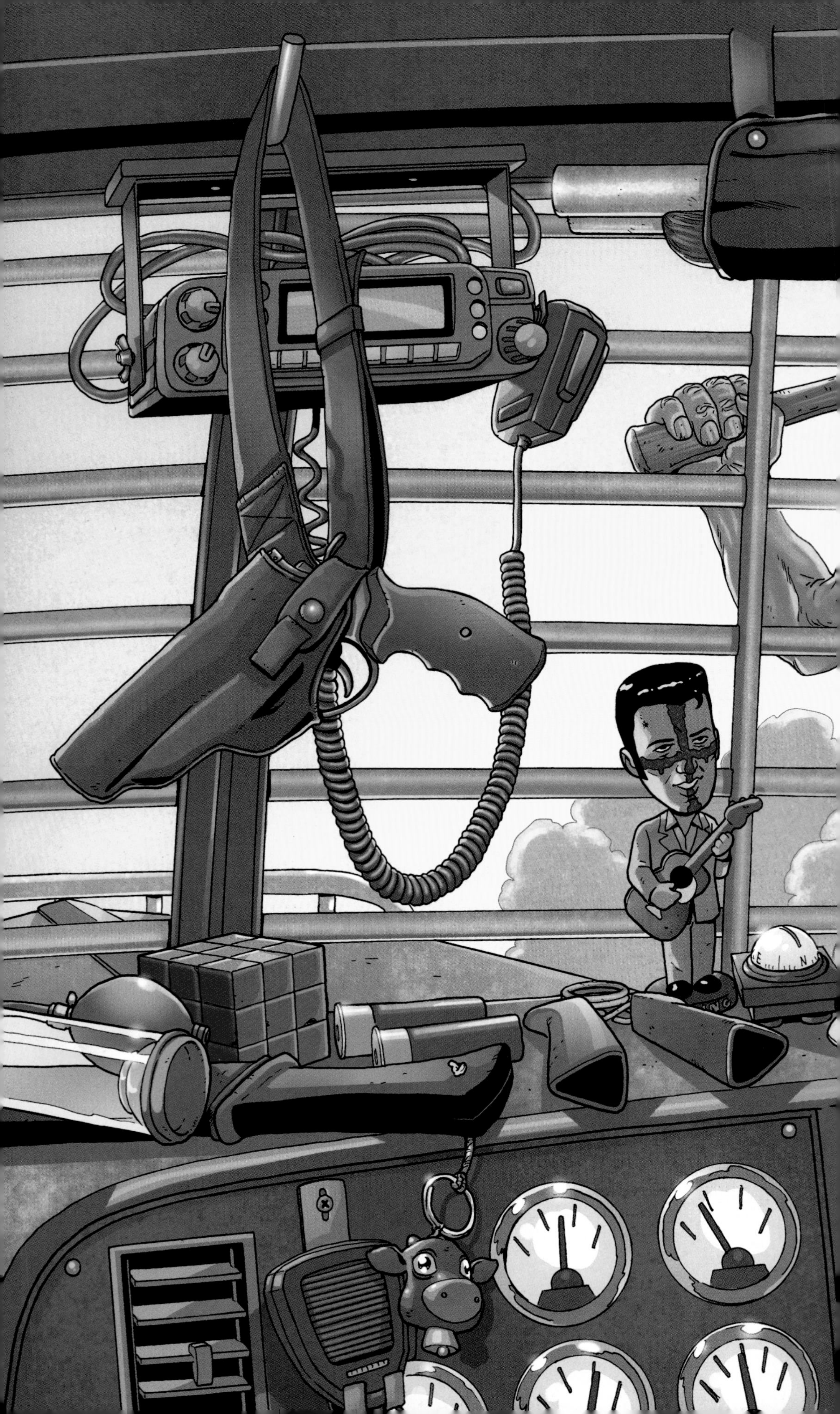

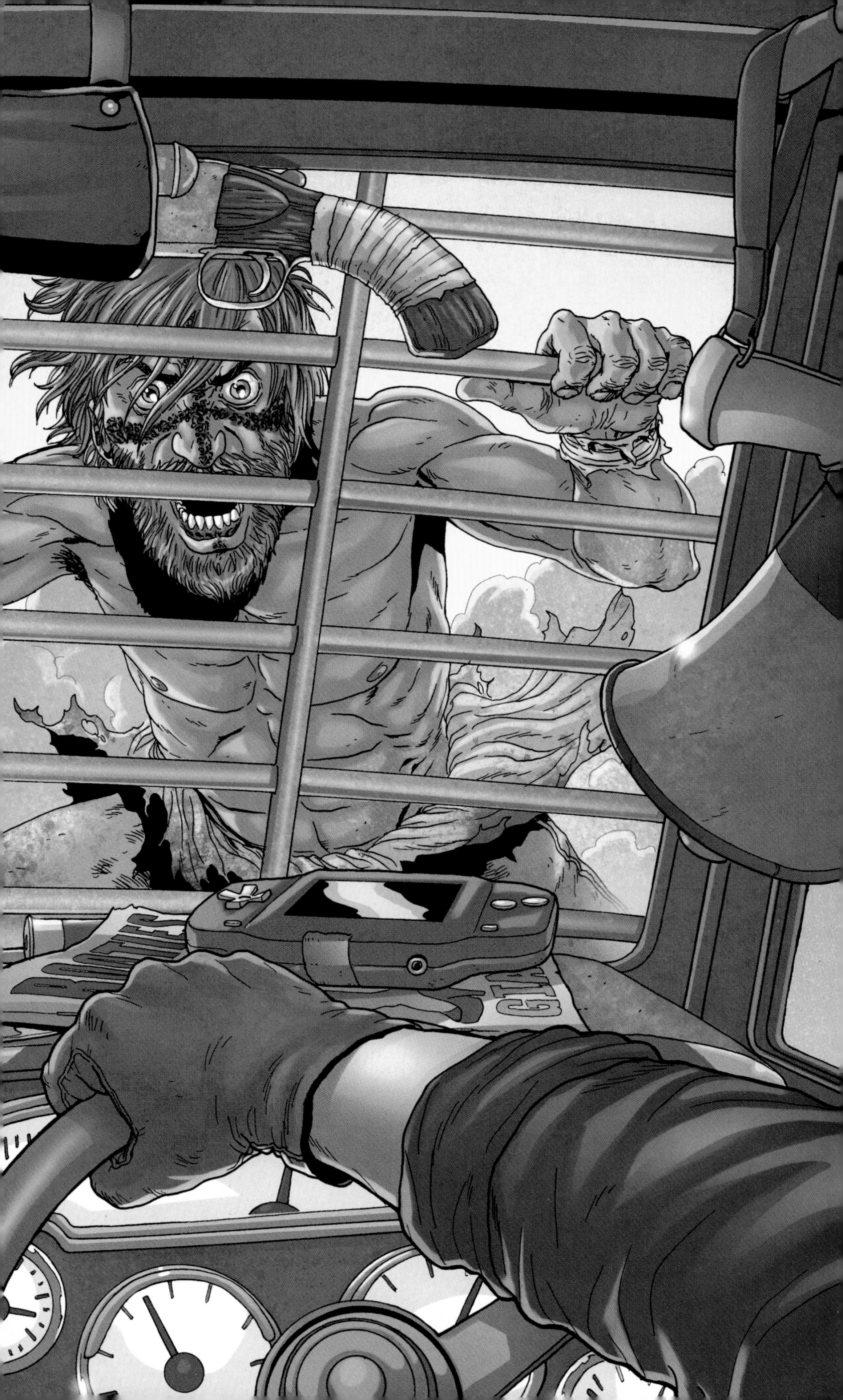

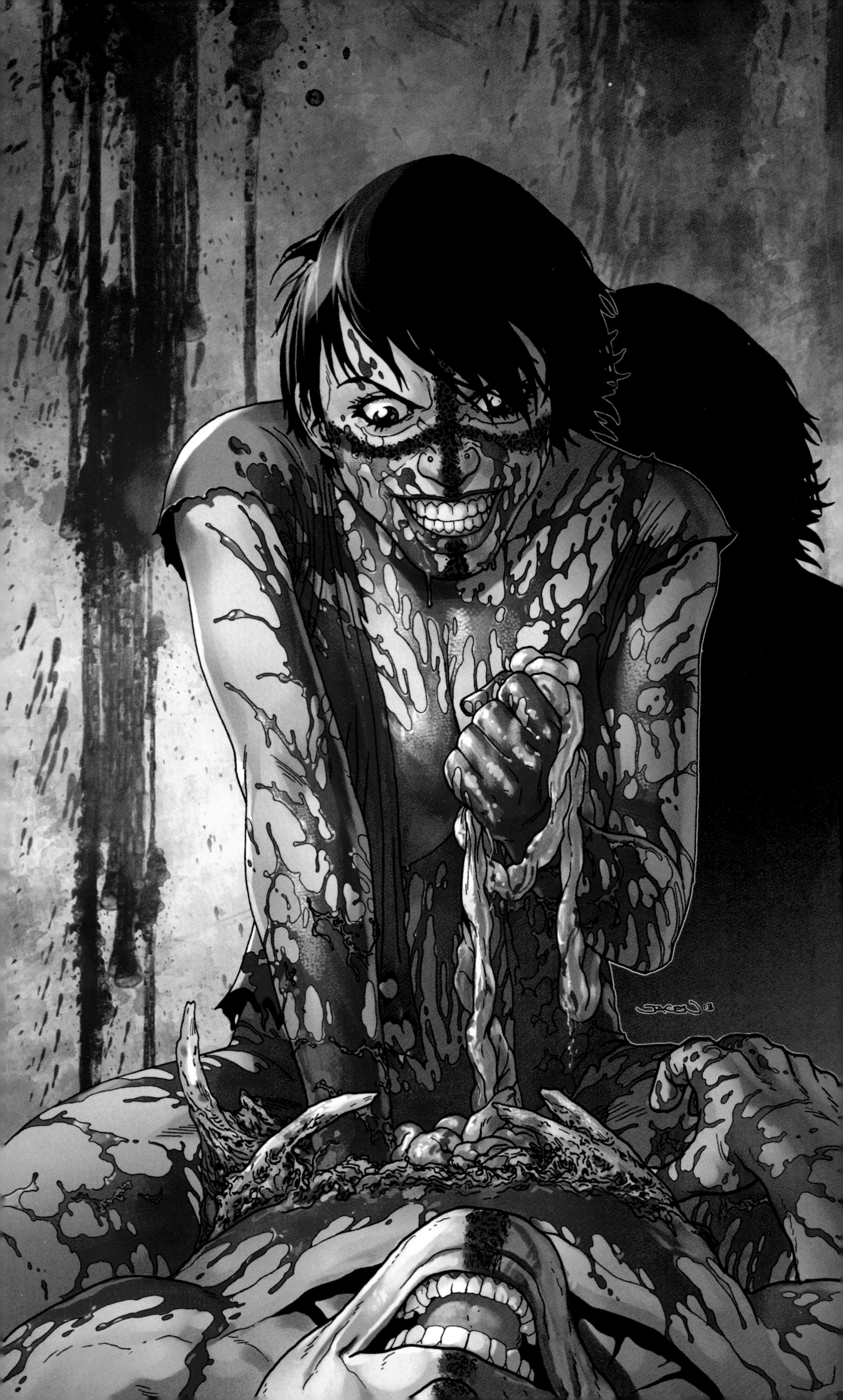